The 2017 Solo and [Small Firm]
Legal Technology Guide

CRITICAL DECISIONS MADE SIMPLE

Sharon D. Nelson, Esq., John W. Simek, and Michael C. Maschke

Introduction by James A. Calloway, Esq.

ABALAW
PRACTICE
DIVISION
The Business of Practicing Law

Cover design by Lachina

Facebook®, Twitter®, LinkedIn®, Google®, Pinterest®, and YouTube® are registered trademarks of their respective corporations.

The materials contained herein represent the opinions of the authors and/or the editors, and should not be construed to be the views or opinions of the law firms or companies with whom such persons are in partnership with, associated with, or employed by, nor of the American Bar Association or the Law Practice Section unless adopted pursuant to the bylaws of the Association. Nothing contained in this book is to be considered as the rendering of legal advice for specific cases, and readers are responsible for obtaining such advice from their own legal counsel. This book is intended for educational and informational purposes only.

Printed in the United States of America.

21 20 19 18 17   5 4 3 2 1

ISBN: 978-1-63425-817-3

Discounts are available for books ordered in bulk. Special consideration is given to state bars, CLE programs, and other bar-related organizations. Inquire at Book Publishing, ABA Publishing, American Bar Association, 321 N. Clark Street, Chicago, Illinois 60654-7598.

www.ShopABA.org

Dedication

Sharon Nelson and John Simek dedicate this book to their children, Kelly, Sara, Kim, JJ, Jason, and Jamie, and to their grandchildren, Samantha, Tyler, Lilly, Henry, Evan, Jordan, Cash, and Parker. Here's to many more vacations together on the Outer Banks—and to welcome a new granddaughter shortly after this book is published.

Michael Maschke dedicates this book to his wife, Summer, and their soon to be family of five. The past few years have been the best of my life. God couldn't have blessed me more than with you and our children.

Contents at a Glance

Table of Contents

Chapter 30: Taking Your Firm Paperless   **323**
by David J. Bilinsky, BSc, LLB, MBA

About the Authors

Sharon D. Nelson, Esq.

 Sharon D. Nelson is the president of Sensei Enterprises, Inc. Ms. Nelson graduated from Georgetown University Law Center in 1978 and has been in private practice ever since. She now focuses exclusively on electronic evidence law.

Ms. Nelson, Mr. Simek, and Mr. Maschke are the co-authors of the nine previous editions of this book (2008–2017). Ms. Nelson and Mr. Simek are also co-authors (with David Ries) of *Locked Down: Practical Information Security for Lawyers* (American Bar Association, 2nd ed. 2016, 1st edition published in 2012) and *Encryption Made Simple for Lawyers* (American Bar Association, 2015). Additionally, Ms. Nelson and Mr. Simek are co-authors of *The Electronic Evidence and Discovery Handbook: Forms, Checklists, and Guidelines* (ABA, 2006). Ms. Nelson is a co-author of *How Good Lawyers Survive Bad Times* (ABA, 2009). Ms. Nelson and Mr. Simek's articles have appeared in numerous national publications, and they frequently lecture throughout the country on digital forensics and legal technology subjects.

Ms. Nelson is a co-host of Legal Talk Network's *The Digital Edge: Lawyers and Technology* and *Digital Detectives* podcasts. Ms. Nelson and Mr. Simek have a regular legal tech column called "Hot Buttons" in the ABA Law Practice Division magazine *Law Practice*. Ms. Nelson was a member of the American Bar Association's Cybersecurity Task Force, and serves on its Standing Committee on Technology and Information Systems. She is now the Chair of the Law Practice Division's Professional Development Board and serves on its governing Council.

Ms. Nelson is a Past President of the Virginia State Bar (2013–14). She is a past president of the Fairfax Bar Association and past president of the Fairfax Law Foundation, past chair of the ABA's TECHSHOW Board, and past chair of the ABA's Law Practice Management Publishing Board. She is a graduate of Leadership Fairfax and served for many years on the Governing Council of the Virginia State Bar and on its Executive Committee. She is the former chair of the Virginia State Bar's Unauthorized Practice of Law Committee and served on both its Technology Committee and its Standing Committee on Finance. She is currently the chair of the Virginia State Bar's Future of Law Practice Committee, its Better Annual Meeting Committee, and the VSB TECHSHOW 2017. She is a member of the ABA, the Virginia Bar, the Virginia Bar Association, the Virginia Trial Lawyers Association, the Virginia Women Lawyers Association, and the Fairfax Bar Association.

In 2015, Ms. Nelson was named by *Virginia Lawyers Weekly* as a member of the Class of 2015's Leaders in the Law. This honor recognizes attorneys and professionals in law-related fields who made outstanding contributions to the practice of law in Virginia, significant achievements through the practice of law, leadership in improving the justice system, and important contributions to Virginia's legal community and/or the community at large.

Ms. Nelson served as a Court Appointed Special Advocate (CASA) for Abused and Neglected Children for five years.

John W. Simek

John W. Simek is the vice president of Sensei Enterprises, Inc. He is a Certified Information Systems Security Professional (CISSP) and a nationally known testifying expert in the area of digital forensics. Mr. Simek holds a degree in engineering from the United States Merchant Marine Academy and an MBA in finance from Saint Joseph's University. Before forming Sensei, he was a senior technologist with Mobil Oil Corporation for more than 20 years, troubleshooting and designing Mobil's networks throughout the Western Hemisphere.

In addition to his CISSP designation, Mr. Simek is an EnCase Certified Examiner (EnCE), Certified Handheld Examiner, a Certified Novell Engineer, Microsoft Certified Professional + Internet, Microsoft Certified Systems Engineer, NT Certified Independent Professional, and a Certified Internetwork

Professional. He is also a member of the High Tech Crime Network, the Fairfax Bar Association, and the American Bar Association. In addition to co-authoring the books cited in Ms. Nelson's biography, he also serves on the 2017 ABA TECHSHOW planning board of the Law Practice Division. He currently provides information technology support to hundreds of area law firms, legal entities, and corporations. He lectures on legal technology and digital forensics subjects throughout the world.

He is a co-host of Legal Talk Network's *Digital Detectives* podcast.

Mr. Simek also served as a Court Appointed Special Advocate (CASA) for Abused and Neglected Children for five years.

Michael C. Maschke

Michael Maschke is the Chief Executive Officer and a digital forensics examiner at Sensei Enterprises, Inc. He is a Certified Computer Examiner (CCE), an EnCase Certified forensic examiner (EnCE), and a Certified Information Systems Security Professional (CISSP).

Mr. Maschke holds a degree in telecommunications from James Madison University. He has significant experience with network troubleshooting, design and implementation, systems integration, and computer engineering. Prior to becoming the Chief Information Officer, Mr. Maschke oversaw Sensei's information technology department, which provided support to hundreds of area law firms and corporations.

He has spoken at the American Bar Association's TECHSHOW conference on information security and is a co-author of Information Security for Lawyers and Law Firms as well as the last nine editions of this book, all published by the American Bar Association.

Acknowledgments

Once again, we welcome our good friend Jim Calloway as the author of the introduction to this book. Jim is the director of the Oklahoma Bar Association's Management Assistance Program. He frequently writes and speaks on legal technology issues, Internet research, law office management and organization, and legal ethics. He is often on the faculty with us at ABA TECHSHOW and is Sharon's cohost on the Legal Talk Network's *Digital Edge: Lawyers and Technology* podcast.

We are very happy that our friend and colleague Jennifer Ellis again agreed to be a contributing author. She has updated her marvelous Social Media chapter for this edition of our book. Jennifer is a social media maven par excellence. You couldn't possibly get better advice.

Thanks to good friends Tom Mighell and Paul Unger, who generously updated their excellent iWin: iPad for Litigators chapter in the book—iPad aficionados will find a wealth of information in that chapter. Tom also acted as a peer reviewer of this book—thanks, Tom, for "volunteering!"

We are again indebted to our long-time friend Dave Bilinsky. Dave is a Practice Management Consultant and lawyer for the Law Society of British Columbia. He contributes an annual chapter, and an invaluable one, on taking your firm paperless. This year, the chapter was co-authored by another long-time friend, Catherine Sanders-Reach, who is the director of Law Practice Management and Technology for the Chicago Bar Association. Brilliant, witty, and insightful, she is one of our go-to resources on legal tech.

Thanks to all the folks from Lachina who did all typesetting, editing, and other tasks that go into a book like this. We appreciate how hard you all worked to get this book "on the streets" in time for the new year and look forward to many years working together.

We cannot leave out our good friend and colleague Allison Shields, who chairs the Law Practice Division Publishing Board and who oversaw the entire journey of this book. Thanks for being so wonderful to work with, Allison!

And thanks to Richard Ferguson, our long-time friend and once again Project Manager for this edition of the book. Richard, we will salute with a "wee dram" when we see the book in print! Thanks for everything, one and all!

Finally, we again thank our colleagues here at Sensei, who carried the load while we were writing and were never too busy to deliberate over recommendations and to offer insightful comments. We don't come to work every day; we come to play, and we really like the folks we play with. Thanks, one and all!

Mike Maschke, Sharon Nelson, John Simek

Preface to the Tenth Edition

What we hope to do with this book is simple: We want to help solo and small firm lawyers find the "sweet spot" of legal technology—the best value for the dollars. You don't need a yacht, and you won't be well served by a rowboat. But there is a happy medium—professional-grade hardware and software that doesn't cost an arm and a leg.

This guide is an annual one, so you can't go too far wrong with our advice. Some chapters will remain almost absolutely current. At worst, we'll only be several months behind the curve. Still, if you can't afford your own legal technology consultant and you are concerned about those who may be selling you snake oil, at least this book should provide you with an overview of recommended legal technology products for solo and small firm lawyers.

As always, the parts of this book that age quickly are the hardware specifications. We are happy to give you our latest specs—just drop us a quick line at sensei@senseient.com. We've given out hundreds of updated specs over the years, so don't hesitate to write!

We do our absolute best to be vendor-neutral. Readers of previous editions will be keenly aware that our advice has changed from year to year as some products excel and others . . . well . . . decline—and sometimes precipitously. We have some exciting new products to talk about this year—nothing moves as fast as technology!

This is the only book we're aware of that deals with legal technology on a collective, annual basis. We are now in our tenth edition, so we must be doing something right. We seem to have a growing, loyal readership looking for independent advice on legal technology and find a yearly dose of that advice compelling. In this book, we provide information on and recommendations for computers, servers, networking equipment, legal software, utilities, cool gadgets for lawyers, and more. We take an in-depth look at the technologies that will be around in 2017 and provide information on how these technologies will shape the way solo and small firm decision makers think about their technology needs.

This year, we have added two chapters at the wise counsel of our Project Manager and friend Richard Ferguson. They are E-mail Providers and Backup Strategies. Though we had touched on these subjects previously, Richard was right—they deserve chapters of their own.

Our recommendations are what we would do in a solo or small practice ourselves. Invest in quality technology that will have a good shelf life and serve you well—that means buying business-grade (not consumer-grade) technology. And don't expect more than the machines can give. A server can be expected to last four to five years; a workstation or laptop, three to four. That's it, folks. As the software also evolves, it demands ever more resources, and the hardware ages both physically and in its ability to handle the new software. Remember the Rule of Three in upgrading: You should be upgrading one-third of your technology each year. Sometimes you can stretch it to four, but if you try to limp along patching things with spit and promises, you are likely going to be in for a "big bang" upgrade, which is acutely painful to the average solo or small law firm. Leasing may help lessen this financial burden (at least on an annual basis), but you lose the option to change course quickly without paying penalty fees.

Be mindful of the fact that this book is written exclusively for solos and small law firms. There is no attempt to include big-firm products or solutions, though many big-firm lawyers have enjoyed portions of this book. In addition, we want to stress that we have included only our recommendations, not all available products. If you don't see a product here, it is because that product is not among our usual recommendations. This is a best-of-breed selection to keep you from being confused by the veritable cornucopia of choices that exist. No one has time to wade through all the choices, so we've tried to give you limited but tested options that work.

We used to say that generally we couldn't serve as your legal technology consultant unless you were in the D.C. area, but we are now providing remote backup and disaster recovery service to law firms anywhere in the country. Today, we are moving folks to the cloud, using a data center in northern Virginia. This means we can now provide IT (information technology) support nationwide and use remote access to connect to any part of your network that is not housed in the data center. Call us if this is an option you want to explore. With all the law firm data breaches that have been reported in the last several years, our Information Security Department has been hopping, investigating data breaches and assessing and securing law firm networks. We also offer employee training and assistance with developing technology-related policies, including incident response plans. More information about our services may be found on our website, www.senseient.com, or you can call Mike Maschke at (703) 359-0700 for further information. Security assessments should be an annual (at least) exercise for all law firms—and they cost less than you might think. In fact, in an effort to be transparent, we have a flat-fee pricing chart at http://cybersecurityva.com/.

We are serious about our commitment to the legal profession and proud of our professional giveback through the American Bar Association. If you have a question, we'll do our best to assist. Just e-mail us at sensei@senseient.com. We appreciate all your comments and suggestions, as they help make each subsequent edition of this book better than the one before. Thanks, in advance, for your continuing help!

Introduction

by James A. Calloway, Esq.

*"The biggest technology issue we face as a profession today
is finding out what technology exists to perform legal tasks
and learning how we can use it ourselves to become
even better lawyers than we were before."*

—Jordan Furlong

*"We are stuck with technology when what
we really want is just stuff that works."*

—Douglas Adams

You might have a difficult time getting some lawyers to admit it, but like most all other businesses today, a law firm is dependent upon its technology.

Today it is practically impossible to effectively manage a law office or your client files without the use of information technology. Yet many in our profession, if pressed, might confess to sharing the view of Texas Supreme Court Justice Don R. Willett (@JusticeWillet) who, when asked what made him decide to go to law school, tweeted in response: "I was told there would be no math."

Many lawyers made the decision to attend law school because they didn't like math, science, or engineering. Now they stare at computer or smartphone screens for most of their working days. Life truly is what happens when you are making other plans.

During the past few weeks, I have had discussions with real practicing lawyers (i.e., not technology consultants with law licenses) about:

- Whether a lawyer has a duty to encrypt e-mail
- How to set up two-factor authentication
- Why lawyers should use speech recognition products like Dragon NaturallySpeaking for much of their dictation
- Incorporating automated document assembly into a small law firm's workflow
- Cybersecurity issues for a small law firm
- Using social media to market a law practice

I also spoke to a room full of judges about how litigators will be increasingly using data-driven analysis of a judge's prior rulings to attempt to predict future rulings.

Articles and posts about whether artificial intelligence or other smart software will someday replace lawyers are fairly common these days.

Several years ago the catchphrase might have been, "It is not your grandfather's (or grandmother's) law practice anymore." Today law practice is different in many ways than even five or ten years ago (e.g., e-filing) and the pace of change is not slowing down.

The "tools of the trade" for today's lawyer almost all require electricity. Many law firms still display rows of law books on the shelves in their library. But often these books have not been updated with pocket parts in several years. No one would really dispute today that competent legal research is performed digitally.

Using digital tools is also the trend in management of client files. Many law firms are finding it more efficient to use digital client files rather than paper client files. The transition to digital client files is certainly more challenging than learning to use the tools of electronic legal research. But ultimately almost all competent lawyers will implement a system for digital client files and all information associated with the client matter will be scanned, downloaded, or saved into the digital client file. Increasingly, those client files will be stored in the cloud. The payoffs will be numerous, including never misplacing a client file or losing an important document from a client file, being able to do a complete data backup of the client file, and being able to work with the documents in the client file from any location.

Your "tools of the trade" today, and in the future, are technology tools. Shopping for these tools can be a challenge. The vendors of these tools present the case that their tool is the absolute best and perfect for your type of law practice.

The *2017 Solo and Small Firm Legal Technology Guide* provides objective reviews of products that you need to successfully practice law. Sometimes this book will help you make a final decision when trying to select the best tool among competing products. On other occasions, this book will help you with a baseline understanding of what a particular product is supposed to help you accomplish.

It is no secret that many solo and small firm lawyers find themselves in an economic squeeze as changes affect the way they have always practiced law. The obvious reflexive response would be to circle the wagons, cut down on overhead, and plan to weather the storm until the climate improves. But, the wisest path is in the opposite direction. Plan for the future of your law practice. Embrace the changes we see happening in the ways consumers make purchasing decisions even while we may privately disagree with some of these trends.

On social media I saw a list of companies and services that didn't exist 12 years ago. I didn't take the time to fact check the list and some may have turned 13 before this book is published. But the list is still pretty amazing: Facebook, Twitter, YouTube, Uber, Airbnb, Snapchat, Instagram, Fitbit, Spotify, Dropbox, WhatsApp, Box, Hulu, and Pinterest. If you are not familiar with what the majority of these companies and apps do, you are failing a test in 21st-century cultural technology literacy.

The point is that big changes in business operations and consumer expectations happen far more rapidly today. Change has come slower to law firms than many other types of businesses. Disruption has hit businesses ranging from travel agents to taxicabs. But many of us believe that disruptive changes in the legal profession are now underway.

Twenty-three states have now adopted the American Bar Association's revision to the Model Rules of Professional Conduct referencing the need for a lawyer to be competent with the technology tools the lawyer uses, according to Robert Ambrogi writing at his LawSites Blog. The official comment to Rule 1.1 on Competence was amended to add the italicized language below:

> To maintain the requisite knowledge and skill, a lawyer should keep abreast of changes in the law and its practice, *including the benefits and risks associated with relevant technology*, engage in continuing study and education and comply with all continuing legal education requirements to which the lawyer is subject.

Ambrogi refers to this as the Ethical Duty of Technology Competence.

And lawyers have already evolved from the position not that long ago of "I barely know how to turn the computer on."

In August 2016, the ABA's Commission on the Future of Legal Services released its Report on the Future of Legal Services in the United States. You can download the report from the ABA at http://tinyurl.com/z52rgv8. This report is required reading for any lawyer who is not actively making plans for an imminent retirement. The report cites the often-quoted statistic that 80 percent of poor and moderate-income people cannot receive legal help they need, and it suggests measures for changing and improving how legal services should be accessed in the future. The report also discusses ways that technology might be used to deliver legal services more affordably.

These changes may well be needed, but it is unwise to believe that they will have no impact on solo and small firm lawyers serving consumers. The obvious conclusion is that many solo and small firm lawyers should now be gearing up with their own plans to deliver legal services more affordably. This involves more sophisticated use of today's already-available technology tools.

The 2017 Solo and Small Firm Legal Technology Guide will not replace a law firm IT director, but annually it provides the information required for the solo or small firm lawyer who *is* the firm IT director, like it or not. It also will serve as an indispensable guide for a local consultant who has the ability to manage a law firm's technology infrastructure, but is not aware of all of the legal-specific technology products that are available today. Some of this book will be read and reread, while other portions will be skimmed or skipped depending on the immediate technology needs of the firm. No law firm can avoid dealing with technology issues today. Lawyers in all practice settings can greatly benefit from this guide.

This guidebook can serve as a law firm's trusted source of basic information as well as in-depth information. It is a quick reference guide to understand where a new product or software release fits into a law firm's overall strategy. The authors of this guide bring their vast knowledge and expertise working with the legal profession to the pages of this volume. It is certainly the most cost-effective technology resource that any budget conscious law firm could hope to obtain.

All of our lives are more intertwined with technology today–as a glance around any public gathering will verify. Lawyer's lives are forever more intertwined with technology.

Your business clients are faced with the challenge of constantly improving their operations and efficiency. They will require similar improvements from the law firms serving them.

Today a litigator must understand e-discovery, a family lawyer must understand social media, and a lawyer advising businesses must have a broad understanding of data security and the specific technology tools that an industry or sector uses. A lawyer may generally rely on an assistant to do e-filing, but must have the training, ability, and confidence to personally e-file an important pleading should the need arise.

The 2017 Solo and Small Firm Legal Technology Guide can help you purchase new tools to replace those that have become outdated or broken. But the highest and best use of the *Guide* is to use it to create change and set your law firm on a path to success by using the tools profiled and information provided in this book to secure your law firm's place in our uncertain future.

CHAPTER ONE

Computers

Desktop Computers

Personal Computers (PCs)

The Dell OptiPlex line of computers continues to offer the perfect combination of performance and business-grade hardware at just the right price. All Dell computers can be purchased with a three, four, or five-year warranty and offer a large selection of available options for protecting your investment. They offer both hardware and software warranty protection of varying levels, along with same-day or next-business-day response for the replacement of failed computer hardware or software.

We strongly recommend the purchase of a three-year warranty—the average life span of a business computer system—with any new computer. Purchasing software technical support, in our judgment, is generally not worth the additional cost, especially when most firms have an IT provider who is familiar with their software and setup and can assist when help is needed, rather than having to rely on Dell for assistance.

Dell also offers accidental damage protection for its computer systems, which covers damage caused by spilled liquids, drops, falls, and electrical surges for a period of three to five years, at an additional cost ranging from $32 to $51. This cost is much lower than in previous editions of this book.

Another option from Dell worth noting is its Keep Your Hard Drive program. Typically, if a hard drive crashes while under warranty, Dell will take the failed hard drive and replace it with a new or refurbished one. Citing privacy concerns—with all the continuing data breaches in the news—Dell now offers its users the ability to keep their hard drives, even in the event a replacement is needed, though at an additional cost. The cost for this option ranges from $13 to $19, depending on the length of the warranty (three to five years), and it is a small price to pay to maintain total control over and responsibility for the sensitive and confidential data on the hard drive. For recommendations on how to securely remove data from a hard drive before disposal, check out the Utilities and Apps chapter.

The following table provides our recommendations for a Dell OptiPlex business-grade computer system with all of the hardware components included.

Windows-Based Desktop Computer

Hardware Component	Recommendation
Computer Model:	Dell OptiPlex 7040 Small Form Factor
Operating System:	Microsoft Windows 10 Professional 64-Bit
Processor:	6th Gen Intel Core i7-6700 Processor 3.4 GHz (Quad Core, 8 MB, 8T, 65W)
Memory:	8 GB 2133 MHz Memory DDR4 Memory
Video Card:	AMD RADEON R7 350X
Hard Drive:	500 GB 3.5-Inch SATA Hard Drive
Optical Drive:	8X DVD+/–RW
Network:	Intel Gigabit LAN 10/100/1000 Ethernet
Warranty:	Three-year basic hardware service with three-year on-site/in-home service after remote diagnosis
Other:	No mouse and keyboard required; no out-of-band systems management; six USB 3.0 ports included

The sixth-generation Intel Core i7-6000 quad-core 3.4 GHz processor will provide more than enough power to support both current and future versions of business-grade software, including the next version of the Windows operating system, throughout the life cycle of the machine. The Intel Core i7 processor has become the standard for business-grade systems. The Intel Core i7 quad-core processor is offered with varying levels of clock speeds, with the 3.4 GHz version currently in the upper range of processor clock speeds offered by Dell for this model of computer system. The faster the processor, the higher the premium for having cutting-edge technology. The amount of memory included in this system is enough to support your business applications, handling even "memory hungry" applications with ease. Eight gigabytes (GB) of memory have become the recommended standard for the minimum amount of memory in business-grade computers, given the low cost and high gain in performance for the upgrade.

The video card included in this system provides dual-link digital visual interface outputs, as well as one high-definition multimedia interface (HDMI) and two display port 1.2 connections. By providing dual interfaces, this graphics adapter allows you to have dual monitors or more, an option we will never go without when purchasing a new computer system. John calls his current setup 2¾ monitors since he has two 20-inch widescreen monitors and a 15½-inch display on his laptop. (Monitors, keyboards, and other peripherals are discussed in subsequent chapters.)

A hard drive plays an important role in the configuration of your computer system because it is the hardware component where your information (files) is actually stored. In short, the better the hard drive is, the faster your computer can read and write your data. This system comes with a 500 GB Serial ATA (SATA) hard drive, which will provide enough storage space for the average lawyer user. The 6 Gbps SATA interface allows for more throughput and higher cache than the previous revisions of the SATA specification. Of note, Dell now offers many solid-state drives for the OptiPlex model line, which will drastically speed up the time in which your computer "boots up," but they are much more costly than SATA drives and offer a smaller overall storage capacity.

When configuring an optical drive for the system, choosing the 8X DVD+/– RW drive will allow you to burn and read data from both CDs and DVDs. The Dell OptiPlex 7040 now includes six USB 3.0 ports (two on front, four on back) and four USB 2.0 ports.

Dell currently offers its OptiPlex 7040 computers preinstalled with either the Windows 7 or Windows 10 Professional operating systems. As of early 2016, Windows 10 has been vetted and is now our recommended choice for business computers.

The three-year on-site parts and labor warranty will cover hardware defects and failures of the computer system for a relatively small cost. The cost of this warranty is built into the cost of the recommended system and should be considered a requirement when purchasing a new computer for your business or firm. Dell provides the consumer with a toll-free phone number to call for technical support, and if any hardware needs to be replaced, Dell will send a support technician to your location to replace the defective part after remote diagnosis. The hardware replacement and labor cost is covered by the warranty, so there should be no additional out-of-pocket costs.

There are some additional pointers to consider when configuring this desktop system. First, most users already have their own wireless keyboard and mouse and don't need another basic USB keyboard and mouse taking up space in the desk drawer. This can be avoided by removing them from the default configuration of this system, and you'll save about $10. For those of you who don't have a wireless keyboard and mouse—you should be looking at upgrading immediately. Our recommendations for a wireless desktop suite can be found in the Computing Peripherals chapter.

Another tip: Dell also includes by default an out-of-band management device, which allows for remote diagnostics by the support personnel. Removing this piece of hardware can save you approximately $30. If you consider yourself to be technically challenged, however, you may want to leave the management device.

For those users who are looking to purchase a new monitor or two, Dell does offer the ability to bundle monitors when configuring your new computer system. If you need a new monitor or two, it may be a good idea to save a few bucks and bundle them with the purchase of your new computer system. Based on a price comparison, it appears that you save about $50 or more per monitor when selecting them at the time of your computer purchase, and we're always looking for ways to save you money! As of this writing, one of the options for monitors is $100 less than Dell's online retail price when bundled—talk about hidden savings!

Keep in mind that, on average, the expected life cycle of a new business computer system is around three years, which is covered by the three-year warranty you purchased. The recommended Dell OptiPlex 7040 Small Form Factor computer can be configured and purchased from Dell's website starting at around $1,050.

Remember that the "sweet spot" in buying computers changes regularly. Our specs will get you close, but they will shift slightly during the lifespan of this publication. You can receive a courtesy copy of our current specs (for workstations, laptops, and servers—PC or Mac) by e-mailing sensei@senseient.com and simply making a request. We are generally able to get our current specs to you within 24 hours during the workweek. We are happy to report that many, many readers are taking advantage of this offer, so don't be shy. We are always pleased to help.

Apple Computers (Macs)

In the past, Apple computers (Macs) were used primarily by businesses with a need for multimedia functions, such as video editing and graphic design—both areas in which Apple systems have always excelled. Usually,

Apple's appearance in an office environment was the result of someone having a personal preference for the Macintosh operating system over the Windows-based system.

Macs are still not as widely used in law offices as Windows-based computers are, but Apple's shift to using Intel-based processors in all of its systems, and the continued popularity of the iPad and iPhone, mean they are chosen more frequently now by solo and small firm lawyers. As a result of the change in processors, Macs can run both the Mac OS X and Windows operating systems on the same computer. In a way, it's like having two systems in one.

A Mac computer can be easily configured to connect to and function on a Windows-based network, including communicating with and authenticating a Windows domain controller.

For those concerned with computer security, Mac systems are perceived to be more secure than their Windows-based counterparts since they are not targeted as often by malware, due to the overall smaller number of Mac users. Some Mac users scoff at the suggestion that their computer should be running some kind of security software for protection. However, they would be wrong; Macs absolutely need security software—Apple itself now says so. Remember, the bad guys who write browser exploits (pieces of malware that take advantage of vulnerabilities in Internet browsers, such as Firefox) don't care what operating system the computer is running. In fact, security companies consistently warn that malware writers who attack browsers are increasingly becoming the real threat, as vulnerabilities in operating systems are less frequently targeted.

In 2015 and 2016, Mac users dealt with zero-day exploits targeting the latest version of the Mac OS X operating system ("Yosemite"), adware/spyware such as MacKeeper that installs unwanted adware on a user's systems, and other exploits targeting QuickTime and Safari.

In 2016, Mac users reported becoming infected with ransomware for the first time. Previously, only Windows-based computers were affected. The ransomware was detected in a downloadable Mac program called Transmission, which is used to share data through BitTorrent's network. The hackers of the ransomware, named "KeRanger," are requesting one bitcoin (about $575 at the time of writing) to decrypt or unlock affected files.

So Apple users, please don't be naive—you, too, need virus and malware protection. In 2012, Apple removed from its website the language suggesting that you didn't need this type of protection, and since then, it has been actively encouraging the use of security software.

Apple's continuing release of security patches, even for the latest version of its operating system, is a clear sign of just how targeted this operating system and its applications are by the developers of malware. For years, we have recommended that security protection suites be installed on all computers, regardless of the operating system.

While they are still not the majority, we are seeing Apple computers make their way into smaller law offices, especially in the solo, stand-alone environment. Now that Apple computers use Intel chipsets, users are taking advantage of the opportunity to better integrate their systems with the Windows world. Some users even run Windows on their Mac computers as the primary operating system. Others use Boot Camp, a free utility provided by Apple with each system, to dual-boot between Windows and Mac OS. With Boot Camp, users can install Microsoft Windows 7, 8.1, or 10 operating system right alongside Apple's OS X on any Intel-based Macintosh computer. Setting up a dual-boot system would be our recommendation, as opposed to running Windows within a virtual machine on a Mac computer.

To run Windows 7 or newer operating systems, you must upgrade your version of Boot Camp to version 4.0 or newer. The most current release of Boot Camp is version 6, which added support for Windows 10. Boot Camp 6 includes support for the following features of your Mac in Windows 10: USB 3.0, USB-C, Thunderbolt, built-in SD or SDXC card slot, USB Apple Super-Drive and the Apple keyboard, trackpad, and mouse.

The Boot Camp software guides users through the processes of creating a new partition of the local hard drive on which to install the Windows operating system and also provides all of the necessary Windows drivers required for hardware functionality. As an alternative to dual-booting with Boot Camp, some users have even purchased third-party products like Parallels Workstation or downloaded Oracle's VM VirtualBox, which allows them to run Windows, Linux, and other operating systems within the Mac OS itself. Virtual machine (VM) software is described in more detail in the Servers and Server Operating Systems chapters of this book.

The iMac desktop systems combine performance and ergonomics by putting the hardware components that make up the system in the same casing as the monitor, eliminating the need for separate components like a tower unit sitting underneath your desk. As a result, the space-saving design allows you to free up both desk and floor space without giving up performance. The following table provides our recommendations for an iMac business-grade desktop system with all of the hardware components outlined.

Macintosh-Based Desktop Computer

Hardware Component	Recommendation
Computer Model:	21.5-inch iMac
Operating System:	MacOS Sierra v10.12
Processor:	Intel Core i5 Quad-Core 2.8 GHz (Turbo Boost up to 3.3 GHz)
Memory:	8 GB 1867 MHz LPDDR3
Video Card:	Intel Iris Pro Graphics 6200
Hard Drive:	1 TB (5400-rpm) SATA Hard Drive
CD/DVD-ROM:	8X SuperDrive (DVD+R DL/DVD3RW/CD-RW)
Network:	10/100/1000BASE-T Gigabit Ethernet Port, 802.11 ac Wi-Fi wireless networking (802.11 a/b/g/n compatible), Bluetooth 4.0
Warranty:	Three-year AppleCare Protection Plan for iMacs
Other:	FaceTime HD Camera, built-in 21.5-inch monitor and stereo speakers, dual microphones, two Thunderbolt 2 ports, four USB 3 ports, Mini Display-Port, Apple wireless keyboard and Magic Mouse 2, SDXC card slot, and Kensington lock slot

The 21.5-inch iMac comes with an Intel Core i5 quad-core 2.8 GHz processor, 8 GB of memory, and the latest MacOS Sierra v10.12 operating system. For an additional $200, this system can be configured for up to 16 GB of memory, which may be overkill for basic business usage—unless you are running a Windows virtual machine from within Mac OS X. If you choose to dual-boot, which is our recommendation, 8 GB of memory should be plenty. The 1 TB 5400 RPM SATA hard drive comes standard and will provide more than enough storage space and hard drive performance for the average lawyer. However, if you feel that you need additional storage space or performance speed, the hard drive can be configured with 256 GB of flash storage or Apple's 1 TB or 2 TB Fusion Drive—a combination flash storage and regular hard drive. The flash storage media will contain the files necessary to boot and load the operating system, dramatically increasing the speed with which the computer system starts up.

The standard Ethernet adapter and 802.11 ac Wi-Fi wireless networking adapter will allow your computer to connect to the business network, whether over a wired network or wireless, even if it's Windows-based. The

AirPort wireless adapter is also backward compatible with 802.11a/b/g/n wireless networks.

The other standard hardware included with the iMac is the built-in Face-Time HD camera, stereo speakers, 21.5-inch LED-backlit display with intrusion prevention system (IPS) technology, four USB 3.0 ports, two Thunderbolt 2 ports, and one SDXC memory card slot. This system also includes one Mini DisplayPort, which allows users to add a second external monitor to their computer system, and the standard Apple wireless keyboard and Magic Mouse 2. The 21.5-inch iMac computer weighs 12.5 pounds and has a depth of about 7 inches, so finding room on your desk for one of these systems is very easy.

Apple's standard warranty with a new iMac provides you with 90 days of telephone support and a one-year limited warranty. We recommend that you upgrade the warranty to the extended AppleCare Protection Plan for iMac, which provides you with telephone and service support for three years. The cost to extend the warranty plan is $169 and is well worth it. The 21.5-inch iMac computer can be purchased from Apple's webstore starting at $1,299.

Laptops

Personal Computers (PCs)

The Dell Latitude line of laptop computers continues to combine performance and mobility in a laptop system that remains at the top of its class. These business-grade laptops are thin and extremely light, weighing less than 4.5 pounds. They are a perfect fit for the mobile lawyer and provide an ideal mobile computing solution. The following table provides our recommendations for a Dell Latitude business-grade laptop with all of the hardware components included.

Windows-Based Laptop Computer

Hardware Component	Recommendation
Computer Model:	Dell Latitude E7470
Processor:	6th Gen Intel Core i7-6600U 2.6 GHz Dual-Core 4M Cache
Operating System:	Microsoft Windows 10 Professional
Memory:	8 GB 2133 MHz DDR4

Hardware Component	Recommendation
Video Card:	Intel HD Graphics
Hard Drive:	M.2 256 GB SATA Class 20 Solid State Hard Drive
CD/DVD-ROM:	None
Network:	10/100/1000 Mbps Ethernet adapter, Intel Tri-Band Wireless-AC 18260 WiGig + Wi-Fi + BT4.1 wireless card
Warranty:	Three-year basic hardware service with three-year next-business-day limited on-site service after remote diagnosis
Other:	14-Inch HD antiglare LCD screen, 65W AC power adapter, four-cell/55 WHr primary battery with ExpressCharge, weight starting at 3.13 lbs., three USB 3.0 ports, HDMI, memory card reader, camera and microphone, fingerprint reader, contactless smartcard reader

The Dell Latitude E7470 comes with a sixth-generation Intel Core i7-6600U 2.6 GHz processor and 8 GB of memory, which should be sufficient to run all of the business applications of a mobile lawyer. The system also comes preinstalled with Microsoft Windows 10 Professional.

The system's fingerprint reader provides the level of security needed to protect your personal files and confidential data. When it's enabled, you can restrict user logon access to either the biometric access or to a user name and password. A fingerprint reader keeps data on the hard drive secure through encryption, with the hardware requiring successful authentication before the data contents can be decrypted. Enabling a start-up or hard drive password in the system's BIOS is a great way to add an extra layer of protection to your system, as is encrypting the hard drive with full-disk encryption.

The Intel HD graphics card supplies crisp, clear graphics to the 14-inch wide LCD display. The 256 GB hard drive will provide more than enough storage space for the mobile user, with a hard drive speed that will supply faster drive performance. There is no internal optical drive included with this model, so if you need to read optical discs, you will need to look at external solutions.

The Ethernet adapter will allow you to connect your laptop to your network when you're in the office, and the wireless network adapter will allow you to stay connected when on the move. The Intel wireless adapter provides connectivity to 802.11a/b/g/n wireless networks, supporting dual-band operation (2.4 and 5 GHz) with data rates up to 300 megabits per second (Mbps). The four-cell battery is an upgrade that will supply the laptop with power longer than the standard three-cell battery and should charge faster as well with the ExpressCharge feature. This battery upgrade is a must-have if you plan to use the wireless network adapter when running the laptop off of the battery, although this will add some slight weight to the unit. Finally, the integrated HD video webcam and digital microphone are great for video-conferences or recording audio, such as podcasts.

The three-year, next-business-day on-site parts and labor warranty is the same warranty described in the Desktop Computers section. The Dell Latitude E7470 can be purchased from Dell's website starting at around $1,700.

If you are particularly clumsy or accident-prone, you may want to consider adding the Accidental Damage Service to your purchase. This plan covers any damage to the laptop, including such things as liquid spills (one client has used this plan multiple times to cover the unwelcome effects of spilling red wine), surges, and dropping the device. It does not cover intentional damage, theft, or normal wear and tear. For the additional $83 to $118, depending on the length of the warranty (three- to five-year options), you will have peace of mind when you set your coffee cup (or wine glass) on the keyboard.

Apple Computers (Macs)

The Apple MacBook Pro is perfect for the mobile lawyer who requires a powerful notebook in a compact and lightweight design. The MacBook Pro laptop comes standard with a widescreen Retina display, built-in FaceTime HD camera, wireless network adapter, and much more. The MacBook Pro laptop is available with 13- or 15-inch screens. Both the 13- and 15-inch MacBook Pros come standard with the Retina display. The MacBook Pro is available in both Silver and Space Gray with glass LED-backlit display with IPS technology. The MacBook Pro can be fully integrated into any Windows-based network without too much overhead and configuration. The following table provides our recommendations for an Apple MacBook Pro business-grade laptop with all of the hardware components included.

Macintosh-Based Laptop Computer

Hardware Component	Recommendation
Computer Model:	15-Inch MacBook Pro
Operating System:	MacOS Sierra v10.12

Hardware Component	Recommendation
Processor:	Intel Core i7 Quad-Core 2.6 GHz (Turbo Boost up to 3.5 GHz)
Memory:	16 GB 2133 MHz LPDDR3
Video Card:	Radeon Pro 450 with 2 GB memory
Hard Drive:	256 GB PCIe-based Flash Storage
CD/DVD-ROM:	None
Network:	802.11ac Wi-Fi wireless networking (802.11 a/b/g/n compatible), Bluetooth 4.2
Warranty:	Three-year AppleCare Protection Plan
Other:	FaceTime HD Camera, built-in 15.4-inch LED-backlit display with IPS technology, stereo speakers, four Thunderbolt 3 ports (USB-C), and display port, Touch Bar with integrated Touch ID sensor

The base 15-inch MacBook Pro laptop comes with 16 GB of memory (minimum amount available) and the MacOS Sierra v10.12 operating system. The Radeon Pro 450 video card provides perfect high resolution to the 15.4-inch-wide Retina LED display, with a maximum resolution of 2880 × 1800 pixels. The 256 GB flash storage hard drive provides enough space to store all of your documents, pictures, and music. The laptop no longer comes with an internal optical drive, so if you need to be able to read and burn optical discs, you will need to look at external solutions. The built-in 802.11 ac Wi-Fi wireless networking adapter will keep you connected on the road, and it supports the 802.11n standard. The adapter is also backward compatible with 802.11a/b/g wireless networks. The aluminum body MacBook is very light, weighing just barely over 4 pounds.

If you need more processing power, this model can be upgraded to an i7 2.9 GHz quad-core processor—for a pretty penny!

The Force Touch trackpad gives you precise cursor control and supports two-finger scrolling, tap, double-tap, and drag capabilities. It also now supports pressure-sensing capabilities. If you have been a lifelong Windows user, be forewarned: There is no right-click button on the trackpad. To right-click on a Mac, you must hold down the Control key while clicking. A tip for former Windows users: Instead of holding down the Control key to initiate a right-click, you can tap the trackpad with two fingers—you just have to enable the option within the Keyboard & Mouse settings. The new integrated Touch Bar replaces the function keys that used to appear at the top of the keyboard, providing users with more versatile functions that change with what you're doing on the screen. Apple has also included Touch ID, enabling instant access to logins and fast, secure online purchases with Apple Pay.

The new Thunderbolt 3 charger allows users to charge and provide power from any of the four ports, and since Thunderbolt 3 is reversible, no matter how users plug in the adapter, it's always the right way!

The sleek and elegant design of the MacBook Pro is what sets it apart from the competition. The design and celebrated ease of use makes the MacBook Pro a smart choice when purchasing a laptop for yourself or your firm. The MacBook Pro configured above can be purchased from Apple's webstore for $2,399.

Netbooks/Ultrabooks

Netbooks and ultrabooks continue to be very popular among mobile users, including lawyers. Essentially, these devices are highly portable mini-laptops. They are much smaller, cheaper, and lighter than most traditional laptops. As with the other computer recommendations, it is impossible to mention all of the available manufacturers and models of ultrabooks and netbooks.

More recently, netbooks have taken a backseat to the class of laptops called ultrabooks. Ultrabooks, which are becoming increasingly popular, are paper-thin laptops (nearly weightless compared to a traditional laptop). Ultrabooks have more robust hardware specifications than netbooks, but they also command a higher price.

Apple released the MacBook Air, an ultrabook considered the first of its class, long before PC manufacturers released the first competitor. Much as the iPad has dominated Android-based tablets, in part because it was first to the market, the MacBook Air continues to be an extremely popular alternative to the regular laptop for a mobile user. It's rumored that the new MacBook line of Apple laptops will ultimately replace the MacBook Air within the next year or so. We will see!

The MacBook Air is offered in a 13-inch model, with configurable internal flash storage capacity available from 128 to 256 GB. The 1.6 GHz Dual Core Intel Core i5 processor is more than capable of handling web browsing and document editing, but not a lot more than that, which is perfect for the mobile lawyer. For power users, the processor can be upgraded to a 2.2 GHz dual-core Intel Core i7 for an added cost of $150. The MacBook Air now comes standard with 8 GB of memory. The battery of the MacBook Air will last up to 12 hours when surfing the web.

If you were to hold the MacBook Air, weighing just 2.96 pounds, you'd never go back to using a standard laptop. The MacBook Air is available for purchase on Apple's website starting at $999.

Tablets

Most users would expect to see the iPad recommended in this section, but keep in mind the iPad is much more of a personal device than it is a true laptop replacement. You will find our recommendations and thoughts on the iPad later in this book, so please don't worry.

Business-grade tablets, those that can truly replace a laptop, are quickly becoming the next big thing in solo and small firm technology. Sharon and John are being bombarded with questions on this very topic at many of the presentations that they give throughout the country—is there a tablet that can actually replace my laptop, while maintaining all of the functionality?

The answer is, yes there is. You can now leave your 4.5-pound laptop and clunky travel bag at home when you need to hit the road.

The Microsoft Surface Pro 4 is truly a laptop replacement. The tablet boasts a 12.3-inch PixelSense touchscreen display with a resolution of 2736 × 1824. The sixth-generation Intel Core processor (m3, i5, i7) is the same processor that you will find in your laptop computer system, and it provides this tablet with more than enough horsepower to run your business applications smoothly. The tablet comes preloaded with Microsoft Windows 10, which means that you can load and run any of your necessary business software—allowing you to get the same functionality out of this device as you can out of your laptop—at just a fraction of the weight!

The device can be configured with 4, 8, or 16 GB of memory and anywhere from 128 GB to 1 TB of storage space. For network connectivity, this device comes with a wireless adapter supporting 802.11a/b/g/n and Bluetooth 4.0 wireless technology. It has both a front- and rear-facing camera, as well as a stereo microphone perfect for videoconferencing. We would recommend that you give serious consideration to the 16 GB memory, 256 GB storage, i7 unit.

The Microsoft Surface Pro 4 tablet can be purchased online from Microsoft's webstore (www.microsoft.com) or from your local electronics retailer starting at $899.

CHAPTER TWO

Computer Operating Systems

Older versions of the Microsoft Windows operating system (Windows Vista and older) are not addressed in this book, mainly because most of the versions are no longer relevant and the majority (Vista is the exception) are not supported by Microsoft, which means they should not be used by business or individuals due to the insecurity of these operating systems. Vista has now entered the "Extended Support" phase that lasts through April 11, 2017—although it's been dead in our minds for years.

Even today, we still come across law firms that are using computers running Microsoft Windows XP. Please note that this operating system is no longer supported by Microsoft and its use should be discontinued immediately. Continuing to use it is regarded by legal ethicists as an ethical violation since it no longer receiving security updates and places confidential client data at risk. Computers running Microsoft Windows XP should be decommissioned and replaced, without hesitation!

Microsoft Windows 7

Windows 7 is the successor to Windows Vista and was made available to the general public on October 22, 2009. Microsoft was ready to move on from the epic failure that was Vista, and finally got it right with the release of Windows 7. It is more "XP-like," emphasizing performance improvements and eliminating the compatibility issues that plagued Microsoft Vista. We have run the various versions of Windows 7 since it was first released as a beta and loved it—as did many of our clients. Recently, this operating system has started to take a backseat to Windows 10, our new recommended choice for new computers.

Windows 7 is available in six editions, but only a few of those are worth mentioning to the solo and small firm market:

Starter Edition—is primarily for small notebooks, such as a netbook. The Starter Edition is 32-bit only, supports only a single processor, and does not support multiple monitors, such as dual displays. This edition was not designed for business use.

Home Premium Edition—comes bundled with Internet Explorer 10 (which is no longer supported) allows for a connection to a home network, and is for home use only. The upgrade (from a previous operating system) retail cost for this edition is $149.99 per license, and the full retail cost for this edition is $199.99 per license.

Professional Edition—includes all the features of the Home Premium Edition, plus allows connection to a company network, such as a domain, and includes a backup-and-restore utility to protect your system. The upgrade retail cost for this edition is $199.99 per license, and the full retail cost for this edition is $299.99 per license.

Ultimate Edition—includes all the features of the Professional Edition, plus BitLocker encryption to help secure your data. The upgrade retail cost for this edition is $219.99 per license, and the full retail cost for this edition is $319.99 per license.

For your business, you will need to purchase either the Professional or Ultimate Edition to install on your computer systems. Obviously, upgrading is less expensive than purchasing a full license. If you have computer systems running Windows XP, the time to upgrade has long passed.

Users may also upgrade their computer systems to Windows 7 from both Windows XP and Windows Vista. However, for users upgrading from Windows XP, you must be careful when performing an upgrade. This upgrade path actually performs a "clean" installation, and the user must back up all programs and data because the upgrade will not retain any of the information. There isn't a prompt during the upgrade process to notify users to back up their data, so this step must be performed before beginning the upgrade process. In other words, there is no direct upgrade path from XP to Windows 7. It is probably best to do a clean install anyway to clean up any past "sins" and remove any leftover files from applications that didn't completely uninstall in the past. You can get some advice about your hardware and software compatibility by running the free Windows Upgrade Advisor (https://www.microsoft.com/en-us/download/details.aspx?id=20). This utility will tell you if your hardware is compatible and what software may need to be upgraded.

If you are upgrading from Windows Vista, most of you will not have to worry about the process of deleting all of your information. As was the case when upgrading from Windows XP to Windows Vista, you need perform a clean install only if you are going to a version that is lower on the food chain (e.g., Windows Vista Ultimate to Windows 7 Home Edition).

Regardless of the upgrade path you take, we always strongly recommend that you back up your system and data before upgrading.

The only other installation scenario with a clean installation is an upgrade from a 32-bit version to a 64-bit version operating system, regardless of the edition. Microsoft released the only service pack for this operating system (SP1) to the public in February 2011, and at the time of its release, it was not a mandatory update. This service pack addressed a number of security issues and fixed a few bugs related to HDMI audio and the printing of XPS documents.

Please note that Windows 7 can no longer be purchased online at the Microsoft Store, but it is still available when configuring a new system from Dell and from other third-party retailers, both online and in brick-and-mortar locations.

Microsoft Windows 8

Windows 8 is the successor to Windows 7 and became available to consumers in early fall of 2012.

The Windows 8 user interface is built based on the Metro design language, featuring a new start screen, Internet Explorer 10, support for USB 3.0, and a new Windows Defender. Windows 8 has also added support for UEFI Secure-Boot, which is a feature used to prevent unauthorized firmware, operating systems, or drivers from running at boot time.

There has been much controversy over the Metro look, replacing the all-too-familiar Windows Start button. The Metro UI environment is tile-based, similar to the Start screen seen on the Windows Phone operating system. The Start button had originally been removed from the taskbar, but was later reinstated with the update, Windows 8.1, released in October 2013.

Windows 8 is available in four editions, three of which are focused on business-grade computers: Windows 8, Windows 8 Pro, and Windows 8 Enterprise. The Windows RT edition is built to run solely on tablet hardware.

Windows 8 has been available for a few years now as of this writing and is headed toward a fate similar to Windows Vista. The adoption of this operating system by businesses was very slow, and even that may be a generous description. We never upgraded our computer systems to Windows 8, and now purchase new computers for our clients with Windows 10 preinstalled.

Microsoft Windows 10

Windows 10, the latest operating system from Microsoft, is the successor to Windows 8 and was released to the public on July 29, 2015. Windows 10 was being offered as a free upgrade for those computers running Windows 7 Service Pack 1 or Windows 8.1 until July 29, 2016. This date has come and gone and users can still get their hands on a no-cost upgrade. Microsoft has continued to provide the free upgrade to Windows 10 for customers that use assistive technologies, which include such features as a magnifier to better see the screen, a narrator to read text aloud, and even keyboard shortcuts. To get the upgrade at no charge, you will need to visit the Windows 10 free upgrade for customers who use assistive technologies web page, which can be found here: https://www.microsoft.com/en-us/accessibility/windows 10upgrade. Currently, Microsoft has not announced an end date of the free upgrade offer for customers using assistive technology.

For all other users, Windows 10 Pro is also offered in retail packaging priced at $199.

Microsoft introduced a universal application architecture across all Microsoft product families including computers, tablets, smartphones, and Xbox One, allowing for applications to be designed and run across all of the devices— similar to the iOS environment. One of the main features that was included was an updated Start Menu (combination of Windows 7 and 8), a new web browser named Microsoft Edge, and integrated support for fingerprint and facial recognition logins. Microsoft's Edge browser is now the default browser in Windows 10 and has adopted the HTML5 specification, dropping much of the support for legacy Internet Explorer releases (meaning websites developed for IE6 or IE7 won't render in this new browser).

Also new to this operating system is the inability for users to be able to selectively install Windows updates. Microsoft now installs all Windows updates automatically. The release of this software has been positively received by the public, but one of the initial criticisms, and a valid one, involves privacy concerns. By default, the system transmits user data to Microsoft or its partners, a troubling setting. For now, it's not easy to restrict what Windows collects. The data can be restricted—it's easier if users don't use the Express Settings during setup, but rather select the "custom install" to turn off some of the data collecting options. As an alternative, you can try one of the free tools to change the settings in a more user-friendly interface (bgr.com/2015/08/14/windows-10-spying-prevention -privacy-tools/).

There is no doubt that Windows 10 is ready for prime time and should be the operating system of choice when purchasing a new computer system or upgrading an existing one.

Mac OS X Version 10.9 (Mavericks) Operating System

Released to the public in late 2013, Mavericks was the tenth major release of the OS X operating system. Some of the new features included integration with iBooks, a new Maps application (Google Maps competitor), a reworked Calendar application, an updated version of Safari, the introduction of an iCloud Keychain, improved notifications, Finder Tabs, and improved battery and performance-boosting technologies.

Mac OS X Version 10.10 (Yosemite) Operating System

Released to the public in October 2014, Yosemite was the 11th major release of the OS X operating system. With Yosemite, Apple introduced a revision to the operating system's user interface, with all of the graphics inspired by iOS 7. While it still possesses the desktop appearance, the inclusion of new icons, light and color schemes, and even new default fonts, Apple put a lot of effort into the upgrading of the look and feel of the software.

Some of the new features of this operating system include the Handoff functionality, which allows the operating system to integrate with iOS 8 devices over Bluetooth LE and Wi-Fi. The Notification center has been revamped and includes new features, such as a "Today" view, and the Spotlight feature is now a more prominent part of the operating system.

Mac OS X Version 10.11 (El Capitan) Operating System

Released to the public in September 2015, El Capitan is the 12th major release of the OS X operating system. El Capitan is the final version to be released under the name OS X; its successor, Sierra, was announced as MacOS Sierra.

All Macintosh computers that can run Mountain Lion, Mavericks, or Yosemite can also run El Capitan. Like previous releases of the OS X software, this version is free to upgrade—so it's a no-brainer to do so!

OS X El Capitan includes features to improve the security, performance, design, and usability of OS X. Compared to the previous release, Apple states that launching apps is 40 percent faster and switching between apps is twice as fast. The latest operating system introduced support for snapping two windows side by side to create a split view, similar to the feature in Microsoft Windows 7. El Capitan also adds multi-touch gestures to its applications like Mail and Messages that allow a user to delete or mark e-mails or conversations by swiping a finger.

As far as security goes, El Capitan has added a feature called System Integrity Protection, referred to as "rootless." This feature protects certain system processes, files, and folders from being modified or tampered with by other processes even when executed by the root user. This feature is enabled by default, which is a great move by Apple—one that previously had been overlooked.

MacOS Sierra Version 10.12 Operating System

Released to the public in September 2016, MacOS Sierra is the latest major release of Apple's Mac operating system for desktops and servers. Now having dropped the Mac OS X naming convention, one of the new features of the latest operating system includes the addition of the Siri intelligent assistant, which can now be used to send messages, search the web, find files, and adjust settings. Also featured is iCloud Drive, which can upload the user's documents and desktop directories and sync them to other devices. Apple has also released a preview of the Apple File System (APFS), which is the replacement for the HFS Plus file system, previously used on Apple computers. This operating system is built for solid-state drives and flash memory, and now natively supports file-system encryption without the requirement of additional software support (FileVault). The new file system is set to be released in full sometime in 2017. Apple has improved the support for communication between Apple devices using Bluetooth and Wi-Fi with Auto Unlock and the Universal Clipboard. With Auto Unlock, users can unlock their user account by holding a paired Apple Watch close to the device. With the Universal Clipboard, users can share their clipboard between MacOS Sierra and iOS 10 devices, including pictures and videos.

Finally with this latest release, Apple has updated and enhanced the Photos application, Safari, and the Messages app, and now includes support for Apple Pay.

Users who have switched on automatic downloads and have enough storage on their Macs will automatically be prompted to get the latest version of MacOS—it will not install without permission. Like previous releases of Mac operating systems, this update is free and should be installed when prompted.

CHAPTER THREE

Monitors

Now that you have your brand new computer or shiny new laptop, you are ready for the task of picking out that brand new monitor—and you can have all the real estate your heart desires these days. The era of 14¬inch monitors is long gone. You might even be able to reclaim some territory on your desk—and actually see some wood for a change—even if you choose to have two or three monitors. We have standardized on two monitors for clients and ourselves, although John has recently started asking for a full-sized third instead of the "partial size" laptop screen!

Choosing a monitor can be an overwhelming task because of all the options and bells and whistles to choose from. If you don't know what you're looking for, you can be inundated with all of the technical jargon that advertisers use to get you to purchase their monitors. We will walk you through the process and explain how to weed through all of the technical jargon, providing you with a solid recommendation for purchasing a monitor.

First and foremost, the days of CRT monitors are long gone. Charities won't even take these monitors as donations anymore, so they can only be recycled at this point. The flat-panel monitor has taken over.

Flat-panel, widescreen monitors have a flat viewing surface that provides a better viewing angle than the curved CRT monitors did. They are also less bulky, taking up only a fraction of the desktop space and weighing next to nothing when compared to the weight of the ancient CRT dinosaurs. Flat-panel monitors have become very affordable.

Flat-panel monitors, like computers, come in all different sizes, resolutions, and features. The flat-panel monitor that we recommend is the Dell E2316H 23-inch widescreen (16:9) WLED monitor. This monitor offers an optimal resolution of 1920 × 1080 at 60 Hz, which will provide you so much desktop real estate that you won't know what to do with it all, even if you follow our recommendation and get two of them. The higher resolution will enable you to view documents, images, and videos with stunning detail, vivid colors, and seamless motion.

This monitor accepts video graphics array (VGA) and DisplayPort (version 1.2a) connectivity, and offers a contrast ratio of 1000:1, as well as a maximum viewing angle of 170 degrees. This monitor weighs about 11 pounds and if needed, can be mounted on a wall using a standard VESA wall mount. The Dell E2316H 23-inch widescreen monitor can be purchased online from Dell's website for $149.99 and comes with a standard three-year hardware warranty. If bundled with the purchase of a new computer from Dell, you may be able to get a much better deal on the price.

If you need a larger viewing area, you may want to consider using dual widescreen monitors. Of course, your computer must have dual-monitor support, which most of the newer computers have by default. Usually, you will find that purchasing dual monitors, or in some cases three monitors, will be cheaper than purchasing a single large one. And anecdotally, we have found that folks who move to dual monitors never want to go back. Certainly, none of the authors would accept anything less than dual monitors—and we are all beginning to covet a third, although we would really need bigger desks, if not a special built-in shelf. We can dream. . . .

CHAPTER FOUR

Computing Peripherals

If you thought purchasing the right computer and monitor was tough, wait until you realize how many options there are when it comes to selecting computer peripherals. Having the right peripherals can make your computing faster, more comfortable, and a better overall, productive experience. Wireless devices have brought peripherals into a new dimension, getting rid of that Gordian knot mess of wires that we all used to struggle to untangle. The following sections provide our recommendations for portable mice, wireless desktops, external storage devices, and speakers. As always, bear in mind that there is a universe of choices. These are our top picks.

Portable Mouse

For portability, those users who travel with laptops and want a nifty little wireless travel mouse should consider the excellent Microsoft Wireless Mobile Mouse 4000. Using 2.4 GHz wireless technology, this mouse connects to your computer with a reliable connection range of up to 30 feet. The nano transceiver that you plug into the USB port of your computer has a slot inside the mouse to store it when on the go. This mouse uses Microsoft's BlueTrack technology to smoothly track the mouse movements on virtually any surface, even on your living room carpet. This notebook mouse also includes the standard back button and scroll wheel, in an ergonomic design that we've all become accustomed to. If you are concerned about the current battery life, the mouse includes an indicator light that will glow red when the batteries need to be replaced—and it only requires a single AA battery, which is included. The battery should last ten months or more before needing replacement. Of course, you do need to look at the light periodically so that you don't end up with a dead mouse and have to scramble for a new battery. This mouse is compatible with both Windows and Mac computers, including the Windows 10 operating system, and can be purchased online from Microsoft's website for $29.95.

Wireless Keyboards

Over the past few years wireless keyboards have become extremely popular—so popular that it's almost impossible to find a USB keyboard and mouse. In fact, it's been so many years since we purchased a stand-alone mouse or keyboard that we no longer provide recommendations for each of these individual devices. We recommend the purchase of a wireless keyboard set instead. A wireless keyboard set is a keyboard and mouse combination that connects to your computer using radio-frequency technology. The keyboard and mouse are powered with standard or rechargeable batteries and transmit their signals to a desktop receiver that is connected to the computer. It requires very little setup to install, and it eliminates the need for cables, which have plagued computer users since the first PC came into existence.

Our recommendation when purchasing a wireless keyboard set is the Logitech Wireless Wave Combo MK550. This wireless keyboard comes with a wave key design that provides superior comfort with full-size and full-travel keys designed for quiet operation. The slight regular curve of the keyboard features consistently sized keys, which lets you type with confidence and ease. The keyboard uses the standard QWERTY layout, so you don't have to relearn how to type, as you do with some of the other curved keyboards. The height of the keyboard is adjustable, with three options for leg height, allowing you to choose the position that's most comfortable for you. The keyboard comes with a cushioned, contoured palm rest to provide comfort to your wrists while you type. The keyboard uses 128-bit AES encryption to secure data as it's transmitted from the keyboard to the receiver, and both the keyboard and mouse use the 2.4 GHz wireless spectrum to connect to the receiver. Logitech claims that the keyboard can operate up to three years before the batteries need to be replaced, and if true, the batteries should last the expected lifetime of the keyboard. The package includes four AA batteries, with the keyboard and mouse requiring two each.

Logitech's wireless laser mouse M510, which is part of the MK550 combination, should operate for up to two years before the batteries will need to be replaced. The laser mouse uses a small infrared laser instead of an LED, which increases the resolution and sensitivity of the mouse. The laser mouse keeps your hands pain-free with the integration of contoured sides and soft rubber grips. The Logitech Wireless Wave Combo includes a three-year limited hardware warranty. This wireless keyboard combo is compatible with Windows 7 or Windows 10. The Logitech Wireless Wave Combo MK550 can be purchased for around $79.99 from your local electronics retailer or online at www.logitech.com.

External Storage Devices

External storage devices are pieces of hardware that connect to your computer using USB, FireWire, eSATA, or some other type of interface and are used to store electronic data. These devices come in all sizes, shapes, colors, and volumes of storage space. They have all but replaced the CD-ROM, DVD, and backup tapes as the leading means to store electronic data because of their portability, low cost, and vast amount of storage space. You should consider some type of secure authentication or encryption for external storage, especially if confidential client information is backed up or stored on these devices. Most products now come with some sort of built-in hardware or software encryption that can be enabled at no additional cost. Just be sure to remember your passphrase, because if you forget it, there's no way to recover your data.

External Hard Drives

External hard drives are great devices for storing media such as videos, pictures, and music and for backing up the data from your internal hard drive. These devices are very easy to install and use, and are relatively inexpensive. Most external hard drives are plug-and-play devices, which means you simply have to plug them into your computer to use them—and nothing else! The drivers necessary for these devices to work are loaded automatically by the operating system. For the volume of information they can store, they are a very good, inexpensive backup solution. Also, lawyers who are otherwise technically challenged seem to do well with this form of backup, which can really be reduced to the push of a button or an automated method that so many lawyers seem to prefer—set it and forget it. The Seagate Backup Plus Desktop Drive is the external hard drive that we recommend for all lawyers and users. The Backup Plus Desktop Drive comes with available capacities of 2, 3, 4, 5, 6, and 8 TB of storage space. The 4, 6, and 8 TB Backup Plus Hub drives include two integrated USB ports on the front of the devices, so that you can back up your files while connecting to and recharging your tablet, smartphone, or camera—even if your computer is powered off. These capacities allow you to select the amount of storage space that best meets your requirements and may provide enough storage capacity to contain backups from more than one computer system. The Backup Plus

Desktop Drive comes with backup software that can be used to automatically back up your data to the device, and it is Windows 10 compatible. You can now even use the Seagate Mobile Backup app to easily back up photos and videos on the go directly from your mobile device to the Backup Plus Desktop Drive.

All of the available models should provide enough storage space to back up all of the data required by most lawyers. If you're looking to back up multiple computers and/or a server, then you probably will need to purchase one of the larger-sized drives—and make sure that you purchase more than one. We recommend that if you're using this external hard drive to back up your company data and files, then you should rotate drives on a weekly or more frequent basis—keeping one on-site and the other one off-site. The Backup Plus Hub drives also include two years of OneDrive cloud storage (200 GBs) for free. This will allow your firm to recover its information in the event of a disaster such as a fire in the office. With the recent rise of ransomware infections, we recommend disconnecting the drive when it is not being used—and keeping an encrypted copy "in the cloud." That way if your computer gets infected with ransomware such as CryptoLocker, your data won't get encrypted and you will have backups that can be used to restore your information.

These devices connect to your computer through the USB 3.0 interface (backward compatible with USB 2.0) and can be placed flat or on their side. The drive is whisper quiet and relatively small in size, so it can sit on your desk or on top of your computer without taking away valuable space. Compatible with both Windows and Mac computers, the drive includes an new technology file system (NTFS) driver for Mac that will allow interoperability between systems without the need to reformat the drive. The Backup Plus Desktop Drive can be purchased online at www.seagate.com for between $99 and $249, depending on the storage capacity, and it comes with a two-year standard warranty.

Flash Drives

USB flash drives (thumb drives) are small, portable storage devices that use flash memory to store electronic data. Currently, they are offered with storage volume sizes ranging from 4 GB to 1 TB. For the most part, USB flash drives with capacities of 4 GB and smaller have been discontinued—in fact, our local computer supply store has all but gotten rid of USB flash drives less than 8 GB! USB flash drives offer many advantages over other portable storage devices, such as the floppy disk, CD-ROM, and DVD. In particular, they are smaller, are more durable, are faster, and can hold more data.

Unfortunately, these devices also pose a great security risk for small businesses and law firms because their small size makes them absurdly easy to lose. This risk can be minimized, however, by using the SanDisk Ultra USB 3.0 flash drive, which comes standard with 128-bit AES encryption to keep data secure.

This model is available with 16, 32, 64, 128, or 256 GB of storage space for your files. Using the SanDisk SecureAccess software, a user can protect access to private files with password protection and encryption. The software creates a file vault (protected folder) on the USB drive, creating a secure storage location for the user to place and keep all sensitive and confidential data. This flash drive is also fast, featuring transfer speeds of up to 100 Mbps.

The SanDisk SecureAccess software is compatible with the Windows 10 and Mac OS X v.10.6+ operating systems, although Mac users will have to download the supporting software from the App Store.

The SanDisk Ultra USB flash drives can be purchased online at https://www .sandisk.com for between $35 and $200, depending on the storage capacity, and all come with a five-year limited warranty. Some of the other online retailers that SanDisk may refer you to in order to purchase its products may have lower retail pricing—so check carefully.

For those users who require top-of-the-line security, look no further than the IronKey Basic S1000 USB device (now owned by Kingston), which comes in 4, 8, 16, 32, 64, and 128 GB versions. We previously recommended the S250, but that USB 2.0 device is much slower than the USB 3.0, S1000. The S1000 can read data at speeds up to 400 Mbps, about 10 times faster than the S250.

This USB device is designed for the needs of sensitive military, government, and enterprise networks and includes XTS-AES 256-bit hardware encryption that has been validated to meet government Federal Information Processing Standard (FIPS) requirements, specifically FIPS 140-2 Level 3. The security features require no software or drivers to enforce, with all the security being handled by the device hardware, and the features are always on.

The device requires that a user authenticate with a password before encryption keys are enabled and data can be accessed. This device is even waterproof! As they tend to be inadvertently placed in washing machines while in the pocket of your pants, this is an excellent feature, though we've not yet put it to the test. This device has a self-destruct mechanism (think Mission: Impossible without the smoke) that will wipe (i.e., permanently and irretrievably remove) the data contents if a user or thief tries to break into the IronKey and enters ten incorrect passwords. The IronKey Personal S250 Secure Drive can be purchased online from Kingston's website (www .kingston.com) for $139 to $849, depending on the storage capacity.

Another great choice for an encrypted USB flash drive is the Kingston Data-Traveler 4000 G2, offered with storage capacity ranging from 4 to 64 GB. This affordable solution provides business-grade security, USB 3.0 connectivity and FIPS 140-2 Level 3 certification, for those firms (or whose clients) that require certified compliance requirements for its hardware. This USB flash drive uses 256-bit AES hardware-based encryption to protect data stored on the drive, and after ten intrusion attempts (incorrect password guesses) the device will lock and reformat itself, rending all of the previously existing data unrecoverable. This device can be purchased online from Kingston's website (www.kingston.com) starting at $53.00 for the 4 GB model.

Speakers and Headphones

Lawyers (and their staff) often tell us that the most important peripheral device they need for their computer is a pair of speakers. They like to be able to listen to music while they work and are adamant about fidelity. Without breaking the bank, reasonable quality desktop speakers can be purchased to provide the user with a clear, true sound. Logitech, a leading provider of speaker systems for computers, makes the Multimedia Speakers Z213. They offer 2.1 stereo sound with a subwoofer, providing enhanced bass, and the speakers come in a slim, stylish profile. These speakers offer quality audio at a reasonable price. The speakers have a stereo headphone jack, an auxiliary input where you can connect your iPod or MP3 player, and integrated controls located on a wired remote. They even include a cable-management system to help reduce the clutter of wires. The Logitech Multimedia Speakers Z213 can be purchased online for around $30 from www.logitech.com.

If you purchase one of the recommended Dell flat-panel monitors, consider adding a sound bar. The sound bar clips onto the bottom edge of the Dell flat-panel and gets its power from the monitor itself. It provides a clean installation and doesn't take up any additional desk space. The model of the sound bar will vary depending on the Dell monitor that you wish to attach the speakers to, so be sure to check out Dell's website to ensure that you select the appropriate model.

CHAPTER FIVE

Printers

Even in the era of the "paperless" office, most law firms still print a lot of documents on a daily basis, probably more than any other type of business. To say that the practice of law tends to be less than green is a massive understatement—although most firms have implemented a recycling program. Nonetheless, it is certainly critical to have a good, reliable printer to ensure that your firm is printing quality documents in the shortest amount of time. In the following sections, we discuss and recommend printers for stand-alone systems, network systems, and multifunctional printers/copiers.

Stand-Alone Printers

The most basic type of printer is the stand-alone printer. This type of printer connects directly to a computer and is not placed on the network. It only has to be capable of handling a single user's print jobs. Even in environments where networked printers are used and recommended, there can be valid reasons to have stand-alone printers—perhaps so the bookkeeper can keep financial records from inadvertently being picked up by someone else. Senior partners may feel their information is so confidential that they want a printer in their office (though their staff often mutter that they are just too lazy to walk down the hall). Many makes and models of stand-alone printers are available to choose from, and each has different performance specifications, features, and available fonts.

The question about whether to use an ink-jet printer is dead. No more ink-jet. We highly recommend going with a laser printer. Ink-jet printers typically result in a higher cost of ownership over the long haul, with ink cartridges printing at a higher cost per page than the average laser printer. There are even studies that show a cost of $3,000–$5,000 per gallon for name-brand ink cartridges. Human blood is cheaper. Laser is better quality and more economical—case closed.

A stand-alone printer can be shared through enabling File and Print Sharing on your local computer, but we strongly counsel against this practice. It creates a host of security vulnerabilities that could compromise not only your system but also your entire network, and it causes a lot of management and configuration headaches for the IT administrator.

When discussing printers with our clients, we are frequently asked, "Should I purchase a color or a black-and-white laser printer?" You will pay a slight premium for a color laser printer, and in most instances, it is not worth the cost when purchasing a stand-alone printer. It is usually more cost effective to purchase a color laser printer to be placed on the local computer network and shared so that more than one user can print to it.

The Hewlett-Packard (HP) LaserJet Pro M201dw black-and-white laser printer is the perfect solution for the stand-alone or network (up to five users) printer. The printer has a built-in Ethernet connection, along with USB and wireless support for network connectivity, and prints in duplex (two-sided) mode by default. This printer prints as many as 26 pages per minute, comes standard with a paper input capacity of 250 sheets, and has a recommended monthly volume of up to 2,000 pages but can support a monthly duty cycle of up to 15,000 pages if needed. The printer has a first-page-out speed of 8 seconds and supports all the common page types, such as letter, legal, executive, and envelopes. This printer comes standard with 128 MB of memory and can connect to your computer using the USB interface. It should be noted that the printer does come with a USB cable, which previous HP models we've recommend have not. For mobile users, this printer is compatible with Apple's AirPrint service, which allows users to print to the device from their iPad, iPhone, or iPod touch—a feature that is quickly becoming a necessity with the increasing number of iPads and iPhones being used in the workplace. Using the HP ePrint app, Android mobile users can print directly from their mobile device as well.

This black-and-white printer was designed for quick business printing and offers a cost-effective solution for personal printing. The printer is both Mac and Windows compatible, including Windows 8 and Windows 10. It also comes standard with a one-year limited warranty. The HP LaserJet Pro M201dw printer can be purchased online for around $199.99 (before discounts) from www.hp.com. At the time of writing, this printer was discounted to a cost of $149.99 on HP's webstore.

If you're looking for tips on how to reduce the frequency with which you have to purchase replacement laser cartridges, there are a few things you can do. First, look into software that automatically removes wasted pages from printing jobs, especially common when printing out content from websites using your Internet browser. This printer comes with software called HP Smart Web Printing that you can install on your local computer, which reduces the wasted pages and space when printing from websites.

Another great tip is to change the print quality to "Draft" if the document is just going to be discarded shortly after printing and not something official that you're going to submit to court. This alone can save you lots of toner.

Networked Printers

Networked printers are used to provide a printing resource to multiple users. Networked printers are generally installed in a central location and then shared throughout the local network. This reduces the number of printers that your firm will need to purchase and administer. The administration and security of these printers can be integrated into your network's security infrastructure, such as through Windows Active Directory for a Windows-based network, and networking a printer is much more secure than sharing it through the File and Print Sharing service. You should consider disabling the remote administration function (via a web browser) for the printer. Remote administration typically means that a specialized website is running on the printer. These web services are rarely secure and fairly easy to compromise. We recommend installing the printer in a central location, which simplifies the management, administration, and security of these devices. Network printers can be shared with the various computers and users that make up your network with very little overhead and effort. Many types of networked printers are available, and depending on your need—low volume, high volume, color—your options will vary. A popular request from many law offices is to have multiple trays for the printer. The capability to have multiple paper types loaded is usually available in the mid-range to higher-end printer models.

Low-Volume Network Printers

Low-volume network printers are designed for workgroups of users having a small to moderate print volume, as high as 5,000 pages per month. These printers are moderately priced and are primarily used to segment printing within offices based on user group or physical location. Network printers have more robust hardware than stand-alone printers to handle multiple jobs from different users at the same time.

The HP LaserJet Pro M402dw black-and-white network-based laser printer is great for a small law firm because it provides users with a highly reliable, cost-effective printer that is capable of handling the expected volume produced by an average small firm. The HP LaserJet Pro M402dw prints as many as 40 pages per minute and has a recommended monthly print volume of up to 4,000 pages. This model also has a monthly duty cycle of up to 80,000 pages. It comes standard with an input capacity of 350 sheets and 128 MB of memory, and it handles all paper sizes. This printer has a first-page-out speed of 6.4 seconds. As an added feature, the printer allows for automatic duplexing for printing double-sided documents. The printer has an embedded gigabit Ethernet network adapter to attach the printer to your local network and a built-in Wi-Fi 802.11 b/g/n adapter for wireless connectivity. This printer also supports Apple's AirPrint service, allowing users to print directly from their iPad, iPhone, or iPod Touch device or using the HP ePrint app, for those using Android mobile devices. For additional security, this printer can prevent unauthorized access with management features including 802.1x authentication and password protection. This model does come with a USB cable.

The memory of this printer can be upgraded if desired, and the printer's drivers are compatible with both Mac and Windows-based systems, including Windows 8 and Windows 10. The printer comes with a standard one-year warranty and includes a CD-ROM with the drivers and software necessary to configure the device. The HP LaserJet Pro M402dw black-and-white laser printer can be purchased online for around $249 from www.hp.com.

High-Volume Network Printers

High-volume network printers are designed for businesses that need the capacity to print a large volume of pages on a monthly basis, and they are usually considered when your firm needs a printer that can produce more than 5,000 pages per month. These devices contain hardware that can handle the volume load and are built to print constantly.

The HP LaserJet Enterprise MFP M630f multifunction printer is ideal for firms that print large volumes of documents on a monthly basis. This printer has a recommended monthly printing volume of 5,000 to 28,000 pages and prints up to 60 pages per minute. The printer comes with a standard input capacity of 1,100 sheets, three paper trays, 1.5 GB of memory, and an embedded gigabit Ethernet network adapter to attach the printer to your local network. The network connectivity can be upgraded to support wireless networks, a must-have option for those firms that use a wireless infrastructure for their local network. It should be noted that the printer doesn't come with a USB or network cable, which will have to be purchased separately if you want to connect the printer directly to a computer. This printer also supports Apple's AirPrint service, allowing users to print directly from their iPad, iPhone, or iPod Touch device if you purchase the wireless option.

For future compatibility, this printer is IPv6-ready, although we have yet to see any clients running IPv6 only. For added security, this printer supports network authentication (LDAP, SMTP) that lets administrators control device access and secure print jobs through user authentication.

The printer comes with a one-year, next-business-day on-site warranty. It is compatible with both Mac and Windows-based networks, including Windows 10. A CD-ROM that contains both printer driver files and software necessary to manage and configure the device is included; in addition, the necessary software can be downloaded from HP's website. The HP LaserJet Enterprise MFP M630f multifunction printer can be purchased online for around $3,499.99 from one of HP's resellers, and it comes with a standard one-year warranty. At this cost, you may want to investigate using your digital copier as a printer, depending on your anticipated monthly print volume and cost per page.

Color Network Printers

Color network printers are essential for any law firm or small business that wants to print a significant volume of documents in color. If the color printer is networked, multiple users can have access to the shared resource, which is far more cost effective than giving everyone a color printer. HP is still the leading manufacturer of color printers in terms of value, selection, overall reliability, and performance. Its color LaserJet printers are reasonably priced and produce high-quality color documents.

For a small business or law firm, the HP Color LaserJet Enterprise CP4025dn printer is perfect for everyday color printing. This printer prints up to 35 pages per minute in black and white or in color and has a recommended monthly volume of 2,000 to 7,500 pages. Its first-page-out speed of less than 9.5 seconds means that the color print job starts almost as soon as it has been sent to the printer. The standard input capacity is 600 sheets, and the printer supports all paper sizes and can be upgraded with an envelope feeder.

The printer comes standard with 512 MB of memory and an embedded gigabit Ethernet network adapter that enables the printer to connect to your local network. If necessary, the memory can be upgraded to a maximum of 1 GB. The printer's drivers support both Mac and Windows-based systems, including Windows 10, and the printer can be networked for easy accessibility. The printer comes with a one-year on-site limited warranty.

The HP Color LaserJet CP4025dn printer can be purchased online for around $1,200 (before discounts) from one of HP's resellers. It should be noted that the printer doesn't come with a USB or network cable, which will have to be purchased separately. That shouldn't be a problem since you will probably connect this printer to a network and not directly to a computer.

The largest operational cost for a color laser printer are the consumables. Color cartridges are not cheap, and color prints can be very expensive. One configuration point to make on all computers networked to your color printers: change the default color setting to black. This will save on the printing and subsequent waste of color cartridges for unnecessary color copies. Users can always override the setting when a color printout is required.

Digital copier manufacturers are beginning to take over the task of color printing. Investigate using a color copier for your color print needs versus a stand-alone color printer, or if you have a large-scale color print job, you may want to consider the costs of outsourcing the project to your local copier store. You might be surprised at the amount of money you could save.

Typically, lawyers lease their copiers. As you work with your copier lessor, which normally provides your supplies, make sure you negotiate a low cost per color copy and pay only for the number of pages that you print. Don't pay for the consumables (e.g., toner cartridges) or maintenance, as these should be included as part of the per-page cost.

Multifunctional Printers/Copiers

Don't you wish there was a single device that you could install on your local network that could do everything your office needs—printing, faxing, scanning, and copying? Happily for lawyers, such devices are becoming a standard fixture today. Multifunctional printers (MFPs) offer the capability to print, scan, copy, and fax from the same device, combining the functions of multiple devices into just one and eliminating the need to purchase them separately. In the long run, purchasing or leasing an MFP can save you the time and money often expended to upgrade and service multiple devices.

MFPs are very expensive and are generally leased because of the high cost to purchase. When looking at whether to buy or lease MFPs, keep some functionality questions in mind:

- Do you want the ability to print in color as well as in black and white?
- Do you need duplex printing?
- Do you want to scan documents to your hard drive, user box, or e-mail?
- Do you want incoming faxes to be sent to e-mail as an image file or just printed?
- Do you want to be able to link the use of the MFP to the firm's billing program?
- What printing capacity do you need?
- Do you need any finishing capabilities (e.g., stapling, folding, three-hole punch)?
- Can users print to the device using their tablet or mobile phone?
- Do you need to implement any security on the unit, and if so, what?
- At the end of your lease, can the hard drive be securely wiped or erased?

The answers to these questions will give your vendors enough detail to provide you with the MFP device that best meets the firm's needs. Your digital copier may already have some of these features installed but not configured. Check with your vendor to see what capabilities your current copier has. In our office, we have a Konica Minolta Bizhub C224e MFP device. It allows us to print both in color and in black and white at speeds up to 22 pages per minute; to scan to hard drive, user box, e-mail, or FTP; and to fax documents, although we do not use that feature. We are able to download our scanned documents from a built-in secure internal website as JPG, PDF, XPS, or TIFF files, as well as scan to an internal e-mail address—which we constantly use. This device has a 3,650-sheet max capacity with dual scanning speeds up to 160 pages per minute.

The Bizhub has advanced security features such as job erase, hard drive sanitizing and lock, user authentication and account tracking, Internet protocol (IP) address filtering, and secure print and scan encryption. Plus, there are options for biometric and HID proximity card authentication, should we ever need these advanced security features. Needless to say, the Bizhub provides us with a secure MFP option. We are huge fans—this is our second model of one of these devices.

CHAPTER SIX

Scanners

Almost as common as printers, scanners have become a necessary piece of equipment in most offices, as more paper documents are being scanned and stored electronically. The drive to a paperless office is still very much under way. The setup and operation of scanners has become simple to the point where even the most novice computer user can do it. Many of the tasks that once had to be performed manually are now automated, and in most cases, the hookup entails connecting a single wire—or none, in the event of a wireless mobile scanner, which we discuss in the next section.

Not often do we have to insert a CD to install software anymore, now that preloaded drivers are prevalent. Network scanners, however, are a little more complex to set up, and configuring them may require the assistance of your IT staff or your IT consultant.

Most desktop scanners communicate with the computer through the USB interface and come with a variety of software to assist in the scanning and file conversion process. Some models come standard with optical character recognition (OCR) software that will read the scanned image and produce a document that is editable and searchable. Fujitsu is a manufacturer of home and business-grade scanners that have been constantly rated the best models for businesses. In the following sections, we make recommendations for both low-volume and high-volume scanners from Fujitsu.

Some law firms may already have scanning capability in their digital copier. As we previously stated, check with your vendor to see if scanning with your copier is a more cost-effective solution than purchasing a stand-alone unit.

Mobile Scanner

The Fujitsu ScanSnap iX100 wireless scanner is the perfect, portable scanner for the mobile lawyer. This mobile device includes a lithium-ion rechargeable battery that can scan up to 260 letter-size documents on a single charge and weighs only 14 ounces. This portable device can scan a single-side color document at 300 dots per inch in just 5.2 seconds. The ScanSnap iX100 is equipped with built-in Wi-Fi to automatically detect the wireless network. In the event you don't have a wireless network or access point, you can use Direct Connect mode to scan wirelessly between the device and your computer system.

This device comes with many different scanning options, allowing the user to "Scan to Folder," "Scan to Email," and a variety of cloud-based options such as "Scan to Dropbox," "Scan to Evernote," and "Scan to Salesforce," to name a few. This device is compatible with both Mac and Windows-based computers and comes with a one-year limited warranty. The ScanSnap iX100 wireless scanner can be purchased online from an Authorized Fujitsu Retailer for around $200.

Low-Volume Scanner

The Fujitsu ScanSnap iX500 Desktop Scanner is a great value for a solid automatic document feeder (ADF) scanner. This desktop scanner scans up to 25 color pages per minute, has an ADF capacity of 50 sheets, and can handle both legal- and letter-sized paper. The scanner has a maximum scanning resolution of 600 × 600 dpi and connects to the computer via the USB 3.0 interface, which is responsible for the increase in scanning speed. This scanner also comes with a built-in wireless adapter, allowing you to scan directly to a computer or mobile device without the need of a cable. This scanner is compatible with Microsoft Windows 7 and Windows 10, and Mac OS X v10.6 or newer. This scanner comes with bundled software that includes Adobe Acrobat XI Standard Edition (Windows version of software), ScanSnap Organizer v5.5, ABBYY FineReader for ScanSnap 5.0, Scan to Microsoft SharePoint v5.0, and CardMinder v5.2.

Adobe Acrobat XI Standard software allows you to automatically convert scanned data into searchable PDF files. Some of the automatic features of this device include auto paper-size detection, auto de-skew, and auto blank-page removal. The auto blank-page removal eliminates the need to edit scanned documents because the scanner has the ability to recognize the deleted blank pages. The ABBYY FineReader software allows you to scan documents directly to applications such as Microsoft Word, Excel, and PowerPoint.

A new feature of this scanner is the ability to scan to the cloud. With the free ScanSnap Connect app, users can link their ScanSnap to their iPad, iPhone, or Android mobile device for viewing on the go. Users also have the ability to scan to Evernote, Google Docs, Salesforce, SugarSync, and SharePoint. Again, as with all cloud services, please use caution and seek the advice of your IT staff when moving client data to the cloud to ensure that your documents are secure.

The scanner comes with a standard one-year limited warranty that can be upgraded to the Advanced Exchange Service program. The Fujitsu ScanSnap iX500 Desktop Scanner can be purchased online from Fujitsu's website (www.fujitsu.com) for $495 and comes with a one-year limited warranty. The inclusion of Acrobat Standard makes this a very worthwhile purchase.

High-Volume Scanner

The Fujitsu fi-5530C2 is perfect for legal professionals who need a high-speed scanner on a modest budget and are serious about scanning documents. The built-in ADF holds 100 pages and scans up to 50 pages per minute (100 images) in 200 dpi in color, monochrome, and grayscale. This scanner comes standard with 64 MB of memory and advanced software tools to allow administrators to centrally manage the scanner more productively and cost effectively.

Using the Fujitsu fi-5530C2 scanner, you can convert any document to Adobe PDF using Adobe Acrobat software, which is not included with the purchase of this scanner. Luckily, most lawyers already have access to this software. This scanner can handle a vigorous duty cycle of up to 4,000 documents per day and can handle documents ranging in size from a business card to a legal document without issue. The Ultra SCSI and USB 2.0 interface allows for simplified connectivity to your computer. The scanner is compatible with Microsoft Windows 7 and 8 computer systems and Windows Server 2012. It should be noted that this scanner is not compatible with Macs. The Fujitsu fi-5530C2 scanner can be purchased online through one of Fujitsu's resellers for around $2,500 and comes with a three-month on-site limited warranty.

This amount of money is a lot for a solo or small firm operation to spend, especially on a scanner. We're sure that your digital copier could provide a less expensive solution for your scanning needs, especially if you have a newer unit that provides a convenient ability to scan to e-mail—which this ScanSnap device does not offer. Consider that before you make a purchasing decision and you might be able to save yourself a lot of money.

CHAPTER SEVEN

Servers

Many small law firms struggle with the decision of whether to purchase a server. For many people, the struggle is with the cost of the hardware. The truth is that most firms are not solely cloud-based and are more of a hybrid type, with some applications or services hosted in the cloud and some hosted locally. Even a hybrid approach requires an on-premise server where users can store their data and applications and where hosted services can be accessed. If a small firm opts against centralized storage or single point of administration, the costs to support and maintain a decentralized computer network (peer-to-peer) will surely be much higher.

Once a server is purchased, configured, and installed, routine maintenance is all that should be required, with the hardware running like a well-oiled machine. There may be some sticker shock with the upfront cost to purchase a server, but over time, the support costs should be considerably less than if you opted not to purchase one and went with a peer-to-peer solution. The good news is that hardware costs keep coming down, so a server for a solo or small firm operation is even more affordable as time advances.

The purchase of a server is one of the most important and expensive decisions you will have to make regarding technology for your firm. A server is the mother ship of the network, so the purchase decision should be made very carefully. It is absolutely not the time to be penny wise and pound foolish. The choice of a server is a business decision—make no mistake about that—and if made with great consideration and thought, it will allow your business to be more efficient from a technology perspective.

Like workstations and laptops, servers come in every make, model, and flavor. Unlike workstations, however, servers are expensive and can consume a large chunk of your technology budget rather quickly. Your firm will need to plan carefully when selecting a server—including discussing future needs and goals—so that the desirable hardware and software components can be identified. Be careful when planning, because you don't want to have to buy a new server every other year. The average life span of a server is four to five years—so start planning (and budgeting) well in advance!

Solo—File and Printer Sharing

The most simple and basic reason for getting a server is for file and printer sharing. Centralizing electronic file storage and administration and installation of printers will save you time, money, and headaches when it comes to maintaining and managing your network. Some servers are designed specifically for the purpose of sharing files, documents, and printers. These servers come with the basic hardware and software and are relatively inexpensive when compared to the mid-range to higher-end servers.

The Dell PowerEdge T330 server was designed for the small business to provide the most basic file- and printer-sharing capabilities. The following table provides the server's hardware and software components, along with some technical specifications.

File- and Printer-Sharing Server

Hardware Component	Recommendation
Model:	Dell PowerEdge T330
Chassis:	Tower
Operating System:	Windows Server 2012 R2, Standard Edition
Processors:	Intel Xeon E3-1270 v5, 3.6 GHz, 8 MB Cache
Memory:	32 GB UDIMM, 2133 MT/s ECC
RAID Controller:	PERC S130
Hard Drive Configuration:	RAID 5
Hard Drives:	Three 1 TB 7.2K RPM SATA 6 Gbps
Network Adapter:	Onboard Broadcom 5720 Dual Port 1 GB LOM
Warranty:	Three-year ProSupport and next-business-day on-site service
Other:	DVD+/-RW Drive

This Dell PowerEdge T330 was customized through Dell's website (www .dell.com) and contains an Intel Xeon 3.6 GHz processor with 32 GB of RAM. This server comes with the Windows Server 2012 R2 Standard Edition operating system. CALs (client access licenses) are needed for each device or user that accesses the server. The three SATA 1 TB hard drives are configured in a RAID 5 (redundant array of independent disks) hard drive configuration for increased performance and fault tolerance. In a RAID 5 hard drive configuration, if one of the hard drives were to fail, the server would continue to operate until the failed hard drive could be replaced. In most other hard drive configurations, if a server's hard drive were to fail, the server would be inoperable until the disk was repaired or replaced. The RAID 5 configuration offers both fault tolerance with the parity hard drive and better performance than most other RAID or mirrored disk configurations. RAID 5 hard drive configurations are strongly recommended for all law firm servers.

In total, this server has about 2 TB of hard drive space available for the storage of electronic data, programs, and other applications. You used to be able to save a little bit of money by reducing the number of hard drives purchased and setting up a RAID 1 hard drive configuration, but since hard drives have come so far down in price, we no longer recommend this as an option. Also, RAID 5 is a more fault-tolerant and flexible configuration.

The onboard dual gigabit network adapters will allow clients to connect to the server at gigabit speeds, assuming the rest of your network components (switches, cabling) are gigabit as well.

One of the most important features to consider when purchasing a server is the warranty. In most cases, you will not need both the hardware and software support. At a minimum, you must include a hardware warranty that will cover the hardware and labor cost to replace any of the components that may fail during the server's life cycle. This Dell PowerEdge server comes with a three-year, next-business-day on-site parts and labor warranty at an included cost of about $400 when bundled with the server hardware. Having a hardware warranty for your server is critical to protecting your equipment, data, and business. This is no time to be miserly. This Dell PowerEdge T330 server was quoted on Dell's website for approximately $2,000 at the time of this writing.

Small Firm—File- and Printer-Sharing/ Hosting Services

When purchasing a server for your network, you must decide what function the server will have in your day-to-day business operations. In addition to file and printer sharing, it's common for small firms to host their company's e-mail. Although you can also host a website, we recommend that you outsource that to a website hosting provider because of potential security, administration, and resource issues. The added hosting services (e-mail and/or web) will require a server with upgraded hardware to be able to provide the necessary resources for the services to operate reliably.

Previously, our server recommendations included those running Microsoft Small Business Server 2011, which, depending on the edition/add-on (Standard or Premium), included Microsoft Exchange Server and Microsoft SQL Server. As of July 1, 2013, in response to small business market trends and behavior, such as moving in the direction of cloud computing for applications and e-mail, Dell no longer offers this operating system as an option. The Microsoft Exchange Server software will have to be purchased separately for those firms that wish to host their own e-mail or you can look at a cloud-based solution, such as Microsoft Office 365, for a hosted solution. An alternative is to order the hardware without an operating system and obtain the Microsoft Small Business Server 2011 software from another source.

The Dell PowerEdge T630 was designed for small firms or businesses that are looking for a cost-effective solution to hosting their own e-mail or website. The following table provides the server's hardware and software components, along with some technical specifications.

File- and Printer-Sharing/Hosting Services

Hardware Component	Recommendation
Model:	Dell PowerEdge T630
Chassis:	Tower
Operating System:	Windows Server 2012 R2, Standard Edition
Processors:	Dual Intel Xeon E5-2643 v4 3.4 GHz, 35 M Cache, 9.6GT/s QPI
Memory:	64 GB RDIMM, 2400 MT/s, Dual Rank
Primary Controller Card:	PERC H330
Hard Drive Configuration:	RAID 5
Hard Drives:	Three 2 TB 7.2K RPM SATA 6 Gbps 3.5-Inch
Network Adapter:	Onboard Intel i350-AM2 Dual Port 1 GB LOM
Warranty:	Three-year ProSupport and Mission Critical 4HR 7?24 on-site service
Other:	Redundant power supply, DVD+/-RW drive

This Dell PowerEdge T630 was customized through Dell's website. It contains Dual Intel Xeon 3.4 GHz processors with 64 GB of memory. The server was customized in a tower chassis; however, the same model is available in a rack-mount chassis for an additional $65. The rack-mount chassis is for those firms and small businesses that maintain their servers and networking equipment in a rack. The processors will supply more than enough horsepower to configure the server as an e-mail or web server, and the 64 GB of memory will allow these services to run smoothly and will prevent the server from lagging or becoming bogged down.

The server comes with Windows Server 2012 R2 Standard Edition pre-installed. CALs will need to be purchased for each device and/or user that wishes to connect to the server. Dell offers a five-pack of device or user CALs bundled with the server purchase for a price of $130.67.

The three 2 TB SAS hard drives are configured in a RAID 5 hard drive configuration and provide about 4 TB of storage space for your firm's applications and data. This PowerEdge server comes with the three-year Pro-Support 4HR 7×24 on-site hardware warranty, which provides three years of four-hour response, same-day parts and labor warranty. The Dell PowerEdge T630 server was quoted on Dell's website for approximately $8,100 at the time of this writing.

Don't forget to consider backup software and any additional applications (e.g., security software, file synchronization, encryption) when configuring the server, because you might get a better discount from the vendor if they are bundled and purchased with the server hardware.

Small Firm—Database/Applications Server

Your firm's software requirements, current and future, will play a big role in determining what hardware and software components your server will need to adequately support your firm in the coming years. So far, we have discussed the hardware and software specifications for a server used primarily for file and printer sharing and one capable of handling basic hosting services, such as e-mail and a website. When planning to use a server to host a database application, case management software, or e-discovery software, you must look at the minimum requirements for each piece of software and then go above and beyond the specifications that vendors provide. What vendors list should be regarded cautiously as a bare minimum. To run well and reliably, the software almost always requires more horsepower.

The recommended Dell PowerEdge T630 server is capable of handling most database and software applications as long as it's configured with advanced hardware to handle the powerful and robust database applications. The server's hardware and software components are provided in the following table.

Database/Applications Server

Hardware Component	Recommendation
Model:	Dell PowerEdge T630
Chassis:	Tower
Operating System:	Windows Server 2012 R2, Standard Edition
Processors:	Dual Intel Xeon E5-2667 v4 3.2 GHz, 25 M Cache, 9.6GT/s QPI, Turbo
Memory:	128 GB RDIMM, 2400 MT/s, Dual Rank
Primary Controller Card:	PERC H730 RAID Controller
Hard Drive Configuration:	RAID 5
Hard Drives:	Three 2 TB 7.2K RPM SATA 3.5-Inch
Network Adapter:	Onboard Intel i350-AM2 Dual Port 1 GB LOM
Warranty:	Three-year ProSupport and Mission Critical 4Hr 7?24 on-site service
Other:	Dual, hot-plug, redundant power supply 1100W, DVD+/-RW Drive

The PowerEdge T630 server was customized through Dell's website and contains Dual Intel Xeon E5-2667 v4 3.2 GHz processors and 128 GB of memory. The processor is faster than the processor included with the server discussed in the previous section.

This server comes with the Windows Server 2012 R2 Standard Edition operating system with Hyper-V capability for virtualized environments.

The three 2 TB hard drives are configured in a RAID 5 hard disk configuration and provide about 4 TB of storage space for applications and data. If more storage space or faster disk read/write speeds are needed, these upgrades can be made when the server is configured to meet your needs, especially if you plan to use virtualization (explained in the following section).

The redundant power supply allows the server to stay powered on in the event that one of the power supplies fails. The server comes with dual embedded Broadcom Ethernet adapters, providing connectivity for up to two networks. The PowerEdge server comes with a three-year ProSupport Mission Critical 4HR 7 × 24 on-site hardware warranty, which provides three years of four-hour response, same-day parts and labor warranty. The

Dell PowerEdge T620 server was quoted on Dell's website for approximately $10,000 at the time of this writing. You can save a little money if you want the next-day warranty instead of the four-hour response warranty.

Virtual Servers

The large push within the IT industry continues to be toward virtualization bundled with cloud services. Microsoft continues to sell more licenses for virtual machines than it does for physical hardware. This is one trend that isn't going to reverse.

Simply put, virtualization means that a single piece of hardware contains and hosts multiple server or desktop images, otherwise known as machines. Virtualization enables the consolidation of data and applications onto a single physical hardware server. The reduction in hardware saves energy, management, and administration effort and reduces overall hardware and software costs, along with rack space, especially if your firm needs multiple servers.

Virtualization is used to separate hosting services and applications, creating independent machines, which allows for one virtual server to be down for maintenance without affecting the others. For example, if Windows updates were downloaded onto a virtual server hosting file- and print-sharing services, this virtual server could be rebooted and have the updates applied without having to bring down or affect the entire host system, keeping other virtual servers online and available to users. It also means that you can quickly "spool up" a virtual machine for testing new applications or services without investing in additional hardware. Virtual servers are also very flexible and can be modified on the fly. Resources (e.g., RAM, disk space, processing power) can be modified while the virtual machine is running. Running short on disk space? No problem. Just go to the management console and add a few hundred gigabytes to the virtual machine's dynamic disk.

Previously, virtualization was not implemented due to the required costs, expertise, and large budget. It was not typically found in a small firm environment; however, this is no longer true. We are recommending that small firms consider virtualization technologies when making server hardware and software purchasing decisions, especially in scenarios where the firm is hosting services such as e-mail internally.

Is server virtualization the best choice for your network environment? Probably, but you will need to answer a number of questions before making this determination.

First, what services and applications are running on your network? If your network is running Microsoft Exchange Server, SQL Server, and a case management application, most likely you will need multiple servers to host all of these services and software. Most case management applications now require a separate server to run on. By using virtualization, you can avoid purchase of another physical hardware server by installing the case management software on its own virtual server, as long as your virtual server meets, if not exceeds, the host specifications required by the vendor of the software.

When purchasing a host system (the server hosting the virtual servers), the most critical hardware options to consider are the amount of memory, number and type of processors, and amount of storage space. For each virtual server, 8 GB or more of memory must be allocated for the virtual server to operate. A larger amount of memory will be needed if the virtual server is hosting a database or other memory-hungry service. This does not account for the amount of memory that the host system will require. For example, if you have a host server running three virtual servers, you will need a minimum of 32 GB or more of memory installed in the host server to supply the host and all of the virtual servers with enough memory resources to operate. To accommodate the necessary hardware, the host system must be running at least the Windows Server 2012 Standard Edition operating system.

When running virtual servers, you will need to ensure that the host system has enough processing capability to handle the processing load. At a minimum, you will want the system to contain Intel Xeon processors with a processing speed of 2.53 to 3.6 GHz. The optimum solution for stand-alone servers is to use Intel Xeon processors with the same speed range, and in virtualization solutions, you will need to have multiple processors with multiple cores. The Xeon processors that are in the servers recommended previously were designed by Intel for virtualization solutions, providing increased virtualization security, reduced storage and network latencies, and acceleration of fundamental virtualization processes throughout the system. The multicore processors combine two or more cores onto a single integrated circuit, providing multiprocessing capabilities to the chip. Multiprocessing allows the execution of multiple concurrent software processes in a system, which is vital in a virtualization solution.

The amount of storage space required to run all of the virtual servers and the host system will vary from solution to solution. When determining the amount of storage space the systems will require, you need to consider the services and applications that will be hosted. For example, a virtual server hosting Microsoft Exchange Server will require enough disk space to account for the current size and future growth of the Exchange Database stores along with the program files and operating system. If more space is needed at a later time, the amount of storage space allocated to each virtual server can be independently configured and modified in real time. For ease of configuration and setup, bearing the cost of additional hard drive storage up front makes more sense than waiting to add more hard drives later. Plus, it's always recommended that the host system and virtual servers have available more than enough hard drive space, so problems with low disk space can be avoided. We have clients who have terabytes of disk space available just for their file- and printer-sharing virtual server. As an alternative to purchasing host-based storage, you may want to look into a storage area network (SAN) device that would provide locally attached storage over a dedicated network, usually over Fibre Channel or iSCSI.

Microsoft offers free server virtualization solutions for Windows Server 2008 and Server 2012. For host systems running Windows Server 2008 or 2012, Microsoft has included the Hyper-V virtualization system with the base installation of the operating system, and this role is installed through the Server Roles interface. Hyper-V enables the consolidation of multiple server roles as separate virtual servers running on a single host system, allowing for different operating systems such as Linux, Windows, and others to run in parallel. For more information regarding Microsoft's virtualization solutions, you can visit Microsoft's website at https://www.microsoft.com/en-us/cloud-platform/virtualization.

Hyper-V was designed with enhanced security features in mind, providing an architecture that is less vulnerable to attack. This software includes a set of management and administration tools that can be used to manage the host and virtual systems' hardware from the same interface. It even allows administrators to migrate live systems from server to server. Windows Server 2012 has an updated version of Microsoft's Hyper-V, which includes such new features as network virtualization, multitenancy, storage resource pools, and cloud backup. The new version of Hyper-V also increases the amount of memory and storage and the number of virtual processors that each machine can be allocated. For more information regarding Microsoft's Hyper-V 2012 R2, you can visit Microsoft's TechNet website at https://technet.microsoft.com/en-us/library/hh833684.aspx.

Depending on the operating system of the host system, a few Microsoft-based software options are available for server virtualization, and they are fully supported. We have observed that the free Hyper-V implementations may have some issues sharing peripheral devices across the virtual machines. As an example, you may not be able to share the USB ports of the hardware with a virtual machine without some kind of workaround, which means that you can't copy files from a USB flash drive from the host system to the virtual system.

Software licensing will also play a role in determining your firm's ability to move to a virtualization environment. To say the licensing is easy to figure out when it comes to virtualization would be a flat-out lie. Microsoft has muddied the waters when it comes to virtualization licensing, because it varies depending on the type of server operating system and the number of processors. Some operating system editions allow you to use the license key on the host and on up to two virtual machines. If you're running a host with Windows Server 2012 Datacenter Edition, you get a feature called Automated Virtual Machine Activation. With this feature, any virtual machine on this host running Windows Server 2012 R2 Datacenter/Standard/Essentials will automatically activate.

There are other alternatives to Microsoft's virtualization solutions, such as VMware's vSphere Hypervisor (ESXi). If you are investigating alternative virtualization solutions, you will need to work with your IT vendor to see what other options might be available. We currently recommend and use the VMware solution instead of Microsoft's Hyper-V solution. VMware has been in the virtualization game a lot longer than Microsoft, and you can share those USB ports with the virtual machines. VMware Tools also offers some other useful and time-saving administration capabilities.

What we do know is this: The cost to purchase the hardware and software necessary to implement a virtualization environment for your network will be significantly less than the cost of purchasing multiple physical servers to fill the necessary roles your applications and services require.

Peer-to-Peer

Many small firms use the built-in peer-to-peer network capabilities of their computer systems as an alternative to purchasing a server. A peer-to-peer network, in its simplest form, is two or more computers that are able to communicate with one another to share files and folders, printers, and applications without using a server to accomplish these tasks. Peer-to-peer networks are commonly used in solo or small firm offices with only two or three computers. The computers, located on the same local network and belonging to the same Workgroup (Microsoft's name for a peer-to-peer network), can access shared resources in the Workgroups to which they are joined. Unless a computer is joined to a domain, it belongs to a Work-group. The default Workgroup name in Windows 7, 8, and 10 is the original WORKGROUP, but you are free to name your workgroup something that may be more appropriate.

Peer-to-peer networks may sound like a good solution for small firms that have only a few computers, but this type of network has some significant disadvantages compared to purchasing a server. First, when networking computers together, you are going to experience a slowdown and incon-sistency in your system's performance. Workstations are not capable of handling concurrent access to their files by other computers. When this occurs, the system's resources are severely taxed, causing disruption to the users. Think of this as a tug-of-war for data. Your computer is trying to use data at the same time that someone else needs it. Because of the inconsis-tency and unreliability of the peer-to-peer network, corruption of shared files, such as case management and billing systems, occurs frequently. Since computers in a peer-to-peer network can be running different operating systems, software incompatibilities between the systems can occur. Manage-ment of user accounts, along with implementing the proper security con-trols to protect sensitive and confidential data, becomes a nightmare—and even more difficult should a breach occur that requires investigation.

The decentralization of critical firm data can lead to unnecessarily complex data backup scenarios, often resulting in important data not being backed up or protected. On top of all the issues above, the need to manage and administer multiple copies of the same software, such as antivirus protec-tion on each individual computer, becomes needlessly tiresome. Software that is centrally managed is much more cost effective to purchase and maintain, as opposed to managing each computer's software suites inde-pendently. Just figure in the added administration costs that your firm will pay its IT provider; this will more than cover the cost of a server—and then some!

There is an inaccurate perception that peer-to-peer networks save money and cost less than client/server networks. However, in the end, this is never the case. Yes, purchasing a server—even a lower-end unit—might seem expensive at first, but the costs of managing and maintaining a peer-to-peer network will always be higher than the costs you would have incurred if you had implemented a server/client network in the first place. The soft-ware licensing costs for peer-to-peer networks can be higher because you are purchasing single licenses. Software that is administered and maintained on independent computers will take more time than if it were centrally managed from a server. Technical support and consulting costs will be much higher in a peer-to-peer environment, a fact that is usually not considered when making the initial decision to purchase and use a peer-to-peer network. For most small network environments, even those involving as few as two computers, purchasing a server to centralize applications and data can save time and money—and the number of headaches you will have to endure in the long run.

CHAPTER EIGHT

Server Operating Systems

Choosing the hardware components is just one step in selecting the right server for your business. The next step is determining what operating system and software will best meet the current and future needs of the firm. There are many variations of server operating systems currently available for both Windows and Mac servers, and they are described in detail in the following sections.

Microsoft Windows Server 2003—Any Edition

Any server running the Microsoft Windows 2003 Server operating system should be decommissioned or upgraded immediately. As of July 14, 2015, Microsoft discontinued support for this version. If you are a lawyer, this means you cannot ethically use this operating system because it is no longer receiving security updates and you cannot reasonably protect your firm's confidential data!

Microsoft Windows Server 2008 R2

Microsoft Windows Server 2008 R2 is the successor to Windows Server 2003. It was officially launched in late February 2008 and built from the same code base as Windows Vista, however, without all the problems that Vista had. Microsoft Windows Server 2008 and 2008 R2 are both now in extended support from Microsoft, which ends on January 14, 2020. Given that end-of-life date compared to the four-to-five-year life span of a new server, this operating system shouldn't be chosen when purchasing a new server.

This operating system includes a lot of new features and enhancements, such as native support for IPv6, new security features such as BitLocker, and an improved Windows Firewall with a more secure default configuration. Also, the manner in which this operating system handles processors and memory is different from previous versions. Processors and memory are now treated as plug-and-play devices, meaning they are "hot-swappable." They can now be removed and replaced without shutting down the server, although sticking your hands into a hot, running server is probably not a very bright idea.

Windows Server 2008 includes expanded Active Directory functionality and a major upgrade to Terminal Services. Terminal Services now supports Remote Desktop Protocol 8.0, which provides the ability to share a single application over a remote desktop connection rather than the entire desktop, as was the case in previous versions. It also provides additional support for multiple monitors and stronger encryption algorithms for keeping data traffic secure.

In previous versions of the Windows operating system, if corruption or errors were found on a new technology file system (NTFS) volume, the volume would have to be dismounted and taken offline for the errors to be corrected. Windows Server 2008 supports a self-healing NTFS format that can detect and fix errors while online without having to bring down the entire system. Microsoft Windows Server 2008 is offered in both 32-bit and 64-bit versions.

Windows Server 2008, like previous versions, is offered in the following editions:

- Standard Edition
- Enterprise Edition
- Datacenter Edition
- HPC Server
- Web Server
- Storage Server
- Small Business Server
- Essential Business Server

Most of the editions listed above would not be considered when purchasing a server solution for a small business or law firm and will not be discussed in more detail in this book. However, the Standard, Enterprise, and Small Business Server editions are described later in this chapter.

In February 2011, Microsoft released Service Pack 1 for Windows Server 2008 R2, which introduced two new features and addressed a number of security issues in this version of the operating system. The two new features, RemoteFX and Dynamic Memory, add support for 3-D graphics within a Hyper-V-based virtual machine, as well as dynamic memory allocation based on the resources the virtual machine requires at any given time. It is recommended that if you're running Windows Server 2008, you download and install the latest service pack from Windows Updates as soon as possible.

Microsoft Windows Small Business Server 2008 Standard and Premium Editions

Windows Small Business Server (SBS) 2008 is based on Windows Server 2008 and includes Microsoft Exchange Server 2007 Standard Edition, Windows SharePoint Services 3.0, and trial subscriptions for Microsoft's new security products, such as Forefront Security for Exchange.

The SBS 2008 operating system was officially launched on November 12, 2008. Like previous editions of SBS, the 2008 version is offered in both Standard and Premium editions. The Standard Edition is regarded as a single server solution for small businesses, your all-in-one operating system.

In one server, you get file and printer sharing, e-mail, web hosting, and the ability to set up a domain for up to 75 users and/or devices. The Premium Edition contains all of the features and software the Standard Edition has, plus a license for the Microsoft SQL Server 2008 Standard Edition. The Premium Edition requires two separate servers, one for Windows Server 2008 with Exchange and the other solely for SQL Server. This requirement is going to be a problem for small firms on a tight budget, but it may be more affordable if used in a virtualized environment.

Windows SBS 2008 is offered only in a 64-bit version due to the requirements of Microsoft Exchange Server 2007, whose production version is 64-bit. This distinction is important when considering your hardware purchase. Make sure you have 64-bit hardware if you are considering using these new server operating systems.

On a more positive note, Microsoft has finally changed the way CALs are purchased for SBS. In earlier editions, CALs could be purchased only in groups of five, ten, or 20 licenses, but not anymore. CALs for SBS 2008 can now be purchased individually.

Dell has discontinued the option of configuring servers with the Microsoft Windows Small Business Server option, so we recommend using the Windows Server 2012 Standard Edition option at this time or purchasing the operating system from another supplier, but understand that it will go out of support much sooner than the more recent versions.

Windows Server 2008 Standard Edition

The Windows Server 2008 Standard Edition was designed to increase the reliability of server infrastructure while simultaneously saving time and reducing costs when it comes to server maintenance.

The Standard Edition comes with enhanced security features to help protect your data and network and includes powerful tools that give you greater network control. Windows Server 2008 Standard Edition comes with IIS 7.5, a powerful web hosting and services platform. The operating system also includes Windows Server Hyper-V—virtualization software designed to support machine virtualization—and an upgraded version of Terminal Services that supports Remote Desktop Protocol 8.0.

In terms of security, the Standard Edition includes tools to improve auditing and secure start-up, and it enables disk encryption using BitLocker. The Standard Edition supports up to 32 GB of memory, four multicore processors, and up to 250 concurrent Terminal Service connections.

Windows Server 2008 Enterprise Edition

Microsoft Windows Server 2008 Enterprise Edition, like its predecessor, is an operating system aimed at medium to large businesses looking for a server capable of handling enterprise-level services.

The Enterprise Edition provides mission-critical applications through such features as failover clustering, fault-tolerant memory synchronization, and cross-file replication. It also features the latest advancements in security and is extremely scalable to support mission-critical applications.

This operating system is recommended for servers that will be hosting database applications, case management applications, or other software that requires more processing power and memory addressing than the Standard and SBS operating systems can support.

Microsoft Small Business Server 2011 Standard and Essentials

Microsoft Small Business Server 2011 (SBS 2011) is the successor to SBS 2008 and is offered in two versions: Standard and Essentials. A separate SBS Premium add-on is available for small firms that require SQL Server.

The Standard Edition is designed for small businesses and supports up to 75 users and/or devices. Like the previous SBS versions, this edition provides a single server solution for small businesses that includes e-mail, remote access, and file and printer sharing. This edition includes both Microsoft Exchange Server 2010 and SharePoint Foundation Server 2010.

The Essentials Edition is designed for small businesses and supports up to 25 users and/or devices. This edition is integrated with Microsoft's cloud services and doesn't require the end user to purchase any CALs. This edition, unlike the Standard Edition, does not include Microsoft Exchange Server or SharePoint Foundation Server 2010.

For those small businesses that need to deploy additional servers on their network to run SQL Server 2008 R2 Standard, the Premium Add-on license is the component that they'll need to purchase. Additional server and SQL CALs are required with this component and will add cost to the purchase, depending on the number of users and computers that need to access this system.

Dell has discontinued the option of configuring servers with the Microsoft Windows Small Business Server option, so at this time we recommend using the Windows Server 2012 Standard Edition option or purchasing the operating system from another supplier.

Microsoft Windows Server 2012

In September 2012, Microsoft released this version of its operating system software to coincide with the release of Windows 8. Server 2012 is offered in four editions, only three of which (Essentials, Standard, and Datacenter) would be considered when purchasing a server for a small business.

Server 2012 includes a number of new and enhanced features that IT administrators will love, including

- A newly redesigned user interface with a focus on easing server management tasks, including the administration of multiple servers from within the same window
- An updated version of Windows PowerShell with over 2,300 commands, compared to about 200 in Windows Server 2008
- A new version of Windows Task Manager
- IP Address Management (IPAM) role for discovering, monitoring, auditing, and managing Internet protocol (IP) address space used on the local network
- An updated version of Windows Active Directory, including simplified upgrading of the Domain Functional Level to Server 2012, a new graphical user interface (GUI), the ability to set multiple password policies within the same domain, and the ability to safely clone virtualized domain controllers
- An updated version of Hyper-V, which includes such new features as network virtualization, multitenancy, storage resource pools, cloud backup, support for an increased number of virtual processors, greater storage capacity, and more memory
- A new version of Internet Information Services (IIS) (version 8.0) used to host websites
- A new file system, Resilient File System (ReFS), that is intended for file servers and improves the features of NTFS

Microsoft Windows Server 2012 R2

Windows Server 2012 R2, released in October 2013, should be one of the operating systems of choice when configuring a new server. This edition, like Windows Server 2012, was released in four editions: Foundation, Essentials, Standard, and Datacenter.

Some of the changes from Windows Server 2012 that were introduced in Windows Server 2012 R2 include

- Automated tiering of frequently accessed files on the fastest physical media
- De-duplication for Virtual Hard Drives
- New version of Windows PowerShell (v4)
- Integrated Office 365 support
- Return of the Windows Start Button
- UEFI-based virtual machines
- Boot from SCSI device option
- Faster VM deployment (50 percent increase in speed reported)

We are currently running this operating system on some of our servers and include this operating system when configuring new servers for our clients. It has our stamp of approval at this time.

Microsoft Windows Server 2016

Microsoft Windows Server 2016 is the latest server operating system from Microsoft and is the successor to Windows Server 2012. This edition was released on September 26, 2016, at Microsoft's Ignite conference and became generally available in October of 2016.

Some of the new features include

- A new version of Windows PowerShell
- Internet Information Services 10
- Integration of Windows Defender
- Improved remote desktop services, including performance and stability improvements
- Active Directory Federation Services
- Soft Restart—a feature to speed up the booting process

Microsoft has included a new installation option called Nano Server, which offers a minimal installation footprint and excludes a graphical interface, support for 32-bit software, and console login. All management of this server is performed through the Windows Management Instrumentation interface and PowerShell. Early testing has showed that the Nano Server has resulted in 90 percent fewer critical security advisories and has required 80 percent less reboots than a standard installation of Windows Server.

It's far too early to recommend this operating system and probably will be a year or more before it's a true Windows 2012 replacement. We're sort of on the bubble with this server version as it is very new. As with any new operating system, you need to make sure all of your other application software is compatible with the new version. We know you're safe to deploy Windows Server 2012 R2, which is probably the better move at this time for a new server installation.

X64 Operating Systems

Until about ten years ago, 32-bit processors dominated the commercial marketplace, and 64-bit processors were found only in supercomputers or very high-end and expensive servers. Now, however, 64-bit processors are standard rather than an option when configuring a server or a desktop computer prior to purchase. The 64-bit operating systems have been developed to run on these processors and offer many advantages over their 32-bit counterparts. In fact, the newer versions of Microsoft's server operating systems are offered only in 64-bit versions.

First, these systems process more data per clock cycle, and second, they offer direct access to more virtual and physical memory than 32-bit systems. These advantages provide for more scalable, higher-performing computing solutions, which is a requirement when running a virtualized environment. There are far fewer device driver issues with X64 operating systems now than when 64-bit systems first appeared on the market; however, it's always important to make sure everything is compatible before migrating from a 32-bit environment to a 64-bit environment.

The current versions of Windows desktop-based operating systems and server-based operating systems are all offered in 64-bit versions, and with most editions, that is the only option.

Mac OS X Server 10.9 (Mavericks)

Mac OS X Server 10.9, nicknamed Mavericks, was released in the fall of 2013 as a downloadable package from the Mac App Store, just like Mountain Lion was. This server app costs only $19.99 for the upgrade; however, you should upgrade to the latest Mac OS X server software, Yosemite, if your current hardware meets the necessary requirements.

One of the new features in the Mavericks operating system is a XCode Server used in iOS development—Caching Server 2, which speeds up the download and delivery of software through the App Store, Mac App Store, and iTunes Store so that copies can be downloaded faster to computers and iOS devices from the local cached resource. Some of the additional new features include Profile Manager—simplifying the deployment and configuration of new Mac computers and iOS devices; File Sharing—using SMB2, sharing files and folders between Macs, PCs, or iPads is significantly faster and easier to set up; and Time Machine Backups—the server can act as a designated Time Machine backup location for all the Mac computers on the network.

Mac OS X Server 10.10 (Yosemite)

Mac OS X Server 10.10, nicknamed Yosemite, was released in October 2014 as a downloadable package from the Mac App Store, just like the previous versions of the server software have been.

Some of the new features include an easier-than-ever ability to share data and folders between Mac, iPad, and PCs using the new superfast protocol for sharing files in OS X Server, SMB3. This new protocol helps protect against data tampering and eavesdropping by encrypting and signing data while in transmission, adding another layer of security protection to your server.

The new Profile Manager simplifies deploying, configuring, and managing Mac computers and iOS devices, including user accounts, and allows administrators the ability to perform push installs of OS X enterprise apps and iOS media assets including PDF, ePub, and iBooks Author files.

The Caching Server automatically speeds up the downloads and delivery of software updates through the App Store, Mac App Store, iTunes Store, iTunes U, and iBooks Store to users on the network whose apps need updating.

Mac OS Server 5

This version of the Mac server, first released in the fall of 2015, is the successor to the Mac OS X Server 10.10 operating system. It was updated to version 5.1 in the spring of 2016 and 5.2 on September 20, 2016.

The latest version of Server 5 includes new features such as

- Supports MacOS Sierra 10.12
- Supports SMB3 protocol for sharing files, which includes protection against tampering through encryption and signing by default
- Supports AES encryption for Kerberized NFS
- Supports Access Control Lists
- Updated Caching Server—reduces the amount of data that needs to be uploaded or downloaded to devices on the network, increasing the speed of delivery and enhanced control over peer replication

- Updated Profile Manager—simplifies deploying, configuring, and managing Mac computers and iOS devices within the network
- OS X Server can act as the designated Time Machine backup location, centralizing backup storage of networked computers
- Improved collaboration tools
- MacOS Sierra and Server 5.2 include support for the Xsan 5 file system.

This latest version of the Mac server can be downloaded directly from the Mac App Store for only $19.99. For the minimal cost, it makes sense to upgrade to the latest server version.

Linux-Based Operating Systems

Linux-based operating systems are similar to Unix-based operating systems and are built on an open-source kernel packaged with system utilities, software, and libraries. The underlying source code of the operating system can be freely modified, used, and redistributed, and it is supported by a community of programmers and volunteers.

Linux is now packaged for different uses, primarily servers, which contain modified kernels along with a variety of software packages tailored to different requirements. Some of the commercially available distributions that are backed by corporations are Fedora (Red Hat), SUSE Linux (Novell), Ubuntu (Canonical Ltd.), and Mandriva Linux. Each of these distributions has versions specifically designed and programmed to run on server-based hardware to provide management, web and e-mail hosting services, and file and printer sharing, along with other services and functionality that are available in both Mac- and Windows-based server operating systems. There are also desktop and mobile versions for each of these versions of Linux, which only hold a microscopic fraction of the desktop operating system market share.

Unless you're a serious technologist, you don't want to go anywhere near Linux-based operating systems. A simple but very true statement.

CHAPTER NINE

Networking Hardware

Networking hardware typically refers to equipment that allows network devices to communicate with one another, but not always. Other types of networking hardware include server racks, cabling, and other devices that help make up the computer network. Here we provide descriptions and recommendations for the most common types of networking hardware that you will require in a solo or small firm computer network.

Switches

A switch is a piece of networking hardware that connects network segments (discrete sections of the network), allowing multiple devices to communicate with one another. For example, if two or more computers are connected into the same switch and are located within the same defined network, the switch will allow these devices to communicate. Switches inspect data packets as they are received and, based on the source and destination hardware addresses, will forward the data packet appropriately. By delivering the packet of information only to the device it was intended for, network bandwidth is preserved, as well as confidentiality, and the information is delivered much more quickly. In comparison, network hubs send the traffic to all ports, irrespective of the destination device, and are rarely seen in a production environment anymore. In fact, eBay may be the only place that you can purchase a hub these days. Unlike network hubs, switches are "intelligent" devices that can operate on more than one layer of the Open Systems Interconnection (OSI) model, such as a multilayer switch. Switches allow traffic to pass through them at speeds of 10 Mbps, 100 Mbps, 1 Gbps, or 10 Gbps, depending on the speeds of the ports.

The International Organization for Standardization created the OSI model as a way of subdividing a communications system into seven layers: Physical, Data Link, Network, Transport, Session, Presentation, and Application. We could write a whole book on the OSI model, but others already have.

Most solo and small law firms will not need expensive high-end network switches for their computer infrastructure. In the majority of situations, a switch is needed only to connect computer workstations to the server and to the router for Internet access. Netgear offers reasonably priced switches in a variety of configurations to meet almost any solo or small firm need. Its ProSafe Gigabit Unmanaged Switch series is a good choice for the solo or small law firm because of the low cost, ease of setup, and reliability. Setup of these devices requires no configuration—just plug in the power and network cables and you're ready to go.

When purchasing a switch for your firm, you will need to determine the number of connections or ports the switch will need. Next, you will have to determine the speeds of the ports that you will require. Will all of your computers need the ability to connect to the server at gigabyte speeds, or will just a handful of devices need that kind of speed? Remember, you certainly will pay more for a 48-port switch with 48 gigabit ports than if you buy a 48-port switch with only two gigabit ports and 46 10/100MB ports. Given the bandwidth of today's networks and applications, it's almost a requirement to purchase a switch with gigabit ports, and the added speed is worth the additional cost. The ProSafe Gigabit Unmanaged Switches from Netgear can be found on its website at www.netgear.com.

These switches are also offered in a 1U rack-mount solution that will fit standard 19-inch racks and are backed by a Netgear ProSafe lifetime hardware warranty.

For those law firms that require or desire tighter security controls over their computer systems and users, a managed switch may be the solution. A managed switch, unlike an unmanaged switch, is a device that can be administered or controlled. Advanced features include the ability to limit how computer systems can "talk" with one another at the physical level (private virtual LANs), advanced performance monitoring, Layer 3–based prioritization, and increased bandwidth control. These switches also support Quality of Service (QoS), which can be used to prioritize certain network traffic over other functions, such as VoIP (voice over Internet protocol) phones. A good cost-effective managed switch for small- to medium-sized law firms is the ProSafe Smart Managed Switch from Netgear. This managed switch can be found on Netgear's website (www.netgear.com) starting at around $200 and can be purchased with differing numbers of ports and connection speeds, depending on the requirements.

As an alternative, Dell manufactures some very cost-effective switches for network connectivity. It has managed and unmanaged versions as well as multi-gigabit port models.

Entry-Level and Intermediate-Level Routers

A router is a computer networking device that connects two or more independent networks—for example, your firm's local computer network and your Internet service provider's (ISP) network. A router's job is to determine the proper path for data to travel between the networks and to forward data packets to the next device along the path—basically to get your data from point A to point B. Routers come in all shapes and sizes and can have different features. For a solo or small firm, the most basic router will often be sufficient to connect the local network to the Internet, as well as to protect computers and other hardware devices on the local network from outside attacks (though there is no silver-bullet solution). A basic router will require some configuration from the default values to communicate with the ISP's network, as well as to strengthen the security and protection it provides to your information systems. Most basic routers are capable of handling only broadband Internet connections, such as cable and DSL, by using the Ethernet port coming from the cable or DSL modem. If your firm has a T1 or any variant of this Internet connection, your ISP will probably provide you with a router.

The increasing number of data breaches has prompted a lot of discussion recently about which router a solo or small firm should use. Whichever router your firm chooses, it must have a built-in firewall, logging capabilities, and an intrusion detection system/intrusion prevention system (IDS/IPS) module. There can be no exceptions. Previously, we recommended a Linksys router as a basic routing solution for solo and small firms. When configured correctly, this device could provide adequate protection for your firm's data and information systems. However, our recommendation has changed.

Today, the bad guys have gotten so good at breaking into law firms that it's becoming increasingly hard to keep them out. When they do get in, most law firms don't realize that they've been compromised for months. And be advised, nothing we recommend, however good it is, is a guarantee that your confidential data will not be breached. For this reason, there is no longer an entry-level routing solution that we can recommend with confidence. Your firm's data is just too valuable.

Given the types of data that your firm stores, such as Social Security numbers, credit card numbers, patient/medical records, and other sensitive client information, the only way to combat hackers and have a chance of keeping them out is through the implementation of a defense-in-depth security strategy. This type of information protection strategy provides security at all levels of your computer network, including the point at which your local network interfaces with the public Internet. For this reason, we recommend the Cisco Meraki line of security appliances, even for a solo lawyer.

The Cisco Meraki line of security appliances provide high-performance connectivity for small businesses and have built-in threat defense, including a proven stateful packet inspection firewall, an IDS/IPS (with Advanced Security License), and an optional content-filtering subscription package to restrict a user's access to undesirable websites that may contain malware and phishing attacks. The Cisco Meraki MX64W security appliance offers a wireless option for those firms that require it. The Cisco Meraki security appliances start at around $400 for the hardware and the Advanced Security License costs about $300 per year.

It's becoming harder to find a router for a small- to medium-sized business that doesn't include wireless 802.11 capabilities, although the Cisco Meraki line has plenty of wired-only devices to choose from. Be careful when purchasing these devices for your firm's computer network, as you may unintentionally open up your network to unwanted guests if your system is not configured properly. The majority of these devices come preconfigured with open, unsecured wireless networks—which may be OK for your guest network, but even most wireless devices now have an option to set up a separate guest network to keep your visitor's computer network separate from the firm's. You can never be too safe. Remember, you also have the ability to disable the wireless capability if you don't need it.

Make sure you consult with your IT vendor on best practices when implementing a wireless network for your law firm. And for heaven's sake, make sure all the default settings are changed. Even "script kiddies" know all the default settings.

Firewalls/IDS/IPS Devices

An intrusion detection system (IDS) is used to detect many types of malicious network traffic and computer usage that can't be detected by a conventional firewall or router. These malicious activities include network attacks against vulnerable services (web hosting, e-mail, databases, etc.), data-driven attacks on applications, host-based attacks such as privilege escalation, unauthorized logins, and access to sensitive files. Privilege escalation is the act of exploiting a known vulnerability in an application to gain access to resources that would have otherwise been protected. When an IDS and an IPS are used in combination, they also can detect and prevent malware such as viruses, Trojan horses, and worms from entering the network.

An IDS/IPS device is commonly placed at the gateway of the computer network so that all incoming and outgoing network traffic passes through it. This allows the device to scan all incoming/outgoing traffic before it is passed on to the destination located on the local computer network, denying the entry of any malicious traffic and prohibiting the exit of any malicious traffic. A firewall has the ability to permit or deny data traffic based on port number, originating or receiving Internet protocol (IP) address, and protocol type, to name just a few, and it is usually based on rules that are set up and configured by an administrator. An IP address is a unique address or identifier assigned to a networked device, such as a computer, that allows the device to communicate with other networked devices. Just think of an IP address as being the same as a home address, which is a unique way to identify your home's physical location.

A firewall device with these described capabilities is critical for the protection and security of your firm's computer equipment and information systems. For those users who have a broadband Internet connection at home, a router with firewall should also be used to protect your home-based computer network from outside attacks. This is especially important for those lawyers who work remotely, because you do not want your clients' data to become compromised while you are working off-site. According to the Internet Storm Center, which is part of the SANS Institute, it takes only 20 minutes or less for an unprotected and unpatched computer connected to the Internet to become compromised. Imagine that the computer is yours and it contains confidential client data. This is the stuff of which nightmares are made.

For this reason, we recommend the Cisco ASA 5500-X Series Adaptive-Security Appliance, which provides a good solution for solo and small firms looking to secure their local computer network from outside attacks. This appliance integrates a world-class firewall, unified communications (voice/video) security, SSL (Secure Sockets Layer) and IPsec (Internet protocol security) VPN, intrusion prevention, and content security services into a single piece of hardware. These devices offer advanced security features such as granular control of applications and micro-applications with behavior-based controls, highly secure remote access, and near real-time protection against Internet threats. Combining all of the functionality into one piece of network hardware eliminates the need to purchase a single device for each function. Using a single piece of hardware saves time in setup and configuration, eliminates complexity, and tremendously reduces the cost to adequately secure your business computer network.

The Cisco ASA 5500-X Series provides intelligent threat defense and secure communications services that stop attacks before they affect your firm's business continuity. The firewall technology is built on the proven capabilities of the Cisco PIX family of security appliances, allowing valid traffic to flow in and out of the local network while keeping out unwelcome visitors. The URL and content-filtering technologies implemented by the device protect the business as well as the employees from theft of confidential and proprietary information and help the business comply with federal regulations such as HIPAA and Gramm-Leach-Bliley. The application control capabilities can limit peer-to-peer and instant messaging traffic, which often leads to security vulnerabilities and can introduce viruses and threats to the network. The implementation of a Cisco ASA 5000-X Series device will deliver comprehensive, multilayer security to your computer network and will help you to sleep better at night knowing your electronic data and equipment are protected. The Cisco ASA 5500-X Series Adaptive-Security Appliance can be purchased from Cisco Systems online at its website (www .cisco.com) or through a distributor.

The cost of the Cisco ASA 5500-X Series device can range in the thousands of dollars, depending on the number of licenses, features, warranty, and support purchased with the product. When purchasing this device, we absolutely recommend that you get SmartNet maintenance. SmartNet allows you access to the excellent technical support personnel of Cisco, hardware replacement for failures, and upgrades to the device operating system.

Make no mistake about it: this is an excellent high-end firewall well worth the investment to protect—as well as possible—your network and confidential information.

Racks

A rack unit or enclosure is a piece of hardware that is used to store, organize, and secure your networking and computing equipment. Most often, rack units are used to hold rack-mount servers and network communication equipment such as firewalls and switches. Many types of computer and networking hardware are offered in rack-mount sizes, due to the need to place and secure equipment within a single physical location. Rack units can be portable units mounted on caster wheels; bolted to the floor; or, if small enough, mounted on the wall. The amount of space that is available for the servers and networking equipment will greatly affect which type of rack to purchase. The leading manufacturers of rack units and enclosures are American Power Conversion (APC) and Chatsworth.

APC NetShelter SX enclosures are rack enclosures with advanced cooling, power distribution, and cable management for server and networking devices. The 19-inch rack is vendor-neutral and is guaranteed to be compatible with all EIA-310–compliant 19-inch equipment, which covers nearly all rack-mountable equipment. The 19 inches refers to the horizontal distance between the mounting screws for the equipment. These enclosures offer large cable access slots in the roof to provide overhead cable egress, which is useful when cable runs come down through the ceiling. The bottom design allows for unobstructed cable access through a raised panel floor, which is common in network data centers. The enclosures are well ventilated with perforated front and rear doors to provide ample ventilation for servers and other networking hardware that require unobstructed airflow to keep systems cool. The front and rear doors can be arranged to open in either direction, depending on the layout of the room. For physical security protection, both of these doors can be locked.

The enclosure contains rear cable-management channels to assist in managing the plethora of cables that servers and network equipment require. The frame design of the NetShelter SX enclosures is made with heavy-gauge mounting rails and casters to provide support for up to 3,000 pounds of equipment. APC's NetShelter SX enclosures are offered in many different sizes (stand-alone, data center, colocation, etc.) and can be purchased with accessories, such as UPS battery backups, retractable keyboard, mouse pad, flip-down monitor, cable-management arms, additional fans, and power distribution centers. The APC NetShelter SX rack enclosures can be purchased online at APC's website (www.apc.com), and the basic enclosures start at around $1,500.

If you're hesitant to spend $1,500 on a piece of equipment just to hold your servers and networking devices, you may be able to find used racks from local businesses that are moving or have been closed, or through your local online classifieds, at only a fraction of the price.

Cabling

Now that you have all of your computer equipment selected and purchased, you will need to decide how to wire your data and voice network and what type of network patch cables to purchase to connect your computers to the network drops (cables from the wall outlet to the hub/switch location). These patch cables come in various lengths and are primarily offered in two different types.

First, you have the category 5e cable, which is not the same as the generically termed Cat 5 specification. Second, you have the category 6 cable, more commonly referred to as Cat 6, along with category 7 cables used for networks requiring data transfer speeds of up to 10 Gbps. Each type of cable has a different maximum throughput speed. As with computers, as time progresses, newer cable standards are developed that can handle greater data transfer speeds. There is even a category 8 cable that was just approved in June 2016, promising a new copper speedway for data centers in the not-too-distant future, and operating up to speeds of 40 Gbps. This new specification is directed toward cabling that will be used by data centers to transport data up to four times faster than they currently do now, using the same type of cable.

The Cat 6 standard cable is now the de facto standard used by businesses, increasing in popularity as more and more networking and computer devices operate and communicate at gigabit speeds. Current data transfer rates and applications operating at speeds of 1 Gbps are starting to push the limits of category 5 cabling; although category 5e cable is rated for gigabit speeds, it should be used with caution. The trends of the past and predictions for the future indicate that data rates have been doubling every 18 months. The category 6 cables offer double the amount of bandwidth capacity of category 5 cables and a better transmission performance. The category 6 cable provides a higher signal-to-noise ratio, allowing for higher reliability for current applications and higher data rates for the future. Analysts have indicated that the majority of new wiring installations are using Cat 6 cabling. This decision is fairly easy because all Cat 6 cabling is backward compatible with Cat 5e cabling.

Just when we thought that we would be limited to 1 Gbps speeds with the current cabling in our office, the IEEE (Institute of Electrical and Electronic Engineers) has approved the 802.3bz standard. The standard was specifically designed to bridge the gap between 1 Gbps (Cat 5e and Cat 6) and 10 Gbps (Cat 6a or 7) and provides for 2.5 Gbps over Cat 5e cable and 5 Gbps over Cat 6 cable. We should be seeing a whole new line of networking products (e.g., switches, routers, etc.) supporting 2.5 Gbps and 5 Gbps connections in the coming year.

Category 7 cabling is only commonly seen in data centers and is not yet widely used in local networks. If your firm is planning on wiring the office for data and voice, it makes all the sense in the world to wire with Cat 6 cabling. Remember, once the dust has settled from the construction, it would be extremely costly to have any type of cabling pulled out and replaced. The approximately 10 percent premium that you currently will pay for Cat 6 cabling over Cat 5e cabling is worth the added cost. As time goes on, the premium is getting smaller and smaller.

Wireless Networking Devices

A wireless networking device allows for communication between devices without being physically connected by wires or network cables. In a solo or small firm, if the investment cost to wire an office space with data cables is too expensive, a wireless solution may be the answer. Plus, who wants networking cables all over the place? This is particularly true in older properties—and may be aesthetically desirable in historic buildings. A wireless network is extremely convenient for lawyers who use laptops, smartphones, or tablets because they can move from their office to the conference room with these devices and still stay connected to the local network and Internet. However, we do not recommend wireless connections while connecting to a database or database applications such as some case management systems. Wireless connections could cause database corruption, which would require a reload of backup data. The cost to purchase a wireless networking device is extremely low, and the benefits gained are worth the small investment. However, do not implement a wireless network without taking the proper security precautions. By default, most wireless routers and access points are preconfigured not to enable encryption. This means that by default, all communications between computers and the wireless device are unencrypted and therefore insecure. How many people have connected their laptop to an unencrypted wireless network so that they could check their e-mail or perform online banking? We see this all the time—even at legal technology conferences!

Wireless networks should be set up with the proper security. First and foremost, encryption should be enabled on the wireless device. You should have separate wireless networks for guests—and the guest network should always be encrypted too! Most wireless devices come preconfigured with either an unencrypted network or a network encrypted using the wired equivalent privacy (WEP) 64-bit or 128-bit algorithm. Ultimately, neither of these solutions is adequate. WEP is a weak encryption algorithm and can be cracked in a matter of minutes using free open-source software. Do not use WEP! Frankly, the Federal Trade Commission and the Canadian Privacy Commissioner have both found WEP encryption insufficient to secure credit card information, so we suggest it not be used at all. Some time ago, Wi-Fi protected access (WPA) using the TKIP (temporal key integrity protocol) algorithm was cracked by a group of Japanese scientists in about a minute. So avoid WPA as well. This means that you should be encrypting using WPA2 only.

If the wireless network is for the firm only, enable MAC (media access control) filtering on the wireless device. MAC filtering essentially limits the devices that may communicate with the wireless device. If the MAC address of a computer's wireless network card does not match an authorized MAC address, then the wireless device will not communicate with the unauthorized computer. Enabling MAC filtration will also stop employees from connecting their personal smartphones to the wireless cloud without authorization, even if they know the appropriate network name and passphrase. This is an added layer of security. Most commonly, wireless routers and access points ship with default network names such as Linksys or Netgear. While in operation, these devices will broadcast their names so that wireless clients can locate the wireless networks. It is strongly recommended, for security reasons, that the default name of the wireless network be changed (not to something identifying who you are—such as TheSmithLawFirm) and that SSID (service set identifier, which is essentially the network name) broadcasting be disabled.

If your router doesn't come equipped with built-in wireless support, there are other wireless solutions available for the solo and small firm that provide reliable and secure network connections.

Linksys continues to be a very popular manufacturer of wireless networking devices for residential users and small to medium-sized businesses. Its products have only gotten better since the company was purchased by Cisco in 2003. In 2013 Cisco sold the Linksys line to Belkin, but the products are still rock solid. The Linksys EA3500 N750 Dual-Band Smart Wi-Fi Wireless Router is an all-in-one Internet-sharing router with a four-port switch. Although this router can be used to connect your local computer network to the Internet, it should be implemented as a wireless access point only in coordination with another firewall/IDS/IPS device. The 802.11n wireless standard protocol is used by this device and offers data transmission speeds up to 300 Mbps. This standard is about six times as fast as the 802.11g standard, which offered data transmission speeds up to 54 Mbps. One of the benefits of the 802.11n standard is that it is backward compatible with all 802.11b/g devices. This router supports the latest wireless security encryption standards, such as WPA2, to keep your data communications secure.

The Linksys EA3500 N750 Dual-Band Smart Wi-Fi Wireless Router can be purchased online from the Linksys website (store.linksys.com) or from your local electronics retailer for around $70.

Wireless device manufacturers continue their push to get consumers to purchase their 802.11ac wireless products. The 802.11ac standard has been approved since early 2014, so it's fine to purchase and use these products. Wireless networks that use the 802.11ac standard will see an improvement in connection speeds and range beyond previous 802.11 standard connections. To use the new standard, all wireless devices will have to be 802.11ac compatible; otherwise, the wireless network will operate using only the same standard as the "oldest" wireless device on your network. Further, to get transmission speeds as fast as advertised, you'll have to be relatively close to the access point, and only a limited number of devices can be connected and using the wireless network at the same time.

If you work in a large office space, in a building with a lot of brick or mesh metal wiring embedded within the walls, or in a cubicle next to a microwave, you can purchase a piece of hardware to extend or improve the wireless signal strength in your office. These wireless range extenders cost around $100 and can be purchased online.

CHAPTER TEN

Miscellaneous Hardware

Aside from all of the computer hardware, software, and networking equipment, many other types of hardware deserve to be discussed. These additional devices can provide mobility, security, or functionality that would greatly benefit a solo or small firm.

Fire Safe

A fire safe is an important and often overlooked piece of hardware to have in your office to protect your backup media, software licenses, and other valuables from destruction during a fire or other natural disaster. And don't put the items in the safe and leave the door open; it is astonishing how often we see this. Let the safe serve its purpose and don't succumb to the temptation of convenience by leaving it open. Most come with a locking mechanism, so take advantage of the added security to protect your firm's information.

It is strongly recommended that you store backups (if you use external media), software licenses, copies of technical contracts with third parties, insurance policies, emergency contact lists, your incident response plan, and other important documents in a fire safe. A fire safe is a relatively inexpensive investment; they can be purchased from your local office supply store for a couple of hundred dollars. There are many sizes and shapes of fire safes, so you shouldn't have a problem finding one that suits your needs. The key specification is the rated internal temperature. The safe may be rated to keep the contents from burning, but it also needs to avoid damaging the contents, such as by melting a tape casing, which is why the internal rated temperature is important. If you keep important business records off-site for redundancy, make sure that this information is stored in a fire safe as well. Your ability to recover from a disaster is only as good as the weakest point in the plan.

Battery Backup Devices

A battery backup device is an electronic device that supplies secondary power in the absence of main power, such as during a power outage. Battery backup devices can also protect electronic hardware from power spikes and dirty electricity. These devices come in all sizes and power capacities, and depending on what devices you are looking to protect, this will affect the size and capacities you choose. APC is the leading manufacturer of battery backup devices used for protecting computers, servers, and other networking hardware and equipment.

It is strongly recommended that every computer within the local network be placed on a battery backup device, such as the APC Back-UPS 350. At our office, we have our computers, printers, routers, switches, phones, and voicemail system all on battery backup devices to protect our hardware investment. This battery backup device will supply your computer system with power for up to five minutes after an outage has occurred. During this time, the battery backup device will communicate with the APC software installed on the computer (bundled with the device) and will instruct the computer to shut down properly and safely. The Back-UPS 350 supports up to 210 watts and has three NEMA 5-15R battery backup outlets and three NEMA 5-15R surge protection outlets. You may elect to have a larger UPS for your computer system in order to achieve a longer run time.

Many computers and servers will experience software or hardware errors after a power outage because they did not have the opportunity to shut down properly—often referred to as a hard shutdown—which is a quick way to lose or corrupt your data. When computers and (horror of horrors) servers go down hard, the result is often not pretty—actually it's more of a catastrophe. There is a great chance for data loss or system failure in the event of an outage. By purchasing battery backup devices for your computers and other electronic equipment, you are protecting your hardware and software investment and avoiding possible IT costs to correct all the problems that might ensue from a hard shutdown. The APC Back-UPS 350 can be purchased from APC's website (www.apc.com) for $79.99.

We've discussed battery backup devices for workstations and laptops, but what about servers? Servers require much more power to operate than a desktop or laptop computer. Therefore, they will require more battery capacity to allow them to operate during a power outage and/or the time necessary to properly shut down. On top of that, they take much longer to shut down properly than a workstation due to the greater number of services and processes constantly running on a server. To properly shut down, the average server will take upward of ten minutes or more if it is hosting multiple virtual machines, so supplying the server with enough power to accomplish this task is important. Certainly, you do not want your server to experience a hard shutdown, because the risk is great for data loss or hardware failure. Battery backup devices for servers can be purchased as a tower unit or rack mountable, depending on what your firm needs to support its server configuration.

The APC Smart-UPS 1500VA is an ideal battery backup solution to protect a single server from the power outages, power spikes, or dirty electricity that can damage the server's internal hardware components. The Smart-UPS 1500VA is offered in both tower and rack-mountable forms and can supply a server with enough power to allow the server to shut down properly. Note that this unit has only enough capacity to supply power to one server and its peripheral devices. If there is a need to purchase a battery backup device for multiple servers, there are models with greater capacities that will be able to handle the load.

As with all batteries, someday they will need to be replaced. Happily, the batteries in these devices are hot-swappable, which means they can be replaced without the need to shut down the battery backup device or the devices connected to the unit. It is important to replace batteries as soon as they fail so that the systems connected to the battery backup device continue to be protected in the event of a power failure, and—trust us—you'll know when the battery needs to be replaced, because the beeping alarm is really loud and annoying. Replacement batteries for these devices can be purchased online from APC's website. Because the batteries in these units are replaceable, this is one hardware investment that you will not be replacing every one to two years. In our experience, these devices will always outlast the life of the computers, servers, or equipment connected to them.

The APC Smart-UPS 1500VA comes bundled with software that can be installed on the server itself to enable the battery backup device to communicate with the server. This is necessary so that in the event of a power outage, the battery backup can alert the software installed on the server of the need to begin the shutdown process. The battery backup device connects to the server through a USB or SmartSlot device. The APC Smart-UPS 1500VA can be purchased from APC's website starting at $569.

You can also purchase an optional network card for many of the larger UPS devices. The network card allows you to connect the communications over your data network and can support multiple servers. You configure the network card with an IP address, and the servers use the APC network shutdown software to "talk" to the UPS for status rather than communicating through the traditional USB or serial connection.

Fax Machines

Even though the need for fax machines has dwindled, they are still often a staple in a law office and do get some use from time to time—we still receive a fair number of faxes, and some clients and institutions insist that we receive information via the facsimile machine. Sometimes there just isn't enough time to scan a document and then e-mail it to a recipient, so instead the document will be faxed—or in some cases, although increasingly rare, the communicating party doesn't have access to an Internet connection. We still see plenty of solo and small firms where there is no interest in learning how to scan. The fax machine is the devil they know, and they don't want to change. So, even with all of the advancements in technology, the fax machine has a continued role. As previously stated, many digital copiers have fax transmission and receipt capabilities. Check with your vendor representative to see if using the copier is more cost effective than purchasing a separate device.

If your firm is in the market for a fax machine, the device we recommend is the Brother IntelliFAX-2940, which is a high-speed laser fax, phone, and copier. This model was designed for multiple users in a small business to easily share the benefits. Its design incorporates a high-capacity front-loading paper tray that makes replenishing the paper a task that doesn't require a degree in engineering to accomplish.

The IntelliFAX-2940 is equipped with 16 MB of memory, allowing multiple faxes to be stored in memory for transmission when it senses the line is free. The 33.6 Kbps SuperG3 fax modem optimizes throughput, transmitting as fast as 2.5 seconds per page. The 250-sheet capacity paper tray is front-loading for easy access, which means less time spent reloading paper. The paper tray can adjust to hold either letter- or legal-size paper.

This fax machine also comes with a 30-page auto document feeder. Access to incoming faxes can be protected through the use of a password, ensuring that only the appropriate parties see confidential faxes. Finally, if your needs exceed or grow beyond faxing and copying, this device comes with a USB interface and can serve as a laser printer capable of printing up to 24 pages per minute. This device comes with a standard one-year limited warranty. The Brother IntelliFAX-2940 can be purchased online at Brother's website (www.brother-usa.com) for around $300.

In the event that you already have a scanner and don't want to purchase additional hardware just to send or receive faxes, you may want to look into e-fax services. E-fax services allow users to send and receive faxes via e-mail or online. One popular provider, eFax, provides users with a local or toll-free fax number to use to send or receive faxes. Received faxes are then available via e-mail or through the browser. Users send faxes using e-mail and the service provider will send the attachment onto the recipient fax machine, providing confirmation of receipt. eFax (www.efax.com) offers a 30-day free trial, followed by a monthly subscription cost starting at $16.95 for receiving up to 130 fax pages and sending up to 30 fax pages a month.

CHAPTER ELEVEN

Smartphones

Smartphones remain the number one tech accessory among lawyers. We all remember the time (it's getting more distant with each passing year) when a lawyer would carry two separate devices, a cell phone and a PDA (personal digital assistant). The cell phone was used to make phone calls, and the PDA was used to keep your notes and calendar. Some even allowed you to view your e-mail captured during the last synchronization with your work computer. Things have changed radically. Smartphones are like laptops—able to perform almost every function a laptop can, and in some instances, more—but at a fraction of the size. Because smartphones have so many capabilities, lawyers in firms of all sizes tend to view them as a necessity—a device they can no longer live or go anywhere without. Smartphones have become computers in and of themselves, with increasing functionality, and in some cases, they are more important to a lawyer than a computer system.

And sadly, they have become a kind of crack, with many lawyers seriously addicted to them and unable to disengage from technology, risking their health and relationships. That aside. . . .

Among business users and especially lawyers, the smartphone debate has evolved into major warfare. Since its introduction and with its growing popularity, the Apple iPhone has grabbed the largest share of the lawyer market, and that is particularly true for solo and small firm lawyers.

According to the American Bar Association's 2016 Legal Technology Survey, Apple's iPhone continues to be the dominant phone used by attorneys. Here is the breakdown:

- Apple iPhone: 73 percent
- Google Android: 23 percent

- BlackBerry: 3 percent
- Windows Mobile: 2 percent
- Don't Know: 1 percent

These numbers have resulted in some major changes over the past few years:

- There are only two major players in the smartphone market (iPhone and Android), and that should continue for the foreseeable future.
- iPhone's usage increased to 73 percent, while all of the other four categories saw decreases in usage—Android's first-ever decline recorded by the survey. By the way, these figures are not reflective of the business world at large—the race between Android phones and iPhone is very close in most other industries.
- Windows Mobile and BlackBerry devices continue to be minor players.

Both the Android and the iPhone continue to split the market share at an almost 61 percent combined share of the market. The BlackBerry is no longer used very much—it has become all but nonexistent in the United States, much like the Windows Mobile phone has become. BlackBerry (the name of the device and the company name) may have been lulled into inaction by its early success, but the hot technology continues to clearly belong to Androids and iPhones. Because BlackBerry is a Canadian company, Canada continues to keep it on life support.

A key functional requirement for any smartphone is the ability to synchronize data with your computer or server. E-mail synchronization is at the top of all lawyers' lists, followed closely by calendar synchronization. The Windows Phone 8 and 8.1, Windows Phone 10, iPhone, and Android phones synchronize with Microsoft Exchange Servers via ActiveSync. This doesn't require any special hardware or software because the function is built into Exchange. However, there are some limitations, such as the inability to synchronize natively with Public Folders over the air. You may have to purchase third-party products to get all of the features you need for over-the-air synchronization of Public Folder items such as Calendar Items, Contact Items, InfoPath Form Items, Journal Items, Mail and Post Items, Note Items, and Task Items. For this task, we use and recommend CodeTwo Exchange Sync (http://www.codetwo.com/exchange-folder-sync/). The cost to purchase and install this product will vary depending on the type of Exchange server that you have—Small Business Server or Exchange Server Standard/Enterprise—but will generally cost under $800 to get you up and running, plus another couple hundred or so for a year of support, which you will want to renew annually.

Your mailbox will synchronize without any additional software. For those firms that don't host their own e-mail, users can set up their devices to retrieve e-mail directly from their e-mail service provider.

Our continuing recommendation for any lawyer (or anybody wanting to keep his or her data secure) is not to use an iPhone. The iPhone security has gotten better, significantly so, but there still are some issues—and the iPhones hold a lot more data than other phones. Those of us in the digital forensics world call them "evidence-rich." Apple just released the iPhone 7 as we are writing this book and the security of that device remains to be seen, although we expect it to be an improvement over previous models as has been historically true.

The new flagship iPhone comes in two flavors, the iPhone 7 and the iPhone 7 Plus running iOS 10. The iPhone 7 is 5.44 inches long; the iPhone 7 Plus is a whopping 6.23 inches long, which is huge for a smartphone. It's almost like you're holding an iPad Mini next to your head—too large for our taste. Both models have an improved splash-, water-, and dust-resistant design and both removed the headphone jack, which is causing a world of controversy.

The iPhone now comes with dual speakers for the first time and is available in five different colors. Lastly, one of the major updates included with the iPhone 7 Plus is the dual camera setup. One camera is identical to the wide-angle lens in the iPhone 7; the second is a telephoto lens enabling 2? optical zoom and far greater depth of field—and even the flash got an upgrade! The lack of a standard headphone jack is bound to annoy some users because the device now uses the Lightning port instead and comes with EarPods with Lightning Connector. You do have the option to purchase wireless AirPods for a whopping $159 instead of using the Lightning Connector EarPods. Supposedly the AirPods will last five hours on a single charge, but Apple's history of poor battery life with iPhones makes us skeptical. It's also interesting to see that Apple has finally dropped the 16 GB model with this release, with the 32 GB model the new "entry level" model. The Home button has been revamped to include haptic feedback and includes a built-in Touch ID fingerprint sensor.

The features of iOS 10 are discussed later in the book in the More from Apple chapter.

Continuing on with the fingerprint scanner that was introduced with the iPhone 5, the iPhone 7 allows users to unlock their iPhone with a fingerprint as well as approve purchases from iTunes, iBooks, and the App Store without having to enter a password. Apple has released multiple fixes for various vulnerabilities as we go to press, but the fundamental insecurity of the fingerprint scanner cannot be fixed. However, it is unlikely that this will present a problem for most users, as there is some level of sophistication involved in compromising the fingerprint. But if you are targeted by a professional, your data is not secure—after all, we leave our fingerprints everywhere we go. In addition, there are stories of suspicious spouses accessing iPhones via fingerprint after their spouse has passed out from a hard night of partying. You can't make this stuff up.

The government has been making the same complaints since the release of the Android Lollipop operating system in 2014 as it has about the encryption of the more recent iPhone models. The encryption of data on these mobile devices continues to prevent the National Security Agency (and others) from being able to access the encrypted contents of these devices, potentially hampering or slowing down their investigations. Anyone concerned with the privacy of an individual's data should be happy that the government is unhappy and should be thankful that we just may have a way to keep the data on our devices secure once and for all—whether from hackers or our own government!

Not much has changed in the security model, or lack thereof, of Apple's iPhone devices. There still are security problems with the current generation of the devices. Within days of each new firmware version released, a new "jailbreak" method has been discovered. Although iOS 4 held up better than its predecessors, iOS 5, 6, 7, and 8 have all been jailbroken. Even iOS 9 and 10 have been jailbroken before being released.

Because we know so many lawyers will (and do) ignore our advice, here's what we recommend:

- Only use the iPhone 6, 6 Plus, 7, or 7 Plus. If you're using any other model, upgrade immediately.
- Upgrade to the latest version of iOS 10.
- Enable a passphrase (not the default six-digit PIN) on the device.
- Enable device wiping upon a set number of unsuccessful logon attempts.
- Do not enable the Touch ID fingerprint reader. Only use a passphrase to unlock the phone.

As of this writing, the iPhone 7, iPhone 7 Plus, and iOS 10 have been released. Given the insecurity of the fingerprint scanner, make sure you configure a strong lock code and not the default six-digit PIN. Even though the FBI is reported to have paid approximately $1.3 million to access the San Bernardino iPhone 5c, security researchers have been able to "mirror" the memory for $100 and brute force every possible PIN. Once the phone wipes, they just restore the memory image and keep trying PINs. We are well aware that our advice is largely ignored here, as the glamour of the iPhone continues to mesmerize the public, including lawyers. It is a very slick phone, but remember that the new ABA Model Rules adopted in 2012 require that you balance the risk of the technology you use against the security of client data! As we write this, 26 states have thus far adopted the changes to the rules.

With the introduction of iOS 5 back in 2012, Apple introduced the iCloud service. When enabled and configured, iOS devices use this service to back up information from your local device to the cloud. The iCloud service removes the necessity to connect your iOS device to your computer and either back up or update your device by using iTunes. All of this now takes place wirelessly, over your mobile data connection or your local Wi-Fi network. However, while convenient, there are some serious concerns with data privacy.

First, consider that all information from your local device, whether the iPhone or iPad, is being sent to Apple for storage. The information may be encrypted by Apple, but it holds the decryption key and will turn the decrypted data over to law enforcement when the right paperwork is supplied. The 2014 Celebgate scandal, in which nearly 500 private photos of various celebrities were leaked to the public, have highlighted the insecurity and dangers of the iCloud, especially if you want to store your nude selfies on Apple's service. To secure your iCloud account from unauthorized access, users should enable and use two-factor authentication—which was implemented in response to Celebgate. When two-factor authentication is enabled, a password alone is no longer enough to access an account—you will also need the six-digit verification code that's automatically displayed on your trusted devices. Even though Apple can currently decrypt your iCloud data, it has indicated that it plans to change the security design to match the iPhone. This means that data will be able to be decrypted only by end-user-supplied credentials and not by Apple.

For any cloud storage provider, whether iCloud, Dropbox, or some other provider, we always recommend that you encrypt the data prior to using and initiating the service. By following this process, the user holds the decryption key—not the service provider.

For iOS devices, an app like BoxCryptor encrypts the files on your local device before the information is synchronized with the cloud storage provider. BoxCryptor encrypts files on the local device using AES-256–bit and RSA encryption, providing the necessary security to keep your files and information secure. This also allows the user to hold and maintain possession of the decryption key, which is very important. This product used to be free, and still is for personal use, but costs $96 per year for a single-user business license.

During the past few years, many vendors of Android smartphones have continued to release phones designed for business use. They include enhanced security and enterprise management capabilities, like encryption, support for virtual private networks, support for more ActiveSync controls, and remote locking and wiping.

In August 2016, Google released version 7.0 of Android, called Nougat. This version includes the default encryption of e-mails and text messages when stored locally on your phone, as well as a new chat app called Allo, which boasts an incognito mode featuring end-to-end encryption. If you use Allo, be sure to enable and use incognito mode. Google has stated that by default, all non-incognito messages will be stored and accessed by Google to improve Allo's "smart reply feature." This is a serious privacy concern that users should be aware of when using this app. Also new is granular encryption support, allowing devices to reboot into a normal functioning state by using just the device keys, allowing the system storage area and the user profile storage area to be encrypted separately. Starting with Nougat, Google also requires all Android devices to use trusted hardware modules for storing cryptographic keys as an added measure of protection against brute force attempts to bypass a user's password, PIN, or pattern.

Besides the security enhancements, Google also included standard multi-window multitasking, updated Notifications, and added a "Data Saver" mode to reduce background data usage and a new application programming interface for high-end Android games.

For those users looking for a smartphone recommendation, we strongly recommend investing in Android phones. We officially made the jump four years ago to the Samsung Galaxy S3 and haven't looked back. We have fallen in love with the Samsung Galaxy line of devices and have used many of the models. The Samsung Galaxy S7 and S7 Edge are the latest available models and are offered with up to 32 GB of internal memory and three different colors to choose from. Please note that Samsung has recalled the Galaxy Note 7 (not to be confused with the S7), which is no longer available for purchase. This device was recalled due to the battery failing, causing some of the mobile devices to catch fire or explode. If you currently have a Note 7, you can learn more about the recall and exchange program on Samsung's website at https://pages.samsung.com/us/note7/recall/index.jsp.

Besides the Samsung Galaxy model line, there are many other Android devices to choose from. It may help to choose your cellular provider first and then see what options it has. We've been to many Sprint, Verizon, and AT&T stores—nowadays, they all pretty much have the same models in stock with many more options available online. For an Android, the Samsung Galaxy S7 is our current recommendation.

On a side note, everyone is familiar with getting spam through e-mail, but how about on the phone? Spam text messages can be costly since most carriers will charge for both text messages sent and received unless you have an unlimited plan. There is no anti-SMS-spam software available to install on cell phones to prevent receiving these messages, but there is a way to block cellular spam, and it's quite simple. The vast majority of spam text messages originates on the Internet and does not come from other cell phones. Why? Because spammers don't have to pay anything when using the Internet to send the text messages. Most carriers, led by AT&T and Verizon Wireless, offer spam SMS-blocking features. To enable this feature, just log in to your online account manager and the options should be available in your account profile. Most cellular providers allow you to block SMS messages only from certain phone numbers and addresses. What are you waiting for? We've signed up. Here are the websites you can use:

- AT&T (mymessages.wireless.att.com)
- Verizon Wireless (www.verizonwireless.com)
- Sprint (www.sprint.com)
- T-Mobile (www.t-mobile.com)

Make sure you pay attention to smartphone updates and security notices, as the number of malware threats targeting smartphones have skyrocketed over the past year. Currently, Android devices are the most frequently targeted by malware due to their popularity, open-source operating system, the relatively lawless Android Market, and the availability of apps from multiple sources.

For Android phones, we recommend a security product called Sophos Mobile Security for Android (https://www.sophos.com/en-us/products /free-tools/sophos-mobile-security-free-edition.aspx). Specifically designed for Android, Sophos Mobile Security identifies malicious or potentially unwanted applications that could result in, for example, data theft, data loss, and excessive network usage costs. If your device is lost or stolen, a remote lock or wipe will shield your personal information from prying eyes.

Even with the rising threat of malware, there are some basic steps you can take to protect yourself. First, make sure that when you're downloading an application, you do so only from Google Play or the App Store. When choosing an application to try or to purchase, be sure to read carefully through the reviews. Also, pay attention to the access permissions that an app requests when you install it, especially on an Android device. Finally, vendors of security software are now offering antivirus and anti-malware products for smartphones. This is software that you should seriously consider purchasing to protect your mobile devices, especially if they contain confidential information, which they most certainly do.

Basic security measures for any smartphone should include strong passwords, passphrases, or PINs; automatic logoff after a set time; encryption of the phone and storage cards; and remote wiping capability. The good news is that by configuring a lock code (PIN, password, etc.) on an iPhone or newer Android device automatically encrypts the contents.

CHAPTER TWELVE

Productivity Software

Having worked with so many solos and small law firms through the years, we know that lawyers are constantly striving to be more productive and thereby increase their billable time. We see a few lawyers (fewer than the number of digits on one hand) who still prefer to use Corel WordPerfect over Microsoft Word, but that number is continuing to approach zero as Corel is becoming more and more of a nonfactor in the productivity software market.

Microsoft Word is what the business world uses and will continue to use for the foreseeable future. There are alternatives, but they all come with some degree of pain and a large learning curve. There are adherents of WordPerfect who are religious in their fervor and others who are evangelical in their admiration for open-source solutions. Whether you are a fan of Microsoft or not, the reality is that Word is the preferred application of the business world, and your clients will expect you to use it. They will not appreciate any conversion problems that may occur if you are using something else. In this chapter, we detail the latest and greatest releases of productivity software that can help lawyers be more productive.

Microsoft Office

Microsoft's latest version of Office, Office 2016, was released about a year ago and has been thoroughly vetted at this point. The software was redesigned to make the most of the Windows 8 and 10 operating systems, work with mobile devices, and strongly push Microsoft's cloud services. It works and runs just fine on Microsoft Windows 10, and it is our current choice and recommendation for a productivity suite.

To compete with Google's cloud storage options, Microsoft designed the new version of Office as a service in which applications and files are primarily stored in the cloud and not on your local computer system. This may come as a shock to most traditional Microsoft users, and lawyers should be aware that this type of service may pose ethical issues depending on how and where their information is actually being stored. However, users also have the ability to store documents on their local computer system.

Each of the three editions of Office 2016 includes the core applications of Word, Excel, PowerPoint, and OneNote:

- Home & Student, designed for families and consumers; core applications only; retails for $149.99
- Home & Business, designed for the small business market; provides e-mail, shared calendars, and web conferencing tools; core applications and Outlook; retails for $229.99
- Professional, designed for enterprise customers; provides advanced business and cloud deployment features; core applications plus Outlook, Publisher, and Access; retails for $399.99

If your firm is using Microsoft Office 2010 or older, we highly recommend that you upgrade to Office 2016 at this time. Office 2013 users should be just fine unless you want to take advantage of the collaboration features of Office 2016.

Microsoft, like a lot of companies, is making a very strong push to get users to the cloud and away from local applications. To accomplish this goal, Microsoft has introduced a software as a service (SaaS) called Office365, which gives users and companies the option to purchase a subscription (monthly or annually) to use the Microsoft Office applications in the cloud, and in some instances, also includes the ability to install and use the stand-alone versions.

The subscription-based Office365 may not be for everyone, but for a solo or small firm, it at least presents another licensing option—rather than having to shovel out hundreds of dollars for the stand-alone versions of the Office 2016 suite. The Business Essentials subscription is entirely cloud-based and costs $5 per user per month ($60 per year), but doesn't include the ability to run Office on a mobile device, such as an iPad, or to install Office on your local computer. This requires you to be connected to the Internet in order to use Microsoft Office, which is a major downside. The Business subscription costs $8.25 per user per month ($99 per year), but doesn't include e-mail hosting (storing your e-mail with Microsoft), which is different than the Outlook application. This subscription plan does allow you to install the full version of Office on your local computer (including Outlook) and use the Office apps on your tablet or mobile device. Finally, the Business Premium subscription costs $12.50 per month per user ($150 per year), includes Office for tablets, and allows for the installation of Microsoft Office 2016 on up to five computer systems per user ($30/license). For a small firm just starting up that is looking to be mobile, shelling out $12.50 per month for your employees to use Office may be easier to swallow than paying up to $400 per copy of Microsoft Office 2016. It's just another option to consider.

In addition to the Business subscription plans, Microsoft offers several Enterprise plans. The top-level Enterprise plan costs $35 per user per month (annual commitment) and includes features that attorneys will love. As an example, Enterprise E3 includes Compliance and Information Protection, including Legal Hold, Rights Management, and Data Loss Prevention for e-mail and files. There are also e-discovery tools to support compliance. The Enterprise plans can get expensive for some solo and small firm attorneys, but some may feel it's worth the extra money just to get Data Loss Prevention for their e-mail. You can see the features for each edition of Office 365 at https://products.office.com/en-us/business /compare-more-office-365-for-business-plans.

We are seeing a lot of solo and small firms migrating to Office365, and in general, we hear that lawyers are very satisfied with the cost and performance.

It should be noted that Microsoft Office 365 includes support for Office 2016 for Macs, which is available for those subscriptions with the ability to install a full version of the Office suite locally on a computer system. One of the other major advantages of Office 365 is the ability for Microsoft to update its applications in "real time," without having to wait to release updates for users to take advantage of new or improved features.

Editing Office documents on tablets (and other mobile devices) has long been a major headache, which could only be overcome by using third-party applications to perform the simplest tasks of opening, editing, and saving documents on the mobile device. Microsoft has finally released Office for mobile devices, including Office for iPad and Office Mobile for the iPhone, Windows Phone, and Android devices.

Office for iPad has been an app that the legal community has been anxiously awaiting. Now it is here. This app allows users to edit and create documents, including spreadsheets and presentations. Office for iPad requires a subscription to Office365; however, Office Mobile is free to download on your Android, iPhone, or Windows Phone. Just remember that an Office365 subscription is required if you want to edit Office files and not just view them.

For those attorneys who require e-mail encryption (most of you should be using e-mail encryption by now), Microsoft has released a service called Office 365 Message Encryption. This service lets users send encrypted e-mails to people outside your firm, regardless of the destination (Yahoo, Gmail, Outlook, etc.). Encryption is critical when sending messages that contain personally identifiable information, credit card numbers, medical records, and Social Security numbers, to just name a few types of sensitive information. Office 365 Message Encryption requires Microsoft Azure Rights Management, which costs $2 per user per month. If you have the E3 or E5 subscription of Office 365 Enterprise, Azure Rights Management is included in the cost, so you automatically get e-mail encryption without having to pay the extra $2 per user per month.

Corel Suite

WordPerfect Office X8 is the latest version of Corel's Office Suite, and it is available in Standard and Professional editions for the business user. WordPerfect Office X8, the successor to WordPerfect Office X7, was released in April 2016. New features of Corel WordPerfect Office X8 include an improved interface, new templates, and enhanced import and export capabilities for Office formats. The components of WordPerfect Office X8 Standard Edition include

- Main Applications
- WordPerfect word processor
- Quattro Pro spreadsheet program
- Presentations slideshow creator
- WordPerfect Lightning digital notebook
- AfterShot 2 RAW photo-editing software

Also included:

- 900+ TrueType fonts
- 10,000+ clipart images
- 300+ templates
- 175+ digital photos
- BrainStorm training videos
- The Pocket Oxford English Dictionary

- WordPerfect Address Book
- Presentations Graphics—bitmap editor and drawing application
- WordPerfect XML Project Designer
- Batch Conversion Utility to convert Microsoft Word documents to WordPerfect documents

Corel X8 is offered in Standard and Professional editions, but the Standard Edition is best suited for serving solo or small firm needs. Unless a solo or small firm needs a database application, there is no reason for it to invest in the Professional Edition.

One of the touted advantages of WordPerfect over Microsoft Word is the Reveal Codes option, which allows users to manage document formatting with a fine-tooth comb. We are constantly amazed when lawyers mention the reveal code "excuse." Perhaps they are unaware that Word actually has a reveal code type display (and Office has since 2007), where the user can see formatting codes.

Even with the new features included with WordPerfect Office X8, we still prefer the more seamless Microsoft Office 2016. Another concern is the integration of WordPerfect with other software in your practice such as case management and document management. You can see a listing of products that work with WordPerfect at http://www.wordperfect.com /us/pages/4500028.html. Corel used to price the software suite at a much reduced cost when compared to Microsoft Office, particularly for business-friendly packages, but that hasn't been the case for many years. Full license and upgrade costs for the two editions are below.

Edition	Full License Cost	Upgrade Cost
Standard Edition	$249.00	$159.99
Professional Edition	$399.00	$259.99

Users who don't need the extensive features of WordPerfect or Microsoft Office might opt to use a product such as OpenOffice.org or LibreOffice (described in the next sections), both of which are free.

OpenOffice.org

Apache OpenOffice.org (formerly just OpenOffice) is a free open-source software office suite that is available for many different operating systems, including Linux, Windows, and Mac OS X. The latest release of OpenOffice.org (version 4.1.2) was in September 2015, and it contains many features and functions that are present in Microsoft Office and Corel WordPerfect Office. This suite was developed to reduce Microsoft Office's dominating market share by providing a free, open, and high-quality alternative. Some of the new features in version 4.1 include comments on text ranges, support for IAccessible2, in-place editing of Input Fields, interactive cropping, and the ability to import pictures from files. The micro release, version 4.1.2, was primarily released to fix a number of security vulnerabilities, and in terms of enhancements, added support for interaction with Microsoft SharePoint.

OpenOffice.org can read and write most of the file formats found in Microsoft Office, which is important if you are going to choose to use a free utility for your productivity software. It also natively supports the standard OpenDocument Format (ODF) and has the capability to read WordPerfect Office, Rich Text Format (RTF), Lotus, and other common productivity file types.

The components of OpenOffice.org work together to provide the features expected from a modern office suite and include

- Writer—word processor
- Calc—spreadsheet application
- Impress—presentation program
- Base—database program
- Draw—an editor used for drawing
- Math—allows for creating and editing mathematical formulas

All of the components of the OpenOffice.org suite look and feel like the corresponding components in Microsoft Office and Corel WordPerfect Office. Microsoft, seeing the need for and popularity of the open-source movement, has sponsored the development of a converter from Office Open XML to OpenDocument format and vice versa. Microsoft and Corel have included add-in support for the ODF file format into their office suite products to allow reading and writing to the format.

However much we all grimace at Microsoft's domination, we do not recommend that you use OpenOffice.org as your primary productivity suite. Because it is developed and maintained by freelance programmers and other companies that make contributions to the project, such as Apache, the software is not very well supported and may not contain all of the features provided by other productivity suites. Over the last several years, developers have abandoned OpenOffice and are now writing code for LibreOffice. As a result, OpenOffice upgrades have slowed to a crawl and LibreOffice keeps enjoying major upgrades. Some commentators even suggest that there are still security vulnerabilities in the current version of OpenOffice that haven't been fixed for over a year because of the lack of developers.

If you are still interested in trying OpenOffice, the current release of OpenOffice .org can be downloaded from the website free of charge at www.openoffice.org.

LibreOffice

LibreOffice has become the open-source office suite replacement for OpenOffice, which is all but now defunct. LibreOffice forked from OpenOffice.org in 2010, and is developed around the ODF format, just like OpenOffice is.

LibreOffice also supports the file formats of most other major office suites, including Microsoft Office.

LibreOffice includes the same six applications as Open Office—Writer, Calc, Impress, Draw, Math, and Base. LibreOffice is supported on Windows, Linux, and Apple computers, and released a viewer application for Android devices with basic editing capabilities in the spring of 2015.

If you're looking at trying one of the open-source office suites, LibreOffice would be our recommendation of choice. You can download the latest version of the free suite, 5.2, from www.libreoffice.org. LibreOffice uses a time-based release schedule for major updates, which turns out to release one every four to eight months—so make sure you check for updates periodically.

Adobe Acrobat

Adobe Acrobat, a family of application software developed by Adobe Systems, uses Portable Document Format (PDF) as its native file format. The PDF specification was originally a proprietary format but is now a published and approved ISO standard. The latest version of Adobe Acrobat (DC) includes Adobe Document Cloud services and is notably different from previous versions. Document Cloud allows users to create, review, approve, and sign documents from any desktop or mobile device. Since the program is integrated with the cloud, a user can begin working on a document on one device and then continue editing it on another. Adobe Acrobat PDF files can easily be created or edited from a mobile device, such as an Apple iPad. The latest update added support for SharePoint-based reviews, including participants using Microsoft Office 2016 (Windows and Macs).

Adobe Acrobat DC allows users to convert, combine, and export PDFs easier than ever. The Export PDF to Word feature has been enhanced, hopefully fixing all of the formatting problems previously experienced when attempting to accomplish this task. The Pro DC version contains all of the features that attorneys love such as Bates numbering and redaction capabilities.

Adobe Acrobat DC is offered in a subscription model as well as a stand-alone solution, without the cloud-based integration. The Acrobat DC subscriptions cost $14.99 per month per user, which includes the desktop version of the Acrobat DC software as well as the cloud-integration and mobile features. Subscribers will also get 20 GBs of cloud storage with their plan.

Adobe has recently released an update to Acrobat DC that enhances the Compare Documents tool, as well as allows users to digitally sign, certify, and verify documents with a Certificate ID. The Compare Documents tool allows users to compare the contents of two documents and highlight the differences between the two, including text, images, annotations, and formatting. Adobe has made it easier to follow prompts to configure a digital ID and add it to a document, allowing the document to be digitally signed.

Users can still opt for the stand-alone version of the Adobe Acrobat DC software at a cost of $449 for the full version of Acrobat Pro DC or $299 for the full version of Acrobat Standard DC. The upgrade versions of these products are priced much lower than the full versions, allowing for users of Acrobat X and XI to upgrade at a fraction of the cost. The cost to upgrade to Acrobat Pro DC is $199, and the cost to upgrade to Acrobat Standard DC is $139. This product is supported on Windows 10 as well as the latest version of Mac OS X. There are some reported issues with Adobe's Creative Cloud applications running on Mac OS Sierra, but it appears that Acrobat runs just fine.

Power PDF

For those users who are looking for an alternative to Adobe Acrobat, our recommendation is to use Power PDF Advanced 2 by Nuance. It is certainly a worthy alternative and is only one-third of the retail cost of Acrobat Pro. Power PDF Advanced has Bates stamping support to create custom profiles for stamping information into headers and footers. There's also an assistant function to convert legal pleadings into PDFs with stamp and line numbering options. Redaction ability is included too. Users may also secure their PDFs with passwords using 128-bit or 256-bit AES encryption and permission controls to protect document viewing, printing, and modifications. The program also integrates with cloud storage providers, allowing users to save their PDFs directly in the cloud. Some of the new features included in the latest version are the ability to covert a PDF file to Office documents, Microsoft Windows 10 touch-enabled input, and integration via Ribbon into Microsoft Office 2016 products.

There are a lot of other features available with Power PDF Advanced 2. Suffice it to say that it has the majority of features present in Acrobat Pro that any attorney would find valuable. The cost is attractive as well. Make sure you take advantage of the 30-day trial to determine if it will meet your needs. It should be noted that this product is Windows 10 compatible.

OCR Software

Optical character recognition (OCR) software translates graphical images into editable text. This capability is used most commonly to edit a scanned document or image. It's widely used in law firms to convert scanned paper documents in a case file to searchable electronic files. OCR software will translate the image to text, such as a Microsoft Word document, which can be edited.

OmniPage Ultimate, by Nuance Communications, Inc., is an OCR software product enabling the conversion of paper documents and TIFF files to a text-based format for amending as needed with prominent business communications software. OmniPage Ultimate can convert scanned images to Microsoft Word, Excel, PowerPoint, Corel WordPerfect, e-mail, HTML, and even to the Amazon Kindle format. The program generates a formatted text document that preserves the layout and format, character, font, and style of the scanned image. This software boasts a 50 percent greater accuracy rate than its competitors when converting, and the updated recognition dictionaries for financial, legal, and medical specialties allow for legal-specific word recognition, which means that you will spend less time editing your legal documents. This software can also process, edit, and recognize over 120 languages—a great feature for those firms with a global presence.

OmniPage supports data capture from a digital camera. The software can "read" a digital photograph, which may come in handy for lawyers who use photographs as exhibits. This software is the first OCR application designed for the multicore-processor computer, taking advantage of hyperthreading to increase the conversion speed of documents. It was also the first OCR software to support Microsoft Office 2007/2010 native formats. When converting legal documents, OmniPage now has a greater ability to recognize formatting such as line numbers, Bates stamps, signatures, and more.

Other new OmniPage Ultimate features worth mentioning include the ability to convert a scanned document into a readable format and send it to an Amazon Kindle, a "one click" toolbar in the Microsoft Office Suite that allows for document conversion with a simple click, and a faster load time than previous versions. OmniPage Ultimate's 3DC technology allows users to capture text with the camera on their mobile device.

Also new in the latest version of OmniPage is the eDiscovery Assistant for searchable PDFs. The eDiscovery Assistant provides the ability to safely convert a single PDF or batches of PDFs of all types into searchable documents without having to open PDF files one by one, giving the user greater flexibility when applying an OCR process to an entire group of documents.

As more and more firms look to use the features the Internet cloud provides, so do vendors. OmniPage includes the Nuance Cloud Connector application, which integrates with Evernote, Dropbox, OneDrive, and Google Drive, allowing users to scan and/or save their documents to the cloud.

OmniPage Ultimate can be purchased and downloaded online directly from Nuance's website (www.nuance.com) for $499.99 for the full version and $199.99 for the upgrade version.

Adobe Acrobat includes an OCR engine too and the ability to batch OCR documents—and not just one at a time. We recommend purchasing Adobe Acrobat first to see if it meets your OCR needs before expending funds on another specialized product like OmniPage.

Voice Recognition Software

Arguably one of the biggest recent advances in productivity software is the continuing refinement of voice recognition software. Dragon Naturally Speaking by Nuance (www.nuance.com) has made voice recognition software a respectable addition to your productivity arsenal. Many solo and small firm lawyers are now using Dragon as their primary composition tool. This is especially valuable for those who are not very accurate or fast typists.

It takes only a short time to train Dragon to your voice, and its accuracy is astonishing. Nuance claims that the latest version is up to 24 percent more accurate than the previous version, which is just incredible given how accurate the previous version of this product was.

Dragon can be used to compose e-mail messages, draft documents in your word processor, and even launch software applications without touching the keyboard or mouse. The software now allows users to search the web and their computers through the use of voice shortcuts.

Along with new formatting and editing commands, the latest version also provides users with the ability to post to Facebook and Twitter by voice and even allows users to use their iPhone or iPad as a wireless microphone, untethering them from their computer.

Some of the new features include

- Support for Windows 10 touchscreen PCs
- Support for WordPerfect X8 and Skype for Business
- Accuracy is improved over the previous version—the new version continues to "learn" your voice and becomes more accurate the more you use the product.
- The software now learns words and phrases you use most.
- Multicore processors provide faster performance.
- Go hands free and headset free—the software now offers multiple microphone options, including those built into the latest laptops, so that you can type even less and not have to use a headset.
- Dictate notes and ideas on the go and transcribe the audio files back at your computer.

This is a great tool and is used by many individuals with disabilities. But make no mistake—this is a mainstream product, and the able-bodied are moving to this technology in hordes!

Dragon Naturally Speaking comes in several versions. We recommend using the Legal or Professional version 15 if you can afford it. The Legal version contains vocabulary specific to the legal profession and carries a price tag of $500. The Professional version is a higher-end package that allows for roaming user profiles and allows multiple custom dictionaries. The Professional Individual version costs $300 and may be purchased from many webstores or directly from the Nuance site. The Premium version 13 package, which is a home version, costs $199.99, and it may be a good, cost-effective alternative for some lawyers as it also supports digital recording devices, smart formatting, and text-to-speech, especially for those just wanting to get started with voice recognition software. At the time of this writing, the Premium version was on sale for $174.99 on Nuance's website. Dragon Naturally Speaking is licensed on a per-user basis. You can install and run it on multiple computers, but you need a license for each user's voice file.

The most important tip about using voice recognition software is to proof any output from Dragon. The speech-to-text is very good, and it "learns" and improves with time, but it's not perfect. Make sure you proofread your documents, especially those that may be submitted to a court.

If you use Dragon on multiple computers, make sure you know how to move your voice files among machines. This will save on the "retraining" time when you use several computers. The process is most appropriate for those lawyers who use a computer at home and one at the office. Moving the voice files between the machines allows you to take advantage of the aggregate training time instead of each machine "learning" on its own.

A key component to the success of voice recognition is the use of a good quality USB microphone headset. We have had great success using a Plantronics 510 headset/microphone system, but they are no longer manufactured. The Plantronics Blackwire 720 Series is available for $149.95 from the Plantronics website (www.plantronics.com) and should be an excellent replacement for the older 510 model. The lightweight headphones with noise-canceling microphone connect to your computer using a standard USB or Bluetooth connection. We recommend the USB connection as Bluetooth wireless is more susceptible to audio errors. The wideband acoustic echo cancellation feature captures a broad range of voice signals for calls that are clearer and more natural sounding, perfect for use with Skype. The smart sensor technology lets you answer calls simply by putting on the headset or pause mobile device media playback by taking it off. This pair of headphones also allows for dual connectivity between your computer and mobile phone, allowing users to take phone calls while using their computer without the need to take off the headset.

CHAPTER THIRTEEN

Security Software

Combined with network firewalls and IDS/IPS (intrusion detection system/intrusion prevention system) devices, security software provides another line of protection in the defense-in-depth information security strategy against malware, including viruses, Trojan horses, ransomware, and other external forces. The defense-in-depth approach to securing your network is the best way to keep your systems safe from both internal and external threats. These threats can be extremely harmful to a law firm network and very costly to remove once an infection has occurred, assuming you've been able to identify that a breach or infection has taken place. Even in a solo or small firm network, your client data is of the utmost importance, and securing your computers, servers, smartphones, and information should be taken very seriously. The top security protection suites providing antivirus, antispyware, and antispam protection for stand-alone computers, networks, and mobile devices are discussed below, with recommendations regarding the setup and configuration of the software.

Stand-Alone

The software selections described in this section are primarily for the computers and laptops of solo practitioners and the home computers that attorneys may use.

We do not recommend stand-alone products for targeted protection, such as antivirus protection. This type of software is not sufficient today to keep your systems protected. The Internet security suites are the only way to go, where you get much more functionality and protection and many more features for your computer at a much more affordable price.

Solos and small firms should definitely consider acquiring a single integrated product to deal with spam, viruses, and malware. Norton's security suite is a top seller for the single computer market. It is highly rated and does a credible job in protecting your computer. However, we don't recommend purchasing Norton for several reasons. It gets average ratings for ease of use, and threat blocking is not on par with the top products. We've also found that it may be difficult to uninstall. We continue to find it, along with McAfee, to be a heavier load on computer processing versus its competition, although not as bad as versions from several years ago.

For those users who want to avoid the problems that may be caused by Norton and McAfee, we recommend using Kaspersky Internet Security, especially if you like your security suites to be hassle-free. This product contains firewall, antivirus, antispyware, rootkit detection, antispam protection, and much more. The antivirus engine that Kaspersky uses has been consistently highly ranked by independent testing labs and it tends to be one of the first to detect malicious code.

The firewall included with this software provides two-way protection, scanning both incoming and outgoing network traffic, effectively blocking any hacker attacks against your system. The automatic exploit protection engine watches program behavior and aims to block zero-day vulnerabilities in the most commonly used software. The anti-phishing engine and URL advisor will keep you safe from drive-by malware while you browse the Internet, and the anti-banner blocks annoying banners and other advertisements on web pages. This product even comes with webcam protection technology that stops criminals from using your own webcam to spy on you. Some of the new features include keeping other applications on your system up to date as updates are available, and as well as providing users with an interface to remove/uninstall software from their computer system.

With all the bonus features included in this protection suite, purchasing this product is a very good deal. Kaspersky is available directly from www.kaspersky.com and costs $49.99 for one-year protection on up to three computers. This is an excellent choice for the small firm environment, and it is Windows 10 compatible.

Enterprise Versions

Enterprise versions of integrated security solutions are designed for small, medium, and large computer networks, and the software administration is performed from the server rather than on each individual computer system.

The client software is installed or pushed from the central server to the local workstations with little or no effort. The server supplies the clients with program and definition updates and provides an interface to centrally manage all clients from a single console. Of course, enterprise licenses are a little bit more costly than purchasing a single license, but not by much. Even with the slight increase in cost for an enterprise license, you'll more than make up for it on the money you will not have to pay your IT consultant to manage and support the product.

Integrated Security Solutions

Kaspersky Endpoint Security for Business protects Windows- and Linux-based servers (including 64-bit versions) and even Mac computers from all types of malicious programs and threats. The product provides protection from threats such as viruses, Trojans, worms, keyloggers, malware, rootkits, bots, and so on. This is now the standard that we are seeing in the security product market. Former providers of antivirus software are providing protection from spyware and other malware, offering a more complete security solution to their business customers and all but eliminating the need for multiple applications to protect your systems from viruses and malware. This software provides real-time protection by scanning all files that are opened and quarantining infected files. The application can scan specified areas of the file system based on preconfigured, scheduled scans or on demand from the administrator. The scanning of critical system areas, such as running processes and start-up objects, helps prevent malicious code from launching, and the ability to scan inside compound files provides an extra layer of protection.

Another great feature of this product is the inclusion of encryption. Administrators may select from full-disk or file-level encryption, protected through the implementation of the AES 256-bit encryption standard. This feature is even supported for removable devices.

Kaspersky Endpoint Security for Business is a scalable security solution, allowing administrators to define the number of instances of the program they would like to run simultaneously to accelerate the processing of server requests. The software offers flexible administration through centralized installation and control. The administration tool can be used centrally to install and manage client applications and, once they are downloaded and installed, to push updates to the clients for rapid deployment of critical security updates.

Endpoint Security for Business, similar to other integrated security solutions, scans not only for viruses but also for other threats and malicious programs, such as spyware and keyloggers. In most instances, this solution can serve multiple functions. We use a Kaspersky security solution on our network systems to provide us with complete malware protection.

By using an integrated solution that is capable of handling both antivirus and antispyware protection, we have one less product to purchase and renew on a yearly basis. The product also allows for different configuration settings depending on the type of network to which the computer system is currently connected, similar to the way Microsoft Windows 8 and 10 handle the different firewall settings.

As the security of smartphones is brought to the public's attention, more vendors are integrating smartphone security with their products. Kaspersky is no different. Endpoint Security for Business protects smartphones from data leaks, malware, and viruses, and it also allows an administrator to lock and wipe the device remotely should it be misplaced, stolen, or lost. Some of the additional key features include GPS tracking, SIM card monitoring, privacy protection, and folder or device encryption. The antispam protection feature works to block both unwanted calls and text messages. For those firms that allow employees to bring their own devices (BYOD) and connect them to the firm's network and data, administrators can use this product to separate corporate and personal data on these devices. Through the creation of "containers," this software can store all of your firm's data within the encrypted work "container" fully separate and apart from your employee's personal information on the device. If a problem were to occur, such as a lost device or unexpected termination, you could wipe the firm's data off of the device without harming the personal information. Integrating security for mobile devices can save you money by not having to deploy a separate mobile device management solution, which could cost thousands of dollars.

Kaspersky Security for Mobile runs on Android, iPhones, Windows Mobile, Symbian OS, and BlackBerry devices.

There is a ten-license minimum purchase for Kaspersky Endpoint Security for Business Select. Cost for the product begins at $44.99 per license and includes technical support and upgrades for a year. This product is Windows 10 compatible. Kaspersky is priced much lower per license than its competition and is an affordable, complete security solution that is rapidly taking over the market. This software product is offered for purchase with one-, two-, and three-year subscriptions. Licenses can be obtained directly from Kaspersky's website (www.kaspersky.com) or from any authorized reseller.

Besides Kaspersky, we also recommend the enterprise product Trend Micro Worry-Free Business Security. It is highly regarded and available in four editions: Advanced, Standard, Services, and Services Advanced. We don't recommend either of the Services solutions, as the entire configuration is set up and maintained by Trend Micro as a hosted solution. All of the editions include antivirus and antispyware capabilities, as well as advanced security features such as the ability to limit or prohibit the insertion and usage of USB devices attached to company computer systems. The software will protect both servers and computers from malicious threats and will automatically change settings on laptops to protect employees when they are out of the office. The software will monitor active processes and applications to prevent unauthorized and harmful changes to your computers.

Unlike the Standard Edition, the Advanced Edition includes antispam filtering for Microsoft Exchange Server as well as multilayered spam protection, and it offers protection for Mac clients and servers. The Advanced Edition also protects mobile devices using Microsoft Exchange ActiveSync. Cost for the product starts at around $38 per license for the Standard Edition and $62 per license for the Advanced Edition, which includes technical support and upgrades for a year. This software product is offered in one, two, and three-year subscriptions, and licenses can be purchased directly from Trend Micro's website (www.trendmicro.com).

Antispam Protection

For antispam protection and an integrated e-mail security solution, we use and recommend Mimecast and love it. If you are not using an enterprise product and have implemented a stand-alone solution, there is probably antispam capability contained within your stand-alone product.

Mimecast's e-mail security solution provides a lower-cost alternative service for e-mail antispam and antivirus without any of the headaches that come with other products, including the products you actually need to install and run on your e-mail server. Note that your e-mail flow will be rerouted so that it goes through Mimecast servers before being delivered to your mail server or e-mail client. You can purchase the Mimecast service directly from the vendor. We use and recommend the Targeted Threat Protection—URL Protect add-on, which protects against targeted attacks and spear-phishing through the real-time scanning of all URLs within incoming and archived e-mails. With this add-on, when a user clicks on a link embedded within an e-mail message, they are redirected to a dynamic page that makes the user aware of the link they're clicking on and reinforces security policies, prior to the user clicking to proceed to the destination address.

There is a secure messaging component that allows users to send encrypted e-mail communications. E-mail solutions and encryption are addressed in Chapter 31, Tomorrow in Legal Tech.

One of the features or add-ins that we subscribe to includes the Large File Send add-on, which allows us to send and receive files up to 2 GB safely without affecting system performance. The Large File Send is integrated with Microsoft Outlook and allows files to be attached directly from the e-mail message window. Large File Send allows senders to encrypt the attachment and provide access keys for users to input in order to download the attachment. Custom expiration dates can be configured and used, setting an expiration date when the attachment is no longer available to the recipient. The authors find themselves using this file sharing add-on more frequently than the alternatives, such as Dropbox. It is simply easier and more secure. It works by "chopping up" the file into smaller segments that are below normal attachment restrictions. Each segment is sent separately to the Mimecast servers where it is reassembled. The user gets a link to download the large file attachment.

Mimecast's solution provides a web-based interface to manage the quarantine, where spam messages are held. Users receive a quarantine message in which they are provided with a summary of the e-mail messages quarantined throughout the day. We have configured notifications of quarantined messages to occur at 8 a.m., 12 noon, and 5 p.m.—three times throughout the work day. From this message, a user can choose to release a quarantined message with just a simple click of the mouse. A user can also "permit" a sender, effectively whitelisting them. Keep in mind that a user can always click on the Mimecast toolbar within Microsoft Outlook to view the current state of the quarantine.

Mimecast also has a "mail bag" feature included with this recommended solution. This feature spools your e-mail in the event you lose your Internet connection or your e-mail server goes down. Once your connection or server comes back up, Mimecast will feed you the e-mail that it held during the outage, which means you won't lose any e-mail even if your server goes down for a period of time. Even while your server is down, you can access your e-mail from the web portal or directly through Outlook by activating Continuity Mode, which essentially connects Outlook to the Mimecast servers. In other words, you will not be without e-mail even when your server goes down. Some may think that is a curse rather than a benefit, so we'll let you choose.

Mimecast has a very good reputation for quality service, and clients seem to be very happy with it. Since we started using this product about a year ago, most of our clients have switched as well (now that Postini and McAfee's antispam services are defunct), and the feedback continues to be excellent. You may need to tweak the default rules a bit upon initial installation since Mimecast is pretty aggressive in blocking messages. As an example, e-mail notifications from our credit card payment processor were getting blocked and we were not receiving copies of receipts—which caused a lot of head-aches, but we were able to fix all of the problems we identified. Modifying the spam rules is easy, but your administrator should take on this task if needed.

Mimecast provides 24/7 technical support; automatic maintenance and upgrades; and a monthly, annual, or multiyear subscription. This product can be purchased directly from Mimecast (www.mimecast.com). You'll have to request a quote directly from Mimecast, and pricing is dependent on the features selected and number of licenses. The more users, the lower the costs. We feel that you are better off purchasing the service through a Mimecast reseller. They will be able to provide and maintain the service for you. If you go directly through Mimecast, you'll have to maintain your own environment, which is very complicated, but powerful. In addition, we highly recommend the Secure Messaging, Large File Send, and Targeted Threat Protection add-on services. You should be able to get the message security and the recommended add-ons for around $20 per user per month.

Ransomware Protection

Over the past two years, we have seen many law firms affected by a type of malware called ransomware. Some of the ransomware that we have come across over the last year include variants of CryptoLocker and CryptoWall. Ransomware is a type of malware that restricts access to a computer system and demands that the user pay a ransom to the operators of the malware to remove that restriction—in short, the malware encrypts the user files on a computer system, making them inaccessible. For a fee, the files can be decrypted. It should be noted that we do not recommend paying any ransom, as there is no guarantee that the decryption key will be turned over upon receipt of payment. That being said, even the FBI acknowledges that folks have to make their own decision about paying up—and the decryption key is indeed usually provided once the ransom is received. To protect against ransomware, we recommend user training, the use of security software, and a well-configured backup solution.

Ransomware has been successful in bypassing some security solutions, such as those listed above. One of the reasons for this is the malware's ability to change, and in most instances, it is actually installed by a user with administrative privileges over his local computer. This software has been documented primarily to infect a user's computer through the inadvertent clicking of links embedded within a spam/phishing e-mail or in attachments to such an e-mail.

However, there are steps a firm can take to protect its systems from ransomware. First, make sure your security software is up to date and configured properly for doing regular scans and actively monitoring your users' computers. Many security solutions have definitions to catch and prevent older versions or variants of ransomware, so it's important to keep these programs running as recommended.

Second, we recommend a product called CryptoPrevent to assist in the blocking and prevention of this malware. CryptoPrevent was designed to protect systems from CryptoLocker and has grown to protect computers against other malware that utilizes the same infection tactics and launch point locations. CryptoPrevent can be downloaded and purchased from the vendor's website at www.foolishit.com/cryptoprevent-malware-prevention/ for $15 per license. This program updates itself automatically as new definitions and signatures are released by the vendor, and it is a product that we have recommended and installed on our clients' computer systems.

Finally, you must have a proper backup solution designed to mitigate the effects of a ransomware infection. Ransomware has the capability to infect or run against any volume accessible from the infected computer, including any directly attached USB drives and even network drives. To combat this, we recommend that users disconnect USB drives directly attached to their computer systems or servers when not in use. Further, we recommend firms utilize an off-site backup solution in addition to having locally stored backups of your data. Backups, whether local or off-site, should always be encrypted. This way, if you were to become infected with a variant of ransomware, you would have the ability to restore the infected data from a recent backup. You want to make sure your solution provides that there is always a "clean" copy of your backup.

CHAPTER FOURTEEN

Case Management

If you still live in the paper world, you may not know that a case management application provides all of the functions that you are probably currently performing. You use a Rolodex or some other type of method to aggregate your contact information. We still see address books at the office supply store, but more and more contact information is collected in an electronic form and synchronized to mobile devices. You have a calendar to schedule events, which may be written in a day planner. You have a file for each client or each client matter. We hope you use a word processor—or at least your administrative assistant does—to generate documents. You track everything you do for each client matter or keep some sort of diary. You probably even generate some sort of status concerning each matter. These are all functions of a case management system.

Even in a world full of smartphones and wireless devices, it amazes us that most solo and small firm lawyers still don't use a computerized case management software application. We've been making that statement for more than ten years. Case management is a must-have for today's modern law office. You may have heard other terms that describe the same type of software. Vendors attempt to differentiate themselves by describing their products with different names. You may hear descriptions such as practice management, contact management, litigation management, and so forth. Bottom line: They are all case management products, although they vary greatly in functionality. Arguably, the term practice management is more inclusive and encompasses what is termed "front office" (case/client information) and "back office" (accounting and billing).

There are several choices for case management, some of which we will cover here. The features vary by manufacturer, so make sure you understand what you're buying. Probably the feature we are asked about most is the integration of e-mail and contacts with case management. Make sure that the product will work with your e-mail system and that you understand how it needs to be configured. The synchronization is getting better, but most of our clients are less than impressed with many of the implementations of synchronization support. For example:

- How does the software deal with a common firm-wide Public Folder Calendar?
- Will the product synchronize with your iPad or smartphone?
- What if you don't have an Exchange server and use hosted Exchange services?
- What e-mail clients are supported?
- Can you access your e-mail using other devices and software, or are you restricted to using only the e-mail interface of the case management software?
- Can you synchronize data with your Google account?
- Will synchronization occur wirelessly, or do you have to connect a cable and manually sync your data?
- Are IMAP (Internet Message Access Protocol) connections supported or only POP3?
- Can you sync everything in your personal mailbox, or are you limited to a subset, such as contacts and calendar only and not the tasks?

There are two mistakes that we consistently see when firms decide to implement a case management system. The first mistake is the failure to require everyone in the firm to use the system. You will not realize the full return on your investment if only a few employees use it. In fact, it tends to cause a whole new set of problems, because sometimes there is crossover between lawyers and cases and some operate within the case management system and some don't. The second most common mistake is the failure to invest in training. Training will allow all employees to use the features of the case management system fully, thereby becoming more efficient and properly organizing all data for a client matter. Simply dumping a case management system into a firm is worse than useless. When you price the software, price the training as well.

As with other sections of this book, we cannot mention or address every case management package or every feature of every product. We mention the most popular and widely used case management packages that we see being used by solos and small firms.

Amicus Attorney

Amicus Attorney (www.amicusattorney.com) from Gavel & Gown Software is a good small firm package that provides a fairly simple approach to case management. The technical requirements are very reasonable and don't require a powerful and expensive computer to run. You have a choice of using desktop software or the cloud solution. Either version would work well for the solo or small firm attorney. The desktop/server version is called Amicus Premium. It is an on-premise solution that can be installed for a single user or on a server for multiple users.

The 2016 Premium Edition uses SQL Server to achieve unlimited user and unlimited data access. The good news is that the Premium Edition comes with an embedded SQL Server Standard Edition Restricted Runtime for use with the Amicus Application Server. This mean you don't have to make a separate SQL purchase unless you want a more robust environment.

For very large-scale installations, a separate SQL server is recommended. SQL Server 2014, 2012, 2008 R2, and 2008 (Standard or Enterprise) are supported. Certainly a consideration is the cost of the SQL server software and the hardware to run it on, which can add a hefty price to the implementation costs, especially if you need a lot of CALs (client access licenses). Both 32-bit and 64-bit versions of SQL Server are supported. We recommend the 64-bit version, which supports more memory than the 32-bit version.

The pricing for Amicus Premium is no longer available on the website. You have to contact Gavel & Gown to figure out how much the software will cost you. However, you can play around with the Amicus Price and Return on Investment Calculator to identify license cost. As an example, if you only enter one lawyer and no staff in the form, it shows that Amicus Premium will cost $849 per seat. Previously, you paid a hefty amount for the first license and then a lot less for additional licenses. With the change to a flat license cost, expect to pay several hundreds of dollars more than before.

Mobility is a real focus for the majority of vendors these days. Amicus is no exception. Amicus TimeTracker is used to connect your mobile phone to the features of Amicus Attorney. You will need Amicus Attorney Premium and a license that include Amicus Anywhere. You can record your time, edit previous entries, see your list, and much more. The data is securely transmitted over the Internet between your firm's Amicus Server and your device. The data stays on your server and is not stored on your mobile device. TimeTracker works with most mobile devices with a modern browser. That includes iPhones, iPads, Android and BlackBerry and Windows phones and tablets, and Windows and Mac desktops and laptops. Amicus TimeTracker is available during the 30-day evaluation period and will always be available if you run Amicus Attorney software that has a valid maintenance plan.

The Amicus Anywhere product is available to provide a secure remote connection to your Amicus Premium environment using a browser. Amicus

Anywhere provides you with a remote access solution and keeps your data under your control on your server and not in the cloud. Amicus Anywhere also includes TimeTracker, which was mentioned above. There is no additional cost for Amicus Anywhere, but you will have to have a maintenance plan in place. In other words, as long as you pay for maintenance (a touchy subject among a lot of users) you'll be able to take advantage of Amicus Anywhere.

Another feature of the Premium Edition is a client portal to facilitate collaboration with your clients. Client portal access is an often requested feature from both attorneys and clients. We are beginning to see more and more case management systems including client portal access. The Amicus Client Portal access gives clients real-time access to selected matter information securely. You can grant specific clients access to designated matter files, specific documents, notes, and events on those files. Clients can upload new documents to their matter files and even add notes to the documents. The Client Portal also enables secure messaging with clients.

In addition to the on-premise solution, there is also an option for a cloud-based implementation of Amicus. Amicus Cloud is a full-featured solution that includes matter management, calendaring, task management, contacts, phone call management, global full-text searching, billing, time entries, expense tracking, reporting, document management, and trust accounting. There are also additional features such as a date calendar, collections assistant, and conflict checker. Amicus Cloud uses the cloud services of Microsoft Azure. It is accessible from any device using a modern browser. The cost for Amicus Cloud is $45 per user per month (billed annually), which is $540 per user per year. You can also opt to pay $49.95 per user per month if you don't want to commit to an annual payment. In addition, hosted Exchange services are available for an additional cost, but you'll have to contact Gavel & Gown to find out how much. These dollars are going to add up quickly, especially if you have more than one or two users. As with any other cloud service, make sure you understand the terms of service when placing confidential client data on a third-party server.

In May of last year, Abacus Data Systems and Amicus Attorney joined forces. The result is a private cloud platform that is a complete virtual private workspace for your firm. The offering is called Abacus Private Cloud and is a fully managed solution. This means that all of your computing needs are in the cloud. Not just case management, but Office 365, firm files, document services, two-factor authentication, and any other application you may need. You'll have to fill out the information request form to get pricing for a custom solution.

A trial version of Amicus Attorney (both on-premise and cloud) is available and highly recommended if you are considering purchase. Try the product first to make sure that it meets your needs and will work in your computing environment. If you are already an Amicus Attorney Small Firm user, you'll need to upgrade to the cloud offering or Amicus Attorney Premium since the Small Firm version is no longer supported.

Time Matters

LexisNexis has a couple of offerings suitable for the solo and small firm market. Time Matters (www.timematters.com) used to be the most popular case management package for solo and small firms (before being purchased by LexisNexis), but we don't see it at very many firms in our area. Time Matters is a very powerful and highly customizable case management application, but it can also be fairly complicated for many small firm lawyers. It is an absolute necessity to purchase training if you are considering implementing Time Matters in your firm. The learning curve is steep but well worth it because Time Matters is truly a feature-rich program.

The current version is Time Matters 15.1. The support document for Time Matters system requirements recommend that you run a dedicated server if you have five or more users. In our opinion and experience, Time Matters requires the installation of a dedicated server no matter how many users there are. The dedicated server can significantly increase implementation costs for the solo and small firm lawyer, but we feel strongly that Time Matters needs a dedicated server for adequate performance of the application. Also, Time Matters is only supported in a local, directly connected environment. This means that the use of any wireless connections or WAN technologies for the application, which prevents most data center implementations, is not supported. The workstations and server need to be connected to the same local network. You could install Time Matters in a data center, but the users would have to use a supported remote access technology. Peer-to-peer networks are not supported, hence further requiring a dedicated server. You can use some versions of Windows (e.g., Windows 7, 8/8.1, or 10) as a server with five or fewer connected workstations. There is limited support for virtual servers, but that shouldn't be a problem if it is properly sized. Perhaps the installation requirements are why we haven't seen any new Time Matters installations for a long time.

Version 15.1 adds more than 30 functional enhancements to the 43 that were included in version 15. Version 15.1 also offers access to LexisNexis Gateway and integration with Chrometa, a passive time keeping solution.

According to the LexisNexis website:

- Time Matters 15.1 also brings support for Microsoft Office 365 OneDrive. With OneDrive access, Time Matters 15.1 customers can broaden their document storage and sharing abilities through Microsoft's powerful cloud storage service.
- Time Matters 15.1 includes support for Windows 10, Microsoft Exchange Server 2016, and Microsoft Office 2016, ensuring an optimal upgrade experience for even more firms.

Last year you could order Time Matters directly from the website, but not anymore. LexisNexis has removed a lot of the publically available information about Time Matters. You have to contact the company to schedule a demo and get additional information. LexisNexis has gone back to its past practice of requiring contact with the sales team. Needless to say, we are not fond of this approach and the lack of transparency. If you are considering Time Matters, we highly recommend taking advantage of the free trial. We also recommend that the majority of solo and small firm lawyers investigate several of the cloud solutions first.

PracticeMaster

A highly rated case management application (and our personal favorite) is PracticeMaster (http://www.tabs3.com/products/practicemaster/practice master.html) by Software Technology, Inc. (STI), which is the choice of most solo and small firms in our area. Version 18 is the current shipping version of PracticeMaster. PracticeMaster comes in three versions: Practice-Master, Platinum, and SQL. The regular version of PracticeMaster contains a number of useful features that most lawyers would desire. Many solo and small firm lawyers think that Microsoft Outlook is a case management program. Not even close. You can view a chart that compares the features of Outlook and PracticeMaster at http://practicemaster.com/products/practice master/pm_comparison.html.

PracticeMaster introduced workflows with version 16. Workflows are essentially triggers that automate tasks within the software. In addition, PracticeMaster has one of the best e-mail integration schemes that we've seen. Smartphone support is excellent as well, especially with Tabs3 Connect.

PracticeMaster and Tabs3 licenses include the first 12 months of maintenance. Perhaps it is a new trend to include maintenance automatically as a way to ensure that users pay for support. The cost of the regular

PracticeMaster version is $600 (including 12 months of maintenance) for the first active user license, and each additional license will set you back another $280. The pricing hasn't changed for the last four years.

In addition to the regular PracticeMaster version, STI offers PracticeMaster in a client server version, which scales to larger implementations. The Platinum version costs $1,320 (including 12 months of maintenance) for the first user license and $365 for each additional user. Don't forget to add the cost of the client server environment when calculating the total cost of the project. As an example, the Platinum server software is required for any client server implementation of Tabs3 or PracticeMaster. This server software could cost from $965 for eight connections and up to $7,475 for 1,024 server connections. An even more robust implementation would be using Platinum SQL Server Software. Cost for the SQL version is $1,320 for eight connections and up to $39,340 for 1,024 server connections.

The good news is that STI has updated its website to calculate the software cost quickly. Just go to the price estimator page (http://www.tabs3.com /products/pricing_info.aspx) and select the products you are interested in, the number of concurrent users, and the number of billable entities if selecting any of the financial packages.

Version 18 of PracticeMaster is the current shipping version and it includes several new features. The Fee and Cost Entry has been modified to be more like Tabs3. The Rate Code and Sales Tax values from Tabs3 are now displayed and can be modified. In addition, "Budget exceeded" now displays when entering fees and costs in PracticeMaster. There is a new Fee Recap icon that has been added to the main toolbar and provides a quick summary of fees entered for a timekeeper on a specified date. There is a new Outlook Synchronization Settings Report, which will aid your IT support personnel in troubleshooting any Outlook synchronization problems. The Form Designer has two new buttons in the toolbar. Magnetic Snaps and Snap to Grid will help with alignment of fields. There are additional enhancements as well. Improvements to Calendar Conflict, Graphical Calendar, and WorkFlows round out the upgrades included in version 18.

In a move to enhance security, the version 18 SQL edition of PracticeMaster has an option to enable encryption to protect your data with an extra layer of security. When you enable encryption, there is no place to enter a user-defined passphrase, which would indicate that STI could technically access the data since it presumably has access and knowledge of the encryption keys. To be fair, someone with knowledge of the encryption key would have to connect to the law firm network or be given physical access to the database. We are beginning to see vendors offering some form of encryption as a way to protect access to the user's data. This is especially important for attorneys who have an ethical duty to protect the confidentiality of their clients' data. It is unfortunate that only the SQL version has the encryption option, where the cost will put it out of reach for the majority of solo and small firm lawyers.

Mobile access requires the Platinum versions of PracticeMaster and Tabs3. There is no additional cost for Tabs3 Connect if you are enrolled in a maintenance plan. With Tabs3 Connect, you have access to Tabs3 and Practice-Master anywhere you can connect to the Internet. This means you can get to your data from your smartphone or other mobile device. You have access to your client and contact information, fee and cost entry, personal and firm-wide calendar, and more. The connection is secured using SSL, and the data resides in your Tabs3/PracticeMaster environment in your office. Because you must have the Platinum Editions of Tabs3 and PracticeMaster to take advantage of Tabs3 Connect, however, the mobile access feature will be out of the reach of many solo and small firm lawyers, which is very unfortunate, especially since Tabs3 Connect is the best remote access solution to practice management data we have ever seen. Tabs3 Connect is a feature of the Platinum version of Tabs3 software. Firms that use the Platinum version of Tabs3 but do not use PracticeMaster have the option to purchase a subscription to the billing features of Tabs3 Connect. The subscription cost is $60 per user per year. You can learn more about Tabs3 Connect by visiting http://www.tabs3.com/products/tabs3_connect/tabs3_connect.html.

Finally, it is highly recommended that you obtain the trial version of PracticeMaster. This will help you determine whether the product is right for your practice and your installed infrastructure. We don't think you can go wrong with this product. It is constantly being improved, and the support is among the best in the industry.

Clio

Clio (www.goclio.com) is a SaaS (software as a service) solution that is used by solo, small, and midsized firms. Access is via an Internet browser, which means it will work just fine on an Apple computer. The maker of Clio is Themis Solutions, which is headquartered in Vancouver, British Columbia. Themis Solutions has the excellent reputation of listening to its customers and constantly enhancing Clio based on users' suggestions. The company also has remote offices in Toronto, Canada, and Dublin, Ireland.

Clio is a full-featured practice management platform. Features such as document management, time tracking, calendaring, tasks, billing, and so on provide a complete solution. The billing component works well for hourly and flat-fee billing. Users have control over billing rates at the activity or matter level. Clio is highly customizable: custom fields can be inserted into any matter file. These custom fields have many different formats, so lawyers can enter dates, dollar amounts, website addresses, and various text types.

Clio can also be configured to synchronize with Outlook and Gmail to provide bidirectional syncing of calendar, contact, and task entries. Clio integrates with many online service providers like Office 365, Box, Dropbox, Google Drive, Chrometa, NetDocuments, Fastcase, CloudMask, Law Pay, QuickBooks Online, and many others. You can see all the apps that integrate with Clio at https://www.goclio.com/features/integrations/. Like many other practice management products, Clio is constantly being improved, as can be seen by the increased integration with third-party products.

Clio Connect is a feature that enables firm members to share resources and collaborate with clients, contacts, or co-counsels easily through a secure web-based portal. This grants clients, contacts, or co-counsels the latitude to review and contribute to relevant matter developments and helps to mitigate associated inefficiencies related to time-consuming communications.

Clio's dedicated iOS application makes it easy to manage your law firm from your mobile Apple device. There's also an Android app for Clio. With the mobile app, you can track your time and expenses, add tasks, look up your appointments and deadlines, and anything else you need to manage your practice from the road.

Another key feature is the ability to use the Amazon S3 cloud for data storage, giving you complete control over your data. Your data is automatically backed up to Amazon S3 on a weekly basis. Once the data is replicated to the Amazon cloud, you have the option of downloading the data to your own computer. It is available to subscribers of the Legacy, Boutique, and Elite plans. There is no additional cost to use this feature other than the cost from Amazon, which is pennies per gigabyte. Clio calls this the Data Escrow feature. Just search the help forum on the website for complete instructions on how to activate Data Escrow.

Besides backing up your data to Amazon S3, you can also export data from the various areas as shown here:

- Bank Transactions
- Bills

- Calendar
- Contact Notes
- Contact Related Matters
- Contacts
- Documents
- Expense Entries
- Matter Notes
- Matters
- Tasks
- Time Entries

Finally, Clio provides extensive support to customers free of charge. In-house telephone support is available 17 hours a day. The same service is also available by e-mail and live online chat. Training webinars are available online, typically three days a week. Clio also offers a library of training articles and videos.

Take advantage of the free 30-day trial to make sure Clio will work for you. Clio has changed its pricing and moved from a flat cost to a tiered pricing model that adds additional features as you move up the tiers. The Starter level costs $39 per user per month (billed annually) and includes the performance dashboard, custom invoices and templates, time tracking, support, and the secure client portal: Clio Connect. The next level is the Boutique offering, which costs $59 per user per month (billed annually). It includes everything in the Starter version and adds accounting integrations, custom fields, UTBMS coding, Zapier integration, API access, data escrow, sortable custom fields, alternative fee billing, payments, and trust accounting. The top tier is the Elite plan, which costs $99 per user per month (billed annually). It includes all the Boutique features plus priority support, originating attorney revenue report, court calendaring rules, matter budgets, and campaign tracker.

There are no longer reduced costs for support staff. Clio considers a user to be a user. That means that a receptionist, paralegal, attorney, and so on will all pay the same price. Discounts are available as a member benefit from more than 30 state and municipal bar associations and the American Bar Association. Be sure to ask your bar association if a discount is available.

Clio is one of our favorite SaaS practice management systems, and we highly recommend it. Several of our clients have converted to Clio and never looked back.

Rocket Matter

Rocket Matter, around since 2007, is another web-based cloud practice management system designed specifically for the legal industry. It also contains a time and billing function, which provides almost all you need for your law practice. Rocket Matter is very popular among Macintosh users, as it is web-based. There really isn't any case management application that is specifically geared toward the Apple user community, so Rocket Matter meets that need through web browser access. You can still use Rocket Matter if you are a Windows shop, since all you need is an Internet connection and a web browser.

Rocket Matter has released an app specifically designed for the iPad. As CEO Larry Port said, "This is not just a companion app to our Web version. It is a full-featured practice management platform." You have the full ability to edit and access contacts, tasks, matters, notes, and so on. Probably one of the most valuable features is that you can operate the app with or without an Internet connection. This means that you can have your full practice management environment with you at the courthouse even if there is no Wi-Fi access to the Internet, which many locations ban or prevent. Any information that you modify or add while you are offline will synchronize with your Rocket Matter environment once you reconnect to the Internet.

Rocket Matter also has a client portal offering, which allows users to create branded portals. You have the ability to share calendar information, documents, and invoices with clients or anybody else. The portal integrates with LawPay, allowing clients to pay their invoices online. Another Rocket Matter feature is the integration with Copy2Contact to add new entries to your contacts. Rocket Matter also integrates with other cloud providers such as Gmail, Google Calendar, Box, QuickBooks, Dropbox, and Evernote.

In 2016, Rocket Matter released a redesigned user interface called Atlas and new workflows. The original interface was programmed to maintain a fixed size to match the normal screen resolutions of the times. Since then, resolutions have increased and monitors have gotten larger too, which left a lot of white space on the sides of the original interface. Atlas is a responsive design and adjusts to match the user's device, taking advantage of the previous white space areas. Navigation has moved to the left side of the screen since most people are right handed and read from left to right. You can bounce back and forth between Atlas and the classic interface depending on your comfort level.

Workflows are aided by the usage of matter templates that can include events and tasks. That means you can assign a template to a new matter and a lot of predefined items will populate automatically. If you are a current Rocket Matter user, we're sure you won't go back to the classic interface once you experience Atlas.

Like many of the other vendors, Rocket Matter has removed pricing information from its website. You have to contact Rocket Matter in order to get pricing information. We are not fond of this practice, which isn't very transparent.

Rocket Matter is a cloud implementation and carries the same issues as other providers. The data is held by a third party even though it is transmitted on an encrypted channel. Like Clio, Rocket Matter is always working on improvements to its product. For example, it now provides offline access to your data. Those who have used Rocket Matter generally give it favorable reviews, and we recommend that solos and small firms that want a cloud solution take a look at both Clio and Rocket Matter. Both are fine products.

Firm Manager

LexisNexis has its version of a hosted case management system, which is called Firm Manager. It appears that Lexis has Rocket Matter and Clio squarely in its crosshairs as it competes in the SaaS market. There are two pricing plans for Firm Manager. The Starter plan is $29 per user per month and the Essentials plan is $44 per user per month. These costs make Firm Manager a much cheaper alternative to other cloud-based case management offerings. Some local bar associations may receive additional discounts, which makes the pricing even more attractive.

Firm Manager continues to add features, making it a worthy contender for your practice management dollars. The Starter edition contains Matter Management, Calendar Sync, Billing, Trust Accounting, and Document Management. The Essentials edition includes all of the Starter features and adds Role-Base Permissions, Integrations (e.g., QuickBooks), Reporting, and Customizable Templates. The partnership with LawToolBox helps managing your court deadlines faster than ever. It calculates court deadlines based on the rules for your state and syncs it all up in Microsoft Office 365. With Firm Manager, you get unlimited online storage for case exhibits, documents, client lists, and more.

Though we have yet to hear of any attorneys in our area using Firm Manager, we're very impressed with its improvements. LexisNexis really wants your business and provides contact and matter import templates. The templates are in CSV format and ensure that any existing data will properly import into Firm Manager. Firm Manager isn't nearly as robust and full-featured as something like Time Matters or ProLaw, so we are pretty sure there won't be a home for some of the data in Firm Manager. The other concern is potential price increases over time, which LexisNexis is known for historically, although the pricing is still very reasonable. Firm Manager finally looks like a good candidate for the solo and small firm attorney and is worth a test-drive. If you are considering Firm Manager, be sure to take advantage of the 30-day free trial to make sure it will meet your practice needs.

MyCase

We are seeing a lot great deal of buzz surrounding another web-based case management product. MyCase is similar to the other products and provides similar functions, such as shared firm calendars and reminders, tasks, contact management, document organization, document assembly, time and billing, and so on. It even has iOS and Android apps to facilitate mobile access. MyCase is also jumping into the lawyer marketing game by providing a MyCase website. Actually, the value of the website is working as a portal for clients to get information about their case, pay their invoices, and securely communicate with the firm. Besides the portal aspects, MyCase looks to be getting into the website provisioning business by building lawyer websites that integrate with MyCase (that's where the client portal feature comes in) and includes a blog, social media integration, Google analytics, a responsive code for mobile device access, and basic search engine optimization. The website feature costs a onetime setup fee of $500 and then $50 a month.

MyCase uses Amazon services to deliver its product to the end user. It runs on Amazon EC2 cloud servers and is backed up using Amazon S3 storage. Data is transferred using SSL encryption and encrypted before being written to disk. Originally, the client access portal differentiated MyCase from the other case management products, but today, the client portals of many of the others function similarly to MyCase.

MyCase now has a one-way integration with QuickBooks Online. There is a onetime fee of $99 to add this feature. Essentially, it takes the accounting data from MyCase and pushes it into QuickBooks. The integration offers transmission of detailed invoice data, recording of payments on invoices, trust account transactions, new customer data, and cash and accrual accounting. Frankly, we're not sure why you would want to implement this feature since it really isn't a synchronization but a one-way push. Typically, integrations with QuickBooks are problematic since you have to make sure the QuickBooks accounts are always mapped properly to the data coming from and to the case management system.

MyCase costs $39 per month for each lawyer and $29 per month for each paralegal or staff member. There is a free 30-day trial, which we recommend you take advantage of. In late 2012, MyCase was acquired by AppFolio, a provider of web-based software for vertical markets. Time will tell if MyCase will survive the acquisition or migrate more to a marketing application rather than dealing with the daily needs of the solo and small firm attorney. We still don't have any clients using MyCase, but the feedback on discussion lists has been positive.

HoudiniEsq

HoudiniEsq is an interesting product in that it offers an on-premise and cloud-based version. The feature set is comparable to the other case management offerings. Document management, workflows, contacts, matters, notes, calendars, invoicing, document automation, and much more are all functions contained within HoudiniEsq. HoudiniEsq integrates with Outlook, Excel, WordPerfect, Acrobat, SoftFile, QuickBooks, OpenOffice, LibreOffice, CalendarRules, BIRT, Google Gmail, and Google Docs.

HoudiniEsq has no user software application; everything is accessed via a web browser. Even the on-premise solution uses a browser to run Houdini-Esq. The on-premise solution does require a dedicated computer to host HoudiniEsq, and the technical requirements suggest that you could get an inexpensive ($300–$400) computer from Best Buy to run HoudiniEsq. Sorry, but we certainly don't agree that a cheap consumer-grade machine should be used to house your critical firm data and the core of your practice. Perhaps spending a couple hundred bucks is acceptable to run the trial and to accommodate one user. The reality is that most firms (even solos) have at least one support person in addition to the attorney. Speaking of a trial, there isn't one. At least not in the traditional sense. The on-premise single-user version is given away for free. It's a full-blown version of HoudiniEsq, but only supports one person.

The cloud version costs $64 per user per month and includes support and updates. The on-premise solution is sized for 1 to 1,200 users. You are required to purchase an annual subscription for each user. There are three on-premise plans. If you are a solo attorney, there is a Solo On-premise offering that is $240 a year. If you have 30 users or less, the cost is also $240 per user per year plus a onetime server fee of $1,280 for every ten users. That means you will pay a minimum of $1,520 for the first year ($1,280 for the server and $240 × 1 users) for the minimum one-user requirement. The annual cost would then drop to $240 a year since you would already have the server software. The maximum 30 users would cost $11,040 [($1,280 × 3) + ($240 × 30 users)] for the first year. Subsequent years would cost $7,200 ($240 × 30 users). If you are at 30 users or more, you are required to move to the HoudiniEsq Elite package. That cost is a onetime fee of $8,160 for each grouping of 30 users and an annual subscription cost of $240 per user per year. Finally, there is a $192 per user per year support fee if there are more than 200 users.

The annual subscription cost makes it much more attractive from a cost perspective than the other case management options for the solo and small firm practitioner. Besides the ridiculous notion that you can run your practice on a Best Buy computer, the user interface was based on Flash technology. The latest version of HoudiniEsq (version 2.0) does not use Flash like the previous versions did.

Others

Additional products are available, but some of the vendors aren't public with the cost or system requirements. We are less than impressed with companies that aren't open about their pricing and technical requirements. Products like ProLaw (Thomson Elite) require you to fill out a contact form so that a representative can contact you about pricing. We are not fond of this practice and recommend a relationship with more open vendors, especially when you are entering this arena and want to make an apples-to-apples comparison.

CHAPTER FIFTEEN

Time and Billing Software

Probably the second most important function of your law practice is billing your clients for services rendered. Practicing law is clearly the most important, but getting paid is second, thereby ensuring the continued success and sustainability of your practice. Lawyers tend to hate the billing process and are not much fonder of the software that helps them generate invoices. Some solos and small firms still generate invoices manually, although their numbers are diminishing. We'll look at several options and try to give you some guidance.

You have a lot of options for generating your bills, from a completely manual system to the fully automatic capture and assembly of invoices. Two components make up the items in your bills. One is time. This component is calculated by taking the hourly rate and applying it to the amount of time spent on a task. You can capture this time manually or automatically while the task is being accomplished. Flat fees are also considered time components, where the dollar amount is applied irrespective of the time spent. The second component is the fixed-cost items of the invoice. This would include such expenses as postage, copier costs, filing fees, courier charges, and any other fixed fees. As with the time components, you can track these expenses manually or automatically (to some level or another) through the use of technology.

We are seeing more and more firms adopting some sort of alternative fee arrangements (AFAs) for their practice. It may be flat fee only or a hybrid type of billing with a flat-fee portion and an hourly portion. AFAs are more complicated to automate because of the various customized rules that may apply. The good news is that many of the software packages are sophisticated enough to handle customized rules and they are getting better and better as time goes by. You may have to deal with some manual override techniques if the billing software can't accommodate a particular AFA scenario.

As in other sections of this book, we'll try to cover a lot of the billing methods and applications that we see being used by the solo and small firm attorneys. This will not be an all-inclusive list, so if your favorite product isn't mentioned, it probably means that we've never seen (or heard of) it being used by solo or small firms.

Manual Generation

Pencil and paper are the simplest way to capture time and expense. With manual generation, however, you must remember to log your time and the number of copies or whatever other chargeable component needs to be tracked. Make no mistake about it, studies have shown over and over again that this manual tracking results in a lot of lost time and expense. Because a lawyer's time equals money, many lawyers are shortchanging themselves by not moving to a technology-based solution.

Nevertheless, if this is what you do, on a periodic basis (daily, monthly, the end of the case, and so forth), you total the charges and generate the bill. Many solo practitioners start by using a word processing package to generate their bills to save some money. These bills are professional enough in appearance but still require manually adding up numbers and multiplying other numbers. Moreover, another method is needed to keep track of payments made by the client and/or transfers of funds from other sources, such as a trust account. As the practice becomes more complicated, the billing process becomes more susceptible to mistakes.

If you must start with a manual method for generating your invoices, invest in billing software as soon as possible to improve your accuracy, maximize your income, and minimize your losses.

Accounting Software—QuickBooks

Some lawyers are actually using a financial accounting package to generate their bills. Certainly the most popular software application we see is QuickBooks by Intuit (https://quickbooks.intuit.com/). Using QuickBooks to generate invoices allows the firm to have a total financial package, where all sorts of financial reports are available. However, productivity reports are not available. You won't be able to determine easily how many billable hours are attributed to a specific individual or how much money you lost due to write-offs. One advantage of QuickBooks is the ability to generate payroll. This may not be a compelling reason for many lawyers, especially given the added cost, complexity, and reporting requirements. In general, it is more cost effective to use a third-party service provider such as ADP or Paychex to handle solo and small firm payrolls. QuickBooks can also handle processing of credit card payments, thereby integrating another piece of the financials into a single product. We hear that most lawyers began using QuickBooks because their accountant told them to. Make sure your accountant sets up your chart of accounts in QuickBooks so you know where certain charges and fees should go. Your CPA should be familiar with financials for a law firm. If not, it's probably time to look for a new accountant.

QuickBooks comes in several different versions—even an online version that allows access from any computer and does not require installation of any software. We don't recommend using the online version, as it requires that your data be stored at Intuit. Your financial data is highly sensitive, and we recommend that you control your own data and not risk compromise by holding it at a third-party site. Consider, too, the possibly severe consequences if the third party is "down" and you can't manage the financial part of your law practice. Generally, cloud service providers are fairly reliable, but there are no guarantees when dealing with technology.

Since QuickBooks is an accounting package, some knowledge of financial principles is helpful. You will need to set up a chart of accounts for your practice. We recommend consulting with your accountant before configuring QuickBooks so that your financial categories are consistent with the accountant's needs and your business needs. If you are new to QuickBooks, consider purchasing a support plan to help you learn the features of the software and get technical help. Many local community colleges also offer evening classes for QuickBooks, which would be a relatively inexpensive way to get some training in how to use the product.

The QuickBooks versions vary in cost based on the capabilities of the software and number of concurrent licenses that are needed. The Pro version costs $299.95 for a single user, and the Premier version cost $379.95 for a single user. You can also purchase the products on an annual subscription basis, where Pro Plus 2016 costs $299.95/year and Premium Plus 2016 costs $299.95/year. Since they are both the same price, why wouldn't you go with the Premium Plus 2016?

The Enterprise version is sold only on a subscription basis with varying subscription levels. The hosted options will allow you to connect from any device at any time. The Silver subscription includes the Enterprise software, U.S.-based customer support, online data backup, automatic upgrades, and advanced reporting. The Gold subscription adds payroll to the Silver edition features. The Platinum subscription adds advanced inventory and advanced pricing to the Gold subscription plan. You can choose to pay the subscription monthly or on an annual basis. Either way, you are required to commit to an annual period for the subscription. The cost for a single user will vary from $128 per month for the Silver subscription all the way to $178 per month for the Platinum subscription. There is a local-only option that does not use cloud services. The local Silver subscription is $84 per month, local Gold is $109 per month, and local Platinum is $134 per month.

Most solo and small firms will find that QuickBooks Pro is more than suffi cient for their needs. In previous years, Intuit offered a three-pack license at a reduced rate over the single-user cost directly from its website. The three-pack is no longer a separate product, and you'll need to order three licenses. The good news is that the traditional multiuser discount is applied. The single-user price is $299.95. Selecting two users will cost $549.95, or $274.98 per user. Three users will cost $799.95, or $266.65 per user.

To enhance its desktop offering, Intuit has QuickBooks Pro 2016 Plus, which is an annual subscription product that includes unlimited support, automated data backup, and upgrades. The cost is $299.95 per user per year. Phone support is available on a 24/7 basis, there is up to 11 GB total storage, recovered data is available up to 45 days, and the updates and enhancements happen automatically. You also receive upgrades as they are released. That would save you from spending money to upgrade with each edition (yearly). The $299.99-per-year cost seems rather high to us, especially since you'll be spending money year after year. We recommend purchasing the standard QuickBooks Pro software and upgrading the version every three years. That will save you several hundred dollars over the life of the software.

The QuickBooks Premier version contains additional features for specific industries and expanded reporting capabilities. As an example, you can track unbilled time and expenses for professional services; set different billing rates by employee, client, and service; and analyze profitability by matter. Intuit has significantly reduced the cost of the Premier version. QuickBooks Premier 2016 is $379.95 per user. Like QuickBooks Pro, there is a QuickBooks Premier Plus 2016 version that includes support, backup, and updates. The cost of QuickBooks Premier Plus 2016 is $299.95 per user per year.

Unlike previous years, there is no upgrade pricing available. In other words, if you owned an older version of QuickBooks, you could get a reduced price for upgrading to the newer version. Not anymore. There is no incentive for being a loyal QuickBooks user. You have to pay the same price as a new user would. Intuit, like many other application providers, is trying to migrate users to a subscription cloud service. That way it gets a constant revenue stream. Microsoft is doing the same thing with Office 365. At some point, vendors will no longer offer local loaded applications and everything will be in the cloud. To that end, there are three versions of QuickBooks Online—Simple Start, Essentials, and Plus. Each edition adds additional features to the previous edition. As an example, Essentials adds instant sales and profit reports as well as manage and pay bills to the Simple Start features. The monthly cost for the QuickBooks Online versions are $15 for Simple Start, $30 for Essentials, and $40 for Plus.

Besides the Windows versions, versions for Macintosh computers are also available.

Accountants love it when lawyers use QuickBooks as their billing software. They can take the QuickBooks data file at the end of the year and generate tax returns with relative ease. However, we don't recommend using QuickBooks for billing for several reasons. First, the invoices are very sterile looking and have very little room for customization. The data is there and clients can understand the information, but the invoice format lacks any capability for graphics, different fonts, custom text to identify different sections, or rearrangement of how the information appears on the page. Showing remaining balances properly is an issue too—a real problem if you want to show trust account balances and transfers or automatically indicate how much of the evergreen retainer needs to be replenished. As previously mentioned, QuickBooks Pro won't provide you with any productivity reports unless you purchase the Premier version. You're going to have to find a different way to determine how many write-down hours an associate had for a month or the amount of no-charge entries by client. In spite of these limitations, we still see a lot of lawyers using QuickBooks.

Billing Specific—Timeslips

Arguably the most popular billing software among solo and small firm lawyers is Timeslips by Sage (www.timeslips.com). Timeslips is a billing-specific software package that generates bills, tracks receivables, and manages trust accounting. We see many Timeslips installations in solo and small firm offices, especially those that have no case management system. Even so, we are beginning to see firms implementing invoicing products that are included with the integrated solutions that we describe later on.

Probably one of the reasons for the popularity of Timeslips is that it can be configured specifically for the legal industry right out of the box and supports the LEDES (Legal Electronic Data Exchange Standard) billing format with the optional electronic billing module. When you first install Timeslips, you select the type of business. This configures Timeslips to use the types of tasks and expenses that are specific to the industry. As an example, when you select the legal profession, default tasks are automatically created that deal with those tasks that are performed in the law office. There will be tasks for consultations, document review, and depositions, and so forth. The expense names are also automatically created and include such costs as copier usage, courier fees, postage, and the like. Trust accounting is also built into Timeslips, which is another reason the software is very popular in solo and small firm offices. You can configure Timeslips to deduct fees earned from the trust account automatically or leave it as a manual transfer process. In addition, Timeslips can automatically create the dollar amount to place on the invoice to bring the retainer amount back to a set level. This is a very popular feature for those attorneys who have evergreen retainer arrangements.

Timeslips is licensed on a per-machine basis. Each computer that needs to access Timeslips will require the purchase of a license. In a small office, it is often the case that only one computer is used to process billing. The timekeepers (typically lawyers) may elect to track their time manually on paper and give the time sheets to the office manager or bookkeeper for entry into Timeslips. This arrangement keeps licensing costs down and allows for growth in the law firm. As the firm grows, additional licenses may be purchased and network access configured for the Timeslips database. Larger firms that may use a terminal server need licenses only for the number of concurrent users. With the expanded interest and implementation of virtual computers, this concurrent license model may be a way to control costs.

The current version is Timeslips 2017 and is compatible with Windows 10. You can purchase Timeslips directly from the website. There are one-user ($699), three-user ($1,399; $466.33 per user), and five-user ($2,099; $419.80 per user) options. Once your selection is in the shopping cart, you can adjust the quantity if you need additional users. However, we suggest contacting Sage directly if you need more than five licenses as additional discounts may be available.

Besides the base standard Sage Timeslips product, there is a Sage Timeslips Premium, which is built on a faster, stable, SQL-based platform. Timeslips Premium contains all the features of the standard Timeslips product and adds Quick Bill functions and the ability to create customer calculated fields on invoices. Timeslips Premium is only available as an annual subscription and comes in three levels. The Silver level includes three support cases per year. The Gold level includes six support cases per year and two one-hour training sessions per year. The Platinum level includes unlimited Premium support, product training, minor data repair, and one major data repair per year.

Service plans are also available for Timeslips, but they are no longer available online. You will need to initiate a chat session to get the support options and costs. If you have never used Timeslips, we recommend that you consider the purchase of a support plan at least for the first year of operation, although it could be a little pricey. After the first year, we do not recommend that you prepurchase any support. Access to the free online knowledge base is usually sufficient to work through most issues that you are likely to experience.

Sage has totally revamped its maintenance plans. You can no longer just purchase access to the support personnel. The offered plans also include upgrades to the product. Effectively, you are paying for software upgrades as part of the maintenance plan, which significantly increases your total cost of ownership. As an example, maintenance plans for previous years would cost a few hundred dollars a year to get unlimited access to tech support. That same unlimited access (also includes free upgrades) now could cost several thousand dollars a year. It's pretty obvious that Sage is including the software upgrade cost when they price out maintenance. The three maintenance plans all include software upgrades. The Business Care plan has three levels—Platinum, Gold, and Silver. The Platinum plan gets you Timeslips upgrades and service releases, unlimited access to technical support, priority calling to the Premium Support Team, the eBilling add-on, unlimited minor data corruption repair, and one major data corruption repair for the year. The Gold plan includes Timeslips upgrades and service releases as well as six incidents of technical support and two one-hour training sessions. The Silver plan includes Timeslips upgrades and service releases as well as three incidents of technical support. The plans are priced based on the number of licenses you have. You will need to contact Sage in order to get exact pricing for any maintenance plan you wish to purchase.

Timeslips can also link with QuickBooks. Setting up this integration is a manual process and can be complicated. You have to make sure that the

Timeslips tasks and expenses have a corresponding QuickBooks account. Permissions (Timeslips and QuickBooks) also need to be considered. If you run a networked version of QuickBooks, multiuser versus single user could also cause some complications with the integration. A reader of a previous edition of this book advised us that Timeslips technical support will not help with any of the accounting aspects dealing with the QuickBooks link, as they feel it is giving financial advice and do not want the liability. Perhaps this is one of the reasons why our clients who use Timeslips and QuickBooks don't bother with the integration and manually input data into QuickBooks if needed.

Some of the providers for case management software have also built links to Timeslips. Contact the provider of the case management software if you are interested in how the link would work and what the limitations are.

Billing Software for Macs

There are not that many legal-specific billing software applications for Mac computers. Most Mac users will migrate toward web-based products for their firms. There are some native Mac applications, but like the Windows world, more and more users are moving toward the cloud.

Bill4Time

Cloud offerings are very popular in the Mac community. All you need is an Internet connection and a web browser. Bill4Time (www.bill4time.com) is one billing package we see used in law offices with Macs. It is a secure hosted environment that is available from any computer at any time. A free 30-day trial will allow you to see if it fits your needs. Bill4Time has a legal-specific version, which contains ABA Task Codes, LEDES export for invoices, trust and IOLTA (Interest on Lawyer Trust Accounts) accounting, document management, online payments, and client portal. Most attorneys will want to get the Legal Solo or Legal Pro version. All of the plans now allow for unlimited clients and unlimited matters. The Legal Solo version limits data storage to 2 GB. The Legal Pro version has a 10 GB storage limit, and the Legal Enterprise version has unlimited data storage. Remember that Bill4Time is just a billing application so limited storage shouldn't be a problem.

One convenient feature of Bill4Time is the mobile apps. There are apps for iPhones running iOS 5.0+, Android 3.0+, and BlackBerry OS 10.2.1. Supported tablets include iPads running iOS 6.1 or later, Kindle Fire 3.0+, and

Android 3.0+. This means you can use your mobile device to enter your time and expenses while out of the office. As we mentioned before, you need to keep track of all your billable activities—otherwise, you are losing money. The mobile app feature is a great way to help maximize your revenue.

Before you commit to spending any money for Bill4Time, take advantage of the free 30-day trial period. You can try any one of the three legal plans for 30 days for free. After the 30-day period, you will need to add credit card information to your account; otherwise, the account automatically becomes inactive.

The Legal Solo version of Bill4Time is $30 per month and includes one user license. You can only add one additional user at a cost of $20 per month. This may be fine for the solo practitioner, but some small firms may need more than two users. The Legal Pro version is $50 per month and also includes one user license. However, you can add unlimited users at a cost of $20 per month for each user. The Legal Pro version also adds Basic Data Import and Invoice Cover Sheet Integration features. Finally, the Legal Enterprise version is $100 per month and also includes one user license. Unlimited users can be added for $25 per month per user. Legal Enterprise includes all the features of Pro, but also adds Unlimited Data Import, Customizable Data Fields, Custom Reports, and Premium Support. We think that $100 per month for unlimited storage and the additional features is a bit much for a web-based billing package. At that price point, we recommend investigating other billing alternatives to include on-premise solutions.

EasyTime

Many of the practice management implementations also include some sort of billing mechanism, so you may not need a separate software application. We'll mention a few of the billing packages that are available for the Mac, but we certainly can't mention them all. One such stand-alone package for the Mac is EasyTime. EasyTime, by Bright Light Software (www.brightlightsoftware.com), runs natively on Mac OS X and does not require any third-party database packages. The current shipping version is 3.0.5, released March 7, 2015, and updated October 3, 2015. It requires MacOS 10.9 or higher. The cost is $240 (same as the last two years) for a single user and $320 (same as last year) for a network version.

Version 4 is now available for download. At the time of this writing (in December 2016), you could still purchase version 4 for the introductory price of $299, but it may change to the normal $400 price by the time of printing this book. You can upgrade to version 4 if you are a current version 3 user for $160.

Billings Pro

Another popular package is Billings Pro (www.marketcircle.com/billingspro/) by Marketcircle. The Billings Pro cost model is based on how many invoices, statements, or estimates you generate per month. The Freelance plan costs $5 per user per month and limits you to five invoices, five estimates, and five statements per month. This plan doesn't seem to be very practical unless you only have a couple of very large clients and don't invoice all that often. The Professional plan is $10 per user per month for unlimited invoices, estimates, and statements per month. Since there is no contract commitment with Billings Pro, we recommend starting with the Professional plan. If it looks like Billings Pro is something that works for your firm, then convert to the Professional Yearly plan, which costs $99 for a full year. Additional users are also $99 per user for the year.

A big concern with the Billings Pro cloud offering is that its data center is located in another country. Your data is stored locally and gets synchronized to servers in Canada, meaning that you can continue to work if the network is unavailable or the servers are unreachable. Some attorneys may feel that storing billing information for their clients in another country is not a problem and accept potential cross-border issues. Of course, Canadian attorneys welcome the fact that the servers are in their own country.

As with most of the products mentioned, be sure to take advantage of the free 30-day trial before purchase.

Integrated Packages

Many of the case management products support integration with billing packages. This means that you enter your information into the case management system and the time or expense is automatically captured for the billing process. There are advantages to using the same vendor for your case management and billing needs. The products are designed to work together and share information in a very efficient manner. However, selecting these all-in-one packages may not give you the best features of each package. If you really want a "best of breed" implementation, then make sure you investigate how the case management and billing packages share the data. Many case management applications provide links to billing packages by other vendors. Be careful to understand how to configure these links, especially if it is a manual process. We've seen clients who added tasks to their case management software and forgot to define the linkage to their billing software. This means that you may not bill for the effort when you use these newly defined tasks.

PCLaw

LexisNexis has a couple of billing options to address the needs of solo and small firm law offices. A very popular package is PCLaw. The current version is PCLaw 15.3 (www.lexisnexis.com/law-firm-practice-management/pclaw/), which includes a mobility function to keep your mobile devices synchronized with Outlook for access to calendar and contact information. PCLaw includes some features that you would expect from a case management system. You can keep track of contacts, calendar entries, phone calls, notes, tasks, and so on. This choice may be a good alternative for a solo practitioner to keep start-up costs down since it includes basic case management functions along with billing in a single package. PCLaw can also be used as the billing component when integrated with the Time Matters case management software.

The full feature set of PCLaw is no longer available on the website. Like other LexisNexis products, you have to complete a form to see a demo or get further product information. The pricing is no longer available on the LexisNexis website for the public to view. As we've mentioned before, this is not a practice that we are fond of, and we recommend using products from vendors that are transparent with their pricing.

Juris is another billing software application offered by LexisNexis. It is typically used by larger law firms or in integrating with Time Matters. We have never seen Juris used in a solo or small firm setting. As with some of the other products mentioned, you have to contact Lexis to get pricing information.

Tabs3

Another popular billing package is Tabs3 by STI. Tabs3 is the companion product to PracticeMaster, which is STI's case management software. Tabs3 pricing is based on the number of billable entities. Like so many other vendors, the cost of the software includes the first year of maintenance. The single-user version of Tab3 is $415 for two timekeepers and increases to $675 for five timekeepers. You'll need to purchase the multi-user version if you need more than one person accessing the data at the same time.

The regular multiuser version is available for two, five, nine, and 19 time-keepers. The cost is $675, $1,340, $1,915, and $3,065, respectively. The Platinum version of Tabs3 costs $950 for two timekeepers up to $15,940 for 100-plus (maximum of 999) timekeepers. STI defines a timekeeper as some-one whose time is tracked in the software.

See the Case Management chapter to learn about the mobility features of Tabs3 Connect, which became available in version 16.2 Platinum Edition. Even though Tabs3 Connect is a "killer" application for mobile access to your data, we don't think many solo or small firms will spend the money to have both Platinum versions of Tabs3 and PracticeMaster along with the requisite maintenance plan to get the feature included for no cost. You also have the option of purchasing a Tabs3 Connect subscription, but you'll still need to have Tabs3 Platinum, which we don't see very often in solo and small firms.

Version 18.1 of Tabs3 is the current shipping version. Most of the enhance-ments contained in version 18 have to do with reporting. The period-based reports are now date-based reports. The following reports are date-based and can be run for previous periods.

- Timekeeper Productivity Report
- Category Productivity Report
- Timekeeper Profitability Report
- Productivity Report by Category for Each Timekeeper
- Productivity Report by Tcode for Each Timekeeper

Another enhancement is the ability to print a receipt in the Payment Entry and Client Funds programs for any form of payment. Previously, only receipts for credit card payments could be printed. The majority of changes have occurred in the optional General Ledger Software (GLS) add-on for Tabs3. GLS now includes a new Account Information Report that mirrors information from the Balances, Budgets, and Journal Entries tabs. Additional GLS features are a new Bank Account Manager to show all bank accounts and credit card accounts. In addition, you can now import bank account transactions into GLS. The supported file formats are OFX (Open Finan-cial Exchange), QFX (Quicken Financial Exchange), and QBO (QuickBooks Financial Exchange). Finally, you can now Undo Reconciliations in GLS. New features in the optional Trust Accounting Software (TAS) include auto-matic trust payments from Tabs3; the ability to combine multiple deposit, EFT, or check transaction into a single item for reconciliation purposes; a new Bank Account Manager to see a summary of all accounts in TAS; and the ability to import bank account transactions using OFX, QFX, or QBO file formats.

Unlike other billing packages, Tabs3 has separated out various financial functions and priced them as individual components. As an example, there are additional components such as trust accounting, general ledger, and accounts payable. This means that you can expand Tabs3 from a pure billing package into a complete accounting package. You can find more information about Tabs3 at www.tabs3.com. We regard Tabs3 as highly as we do its case management counterpart, PracticeMaster. It also consistently receives high ratings from legal software experts.

Final Thoughts

One of the higher-level (expensive) billing alternatives is provided by Pro-Law, which is a Thomson Elite product. ProLaw is an integrated package, and the billing component is not available as a separate function. Very few solos and small law firms have chosen this route in our experience.

Most of our clients who use stand-alone applications have chosen Quick-Books or Timeslips for billing, and they are generally quite happy with what they have chosen—although everything has a learning curve. All of these vendors are happy to let you sample their product in one manner or another, so don't hesitate to try before you buy. Also, if you aren't keen on accounting, talk to your friends who are equally numbers-challenged and see what has worked for them. In many cases, the choice has been made by someone at the firm who is going to perform the accounting or bookkeeping functions, and that's fine. As long as you stay with one of the "majors," you won't be left scrambling to find someone who knows your obscure time and billing package if that person leaves.

CHAPTER SIXTEEN

Litigation Programs

Several programs can automate certain litigation support functions, and while they offer different features, they fall into two general categories: case organization programs and courtroom presentation programs. Case organization programs are databases that are set up to analyze and manage facts and evidence. The common ones include LexisNexis Concordance (www .lexisnexis.com/en-us/litigation/products/concordance.page), LexisNexis CaseMap (www.lexisnexis.com/en-us/litigation/products/casemap.page), and Thomson Reuters Case Notebook (legalsolutions.thomsonreuters.com /law-products/solutions/case-notebook).

Summation (http://accessdata.com/solutions/e-discovery/summation) is a case organization program now provided by AccessData. The current product is just called Summation. It is now web-based and provides a single tool for managing all postcollection stages of e-discovery. AccessData describes Summation as combining native and image file ingestion, data processing, early case assessment, fact and transcript management, and final review.

These programs help you organize and review the information for your case. You can accomplish various tasks such as tagging for privilege, creating privilege logs, identifying responsive documents, and so on. They are typically installed on-premise on your own hardware, but some also offer cloud solutions. More and more companies are now offering cloud-based electronic discovery platforms where you upload electronic files for review and ultimate production. Law firms are embracing these cloud solutions, which can be very cost effective and don't have the technical headaches of on-premise solutions.

CaseMap from LexisNexis is one of the most popular case organization packages for solo and small firm lawyers, given its lower cost and ease of use.

Several of the cloud-based offerings we see used by solo and small firm lawyers are Logikcull (logikcull.com), DigitalWarRoom (http://www .digitalwarroom.com/), Lexbe (http://www.lexbe.com/), and Nextpoint (http://www.nextpoint.com/).

Trial presentation programs manage and display electronic evidence, including exhibits, video and text depositions, sound files, and more. They facilitate quick access during trials and hearings and include on-the-fly annotation, such as highlighting and callouts. Trial presentation programs include TrialDirector (www.indatacorp.com/TrialDirector.html) and Vision- ary products (http://www.visionarylegal.com/products/productslist.aspx ?groupId=1). Sanction (http://www.lexisnexis.com/litigation/products /hearings-and-trial/sanction) is a very popular and well-known litigation software application of LexisNexis.

The above-referenced products are full-featured and can give a lot of whiz bang to the presentation of evidence at trial. The reality is that today's jurors want to see trials that seem like they are watching TV. They expect fancy effects, transitions, callouts, and quick access to exhibits. The day of the document camera is fading, although by no means gone. Annotations similar to the "John Madden marker" are finding their way into courtrooms across the country.

More maturity is now evident in the trial presentation packages for the iPad. Products such as TrialPad (http://www.litsoftware.com/trialpad/) by Lit Soft- ware turn the iPad into a presentation tool for litigators. Since we are seeing so many litigators equipped with an iPad, we highly recommend starting with TrialPad for your trial presentation software. For $129.99, you can't go wrong by giving it a try. TrialDirector for the iPad is a free download from the App Store, but is a quite limited version of the flagship product for the PC. It's pretty much a no-brainer to try the iPad app since the data is easy to transfer and it's free. Free is a good price for the solo and small firm attorney, though reviews indicate that inData Corporation has a long way to go with its iPad application. Try it out, since you have nothing to lose, but we'll guess that you will end up using TrialPad instead. There are some other "competitors" to TrialPad, such as ExhibitView. We feel that TrialPad has maintained the beachhead for iPad trial presentation software. Unless you have a compelling, specific reason to use one of the other products, it appears that TrialPad is the product of choice for the majority of litigators.

Most of the above-mentioned products have free downloads for a trial period or online demos. Although we do not review them in detail, they should be considered by lawyers with litigation practices. Be sure to read the iWin: iPad for Litigators chapter by Tom Mighell and Paul Unger, which includes more details about litigation products that are available for the iPad.

CHAPTER SEVENTEEN

Document Management

Document management software solutions can be relatively expensive for the solo or small firm operation, although there are some cost-effective alternatives. Several of the better-known document management products tend to be used more for enterprise-size companies because of their cost and complexity. As the industry matures, vendors are merging the functions of document management, content management, and knowledge management. This is especially true as electronic files are becoming a critical component of discovery. You may see applications described as document management systems, content management systems, knowledge management systems, or even enterprise content management systems. Just because a vendor chooses to describe its product using particular words doesn't mean there is anything unique or special about it. In general, all of the terms previously mentioned are used for applications that organize information. The hot topic of late is information governance (previously known as records management). It's a very specialized operation of document management. Information governance classifies information and has rules for retention periods according to business requirements and appropriate laws and regulations. We're not going to address products that are used in the specialized world of information governance applications.

The main purpose of a document management system is to organize information into a usable and searchable form. How many times have you looked for a file or document but couldn't remember the name or location? A document management system allows for fast and easy access to the data, whether in paper or electronic form. It also provides access control and enforceability of rules. As an example, perhaps one of your rules is that every document has a specific category (programmed ahead of time) tagged to it. This makes for consistency and removes the human error in typing or misspelling the category tag. In addition, security is another feature of document management systems. Typically, you can set security access to particular matters, specific types of files, or even unique files themselves. One person could have full control over a document, whereas another might be able to view the content but not modify it.

DocuShare

We will mention just a few of the products that are available, but understand that document management systems are not generally designed for small-scale operations. Xerox's DocuShare (docushare.xerox.com) has been around for many years. Pricing is available directly from Xerox or through partners. An entry-level version of DocuShare (DocuShare Express) is now available for small to midsized office installations, which starts at a few thousand dollars for ten users. The current version (DocuShare7) requires a 64-bit server, which would significantly increase costs if you didn't have one available. DocuShare may be a viable alternative, especially if you already have a Xerox copier that you could use for scanning documents. Be sure to take advantage of the free 30-day trial if you are considering acquiring DocuShare.

iManage

It is really hard to stay current with a product that changes names and companies so many times over its life. Several years ago, we knew it as Interwoven. Then it was known as Autonomy iManage WorkSite. Autonomy then became an HP company, and the product name changed to just WorkSite. Today, a management buyout of the business from HP leaves us with the current name of iManage Work. As with DocuShare, expect to pay thousands of dollars for this system. It is a highly regarded document management environment (if you can remember the name) but is also geared more toward the intermediate to large-scale firms.

Worldox

The most popular and most used document management system for solo and small firm operations is Worldox (www.worldox.com). Worldox is licensed on a concurrent-user basis and not per seat. The current shipping version of Worldox is GX4. GX4 Professional is the standard network client server installation that has been around for ages. It is the traditional desktop version. The next version is Worldox Enterprise, which is adapted for multi-office, remote access environments. It is typically hosted at a data center and has full communication with local applications, including Microsoft Office, Outlook, and third-party products such as case management. The final version of Worldox is a SaaS hosted solution called Worldox Cloud. With the Worldox Cloud solution, your data is hosted on Worldox servers in its data centers. GX4 utilizes Active Profiling technology for ease of use and automation, enabling you to manage, share, and access all your digital content effortlessly. Worldox GX4 also facilitates effortless content sharing with connectors to industry standard applications like Citrix ShareFile and Legal Anywhere.

The cost for Worldox GX4 Professional is $460 (same as last year) per concurrent user, which makes it very affordable for solo and small firms, especially since there are no minimum seat purchase requirements. Annual maintenance is $97 per license and is mandatory for new orders. No separate server is required, and the indexer can be run on any workstation-class computer. The computer resource requirements for Worldox are very light when compared to other document management systems. The application is very robust and easy to use, hence its popularity within the legal community.

Worldox Enterprise is intended for multiple offices and remote access environments. It looks and acts just like the local desktop (GX4 Professional) version. You must contact Worldox to get pricing information at this time.

Worldox also offers a Web Mobile addition to the Worldox software. The mobile edition gives you access to your documents from multiple devices and locations. It currently supports a wide range of devices, including any web browser notebook or desktop, iPads, BlackBerry smartphones, Android devices, iPhones, Treos, Windows CE PDAs and cell phones, and many Internet-ready smartphones and other devices with Java script support built in. There are two pricing models for the mobile access. For $30 per user per month (billed quarterly), you can implement the SaaS hosted solution, which installs the proxy software on your indexer. You can reduce the cost to $25 per user per month with a one-year prepayment. You can also install it on your own server, but the costs start to climb quickly. You will need a server license ($1,495), user licenses ($65 per named user), and annual maintenance ($15 per user and $300 per server per year). If you need a proxy server, you may need to expend additional money for a proxy server license ($600) and proxy server maintenance ($120). Doing the math, it will cost you $2,195 for five users in the first year without a proxy server and $2,915 with one proxy server. Years two and beyond would be $375 per year for the maintenance charges for the five-user system without a proxy server. Installing your own Worldox/Web Mobile server makes financial sense if you plan to use it for two or more years.

Worldox also includes a Legal Hold feature. The Legal Hold feature will be a great benefit for firms and companies as part of the litigation process. If you are in litigation or if litigation is reasonably anticipated, you have a requirement not to destroy any potentially relevant evidence. Legal Hold will let you assign rights and restrictions to files. You can even create restricted-access security groups so that only authorized employees can access the designated files. In addition, each action is tracked to create an audit trail showing who did what to which file. The key feature for Legal Hold is the ability to "lock" a file so that it cannot be changed. Do be forewarned that this is not complex "litigation hold software," which includes many more features.

Worldox also integrates with Sony's Digital Paper device. Worldox will sync documents and notes with the Sony Digital Paper device using the included USB cable or will sync documents and notes wirelessly through a box.com account. Case management systems (see the Case Management chapter) are also used to provide a certain level of document management. Your electronic files are referenced to a client or client matter, making them easily accessible at the click of a mouse. A key point to remember about true document management applications is their stringent enforcement of the classification rules. The user must use the system within the configured rules, which sometimes frustrates people because of the rigid requirements. In contrast, applications that are not specifically document management software aren't restrictive or mandatory. The danger is that data may be lost or misfiled when the rules are not stringently enforced. Worldox is an excellent choice for document management, as it integrates with almost every case management system available. It consistently receives good reviews from legal software experts.

Matter Center

Microsoft is getting into the practice management game. Matter Center for Office 365 was formally announced at the ILTA annual conference in Las Vegas during August 2015. Matter Center was originally used internally by Microsoft's legal team. Matter Center for Office 365 is a SharePoint-based document management and collaboration solution. Matter Center will not be directly available from Microsoft as a delivered product. Microsoft will distribute Matter Center through various IT providers that serve the legal market. It is currently available via GitHub, which is an open-source community for software development.

According to our friend and colleague Bob Ambrogi, Matter Center has the following features:

- Access anytime, anywhere. Just like Office 365, Matter Center is available across PCs, tablets, and phones and across Windows, Apple, and Android devices. You can access matters and documents either online or offline using OneDrive for Business.
- Real-time collaboration. Using the automatic version control feature of Office 365, you can simultaneously edit documents with multiple people inside or outside your organization.
- Easy search and data visualization. Search, preview, and find matters and related documents across all cases directly within Outlook and Word. Power BI (business intelligence) can be configured to visualize your matter data.
- Pinning and tagging. Track or pin frequently used matters and documents and connect to Delve to provide personalized experiences about who on your team is working on them.
- Security compliance. Control who can access, review, or edit a document. Get the same enterprise-grade security, management, and administrative controls as Office 365.
- Flexibility and control. By offering Matter Center through an open GitHub repository, customers and partners can build or extend the technology to meet specific customer needs faster.

In order to take advantage of Matter Center, you must have a subscription to Office 365 and Azure.

Acrobat

Many solo and small firm offices are equipped with Adobe's Acrobat product. The latest versions of Acrobat provide the ability to manage documents. The collaboration components within Acrobat are used to organize and reference files in a manner similar to other document management systems.

Web-Based

Web-based document management systems are becoming very popular. The cost per user is typically more than purchasing a product for use within your firm, but you save on the hardware and internal support costs. The vendor provides the back-end hardware and software for the management of your documents. The nice part about web-based document management systems is that the information is accessible from any computer with an Internet connection. The bad part is that the vendor is holding your data and you are subject to the reliability of the Internet connection. If you elect to use one of the online document management systems, be aware of the security precautions for client data that is being held by a third party. At a minimum, make sure that the connection for accessing the documents is encrypted and that the data is stored in an encrypted form on the provider's equipment. You should also make sure that you have a copy of the data in your hands to avoid being "held hostage" by the third-party provider. And yes, we've seen that happen. More and more vendors now offer cloud solutions in addition to their traditional on-premise solutions.

NetDocuments

NetDocuments is a popular SaaS provider for document management. Many law firms, small to large, have had great experiences with NetDocuments. We have heard lawyers say that it was very easy to install and configure. In one case, a lawyer converted his firm (tens of thousands of documents) over to NetDocuments in a weekend all by himself.

NetDocuments provides all of the features you would expect in a document management system, in addition to matter-centric work spaces, e-mail management, collaboration, and mobile access.

NetDocuments has cloaked its pricing and capabilities. You can no longer determine the costs or features of its offering. You are forced to contact the company for information or to request a demo. As we've previously stated, we are not fond of this lack of transparency.

Plain Folders

Finally, a very simple form of document management for solo and small firms (though not what we would recommend) is to follow a standard folder and file naming convention along with search software (see the Utilities chapter for search tools). Besides the potential cost for search software, this is a very low-cost solution. Some lawyers will use the search capabilities of Windows or Mac before even investing in supplemental search software. Typically, folders are named on a client or client-matter basis. Files are then given a very descriptive name, such as <client name> followed by the file purpose and sometimes the date. As an example, "Kennedy request for admissions.doc" would be the filename for your request for admissions in the Kennedy matter. This is a very manageable method to organize data when your practice is small. As your practice grows, search software may be needed to assist in finding particular files pertaining to specific issues.

Searching

Search software such as dtSearch or X1 (see the Utilities and Apps chapter) can be used to index the files within your client folders so that you can quickly find the desired document. As an example, you may be looking for the document pertaining to the request for electronic evidence or something concerning a partner's Nexus smartphone.

If you are considering the purchase of a document management system, Worldox is an excellent first choice. We have implemented this software many times, and clients are always happy with it. We have become big fans over many years. No matter what product you are considering, see whether there is a trial version available, or at least participate in a demo of the product, to determine if it meets your firm's needs.

CHAPTER EIGHTEEN

Document Assembly

Essentially, document assembly software automates the creation of legal documents that are used repeatedly. This includes such documents as wills, leases, contracts, and letters. You can think of document assembly as templates that can be used over and over. This shortens the time for document preparation and increases the efficiency of your practice. If you use flat fees, document assembly can be a godsend.

Document assembly software can be specialized for a particular industry or can be generic. As an example, specialized document assembly software is typically used in estate planning and tax preparation. In those situations, the user answers questions in a survey type of form and then the required documents are generated using the answers provided. If you have ever used one of the personal income tax programs (e.g., TurboTax, H&R Block), you've seen how document assembly works. You may see the term "document automation," but it means the same thing as document assembly for our discussion.

HotDocs

In law firms, the top three document assembly packages according to the ABA's 2016 Legal Technology Survey Report are HotDocs, ProDoc, and Microsoft Word. HotDocs (www.hotdocs.com) is the most popular document assembly software by a large margin. HotDocs is a very powerful solution and has significantly matured over the years. HotDocs is composed of many different products, such as those used for template creation, cloud-based access, desktop template distribution, and centralized server-based distribution to the users. HotDocs Developer 11 is one of the most powerful platforms for document automation and allows you to convert word processing documents and PDF forms into document generation process applications, otherwise known as templates. You create a template and determine what text to include or exclude, depending on the answers entered by the user. This is the survey type entry that was described earlier. The presentation walks you through the questions to gather the data needed to generate the document. The current version supports Microsoft Word 2007, 2010, 2013, and 2016 and WordPerfect X4, X5, X6, and X7. HotDocs User 11 is the other desktop product, and it is used to generate finished documents. With HotDocs User, you complete interviews and generate documents.

As with other application software these days, HotDocs is available in a browser version too. The product, HotDocs Server 11, allows for document assembly using a standard web browser. This is particularly helpful for remote users and means you can deploy templates via the Internet. HotDocs Server 11 must be deployed in conjunction with a web application. HotDocs Workplace is a web application designed to run with HotDocs Server. Hot-Docs Workplace will let you organize and access HotDocs process apps and provides options for creating a new answer file or selecting an existing one.

HotDocs also has a SaaS (software as a service) offering, which extends the browser-based document generation to the small and midsized firm. The HotDocs Cloud Services are hosted in Microsoft's Azure cloud and provide state-of-the-art data security and on-demand document generation in any modern browser on any device from within the context of any standards-compliant web application capable of making web service calls. Cloud Services could be used by firms that need browser-based document generation, prefer a hosted (subscription-based) solution, and want to integrate HotDocs interviews into existing web applications. Cloud Services is available at a monthly subscription rate, but you'll need to contact HotDocs to get a quote.

Pricing information is no longer available on the HotDocs website. You must speak with a HotDocs representative to customize you document generation solution. We'll continue to say that we hate the lack of transparency when companies hide pricing information and make you contact them. A free 30-day trial for HotDocs Developer is available directly from the website.

ProDoc

ProDoc (www.prodoc.com) is another document assembly application that is a legal resource from Thomson Reuters. One of the interesting features of ProDoc is how the licensing works. ProDoc is licensed on a subscription basis. The basic subscription license allows for usage on three computers or by three concurrent users. If you install ProDoc on a network, the licensing enforces the three-concurrent-users limit. You can only install ProDoc on three computers if they are stand-alone and not running in a network installation. You can add additional licenses for a small additional fee. The software is licensed for a single firm at one location. If you share office space with another firm, then each firm needs to purchase its own subscription to ProDoc. Pricing used to be transparent and easily determined from the ProDoc website. Not any longer. When you shop for ProDoc products, you are forced to fill out a form so that a Thomson Reuters representative can contact you. When a vendor goes from transparent pricing to "hiding the ball," it makes us wonder how many other things will be surprises.

The ProDoc forms are state-specific and currently only available for California, Florida, Texas, and Texas e-filing. There is also a national package available as a supplement library with links to parent BTS (Business Transactions Solution) forms on Westlaw. There are various document assembly systems available for the supported states. Be sure to check the website to see what modules are contained in each package and that your particular practice area is covered.

Microsoft Word

We were surprised to see that Microsoft Word is tied with ProDoc as the second most popular document assembly product according to the ABA's 2016 Legal Technology Survey Report. While Word is not technically a document assembly application, you can automate functions to generate documents. You would use macros and form fields as template documents to provide some consistency and automation.

Final Words

HotDocs is the clear recommendation for solo and small firm lawyers wanting to embark on document assembly. As a generic package, it is very well suited for any type of law practice. HotDocs integrates with many document management and practice management packages. There are many choices for technical support, including HotDocs Wiki, HotDocs Forum, HotDocs Resource Center, and HotDocs Documentation. HotDocs resellers are the primary method for consulting and product acquisition.

CHAPTER NINETEEN

Cloud Computing

Everybody is talking about the cloud—in the legal profession and elsewhere. You can't go a single week without there being some mention of a new cloud service offering. The really scary part is that many users don't know what it means to use cloud computing and believe that the weather affects the "cloud." That's not a joke—almost half of Americans believe that.

For our discussion purposes, the cloud is generally viewed as an external computing resource that is typically accessed via the Internet. You can participate in cloud computing by putting your own equipment in a secure data center and accessing your data (and perhaps applications) via the Internet. If you don't use your own equipment and software but elect to purchase applications through third parties, then you are using a SaaS (software as a service) solution. To make it easy to understand, imagine that you don't own a copy of Microsoft Office; you simply go to a site on the Internet where you are, by subscription, allowed to use Office. The resulting data is held by the provider, not you. This is exactly the environment that Microsoft is pushing with its Office 365 product.

Stats from the ABA Legal Technology Research Center's 2016 survey of ABA lawyers:

- A web-based software or solution was used by 38 percent (compared to 31 percent in 2015, 30 percent in 2014, and 31 percent in 2013).
- Small firms (two to nine attorneys) were the most likely to respond affirmatively at 46 percent.
- Among those who had not used cloud computing, 42 percent said they did not intend to use the cloud in the future.
- Of those who had not used cloud computing, the concerns they cited were:

- 63 percent: confidentiality and security concerns
- 54 percent: concerns of having less control of your data because it's hosted by the provider, not on your own server/computer
- 50 percent: unfamiliarity with the technology
- 39 percent: concerns of losing access to and ownership of your data
- 31 percent: cost/effort of switching from your current solution
- 28 percent: cost of services
- 25 percent: preference for owning software rather than paying a monthly subscription
- 24 percent: non-web-based software programs you use are sufficient for current needs
- 24 percent: lack of professional responsibility/ethics guidance
- 20 percent: uncertainty over longevity of vendor
- 18 percent: concerns about the inability to integrate with the other software in your office
- 17 percent: lack of control regarding software upgrades
- 6 percent: available products lack desired or necessary features
- 6 percent: lack of reliable Internet connection
- 5 percent: fear of vendor turning data over to law enforcement

The traditional client/server model puts total control in the hands of the law firm. The data is held internally, and access is controlled by the firm. You can choose to encrypt the data locally, which we recommend, or leave it in plain text. Either way, it is within the technology walls of the law firm and not directly accessible by any third party.

In contrast, the SaaS model puts your data in the hands of a third party. This is not necessarily a bad thing, but do you really know if the information is safe? Your contract with the provider may specify that the data be stored in encrypted form, but what if a disgruntled employee has access to tools that allow him or her to decrypt the data and sell it to the other side in a major lawsuit? An ongoing concern for lawyers, in light of the Edward Snowden revelations, is whether there is a government "back door" that allows it access to your data.

When you contract with a SaaS provider, you are required to accept the service as it is delivered to you. This means any upgrades or bug fixes will be implemented by the provider. Sound like a good thing? Perhaps not. What if the upgrade breaks integration with another product that you use? As you can see above, 17 percent of respondents cited lack of control regarding software upgrades as a reason to avoid the cloud.

Besides the data security and access concerns for the SaaS model, the financial stability of the provider may be a consideration, but it is becoming less of an issue as more and more vendors are providing cloud solutions. Still, 20 percent of respondents to the 2016 Legal Technology Survey are concerned about the longevity of the vendor. Even if you have adequate notice that the vendor will stop providing a contracted service, the cost to migrate your data to another provider or bring it back in-house can be significant. This brings us to the topic of exit strategy. At some point, you will likely want to bring the function back within your IT control or move to another provider.

The contract should provide for specific costs and timetables to facilitate the move. It should also specify what file format you will get your data in. Will you get a copy of the complete SQL database along with the schema or just a comma delimited text file?

Another issue is the stability of the communications network. By design, you are dependent on the speed and quality of your Internet connection. Smart firms will have dual network connections to the Internet, although this will mean an increase in cost over what is normally installed at the firm. The Internet connection must be available at all times; otherwise, you will not have access to your data. There aren't many judges who are sympathetic to your problems if you miss a filing date because your Internet connection went down. And Internet connections, as we've all miserably learned, do sometimes go down—and always without notice.

To be fair, let's look at the upsides of using the cloud . . . and yes, there are some compelling upsides.

There can be some financial advantages to contracting service to a third-party provider. Your investment in hardware and software is minimized, since you are really only passing keyboard, mouse, and screen data over the communications link or accessing the application via a web browser. The actual processing occurs at the cloud provider. All configuration and data hosting are external to your firm's infrastructure. Costs for the SaaS model can be based on the number of users or the amount of data storage volume. Either way, it is fairly easy to identify and budget for the cost of the service, which is a big selling point for a lot of firms. However, to get these "stable" price points, the contract terms are typically three to five years. This means that the firm must make a pretty long commitment to using the SaaS model and the specific provider.

The alternative to the long contract term is a much shorter subscription model. Many cloud service providers are now providing solutions where you have to commit to an annual subscription. Some are even offering month-to-month subscriptions. Typically, the shorter the commitment period, the higher the cost. As an example, many cloud-based case management applications won't make you commit to more than a year.

Another advantage to the SaaS model is the rapid reaction time to changes. It is very fast to add new users or to increase the amount of space for data storage. By the same measure, it is very fast to decrease the number of users or amount of storage space. This means that you are more flexible in controlling your costs. If your firm is in contraction mode, you can reduce expenses, assuming that the contract doesn't tie you to a minimum amount. Many firms like the mobility aspect of the cloud model, since they can access the applications from any machine with an Internet browser. Typically, there isn't anything special that needs to be installed on the client computer. The user needs only a browser and perhaps some type of plug-in to access the application. This means that it is easy to gain access to the firm's data from the office, the home, or an Internet café in the Bahamas.

Too often, all costs and all risks are not considered when analyzing a cloud solution. The cloud ballyhoo has drowned out all reasonable objections. We originally moved slowly and carefully in moving clients to cloud solutions, but we do understand that some cloud services make sense for the solo and small firm attorney. More on that later. Client/server solutions can be clearly defined from implementation through the life of the solution. You control the implementation, configuration, and ongoing costs. While you can contractually specify some costs with a cloud provider, future upgrades and exit conversions may tip the financial decision.

You may also hear of two other cloud solutions. Platform as a Service (PaaS) and Infrastructure as a Service (IaaS) are two additional cloud computing services. With PaaS, the client creates software using features and capabilities as available from the provider. Most law firms will not entertain the PaaS model. With IaaS, the necessary infrastructure is supplied by the solution provider. It owns and controls the equipment, operating system, network, and so on, and you load your applications onto the services. Think of it as having your data and applications running on "rented" hardware.

Contract Considerations

Now for a show of hands. How many readers have actually read the terms of service or terms and conditions for a cloud provider service? When we ask that question at continuing legal education programs, you could count the number of raised hands with the fingers on one hand. Shame, shame, shame. As lawyers, you should be reading the contracts and the terms that you are agreeing to. Fear not. We'll point out some of the items and considerations you should be looking for in contracts with service providers.

Where will the data reside? Will it be in the United States or in some foreign country? Can you specify where the data will reside? Certainly, we would recommend that the data remain in the United States, which would avoid any cross-border issues and having to deal with international laws. And yes, even with the Snowden revelations, we don't want data in privacy-focused Europe where we don't know the laws and would potentially need a European lawyer to help in the event of a problem. "Better the devil you know," as we say ruefully.

- Is the data encrypted in storage and in transmission? Encryption will help protect the confidentiality of the information. The majority of cloud providers will encrypt the data in transit (e.g., SSL connections), but not necessarily at rest while it sits on their servers.
- Who controls the encryption keys, and is there a master decryption key? Just because the data is encrypted doesn't mean it is accessible only to you. Services like Dropbox encrypt the data in transit and while it is stored on their servers; however, they hold a master decryption key and have the ability to decrypt your data. Services like Spider Oak allow you to define the encryption passphrase, and they have no master decryption key. The good news is that there exists technology where the end user controls the encryption key and not the service provider.
- Who can access your data? This may not matter if you control the encryption, but it is worth knowing your exposure.
- What is the exit strategy? This was referenced above. Is there a cost? What form will the data be in? How long will it take to get your data? You certainly don't want to be held hostage by the vendor when trying to leave its service.
- Who owns the data? It seems like it should be a silly question, but is the data really yours or can the provider access it and redistribute it?
- What about data breaches? Make sure you understand who is responsible should there be a data breach. Who makes and pays for the data breach notifications? Will the cloud provider pay for any identity theft monitoring if required? Does the provider have adequate cyberinsurance coverage?
- Is your data stored on separate physical devices, or are you comingled with other cloud customers? Comingled storage puts you at risk should the authorities want to seize equipment for a cloud customer that you

share storage with. Think of the Megaupload situation, in which many businesses went bankrupt when the authorities seized servers in a criminal investigation and their data was commingled with the company being investigated.

Private Cloud Solution

We think that moving your data and applications to a secure data center is a much better solution for most solo and small firm lawyers. Think of it as the best of all worlds. It's your data and software running on equipment that you own and control. If you don't like the data center, you can always move or bring it back in-house. The costs are even more predictable because you control any upgrades. We have purchased rack space at data centers over the last several years and moved our clients' equipment into the secured racks. Not long ago, weather conditions in our area (a massive snowfall and a drenching storm that had folks without power for weeks) made more firms cognizant of business continuity solutions. Data centers have redundant power (generators too) and Internet connections. This means that weather conditions will not affect your ability to access your data and applications. Data centers generally guarantee at least 99.999 percent (called the five nines) uptime. Remember, though, that your own equipment could fail and you are still dependent on your local Internet connection. However, if your power in the office and at home is down, you can drive (as one of our clients did) to a Starbucks a few miles away and be back in business using a VPN.

As you engineer the architecture to implement a private cloud (some may call it a hybrid solution), be particularly aware of any software applications that contain databases such as your case management software. Database access using the Internet as the network is extremely risky and will typically result in corrupted data. You may have to implement a terminal server–type connection so that you run the client software from equipment at the data center instead of "dragging" all the data between your computer and the server over the Internet. Your IT consultant can help you determine the right connection scheme for each of your applications to achieve the greatest stability for your needs.

Bottom line: Although we don't regret our initial caution with moving law firms to the cloud, we feel we have now solved most potential problems and that the law firms can feel comfortable that they are complying with ethical requirements when storing confidential data in the cloud. We are now actively moving more and more clients to the cloud, though using the client's hardware rather than the cloud provider's. If you feel that you need to investigate and research SaaS vendors, we describe a few in this book. We just ask that you do it carefully and ask the right questions before making your decision.

We believe that many cloud providers actually offer better security than law firms themselves. There's some truth in that, and we are therefore moving in the direction of recommending cloud solutions from proven providers with good track records. Finally, be sure to check with your bar, as a number of states now have ethics opinions regarding cloud computing. If you're wondering how states are dealing with the cloud from an ethical perspective, the general view is that it is acceptable to use the cloud as long as you investigate the provider, particularly making sure that confidential client data will be adequately protected. An excellent resource is provided (free of charge) by the Legal Technology Resource Center of the American Bar Association available at http://www.americanbar.org/groups/departments _offices/legal_technology_resources/resources/charts_fyis/cloud-ethics-chart .html, where you will find a list of cloud ethics opinions for the various states. Remember that, ethically, you are outsourcing when you contract with a cloud provider, so the ethical rules relating to outsourcing also apply.

New for 2016: On March 17, 2016, the Legal Cloud Computing Association released the first set of cloud security standards crafted specifically for the legal industry at ABA TECHSHOW. It is a short document containing 21 standards—and easy to read. You can review the document at http://www .legalcloudcomputingassociation.org/standards.

CHAPTER TWENTY

Collaboration

Collaboration may or may not be at the top of your list, especially if you are a solo lawyer. However, we're sure you will have occasion to deal with other lawyers or even have a need to collaborate with your clients on a case. There are some great technology solutions that allow for collaboration—and solutions are multiplying week by week. These are just a few of the primary tools available for sharing information and working in a collaborative mode.

Social networking is a collaboration area that is gaining in popularity. Facebook has won the social networking war and is now being used extensively for business purposes. Twitter and LinkedIn are also very popular, with many lawyers preferring LinkedIn as a network for professionals. So what are the top social networking sites? If you consider popularity as number of unique monthly visitors instead of registered users, Facebook is still the "800-pound gorilla." After Facebook is Twitter, LinkedIn, Pinterest, Google+, Tumblr, and Instagram—although the order changes a bit from year to year. While Google+ has not died, it seems pretty moribund to us from a business point of view.

Some lawyers are getting business through social media sites, and others are raising their visibility with potential clients or colleagues who might provide referrals. Still others have obtained opportunities to write or speak on their area of expertise. See the the chapter Social Media for Lawyers—An Overview for more information on how lawyers are using these new applications.

We're also seeing an increase is collaboration with clients by using client portals with cloud service providers. More and more of the case management vendors have client portals so that clients can collaborate with their attorneys and even gain access to documents and other information for their matter.

Google Drive

Probably one of the best-known of the collaboration tools is Google Docs, which is now an offering within Google Drive. Google has repackaged its offering, and what used to be considered a suite is now separate applications known as Docs, Sheets, and Slides, all accessible within Google Drive. Actually, you can bounce around to a bunch of the Google offerings from each of the applications. As an example, from Drive, you can get to Docs, which can access Slides and Sheets. Docs also has a return path to Drive. Other Google offerings are also accessible, such as YouTube, Maps, Photos, and Gmail, Google+, Wallet, Hangouts, and so on. The popularity of this cloud product is no doubt due to the fact that it carries the favorite price tag of all lawyers—it is completely free. The applications allow you to work on a document, spreadsheet, or presentation with others and see the modifications in real time. You just use the web browser on your computer with your Internet connection. There are even enhanced features that you may not be aware of.

You do need to have a Google ID to use Google Drive and Google Docs. Just go to https://drive.google.com and enter your login information. You can also create an account from the main entry page. Besides creating your files from scratch, the Google apps allow you to upload files you've already created on your computer. Documents can be downloaded to your computer as .DOCX, .ODT (OpenDocument format), .RTF, .PDF, .TXT, .HTML (zipped), or .EPUB (EPUB Publication). Spreadsheets can be downloaded as .XLSX, .ODS (OpenDocument format), .PDF, .CSV (current sheet), .TSV (tab separated values), and HTML (zipped) files. Presentations can be downloaded as .PPTX, .PDF, .SVG (Scalable Vector Graphic), .PNG, .JPG, or .TXT files.

If you are used to the way Dropbox operates, you will not have any trouble with Google Drive. The easiest way to synchronize files and work on your spreadsheets, documents, and so on is to install the Google Drive application to your computer. Once it is installed, you will have a folder to drag and drop files into. They will then automatically get synchronized with your Google Drive storage. Google gives you 15 GB of free storage when you create your account. If you need more than that, there are several levels of storage subscriptions. Monthly pricing for additional storage is 100 GB for $1.99, 1 TB for $9.99, 10 TB for $99.99, 20 TB for $199.99, and 30 TB for $299.99.

By default, files are not shared until you make them shareable. This is certainly the preferred security policy and keeps your data private unless you make a conscious decision to share the information. Once you've created or uploaded a file to your Google Drive, you configure how the file is shared.

Your first option is to set what access is allowed via the link. The default is "Private—Only you can access." Selecting the "Change . . ." option lets you modify the access. Selecting "On—Public on the web" means anyone can access the file or folder on the Internet through search results or the web address without logging in. Selecting "On—Anyone with the link" means anyone who is given the link to the file or folder can access it without logging in.

Besides determining how the link is shared, you can also change what a user can do with the data. The creator of the document is tagged as the owner and can obviously do anything. Once you share the file via a link, you can define what the user can do with the file. The choices for access are "Can edit," "Can comment," and "Can view." This gives you some level of granularity in the access and visibility options. When you share a file, the default access is "Can edit." By default, people who can edit your shared files and folders can also

- Change sharing settings
- Share the file and folder with other people
- Copy, print, or download the file

In other words, you pretty much lose control if you keep the default sharing values. Not to worry. You can change the default action by selecting the "Advanced" option. You will then have the opportunity to "Prevent editors from changing access and adding new people" and "Disable options to download, print, and copy for commenters and viewers." You can select one or both options.

As a practical point, multiple people can collaborate on a file and everyone doesn't need to have the same software or version. You can go online and create a file to start the process. Once completed, perhaps you download the file as a .docx file, since you use Word as your word processor. Another person downloads the .rtf version that he reads in an old version of WordPerfect and a third person downloads the .odt version because she uses OpenOffice. Each person downloads the same information but in a different file format to match what's used on each computer.

Rather than downloading the file, users can directly manipulate the file contents within the browser. Changes are immediately seen by all users in real time. This means everyone is working from the same information and you won't get out of sync by people downloading and uploading different versions at different times. Certainly the preferred method of collaboration is to edit using the browser.

The current version of Google Drive now supports mobile access. As smartphones become the computing platform of choice, Google has developed additional methods for you to get to your information. Currently, Google Drive is accessible from an Android phone or tablet running Android 4.1 or higher. For an Apple device, you need to be running iOS 7.0 or above. The Google Drive app is what facilitates access to the Google files from your mobile device. You will need to install the Google Drive app to your Android or Apple mobile device. There are also separate apps for Docs, Sheets, and Slides. Just access the files from your Google Drive app and the changes are synchronized across all devices connected to your Google Drive. You can access Google Drive from other mobile devices by using a browser and going to the mobile web at https://drive.google.com.

The caution with Google Drive is that the data is being held by a third party. Obviously, you would not want to use it to work on highly proprietary information such as a patent application. Even though you can control who has access to the files and what they can do, Google still holds the "keys" to all of the data. Google has had some highly publicized security issues over a period of years, so it is wise to consider what data you store there.

There have also been some recent stirrings over Google's privacy policy and what data Google accesses. We remind readers to review the terms of service and privacy policies for any third-party-provided service, including Google. Apparently, there were a ton of folks that never read the terms and got all upset when they heard that Google scans the data you create and deposit on its servers. This is true for the free services that Google provides, such as Gmail and Google Drive. However, Google Apps for Work (previously known as Google Business Apps) does not have the same terms of service. In fact, the terms of service for the Apps for Work have specific confidentiality provisions, where Google will protect the data. They will also notify you if they are required by law to disclose confidential information so that you have an opportunity to challenge the disclosure (unless they are under a gag order pursuant to the Freedom Act). You should note that Google Apps is also HIPAA-compliant, but you must first sign a Business Associate Agreement with Google.

There are now two offerings for G Suite (formally known as Google Apps for Work). The base version is called G Suite Basic and costs $5 per user per month. Google no longer offers a discounted rate if you commit to 12 months of service. All plans are monthly plans. You get the following features with the basic version:

- Business e-mail addresses (name@yourcompany.com)
- Video and voice calls
- Integrated online calendars
- 30 GB of online storage for file syncing and sharing
- Online text documents, spreadsheets, and slides
- Easy-to-create project sites
- Security and admin controls
- 24/7 phone and e-mail support

The second offering is called G Suite Business, which costs $10 per user per month. The G Suite Business plan contains everything in the basic plan and adds the following:

- Unlimited storage (or 1 TB per user if fewer than five users)
- Advanced admin controls for Drive
- Audit and reporting insights for Drive content and sharing
- Google Vault for e-discovery covering e-mails, chats, docs, and files
- Easily search and export to different formats
- Archive all e-mails sent by your company
- Set message retention policies
- Place and enforce litigation holds on inboxes

Vault is an add-on for G Suite that lets you manage, retain, archive, search, and export your organization's e-mail and chat messages for your e-discovery and compliance needs. You can also search and export your organization's files in Google Drive. Vault is entirely web-based, so there's no need to install or maintain any software. Vault is included with G Suite Business or you can buy Vault licenses for an additional $5 per user, per month. Since Vault is a $5 a month add-on, why not just go with the G Suite Business version and get additional administrative controls and e-mail options?

Acrobat

Today, more and more lawyers have Acrobat (www.adobe.com/products /acrobat), especially if they e-file court documents. Acrobat allows for collaboration with PDF documents, so you can conduct shared document reviews that allow the participants to view one another's comments. Adobe has radically changed the Acrobat product with the release of Acrobat DC. It is much more cloud-driven and part of the larger offering called Adobe Document Cloud. Document Cloud will let you create and edit documents from any mobile or desktop device. The intent is to have documents available in the cloud so that you can have anytime access.

Acrobat DC is sold on a subscription basis, as is Document Cloud. You can also get Acrobat DC as a stand-alone product, but it has fewer features than the cloud option. All of this can be very confusing. Just remember that the version lawyers should be using is the Pro version. Lawyers should opt for the Pro version primarily for the enhanced security, Bates stamping, and redaction ability. Acrobat DC Pro allows you to create a document that your clients may find useful. It allows Adobe Reader (the free reader version) users to participate in reviews with complete commenting and markup tools, including sticky notes, highlighter, lines, shapes, and stamps. This means your clients (or other lawyers, for that matter) don't have to purchase Acrobat to collaborate with you. Sharing of documents can occur via e-mail transmission or through Adobe Document Cloud.

The desktop versions of Acrobat are no longer available from the Adobe site. You'll have to purchase them from a retailer such as Amazon or Best Buy. The retail price for Acrobat DC Standard desktop version is $299 and Pro is $449. Acrobat DC is available in two subscription plans. The subscription for the Acrobat Standard DC is $22.99 per month, or $12.99 per month with an annual commitment. As we've mentioned, lawyers should be using the Pro version. The Acrobat Pro DC subscription costs $24.99 per month or $14.99 per month for the annual commitment. The extra $2 a month for the Pro version is well worth the cost, especially considering all the advanced features you'll get. Adobe also offers a free trial download from its website. Like the other products we recommend, use the trial first if you are unsure of your purchase commitment.

Microsoft Word

Another collaboration tool is the Track Changes feature of Microsoft Word. With this tool, you can see the modifications made by each user who modifies the document. The caveat is that the software must be configured to identify the user properly. Some preloaded Office installations have the user configured as something generic, like "Owner" or "Satisfied Customer," and not the user's name. If you use Office 2007, open Word 2007 and click the Office button in the upper left, select the Word Options button at the bottom, and see the user information in the Popular menu choice. Word 2010, 2013, and 2016 users select File and then the Options menu choice. You then enter your name and initials in the "Personalize your copy of Microsoft Office" section. Once this option is properly configured, the user information will show properly with the tracked changes. The user also has the ability to insert comments in addition to modifying the document contents. Do not strip the metadata (as you might normally do for confidentiality reasons) from the document if you are sending it to another party for collaboration. Removing the metadata also removes the tracked changes, so the recipient will not see the intended modifications. When you have the document ready and want to send it to a client, scrub the metadata at that point.

SharePoint

SharePoint is Microsoft's solution for collaboration. Basically, SharePoint is a web-based server environment that allows the end user to collaborate on data that is managed through a SharePoint server. There is no special client software needed, as access is accomplished via a browser. The current version is SharePoint 2016.

SharePoint 2016 is considered to be expensive for most solo and small firm operations, especially for new installations. Besides the cost of the server hardware, you will need the server software and client access licenses (CALs). Microsoft has attempted to simplify the previously confusing licensing model for SharePoint. The on-premise solution is licensed using the server/CAL model. SharePoint Server 2013 is required for each running instance of the software, and CALs are required for each person or device accessing a SharePoint server. There is even an option for enterprise CALs if you need a very robust and flexible SharePoint environment to take advantage of Microsoft's Business Solutions or Business Intelligence for Everyone features not available with the standard CALs. Suffice it to say that it is all very complicated and can get rather expensive. If you need the services of a full-blown SharePoint server, you may want to consider some of the hosted solutions, which should be a lot more affordable for a solo or small firm office. Microsoft offers SharePoint Online, which is licensed on a per user basis and starts at $5 per user per month (Plan 1) for the basic set of features and $10 per user per month (Plan 2) for more advanced features such as enterprise search, e-discovery, ACM, Compliance, and so on.

Microsoft is continuing to push SharePoint in a major way. It keeps threatening to remove the Public Folders function of Exchange with each new release and force users to go with a SharePoint installation to get the same features you currently get with a base Exchange installation. We thought this was going to happen with the release of Exchange 2010 and then Exchange 2013, but we are happy to say that the Public Folders function is still there. Since Microsoft has been making this threat for many years, we have no reason to suspect that Public Folders will be removed from future Exchange versions.

We've written about SharePoint in the last several editions of this book. Microsoft continues to hype it, but we don't see much traction in the real world, especially for solo and small firm attorneys. Surveys show that 78 percent of the Fortune 500 companies are using SharePoint, but only one of our clients has it installed and we don't see that SharePoint is worth the expense, especially for an on-premise solution. Many solo and small firm practitioners use cloud solutions instead of investing in a complex SharePoint environment. We agree with that direction and don't think SharePoint is going to change the world, as Microsoft has often predicted.

Office 365

Microsoft Office 365 is giving Google a run for its money. Office 365 is really a web-based productivity suite that also contains some collaboration capabilities. The solution is a subscription-based service, so the out-of-pocket cash flow is very reasonable. There are several subscription plans available, depending on the number of users and any advanced features that may be needed. The company is trying to steer users toward a subscription model and away from the traditional retail software packages. As we've mentioned elsewhere, it seems as though a lot of vendors are following Microsoft's lead and traditional locally loaded applications are slowly being phased out in favor of cloud subscription offerings.

Solo and small firms will probably opt for Office 365 Business Premium, which is geared toward small businesses and can handle up to 300 users. The cost is $15 per month per user (billed monthly) or $12.50 per month per user with an annual commitment, which is very affordable. It includes access to business class e-mail, shared calendars, 1 TB of OneDrive for Business storage space per user, the ability to use your own domain name, web conferencing, and document sharing. You also have the ability to have Office on your desktop on up to five PCs or Macs. The Office applications include Word, PowerPoint, Excel, Outlook, OneNote, Publisher, and Skype. With the desktop version, you can work on your files while offline. Once you are connected to the Internet, all of your work will automatically sync. For you e-mail junkies, each user gets a 50 GB mailbox with the ability to send attachments of up to 150 MB in size. We recommend starting with the month-to-month plan, which can be canceled at any time without penalty, and then convert to the annual plan if all goes well.

Workshare

We don't see Workshare very often in the solo and small firm environment. When we do, it is because of the document comparison feature. Workshare also offers the ability to share files securing and remove metadata. The Comparison Edition cost $15 per user per month (billed annually). The Sharing Edition cost $34 per user per month (billed annually) and allows you to compare documents, access them on any device, and share and work on them with others.

A September 2016 announcement teams Worldox with Workshare to provide document sharing and collaboration. The offering is called Worldox Connect Powered by Workshare. As colleague Bob Ambrogi describes it, "[T]he product will allow users to securely share folders and documents with colleagues, clients, experts and others. Sharing includes digital rights management enabling users to prevent recipients from downloading or editing documents. All versions, activity, and comments regarding the document are logged and saved back into Worldox." Pricing has not been set, but the integration will make for an excellent collaboration, especially if you already use Worldox for document management.

Skype

Many users are familiar with the VoIP (voice over Internet protocol) solution called Skype. Skype is now owned by Microsoft, and things seem to be going along fairly well. Telephone calls are free between Skype users. You can opt for pay plans if you need to call mobile or landline numbers, and the cost is very reasonable. Skype for Business is even included in your Office 365 subscription for no additional charge.

Unlimited calling to United States (United States, Guam, and Puerto Rico) or Canada landline and mobile phone numbers is only $2.99 per month. You can save 5 percent if you pay every three months or 15 percent if you pay annually. Other plans are available if you make frequent calls to other countries.

New features with Skype make it an excellent tool for collaboration. Video conferencing is now supported within Skype. You can create a low-cost or no-cost video conference call in just a few seconds. Many laptops now have a video camera built into the screen case, and there are Skype apps for mobile devices such as iPhones, iPads, iPod Touch, Kindle Fire, Windows Phone, BlackBerry, Amazon Fire Phone, and Android devices. Finally, you can share files through Skype as well. File sharing, video conferencing, and free teleconference calls via the Internet make Skype a great low-cost collaboration tool.

Beware of security issues, though. We learned in 2013 that Microsoft was routing Skype calls through its servers, contrary to previous practice. Also, researchers have proven that Microsoft accesses users' content within Skype. Finally, documents revealed by Edward Snowden state that Microsoft has cooperated with the National Security Agency (NSA) and actually decrypted data at the behest of the NSA. We do not recommend using Skype for confidential conversations or file sharing.

Dropbox

Dropbox is not just for file synchronization between your computer and mobile devices. We have seen a tremendous increase in Dropbox being used to share files among multiple parties and even as a vehicle to produce evidence in discovery. You can create a custom folder within Dropbox and share that folder with multiple people. Only those that you authorize can have access to the folder contents. This means you can collaborate with co-counsel, consultants, experts, and even opposing counsel.

Dropbox is free for the initial 2 GB of storage. You can purchase additional storage starting at $9.99 per month for 1 TB or $99 if you elect to be billed annually. There are also offerings for business users. At a cost of $15 per month per user, you get unlimited storage and file recovery. You also get enterprise file-sharing controls with central administration, Active Directory integration and much more. Dropbox transmits the data in a secure fashion using SSL and also stores it in encrypted form on its servers. However, Dropbox holds the encryption key and can decrypt the data should it receive a valid court order or law enforcement request. Therefore, you should consider Dropbox to be an insecure service and not use it for transmitting any confidential or sensitive information. That doesn't mean you can't use Dropbox to share confidential information. Your data is safe if you encrypt it *before* you deposit it in Dropbox. That way you control the encryption key and not Dropbox.

Desktop Sharing

Several products enable you to share your desktop with other people, and sharing your desktop may be a good way to collaborate on a document or share pictures of an accident scene. Products like Webex, TeamViewer, join.me, and GoToMeeting allow for desktop sharing. If you elect to use desktop-sharing products, be advised that you may not be able to determine if the remote party is recording the session. You may want to get agreement and confirmation from all parties that they are not recording the session, especially if you don't want it recorded or you want to be the only one with a record of the session. In addition, be wary if you give control over to a remote user, as they may be able to transfer data from your computer without your knowledge. We would recommend that you "push" your desktop to the remote parties and not let them take control.

CHAPTER TWENTY-ONE

Remote Access

Most lawyers today are road warriors. If their entire office is not on a laptop or smartphone, a good chunk of it is—and the rest is accessible through remote access. Whether in court, on vacation, on the road, or in a meeting, lawyers need access to their e-mail, calendar, appointments, and files—and they need access fast.

Many lawyers have discarded workstations entirely, using only their laptop and a docking station at work and tablets and smartphones while on the move. Others have both a workstation and a laptop. The popularity of laptops and other mobile devices has zoomed in the last decade, to the point where the lawyer without a laptop or smartphone is a rarity. Our new mobile lawyers are now equipped with technologies that allow them to be as productive on the road as they are in the office, minimizing downtime and keeping those billable hours (or productivity hours, in the case of the alternative billers) up. Many clients and colleagues have a strong expectation that lawyers will be constantly accessible via e-mail—even, sadly, while on vacation. We privately joke (and lament) that vacations are times when our mobile devices get a nice view of the beach. Many clients will disregard your out-of-office message and will expect a quick response. So how do we stay in touch with the office when on the road?

Virtual Private Networking

A virtual private network (VPN) connection is a secure communications network tunneled through another network such as the Internet. The VPN connection allows a user to connect to the office when working remotely. The communications tunnel encrypts the data traffic between the remote user and the office network, maintaining the security of the information as it is passed back and forth. This is extremely important for law firms whose law-yers work on client files while traveling or while away from the office and have to download a local copy of a client file to work on. Best of all, the VPN service software is included with Microsoft's server operating systems and the VPN client software is included with Microsoft operating systems at no additional cost to the user.

The average lawyer is likely to be dumbfounded when confronted with setting up a VPN, especially if third-party software and a certificate are required, so this is best left to your IT consultant. However, it is not terribly expensive, and it offers terrific security for your data. The greatest advantage of VPNs is that they are multiuser, whereas other methods are one-on-one solutions.

If you're traveling and don't have access or the ability to create a mobile hotspot—which is the preferred, secure way of accessing the Internet when traveling, you should always fall back on a VPN. A VPN service such as VPN Unlimited (www.vpnunlimitedapp.com) allows users to create an encrypted connection to the Internet, which is important if you're planning on using the "open" wireless network at your next legal conference or meeting. This app can be installed on your mobile device or computer system, and allows for complete anonymous, secure Internet access. This subscription service is offered in packages for purchase in as few as seven days (for a quick trip to the beach) or several months or years and even an Infinity package that never expires. The pricing ranges from $1.99 for seven days to $129.99 for the Infinity subscription, and is one that the authors use on a regular basis when traveling.

If you are confused as to which VPN service you should use, there is a resource that compares over 150 VPNs. It is available at https://thatone privacysite.net/. The comparisons help you determine what features are most important to you. Does the provider log information about your con-nection? Is the pricing reasonable? What is the security level? The charts are in easy-to-understand color codes, where green means good.

GoToMyPC

GoToMyPC is a remote connection service that allows you to connect to your work computer when you are away from the office. This service is a great alternative if you're a solo practitioner or if your law firm does not have the ability to set up a VPN-type connection for remote users (for example, if you don't have a server). Like a VPN connection, data communications between the client and the host are encrypted and secured. To connect to your work computer, software must be installed and running on the host machine (the computer you wish to connect to), and both the client and the host computers must have Internet access. The GoToMyPC website maintains contact with the host computer, so the IP address of the host is always known. This is critical: This solution works even if the host has a dynamic Internet connection (constantly changing IP address) instead of a static one, which remains constant. No modifications to the configuration of your firm firewall will need to be made to get GoToMyPC up and running.

Users can even connect to their work computers (Mac or Windows) from a tablet or smartphone. Apps are available for Android, iOS, and Kindle Fire devices.

GoToMyPC costs as little as $12 per month for one computer license when billed annually. There is a monthly plan, but the cost jumps to $14 a month. There is no limitation on how often you may connect to your host computer, and you are allowed to connect to your host computer from any device. For each additional computer to which you wish to connect, there is an additional charge per computer. The software requires little setup and configuration and can be purchased online from GoToMyPC's website at www.gotomypc.com. This software is more costly than its competitors, so be sure to check out all of your available options before selecting which remote access solution to purchase. GoToMyPC also has a 30-day free trial, so take advantage as you experiment to find which remote access solution works best for you!

LogMeIn

LogMeIn Pro is a remote access solution that is very similar to GoToMyPC. The software works the exact same way, with the service provider maintaining the IP addresses of host computers. This is another good solution for those firms with dynamic (constantly changing) IP addresses. With this service and very little effort, you can gain seamless and total access to your office PC (Mac or Windows) from any computer with an Internet connection. To connect, a user logs in to the LogMeIn website (or uses the app downloaded to her mobile device) and the connection to the host computer is made automatically. Some of the features include remote printing, the ability to transfer and share files between the connected computers, and the ability to map network drives to your local computer. Just like GoToMyPC, this service is extremely secure, using 128-bit to 256-bit SSL end-to-end encryption. Compared to GoToMyPC ($144 when billed annually), this remote access solution is slightly higher at $149 per year, but allows a user to access up to two different computers, instead of just one with GoToMyPC.

This service also supports connecting to your work computer from your iOS or Android device. We've used the iPad app, and it works as advertised—easy to use, great with the touchscreen, and very convenient.

A LogMeIn Pro subscription will need to be renewed annually. There is no longer a monthly plan to choose from. This service can be purchased online from LogMeIn's website at https://secure.logmein.com. We strongly recommend the use of this product for remote accessibility because of its ease of use and ability to access two computers instead of just one. Like GoToMyPC, LogMeIn offers a free trial, so we recommend taking the product for a test-drive before purchasing it.

TeamViewer

TeamViewer Business Edition is a remote access solution on steroids. It contains a number of features that are not available with LogMeIn or GoToMyPC. Although it's a onetime purchase, it comes with a hefty price. Just like the two remote access solutions described above, TeamViewer works flawlessly behind network firewalls and is a good solution for firms that use dynamic IP addresses. While TeamViewer is not difficult to install and run, the connecting computer will need to download, install, and run the client application, which, in our experience, may be a bit more confusing and cumbersome for lawyers to perform rather than just logging in to the service with the web browser. However, once the local application is installed, it's very easy to use.

Some of the additional features include

- Multiplatform support, including Mac OS X, Windows 10, and Linux computers
- iOS, Android, Windows 10 Mobile, and BlackBerry support
- Communication tools that allow users to connect with each other through video chat or VoIP (voice over Internet protocol)
- Onetime charge for a lifetime license; no recurring yearly costs
- Integration with OneDrive for Business
- The ability to transfer files securely
- File box for common file sharing

- Microsoft Outlook calendar integration
- The ability to record meetings
- Space for up to 25 meeting participants

Mobile device support is offered for iOS, Android, and Windows 10 Mobile, but users will need to purchase the TeamViewer Premium license, unlike the included mobile support offered in both of the LogMeIn and GoToMyPC alternatives to this product. TeamViewer Business can be purchased online from www.teamviewer.com, and a single lifetime business license for one computer costs $809. This version allows users to install the TeamViewer software on as many devices as they wish, but only allows for one session at a time—no concurrent usage by multiple users or to multiple computers, and it also doesn't include the ability to remotely support mobile devices.

Mobility Tips

Besides providing remote access solutions for the legal road warrior, we wanted to include some useful tips to think about before heading out on the road:

- Pack a surge protector. It doesn't matter what brand. You never know when you will need more than two outlets to power all of your devices and to protect your electronic devices from power surges and dirty electricity.
- Purchase a lock for your laptop. Ninety-nine percent of laptops have a Kensington security slot, and it's prudent to use it. Kensington locks, such as the MicroSaver DS Notebook Lock, can be purchased online from Kensington's website (www.kensington.com) for around $50—a small price to pay to keep your laptop secure.
- If you use a wireless Bluetooth mouse, be sure to pack extra AA or AAA batteries.
- Pack a spare cell phone charger and tablet charger with an extra sync cable. You shouldn't travel without either one.
- Pack an AC extension cable. This will come in handy when you are far away from a power outlet.
- Keep an AC power adapter for your laptop in your bag. You never know when you might need one.
- If you're traveling internationally, be sure to pack multiple converters so that you can connect your devices. In the United States, we operate on a system that runs at 120 volts. Be sure to check the voltage of the country you're visiting before leaving and find out whether your power supplies will auto-convert. You may not need

voltage convertors if the power supplies auto-adjust, but you will need the plug adapters to match the outlet connections.

- It is always a good idea to have a hard copy printout of your hotel reservation and itinerary, in the event your mobile device stops working or isn't accessible when you need it. If you are using your mobile device to keep track of your itinerary, try using an app like TripIt, which can track all your travel arrangements, including your flights, hotel, and rental car information, and will eliminate the searching of your e-mail for your travel plans. How nice is it to have all of the information in a single place? Plus, another great feature is that this app allows you to share your itinerary with family and friends.

- Another tip for international travelers: Leave your cell phone at home. Roaming charges can be staggering and can be initiated even if you're not actively using your phone. Do you really trust putting your phone in airplane mode?

- Keep appropriate video adapters with your laptop in your laptop bag. You never know when you might need to connect your laptop or tablet to a TV or projector for a presentation.

- Pack headphones to keep the noise out. Have you ever tried to be productive on an airplane? It's hard when the person next to you can't stop talking. Just plug in your headphones and your problem is solved. You can even listen to relaxing music while you work. For those who want wireless Bluetooth headphones, check out the Jabra Revo Wireless, costing about $200, which can be found on Jabra's website at www.jabra.com; however, you won't be able to use these during takeoff and landing because they are transmitting devices. For music aficionados, the Bose QuietComfort 25 Acoustic Noise Cancelling headphones offer top-of-the-line headphone technology and include the noise-canceling circuitry that you hear everyone talking about. The downside, though, is the price—very, very expensive at around $300. The authors are particularly fond of the Bose QuietComfort 20 earbuds. They are small and lightweight and have amazingly effective noise-canceling capability. However, they are also pricey at $300.

- Back up your data to an external hard drive or the network server. If your laptop crashes or is stolen, you will want a recent backup of your most important files.

- Encrypt your hard drive and data. There are many software tools available to do this, such as PGP and PC Guardian. In the event your laptop is lost or stolen, your data is protected. Configure a power on or BIOS password on your computer, if available. Again, this adds another layer of data protection. One point to note, however, is that if you're traveling internationally, encryption is illegal in some countries, which could lead to the confiscation of your encrypted devices—so be prepared and know the local laws. In some cases, it may make more sense to leave your data at home and connect remotely to your system to access your information, rather than to take it with you.

- If you have a tablet, be sure to password-protect your device with a passphrase. PINs aren't as secure and can be easily cracked. On an iPad, a passphrase requirement on the Lock Screen will enable encryption of your data. On Android devices, you can encrypt your data as well by using a lock code or through the configuration settings for older OS versions.

- If you have a smartphone with a data plan that allows device tethering or a mobile hot spot, take advantage of the data service you have already paid for and tether your laptop or tablet with your smartphone for Internet service. Avoid paying daily hotel fees for an Internet connection if it's not provided free during the course of your stay. However, data overage charges from your wireless carrier can be expensive, so it's best not to stream the movie at the top of your Netflix queue while tethered unless you truly have an unlimited data plan.

- Encrypt your USB flash drives and external hard drives.

- Disable your wireless auto-connection feature within the Windows operating system. Most laptops with wireless cards will automatically connect to any unencrypted, open wireless network when your default connection is unavailable. If by chance your device does connect to an open wireless network, never log in to any e-mail or bank account when using an unsecure connection.

- Before leaving the office, make sure that your security software has the latest updates and definitions to protect your devices while you're away. The same applies to Windows updates.

- Download and install an app to track your club membership cards so that you don't have to carry all that plastic around with you. The one that we like the most for iOS and Android mobile devices is the Key Ring Rewards Cards app. It not only allows you to enter and store your club card or membership numbers but also generates a bar code that can be scanned should one be required. You might as well get miles points and hotel rewards while on the go.

- Another great app to download and use on your mobile device is GateGuru. This app comes in handy when your flight has been canceled or delayed, and you're looking for a few hours to kill. This app provides maps of all major airport terminals, including restaurants and stores, along with reviews allowing you to find a bar or restaurant in which to relax and unwind until your flight.

- For Android users, Google's Wi-Fi Assistant app uses free and available hotspots to connect your mobile device to the Internet. It also secures your data through the usage of VPN service managed by Google. Free, secure Wi-Fi sounds like a great idea and reduces carrier data usage at the same time!

These are just a few of the recommendations we have for the legal road warriors, all based on our own experiences traveling. We hope you find them useful.

CHAPTER TWENTY-TWO

Mobile Security

Technology advances in this area have come at warp speed. We're old enough to remember when dial-up was the only way you could connect to the Internet and cellular phones were almost as big as a briefcase. We can't remember the last time we even saw a modem as an option when configuring a laptop purchase. Wireless, whether using Wi-Fi or a 3G/4G data connection with your cellular carrier, is the preferred method of connectivity in the modern age. More and more hotels, motels, conference centers, coffee shops, bookstores, cafés, and so on, are offering wireless access solutions, many without charge. The question is . . . should you use the free Wi-Fi?

Software

Before we jump into the boring details, let's cover some solutions that should be on your laptop no matter what other technology you use for remote connectivity. It goes without saying that you should have some sort of all-in-one security solution installed on your laptop. It should be configured to check for automatic updates and to perform a periodic full scan (we do weekly scans) to catch anything that may have "landed" before the signatures were updated. It would be just your luck to catch a virus or other malware on day one and be the first kid on the block to suffer the effects. Most of the current Internet suites also analyze the computer operation and identify activity that could be virus-like or some process trying to access something it shouldn't. This type of real-time monitoring provides added protection beyond mere signature files. Normally, the all-in-one security product will contain security features like antivirus, anti-malware, firewalls, spam control, and anti-phishing. Don't leave home without it. Software solutions for your smartphone and tablet are also available, but we'll discuss those later.

Encryption

Secure mobile computing must contain some method of encryption to protect valuable personal and client data. We prefer whole disk encryption. This means everything on the hard drive is encrypted and kept secure. We don't have to remember to put files into special folders or on the encrypted virtual drive. All too often, people are in a big hurry and may not save their data in the special protected encrypted areas, leaving the information vulnerable. With whole disk encryption you don't have to think. Save the data anywhere on the drive and it's protected.

In addition, without whole disk encryption, artifacts of the decryption passphrase could be present in various places (e.g., master file table, Page File, temp files, unallocated space). Forensics can extract these artifacts and make it probable that the passphrase can be determined. Many of the newer laptops have built-in whole disk encryption. To state the obvious, make sure you enable the encryption; otherwise, your data won't be protected. Also, encryption may be used in conjunction with biometric access. As an example, our laptops require a fingerprint swipe when powered on. Failure at that point leaves the computer hard drive fully encrypted. A very comforting thought if laptop thieves, who constitute a large club these days, make off with your laptop.

If you think we are being too cautious, bear in mind that a laptop goes missing every 50 seconds in the United States. In 2016, PCWorld.com reported that one of ten corporate laptops will be stolen each year, from cars and other forms of transport, from hotels, airports, and restaurants—and the list goes on. We mean it when we say, "Be careful out there." Also, don't forget to encrypt your USB flash drives. Unfortunately for us good guys, these devices are easily lost and almost always contain our valuable data.

Wireless

What's next? We won't cover modem access in the traditional sense, since dial-up isn't desirable, effective, or even available these days for most travelers. Wireless is the norm for all the road warriors. There are two basic types of wireless access you'll encounter. The first type is generically termed a "wireless hot spot" and is what you find at your local Starbucks, fast-food establishment, hotel, or airport. You may or may not have to pay for these wireless connection services. Many businesses are offering free wireless as a way to attract customers—heck, even McDonald's offers a free wireless hot spot. Most of these hot spots are unsecured and wide open. This means it is possible for your confidential data to be viewed by the customer at the next table or the person sitting on the park bench outside the café if you are not encrypting the traffic.

Does this mean you shouldn't use any of these wireless clouds? If you have a choice, we would say these clouds are best avoided by those who are technology averse and don't understand how to operate securely in an unsecured cloud. Read on and determine whether you can safely be trusted to do what follows.

See if there is an option to have a secure connection to the cloud. This would be indicated if you use https:// (note the s, denoting "secure") as part of the URL. Typically, website connections are unsecure and do not provide an encrypted session like the https:// connections do. Be especially careful if you have to pay for the wireless connection. Be wary when you are at the screens that have you input your credit card and billing information. Do not enter any of this sensitive information without an https:// connection. Once you've established a connection to the wireless cloud, be sure to use your VPN or other secure (https://) access to protect your transmissions. Also, when connecting to a secure website, if you're presented with an error message referencing a SSL certificate error or invalid certificate, proceed with extreme caution or, better yet, don't proceed at all. The good news is that more and more browsers are helping to limit access to nonsecure sites. Chrome is especially aggressive in this area.

Some hotels may give you a wireless cloud that is already secured. Typically, these wireless implementations use WPA (Wi-Fi protected access) or WPA2 to secure your connection and data. The cloud will be visible to your computer, but you will be required to provide a password before your computer connects. Once connected, the data you transmit will be encrypted and secure. However, know that WEP (wired equivalent privacy) and WPA have both been cracked. This means there are insecure methods of encryption. You should only be connected to and using WPA2 Wi-Fi clouds for secure wireless communications.

One scheme we see all the time: You are in a hotel that requires you to pay for Internet access. But when you ask your computer to show "all available wireless networks," it will display something like "free public wireless" as a network name—or something else that sounds innocuous, usually using the word free to entice you. Beware—these are often data thieves offering up an insecure cloud for the sole purpose of making off with your data. You can get the "free Internet"—but at a terrible price. Never be tempted by these clouds.

AirCards

Another wireless connection method is commonly called an AirCard. These are cards that are used to connect to the high-speed wireless networks of cellular phone providers. We're pretty sure you've seen the cellular providers advertising their 3G/4G networks. You may see terms like EDGE or EV-DO to describe the older 3G networks and WiMAX or LTE to describe the latest 4G networks. Don't be swayed by vendors' claims for speed and availability. Make sure that you will be able to have service in those areas you travel to the most. Reliability is another consideration, as is whether you already have a cellular plan.

The AirCard itself is a hardware device that you can externally connect to your laptop or select as a built-in option when configuring a new computer system. External AirCards come in both USB and PC card formats. These cards can be used on any laptop with USB ports or PC card slots. Some laptops and netbooks have the electrical circuitry built in, so no additional hardware is required. The built-in capability means you have nothing to lose, but it is "married" to the laptop and can't be transferred between machines. Further, you would also be stuck with a single cellular vendor, as each vendor's radio is different. The external AirCards can cost several hundred dollars, but most providers offer significant discounts. Of course, you will also need a data plan from your cellular provider.

Also, it should be noted that if you have multiple devices that need Internet access, rather than purchasing a subscription for each device, which can be very costly, you can invest in something like the Verizon Ellipsis Jetpack MHS815L or another mobile hot spot. These devices create a local wireless network that can provide Internet access (over the cellular network) to up to ten devices. Verizon offers the Ellipsis Jetpack for $29.99 with a two-year commitment that can connect up to eight Wi-Fi enabled devices.

Frankly, you should be using the "hot spot" capability that is built into your smartphone. That means you don't have to carry around or pay for another piece of equipment. Like the dedicated AirCards, the data connection is encrypted between the smartphone and the cellular carrier. We haven't seen an AirCard in some years as more and more lawyers use their smartphone as a Wi-Fi hot spot.

Public Computer Usage

A word of warning here. Be very careful about using a public computer, such as those in a library, an Internet café, or the business center of a hotel.

Even if you are only accessing your web-based e-mail account, the data is temporarily written to the local hard disk. There is also the risk that some keystroke logging software is installed on the computer, thereby capturing everything that you do on the machine. Studies have shown an average of seven pieces of malware on these public computers.

Does that mean all public computers are off limits? Not at all. Just don't do anything on the computer that would reveal your identity or expose private information. Even using a hotel business center computer to print your boarding pass would reveal your airline user ID and password. Another reason to travel with your own equipment.

Smartphones

Want to know what the most secure smartphone on the market is? That really isn't the right question. The question should be: What smartphone can be made the most secure? The answer is an Android phone. Because of its design architecture, Android can be configured with enhanced security settings as well as installing security software to protect the OS. You can't do that with an iPhone. It's pretty clear that the iPhone was designed as a consumer phone first, with security an afterthought. However, the latest versions of iOS on the newer iPhones have improved security to the point where it more closely approaches the other smartphones in protecting data. Also, Apple announced that with the release of iOS 10, it would give application developers access to more core functions of the operating system. This means that third-party developers finally have an opportunity to produce software that can further increase the security of the iPhone, iPad, and so on. It still doesn't change the fact that the iPhone holds a tremendous amount of data, unbeknownst to the user that is orders of magnitudes more than any other smartphone. In other words, the iPhone is very evidence-rich. One day, we'll have to record a video of the "happy dance" we do when iPhones come into our forensics lab. While the latest models are encrypted by default when locked by a PIN or biometric, remember that a court (at least in a civil case) may order you to turn over "the keys" to your device.

At a minimum, everybody should have a PIN code programmed into her phone to prevent unauthorized access, along with a fairly short time-out period. It doesn't do much good to have an unlocking PIN and then have 30 minutes pass before the phone relocks. We know it's a pain to constantly punch in the unlock code, but that will keep your data from being accessed by prying eyes. Better yet, it will stop someone from installing spyware on your phone that can effectively trap all of your communications (voice calls, e-mail, text messages, etc.). For those devices that offer a passphrase alternative to the PIN, such as the iPad or iPhone, this would be the preferred choice to secure your device. Why, you might ask?

A passphrase can be longer than a PIN and can contain nonnumeric values, vastly increasing the strength of the protection. In fact, we do not recommend that any iPhone or iPad be configured with the very weak default six-digit PIN lock code.

Encrypt the phone! This is easier to do than you think. Enabling a lock code on the iPhone or iPad automatically encrypts the device. The latest several versions of the Android operating system have built-in encryption. Just check the box to encrypt the device within the Security settings. You may need a third-party application if you are running an older version of the Android OS. Actually, if you are running an older version of Android that doesn't have built-in encryption, it's time for you to replace the phone. There are significant security vulnerabilities in the older versions of Android and iOS. You really don't have much to worry about if you are using the latest versions of iOS or Android devices since they are encrypted by default.

Besides PIN-protecting your phone, make sure you encrypt any memory cards or just don't store any sensitive data on them. We're talking about the SD, micro SD, and similar cards that you can insert into the smartphone to increase storage capacity. There are programs available for some models that allow you to encrypt the card contents if the feature is not already built into the phone. The point is, you don't want any confidential information to be accessible on the card if you lose your phone. The PIN will protect the phone access, but the "bad guy" will pop out the memory card and read it from his computer if it is not encrypted.

You should also have security software installed on your device no matter what operating system is running. Despite what some Apple "geniuses" say, Apple products are just as vulnerable as other products and require security software. The antivirus software you use on your computers probably has versions for your smartphones too. This means you can centrally manage all your computers and mobile devices too. As an alternative, we recommend you investigate security software from Lookout, Trend Micro, or Sophos.

Finally, investigate the ability to wipe the data from the smartphone remotely if it is lost. You should have the phone configured to wipe automatically after a set number of invalid unlock attempts. This will clear the data even if you are not connected to a cellular network. Remotely wiping the device on demand requires that it be in communication with the cellular data network. Configure the "Find my iPhone" function within the iCloud settings on an iPhone or iPad. Android devices can use the free Lookout application for the remote wipe function. Google has a new app called Android Device Manager that will help users locate or remotely wipe their phone. You must enable Android Device Manager from the Google settings on your phone and associate the phone with your Google account. Remember that the remote wipe feature is for the memory within the phone itself and may not wipe the memory cards we spoke about earlier.

Flash Drives

USB flash drives are those small portable devices that attorneys (and others too) use to transfer data between computers. They are also known as thumb drives. They are inexpensive and vary in capacity from several GB up to several hundred GB of storage space. Since they are portable and small, it is very easy to lose them. This is where encryption is your friend. If you intend to store confidential client information on a flash drive, make sure that the device is encrypted. Some encryption software for your computer can also be used to encrypt the flash drive. There are also flash drives that have built-in encryption capabilities. The DataTraveler series from Kingston and IronKey are good choices for encrypted flash drives.

Final Words

The options and requirements for mobile security have certainly changed quickly over the years. Talk to us next year and we're sure the world will have changed again. For now, make sure that you are aware of all the issues related to secure data transfer and that you are not relying on antiquated knowledge. You must assume that there is absolutely no protection of the communication stream between your laptop and your remote device. We've seen hotel networks that didn't have a firewall, so all traffic was allowed to flow through. We immediately saw probing attacks on our computers, which were stopped by the firewalls on our laptops. It's the wild, wild West out there, and you're the only marshal in town. Good luck, Wyatt.

CHAPTER TWENTY-THREE

More from Apple

Apart from the information conveyed previously about Mac laptops and desktops, we want to offer you additional Apple recommendations in light of the continued interest lawyers have shown in potentially switching to Mac computers. Many lawyers may have never used a Mac, either in their personal life or for their job, but most have used one Apple product or another. Most are familiar with the very popular iPhone and iPad. Many people continue to argue that Macs are ready for prime time, to take on Windows-based PCs in the business setting. From a hardware standpoint, Macs are just as good as, if not better than, PCs. You can't really tell them apart since Macs made the switch to using Intel-based processors. The major difference now is the operating system, which is still the main obstacle preventing Macs from gaining a greater piece of the pie in the business marketplace—but this may changes as more solo and small firms move their services to the cloud.

Frankly, the main problem lies with software compatibility with Macs. Most law firms, no matter the size, use legal-specific software on a daily basis to do their jobs. Whether you're looking at case management, billing, or trial-related or practice-specific software, most vendors still do not make versions for Macs. However, this argument is becoming more of a nonissue as vendors move their applications to the cloud. But for lawyers who use a computer just for word processing, Internet research, filing of motions, billing, and accounting, a Mac could suit these functions perfectly.

However, centralized management is much more difficult, if not impossible, in a Mac environment. Group policies and multiple third-party tools enable a very cost-effective way to distribute updates and restrict abilities in a Windows environment. The lack of native ability for centralized control and restrictions of Macs makes them less desirable (and much more costly) to deploy in an enterprise setting. Macs are more expensive to maintain because you have to touch each individual Mac to make changes or install updates. The lack of native centralized control is a large reason you see Macs in solo and small law firms and not uniformly implemented in larger firms. You can purchase additional products to manage Macs in an enterprise, but now you're adding cost and complexity. Below, we discuss some Mac-specific hardware and software solutions that may come in handy if you are or want to become a Mac user.

Hardware

Apple iPad

Year after year, Apple continues to provide its fanboys with more and more enthusiasm about the next version of the iPad, and it has continued to find ways to improve this great device.

In September 2015, Apple released the iPad Pro. This behemoth device, larger than any previously released iPad by almost 3 inches, is targeted toward businesses, with its sights set directly on the Surface Pro market share.

This device comes with either a 9.7 or 12.9-inch Retina display and nearly double the CPU performance of the iPad Air 2. This device is powered by the A9X, a 64-bit, third-generation chip. The 12.9-inch LED-backlit wide-screen multi-touch display boasts a resolution of 2732 × 2048. The refined multi-touch technology adds another dimension to the user experience. The camera has been upgraded to 8 MP and can record 1080p HD video at 30 frames per second. This device also contains four speakers.

The iPad Pro comes with a built-in Wi-Fi network card with two antennas supporting the 802.11ac protocol, enabling the device to connect to wireless networks, and the 4G model comes with a broadband AirCard and GPS locator. The device also includes Bluetooth 4.2 capability and a 38.5 watt-hour battery lasting up to ten hours, even when continually surfing the Internet. This version of the iPad is available with 32, 128, or 256 GB of internal memory at a starting cost of $799.

Since the release of the iPad Pro, Apple has released the next version of its iOS software, version 10, which comes preinstalled on all new iPad devices.

Some of the new features of iOS 10 include

- Updated and improved Siri, including the availability of integration with third-party apps
- Rise to Wake feature: just pick up your iPhone and it will wake up
- The Slide to Unlock feature has been replaced with "Press Home to open"
- Rich lockscreen notifications, including the usage of the 3D Touch to show hidden menu actions
- Revamped Control Center
- Availability of widgets and camera on the Lockscreen
- Updated Maps and Music
- New Home app to control all household devices, "iOT"

In our opinion, the last revolutionary change to the iOS software was iOS 5, when Apple introduced its iCloud service. The iCloud service allows users to synchronize their music, photos, apps, documents, bookmarks, calendar, contacts, e-mail, and other data between multiple iOS devices. As a cloud service, Apple will actually store this data for you in an online account associated with your Apple ID. As with many Apple products, we have determined there are a number of security and privacy concerns with using this service. If you don't believe us, just read the terms of service—we did, and we will not use this service for anything business related. If you have enabled iCloud, be careful with what information you choose to synchronize with Apple. A lot of celebrities now understand that after the Celebgate debacle of 2014, when naked photos of them flooded the Internet. That's all we will say. We only have the Find My iPad feature configured in iCloud so that we can locate the device if lost. Unfortunately, that also means Apple knows where our iPad is at all times.

If you must use the iCloud service, even if only for personal use, we recommend implementing two-factor authentication with this service to provide an extra layer of protection against unauthorized access to your account.

Today, lawyers frequently use the iPad for court or meetings, rather than lugging around a laptop. Originally thought to compete against e-book devices such as the Kindle and Nook, the iPad has actually established a new class of devices that compete against smartphones, netbooks, smaller laptops, and ultrabooks. Lawyers are drawn to the functionality and portability of the device, and we believe their interest will only increase as future generations are released.

Tom Mighell, lawyer and iPad expert, has three wonderful books available to assist lawyers who need help in understanding how to best use the iPad in their practice of law. The three books—iPad in One Hour for Lawyers (make sure you get the third edition), iPad Apps in One Hour for Lawyers, and iPad in One Hour for Litigators (make sure you get the second edition), can be purchased directly from the ABA's webstore and should be considered an invaluable resource for lawyers who are looking to test-drive their iPads at work. You can get all three for less than $150, which is quite a deal!

Having given many lectures on the use of the iPad, we can tell you that this was the largest CLE magnet for the past several years. Although things have slowed a bit, it is clear that the iPad is the tablet of choice for most lawyers. As one of our attendees said while proudly brandishing his iPad, "This is a game-changer."

Apple Watch

Released early in 2015, Apple has entered itself into the field of wearable technology with the release of the Apple Watch. In September 2016, Apple announced the release of the Series 2, or second-generation Apple Watch.

This release completely updates the capabilities of the Apple Watch with the inclusion of a GPS chip inside the casing. So now if you head out for a run you no longer need to lug around your iPhone as well. With the release of a new Swimming app, the Apple Watch is now waterproof up to 50 meters, so go ahead and jump in the pool with it on—it will even track your laps!

There is a new ceramic finish that joins the aluminum and stainless steel cases. The very expensive gold case has been retired. There are also a number of different watch bands available from a variety of designers—Hermes, Nike, and so on—to upgrade the look and feel of your device.

Finally, Apple has made the display twice as bright as the original display, at 1,000 nits. You should have an easier time reading the watch display in sunny weather!

The price of the Apple Watch starts at $369 (ouch!), almost $20 more than the entry-level model of the first generation, and will still need to be paired with an iOS device (iPhone, iPad, or iPod Touch) in order to function fully. At that price, John will keep his solar-energy-charged Citizen Eco-Drive dual time zone watch and avoid having to search for an outlet before going to bed. Why do we include a watch in this book? Because lawyers are starting to use smartwatches to read and respond to texts and e-mails. How useful these watches will be to lawyers is as yet unknown, but wearable tech is a trend worth watching. Apple is making progress—but it's not quite there yet as a phone replacement, and Sharon notes she sees very few lawyers wearing these watches.

Touchfire Case with Keyboard

Some have labeled this keyboard the accessory that turns the iPad into a true laptop "killer." We won't go that far just yet, as we will have to see how much businesses adopt the usage of the iPad Pro, but we are still impressed with this piece of hardware.

This lightweight Bluetooth keyboard is actually a superthin keyboard overlay and not a separate external device like other Bluetooth keyboards. It attaches to the bottom half of your iPad with built-in magnets. This device provides tactile feedback when pressing the patented 3-D keys, enabling users to type much more quickly than on the flat keyboards often used with the iPad.

The Smart Case has a dozen typing and viewing positions to choose from and the keyboard is stored safely behind the iPad when not in use. The Touchfire Case comes with a built-in magnetic mount that allows the iPad to stick to any ferrous metal, such as a refrigerator or a metal-backed whiteboard. The included speaker redirector boosts the iPad's volume to the front by 50 percent.

In terms of compatibility, this device works with all generations of the iPad. If you want to try out this accessory, you can purchase it for $69.99 on the vendor's website. It is offered in four colors: blue, black, red, and light gray.

AirPort Extreme

Apple's AirPort Extreme is its wireless solution for home, school, and business. The wireless router plugs directly into your cable or DSL modem and connects you wirelessly to the Internet. This new version of router supports the 802.11a/b/g/n protocols, including the new 802.11ac standard, which provides data rates of up to 1.3 Gbps—triple the previous 802.11n standard. The wireless router supports NAT, DHCP, and VPN pass-through, allowing users the capability of connecting to their office network from home. The AirPort Extreme comes with built-in security features such as a NAT firewall, WPA (Wi-Fi protected access), WPA/WPA2 and WEP encryption, and MAC address filtering. The router contains one GB Ethernet WAN port for connecting to a cable or DSL modem and three GB Ethernet LAN ports for connecting computers or networking devices. This device supports up to 50 users.

The built-in USB port is provided to connect a printer or hard drive that is shared with other users on the local network. The AirPort Extreme is both Mac and Windows compatible; is 64 percent smaller than its predecessor; is only 6.6 inches from top to bottom; and comes bundled with software, a power cord, and documentation. The AirPort Extreme can be purchased directly online from the Apple Store (store.apple.com) for $199.

AirPort Express

The AirPort Express is a portable wireless router, perfect for taking with you while on the road. However, this device has limited functionality in a business setting, allowing only 50 devices to connect to it at a time. The small wireless router is extremely portable, about the size of a postcard, and weighs less than 8.5 ounces. The router supports the 802.11a/b/g/n protocols and offers simultaneous dual-band 802.11n, transmitting at both the 2.4 GHz and 5 GHz frequencies at the same time. This provides 802.11n support no matter which band your wireless devices use. This wireless device is great for hotels, supplying your laptop with wireless Internet so you can surf from any location in the room.

The device has a built-in USB port for connecting a shared printer and an Ethernet port for connecting to your DSL and cable modem or your local network. The built-in wireless security supports WPA/WPA2, WEP, NAT, MAC address filtering, and time-based access control. The AirPort Express is both Mac and Windows compatible and comes bundled with the necessary software to get your computer connected to the wireless network. The device even allows the option for a guest network that provides users with access to the Internet, but not other parts of your local network such as your computers, printers, and network-attached drives. The AirPort Express can be purchased directly online from the Apple Store (store.apple.com) for $99.

AirPort Time Capsule

Looking for a solution to back up your files automatically? Time Capsule works seamlessly with Time Machine, backup software included with the Mac OS X operating system. Time Capsule is simply a wireless router with a built-in hard drive used for storing backups of your files. Using the Time Machine backup software, the application will back up your files and folders automatically, without user intervention. The data is backed up over the local wireless network to the Time Capsule hardware device.

Time Capsule can be purchased and used solely as a backup solution, or it can also provide wireless Internet connectivity to your local network. It has the same built-in features and functionality as AirPort Extreme. Time Capsule is offered in two models, with storage capacities of 2 and 3 TB. Time Capsule, like the AirPort Express, supports the new 802.11ac protocol, offering data rates of up to 1.3 Gbps. This device can be purchased directly online from the Apple Store (store.apple.com) starting at $299 for the 2 TB model.

Apple Magic Keyboard

The Apple Magic Keyboard uses Bluetooth wireless technology, eliminating the need for obstructive and unfriendly wires to connect your keyboard to your computer. The wireless keyboard comes in a low-profile anodized aluminum frame that matches the Apple theme and takes up 24 percent less space on your desktop than full-size keyboards. The keyboard contains function keys for one-touch access to Mac features and has power management features to conserve the batteries when not in use.

The Apple wireless keyboard requires Mac OS X version 10.11 or later, contains a rechargeable battery that lasts up to a month or more between charges, and can also be used with the iPad. It can be purchased directly online from the Apple Store (store.apple.com) for $99.

Apple Magic Mouse

Like the Apple wireless keyboard, the Magic Mouse uses Bluetooth wireless technology to connect the mouse to your computer. Laser tracking allows you to use the mouse on a number of surfaces while maintaining the precision and accuracy of tracking movement. The mouse uses multi-touch-sensitive technology to detect both right and left clicks, and the innovative scrolling ball allows for 360-degree scrolling capabilities. The mouse is powered with a rechargeable battery, and when paired with the Apple Magic Keyboard, allows you to work wire-free at your desk. This wireless device requires Mac OS X version 10.11 or later to operate. Sorry, folks, but there is no mouse support for the iPad, so this is limited to working with Apple computers only. The Apple Magic Mouse can be purchased directly online from the Apple Store (store.apple.com) for $79.

Apple iPod

At one time Apple's most successful hardware device, the iPod has sold over 350 million units since its creation in 2001, and this number released by Apple hasn't been updated since 2012. It has only been supplanted by the iPhone in total sales within the past few years. In fact, since the summer of

2015, Apple has removed the iPod from its menu bar and replaced it with the Music heading. You have to go to the Apple Store in order to view information about the iPod devices and/or visit the page directly at www.apple.com/ipod.

The portable digital-file-playing devices are the most popular handheld multimedia devices in use today, and some models can be used to play and shoot video, take pictures, play podcasts, and even play games. All models are capable of playing music. The iPod is available in three models: Shuffle, Nano, and Touch. The iPod Shuffle is the smallest, with no display screen, and is available in a 2 GB size. The Shuffle allows you to shake the device in certain positions to change the song, play the songs in order, or shuffle the order. The newest version also includes a new VoiceOver function that will tell you the song or artist you're listening to. The iPod Shuffle costs $49 and is available in six different colors.

The iPod Nano is one of Apple's more popular devices and has just recently had a makeover. The current version of the Nano includes a radio tuner with live pause functionality, VoiceOver, and even a pedometer. Some of the new features include a 2.5-inch multi-touch display, the ability to play video, Bluetooth 4.0, Nike+ support, and the Apple EarPods. This device has been updated with Apple's new Lightning connector pin. The iPod Nano is offered in six bright colors, and it is available only with 16 GB of storage capacity. The cost is just $149. Flash memory is used in the Nano, making it ideal for workouts at the gym.

The iPod Touch is probably the most versatile iPod, providing users with a way to listen to music, watch videos, and play games, as well as surf the Internet and check their e-mail. Like the Nano, the iPod Touch just went through its own refresh. The latest version is much thinner and lighter than the previous models, weighing just 3.1 ounces. It comes with a four-inch Retina display, upgraded iSight 8-megapixel camera, upgraded A8 chip with 64-bit architecture, and the Apple EarPods. The iPod Touch has a four-inch diagonal color display and a touchscreen interface, and it is available in 16, 32, 64, and 128 GB sizes. The iPod Touch even has a built-in Wi-Fi network adapter supporting 802.11ac network connections. The device also includes Bluetooth 4.1 and Nike+ support. The iPod Touch costs anywhere from $199 to $399, depending on the model capacity.

All of the iPod devices can be purchased online from the Apple Store or at your local electronics retailer. The devices are both Windows and Mac compatible, and they connect to your computer using a USB connection.

Software

Microsoft Office 2016 for Mac

Microsoft Office for Mac 2016 is the latest version of Office for Macs and includes better compatibility across platforms, improved collaboration tools, and an improved user interface. Microsoft Office for Mac includes Word, PowerPoint, Excel, Outlook, and OneNote. Some of the new features include new Online Template files; a redesigned interface and sharper graphics to take advantage of the Retina display; the ability to navigate documents and files using multi-touch gestures; and the integration with OneDrive, One-Drive for Business, and SharePoint. One of the improved features in this version that lawyers may find useful is the co-authoring feature, which enables several people to work simultaneously in the same Word document at the same time.

Like the Windows-based counterpart, users are able to opt to subscribe to Office365 instead of purchasing the stand-alone version of Office for Mac. Depending on the subscription level, users may be able to install Office for Mac on up to five computers.

The stand-alone version of Office for Mac 2016 requires Mac OS X v. 10.10 and can be purchased from Microsoft's webstore (www.microsoftstore.com) for $229.99 for the Home & Business edition.

Toast 15 Titanium by Roxio

Toast 15 Titanium is the latest version of Roxio's long-running disc-burning software for the Mac. With this software, you can burn video or data to CDs or DVDs. This version gives users the ability to burn high-definition video to Blu-ray discs and record content directly from their screen with Live Screen Capture. Toast even allows a user to capture streaming audio from any website and then transfer the audio to an iPod or any other iOS-based device. The software has built-in basic features, such as the ability to compress, convert, and compile video in most formats, along with backup software that can be scheduled to back up your data. Features new to this version include the ability to extract clips from any DVD video and convert them to a format of your choice, to convert audiobook CDs for playback on iPod devices, and to build your MP3 library with the automatic capture and tagging of Internet audio. New to this version is the capability for users to convert video recorded on their TiVo DVRs, EyeTV tuners, and Flip Video camcorders to play on their iPad, iPhone, or video game consoles. Users can even share their video compilations directly to YouTube, Twitter, Google+, and Facebook.

This latest version added support to trim video clips with a new, simple video editor. Roxio also include a Secure Burn option that allows users to encrypt files on removable media with the selection of this option.

The software can be purchased online from Roxio's website (www.roxio.com) for $99.99.

Norton Security for Mac

Every Mac user needs to protect his or her computer from viruses and other threats. Using antivirus protection on a Mac is no longer an option; it's a necessity. Norton Security has an edition specifically for Mac computers that offers protection from the latest viruses, spyware, rootkits, and other web-based attacks. Norton Security is compatible with the previous two versions of Mac OS X, which would be 10.11 and 10.10.

The antivirus protection can automatically scan and clean downloaded e-mail files and attachments and provide real-time protection and removal of viruses and other threats.

Some users still believe there are no viruses or threats for a Mac. Not so. Just look at how many systems were infected with the Backdoor.MAC.Eleanor malware, MacDefender, or Flashback Trojan over the past few years. These were such a problem that Apple released security patches just to address these specific threats. There are many other documented viruses and vulnerabilities that are specific to Macs and many more that are operating system–independent. The message here is to get and install a full-blown (not just antivirus) security solution. You should never use a computer on your business or home network without the proper security protection, even if it's a Mac. Apple itself removed from its website (rather late, in 2012) language suggesting that it was impervious to malware. Norton Security can be purchased online directly from Symantec's website (www.symantec.com) for $39.99 for a one-year subscription.

Kaspersky Internet Security for Mac

For users looking for an alternative to Norton Internet Security, Kaspersky has a great product called Kaspersky Internet Security for Mac. We use Kaspersky's security software on our networks and have tried this product on our Mac laptop, and it works as advertised. This software offers real-time protection against malware, phishing, and malicious websites, as well as antivirus protection and parental controls. This product requires Mac OS X 10.7 or higher to run. This product can be purchased online from Kaspersky's website (www.kaspersky.com) for $49.95 for a one-year subscription.

Intuit Quicken 2016 for Mac

Intuit Quicken for Mac offers a complete personal financial management package, providing immediate access to your accounts from a single location. By using Quicken, you can better organize your financial information and easily track your finances. Quicken provides a simple way to track and enter expenses without launching the entire application through the Quick-Entry Dashboard Widget. Some of the new features allow you to check your account balances and budget on the go using the free mobile app, which syncs the data between your phone and your computer. Users can also pay bills directly from within Quicken. The new 12-month budget feature allows you to customize your budget with the labeling of expenses and easily track spending and income against the plan to stay on target. The Portfolio Time Machine allows you to see holdings and value at a particular date and time, and a new feature is provided that allows users to transfer money between different accounts within your bank. Finally, this product also allows you to see all of your accounts in one place. The software will run only on Intel-based Macs using 10.10 or higher.

Quicken users can export their basic tax information to TurboTax and other applications that can read a TXF or QXF file.

If you need to switch your data files from Quicken Windows to Quicken Mac, there is a single-click walk-through conversion feature that will do it all right on your Mac. No Windows computer is required to use this conversion feature.

Quicken 2016 for Mac is the latest version of the software from Intuit that is available for purchase and download on its website (www.intuit.com) for $64.99.

QuickBooks 2016 Desktop for Macs

QuickBooks, another financial and accounting package from Intuit, has an edition for Macs. QuickBooks 2016 Desktop for Macs can be used to organize your business finances. This software package will also track and manage your business expenses, invoicing, and payroll from a single financial application. QuickBooks for Macs can synchronize your contacts directly with the Mac OS X Address Book and set reminders in iCal. This software is compatible with Mac OS X v. 10.10 or higher.

Some of the new features added and improvements made in this edition include

- Faster launch time and better performance
- Ability to print directly on envelopes
- Users can resize columns on invoices and other forms
- Timesheets are easier to fill out

QuickBooks 2016 Desktop for Macs can be purchased online from Intuit's QuickBooks website (www.quickbooks.intuit.com) for $219.95 for a new license. Two- and three-user versions are also available for purchase on the website.

Symantec Drive Encryption for Mac OS X

PGP Corporation (now owned by Symantec), a leading vendor of hard disk encryption software, has released an updated version of its hard disk encryption suite compatible with Mac computers (previously called Symantec Full Disk Encryption for Macs). Symantec Drive Encryption software provides comprehensive, nonstop disk encryption for Macs, securing data on desktops, laptops, and removable devices. A user name and passphrase are required to decrypt the contents of the hard disk, protecting the data from unauthorized access. Symantec Drive Encryption requires Mac OS X version 10.8.4 or higher and only runs on Intel-based Macs. Symantec Drive Encryption can be used to provide quick, cost-effective data protection for information on hard drives and removable media. Any lawyer using a Mac laptop should definitely have this software installed to protect sensitive and confidential information. An alternative is to enable File Vault or File Vault 2, which is included as part of the Mac operating system.

Symantec Drive Encryption software can be purchased online directly from Symantec's website (www.symantec.com) for $85 for a single license with one-year upgrade assurance.

Apple iTunes

If you've ever owned an iPod or older version of the iPhone or iPad, then you're certainly familiar with Apple iTunes. It is Apple's most popular software product, mainly because it was necessary for managing your digital music library on your iPod, iPhone, iPad, or other Apple iOS device. The newest version of iTunes allows users to download more content with their purchased songs, such as the album cover, band pictures, and even song lyrics. Using the Home Sharing feature, users can share their digital libraries with up to five authorized computers in their home, allowing them to share purchased music files across multiple computer systems. Apple now allows you to follow your favorite artists and view what music your friends are downloading and listening to. A new feature called iTunes Match lets you store all of your music in iCloud—even songs you've imported from CDs—synchronizing your music across all of your iOS devices. iCloud provides users with the ability to access their music, TV shows, apps, and books from multiple devices without the need to synchronize files manually using iTunes across multiple iOS devices.

Using the iTunes Store, users can download apps, music, videos, podcasts, and more and then synchronize them to their devices, such as an iPad or iPhone. Users can subscribe to podcasts, and without any user input, the iTunes application can download the latest shows as they're made available. We use this feature a lot when it comes to managing the legal technology podcasts to which we subscribe and constantly monitor.

Apple's new Music service, which was released in 2015, allows users to subscribe to and stream any track within Apple's music library. Currently, Apple is offering a three-month trial membership for the service. Once the trial period ends, membership is currently priced at $9.99 per user per month or $14.99 for a family membership per month.

Apple iTunes is available as a free download for Mac OS X and Windows 10 from Apple's website.

Apple Pay

Apple Pay is a mobile payment and digital wallet service provided by Apple that lets users make payments using the iPhone, iPad, or Apple Watch devices at physical stores, within apps, or on the web. This service doesn't require Apple-specific terminals and is compatible with Visa's PayWave, MasterCard's PayPass, and American Express's ExpressPay terminals for in-store purchases. To use this service, users must register a credit card with Apple Pay. This service uses near field communication (NFC) to communicate with the payment terminals and is increasing in popularity as users move to paying with their mobile devices rather than fumbling for their wallets. A listing of major retailers that now accept Apple Pay can be found on Apple's website at http://www.apple.com/apple-pay/where-to-use/. As more and more retailers begin to accept this form of payment, the usage of this payment method will only increase.

CHAPTER TWENTY-FOUR

iWin: iPad for Litigators

by Tom Mighell, Esq., and Paul Unger, Esq.

Introduction and Tour of iPad

In the six years since Apple released the iPad, it has firmly established itself as a very useful tool for lawyers, and one of the biggest innovations in legal technology to come along in some time. The iPad's design is ingenious and handsome. Its functionality is equally as nice and continues to improve as legal software developers create new and innovative apps for lawyers. Indeed, the iPad remains the tablet of choice for legal app developers, far outpacing Android and Windows tablets in the number of legal apps available.

Tablets are now integrating themselves into the workflow of lawyers, irrespective of firm size or practice area, and nowhere has this been more apparent than for litigators. Whether you need to take notes, mark and handle exhibits, or manage deposition transcripts, these little computers can supercharge your trial practice. But the iPad can make any lawyer more productive, regardless of practice; while we primarily discuss how litigators can use tablet computers to enhance their day in court, we will also provide a general overview for anyone interested in using the iPad (see Figure 24.1) in your practice.

Why Use an iPad in Your Practice?

We like to describe the iPad as an "instant-on" computer that you can control with your finger. There's no booting-up process, and no keyboard is

Figure 24.1. An iPad

needed (but as we'll discuss below, you'll still want to have one). It provides instant access to information traditionally accessed from your desktop computer or laptop.

Although the iPad's initial purpose was thought to be as a "consumption" device—a tablet used primarily for reading and accessing information and very light typing—its ease of use and big screen is so addicting that it evolved into a tool that can do so much more, especially for lawyers. And now that Apple boasts the new iPad Pro, which can replace your laptop completely, some "lighter" users of computers may want to consider whether it makes sense for you to go all iPad, all the time.

Further, with the release of the iPad Pro and Apple Pencil, we are hard-pressed to find a better writing experience. It is so similar to writing on paper that we have both almost completely stopped writing on paper legal pads. The benefits of an electronic legal pad are huge. You will enjoy the best experience with the 12.9-inch iPad Pro because it mimics the dimensions of an actual legal pad. Paul uses it almost exclusively for legal pad note-taking, then just e-mails himself the PDF version of the notes and saves them within a document management system or electronic client filing structure. We have compared the writing experience with a Surface Pro and really enjoy the experience on the iPad with Notability much more. It's just plain easy and enjoyable. Using the Apple Pencil is incredibly natural and easy. It charges in minutes and holds its charge quite well. We're not sure why they call it a pencil because it is truly a pen, pencil, marker, highlighter, and so on, of any color or point size. Even without the Apple

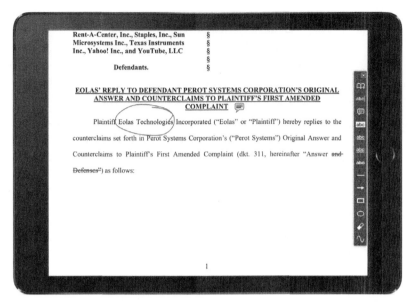

Figure 24.2. Viewing Documents

Pencil, if you carry around a legal pad and a lot of paper in a legal file or Redweld, the iPad can become your legal pad and digital folder. It is truly redefining the idea of the "paperless law office," allowing you to carry most of your office around with you, all in a very small, light device. For courtroom work, the iPad can be used to access exhibits, pleadings, legal research, depositions, and just about any document you might need in hearings or at trial (see Figure 24.2).

Trial presentation apps are available for the iPad that make it easy to display those exhibits on projectors or monitors (wired or wireless) in the courtroom.

Overview

If you want to learn more about using the iPad, check out Tom's books *iPad in One Hour for Lawyers* (3rd edition) and *iPad in One Hour for Litigators* (2nd edition), both published by the ABA and available in the ABA webstore.

Why Use an iPad in the Courtroom?

Certainly, most of you have seen an iPad at this point (see Figures 24.3 and 24.4). Although Apple believes you can ditch your laptop or desktop and go "all iPad," we aren't completely convinced. For those of you who rely on

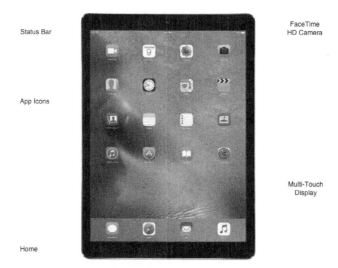

Status Bar

FaceTime
HD Camera

App Icons

Multi-Touch
Display

Home

Figure 24.3. Front View

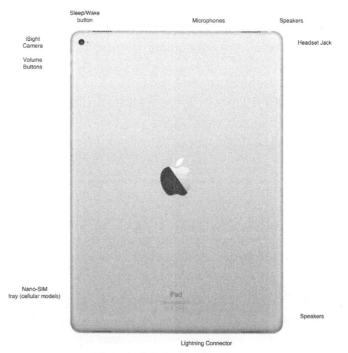

Sleep/Wake
button

Microphones

Speakers

iSight
Camera

Headset Jack

Volume
Buttons

Nano-SIM
tray (cellular models)

iPad

Speakers

Lightning Connector

Figure 24.4. Back View

Microsoft Office, Adobe Acrobat, and various practice management tools in your practice, the iPad has some definite drawbacks as a computing tool. For those who use Microsoft Excel or any other spreadsheet application, a full PC or Mac would be a much better tool. However, we would argue the iPad is *the* ideal courtroom tool, because (1) it is so light and easy to hold and operate, and (2) it is very easy to understand and use, with little training required. (In fact, if you already use an iPhone, you'll be able to start working with an iPad right away.)

Among the often-cited negatives of the iPad are (1) that it has no USB port for plugging the tablet into other devices and (2) that the battery is not removable or replaceable. One of the reasons that the lack of a USB port is not troubling is that the iPad comes with Bluetooth capability, so keyboards, printers, and other devices can be connected wirelessly to the device. Also, a number of cloud providers (Dropbox, Box, and SpiderOak, among others) make it easy for you to access all of your documents online, without needing to connect your iPad to anything. Further, a full charge on an iPad will last about ten hours, meaning you can usually get through a full day in court without having to recharge (but make sure you bring charging cables, just in case).

The new iPad Pro now comes in two flavors. The 12.9-inch model offers a large screen by iPad standards, similar to a small laptop. The 9.7-inch model is the newer brother to the iPad Air 2, and is nearly half as light as the 12.9-inch version. Apple still offers the iPad Air 2 as well as a new version of the iPad Mini, but we recommend the iPad Pro for the litigator. The larger screen of the 12.9-inch model does allow you to do more when working with documents, legal research, and notes in court, but the 9.7-inch iPad is an excellent choice as well. Note: Apple's iOS 10 operating system, released as this book is published, will not support early versions of the iPad, including the iPad 1, 2, 3, and original iPad Mini—so take our advice and use a newer model.

In our opinion, the iPad's ease of use explains why these tablets are rapidly catching on with trial lawyers. A laptop, netbook, or even the "traditional" convertible tablet PCs, which are useful at counsel table, cannot be carried around the courtroom easily when the lawyer is standing at the podium or addressing the jury. We firmly believe the iPad is the preferred mobile device for trial lawyers, because the apps designed for use in the courtroom are very powerful, but also simple enough that they will not distract from actually trying a case.

Essentially, the iPad is just a little heavier than a paper legal pad and not nearly as heavy as the lightest netbook or laptop.

When selecting a jury, it doesn't make sense to question a jury pool while keyboarding your responses into a traditional computer; there's probably no better way to get jurors to clam up and give them the impression that the lawyer is transcribing their personal information. (This is true even though the court reporter may be quietly transcribing it in many cases.) The iPad, however, is ideally configured to take notes on your jury panel, either within a jury selection app or your favorite note-taking application.

Let's take a look at some of the ways a litigator would benefit by using an iPad, from initial receipt of a lawsuit all the way through the jury verdict.

Deadline Calculators

DocketLaw

(Free w/Subscription, http://bit.ly/1nVjjUZ)

CalendarRules' DocketLaw is a rules-based legal calendaring app for the iPhone and iPad. It provides legal professionals with the ability to calculate dates and deadlines based on a customizable database of court rules and statutes. The subscription-based app offers state, federal, bankruptcy, appellate, local, judges, and agency rules for all 50 states.

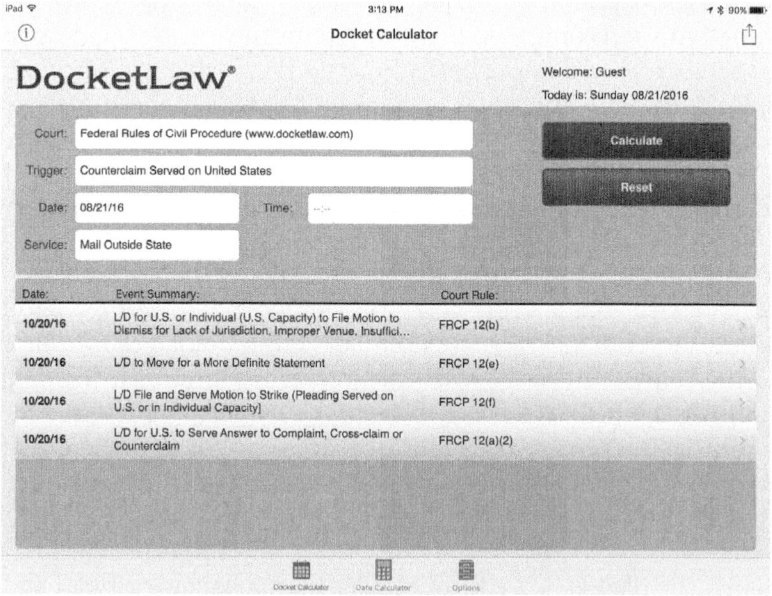

Figure 24.5. DocketLaw

Once you select the court and choose a triggering event (e.g., service of a motion to dismiss or receipt of a complaint), the application will display a list of all events and corresponding dates and deadlines based on that event, along with a description of the corresponding rule. You can add these deadlines to your iPad's calendar app, or e-mail them to clients or others straight from the application.

Lawyer's Professional Assistant

($4.99, http://bit.ly/x5j7Fq)

The Wolfram Lawyer's Professional Assistant (see Figure 24.6) is a reference tool that takes advantage of the company's "Computational Knowledge Engine" to help lawyers with calculations that may be relevant in their practice. Some of the features include

- Calendar computations
- Legal dictionary
- Statutes of limitations for each U.S. state (see Figure 24.7)
- Visa types, including basic requirements, common issues, and extensions and limits
- Financial computations, including fee calculator, settlement calculator, current interest rates, historical value of money, and federal U.S. tax rates.

Figure 24.6. Lawyer's Professional Assistant

Figure 24.7. Statute of Limitations Screen

- Crime rates and history for specific crimes, as well as state and national average comparisons
- Demographics of population and economy for a specific city
- Investigative information, including weather, company information, IP lookup, and blood alcohol calculator
- Damages and estate planning computations for occupational salaries, cost of living, life expectancy, and present or future value

Note: This app has not been updated in over two years, which suggests the app developer is no longer interested in supporting it. We believe the app is still useful, because it is primarily an interface drawing data from the constantly updated Wolfram database.

Depositions and Documents

TranscriptPad

($89.99, http://bit.ly/w7JGHt)

For reviewing and annotating depositions, it is hard to beat an app like TranscriptPad. It does several things very well: (1) You can ditch the bankers boxes full of transcripts, and instead store and organize transcripts by case easily on the iPad; (2) search single transcripts or all transcripts in a case

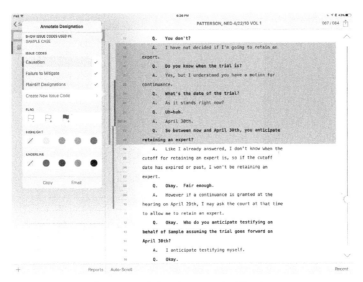

Figure 24.8. TranscriptPad

for key words or phrases; and (3) create issue code and designation reports based on what you review and highlight/tag. It is extremely easy. Once you have taken your depositions, you can load all of the transcripts into TranscriptPad via e-mail, Dropbox, Box, or Citrix ShareFile. The app only accepts text transcripts, so be sure to ask your court reporter for the deposition in TXT format, or convert them to TXT using the free viewer provided by the court reporter. Once it's loaded, you can easily search text, or simply review the testimony, and highlight (or code) the designations with the issues you want to include (see Figure 24.8).

When you complete your designations, it's simple to e-mail them to co-counsel, the judge, your client, or others (see Figure 24.9). If you use TrialDirector or Sanction for evidence presentation, you can also import your designations directly into those tools from TranscriptPad.

DocReviewPad

($89.99, http://apple.co/1KPm8qz)

There aren't many apps that allow you to review large volumes of documents, annotate or otherwise code them, and then Bates stamp all of them with the touch of a button. DocReviewPad is a relatively new app that makes it easy to import, review, code, and then export your documents into TrialPad or some other format for use at trial.

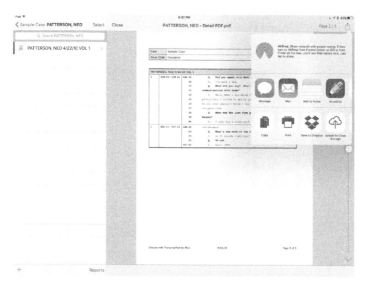

Figure 24.9. TranscriptPad E-mail

Jury Selection/Tracking

iJuror

($14.99, http://bit.ly/xJFIOT)

iJuror is an app developed to assist with jury selection (see Figure 24.10). Features include

- Tap the seats to add juror information
- Track patterns

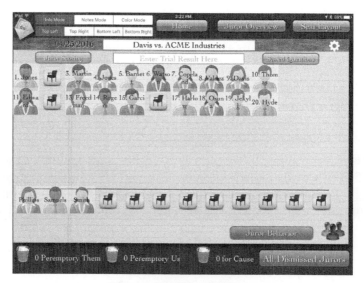

Figure 24.10. iJuror

- E-mail the jury information to any e-mail address
- Configure seating arrangements for up to 96 prospective jurors
- Get easy access to popular social networks to conduct quick research on potential jury members
- Add notes as the trial goes along, and score jurors based on their answers to voir dire questions
- Name view provides quick access to names and notes.
- Drag and drop to choose jurors
- Drag and drop to choose alternates
- Drag and drop to dismiss jurors

Honorable Mentions

- **JuryStar** ($9.99, http://bit.ly/S38DSJ). Similar to iJuror, but it requires you to manually enter a lot more information.
- **JuryTracker** ($1.99, http://bit.ly/xpvyuO). This app goes to work after you have selected your jury; it works as your "personal jury consultant" to help track the reactions of jury members throughout the trial (see Figure 24.11).

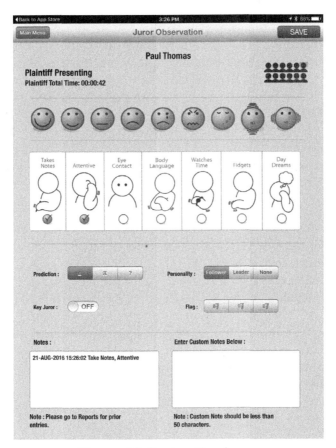

Figure 24.11. JuryTracker

Evidence Presentation

TrialPad

($129.99, http://bit.ly/1BOrw5o)

TrialPad is a legal document and exhibit management and presentation tool originally developed for lawyers to use in the courtroom. Lawyers and other legal professionals also are finding other great ways to use the app, including client presentations and law school lectures. With TrialPad, you can organize, manage, annotate, and store your documents and video while leveraging the portability of your iPad. It is designed to work like full-featured tools such as Sanction or TrialDirector; however, because the iPad is not as powerful as your laptop, TrialPad does not offer all the functionality of traditional trial presentation software. But for many types of trials and hearings, TrialPad is the ideal presentation tool.

TrialPad differs from programs like PowerPoint or Keynote in that the presenter can present documents, images, and video in any order. It's possible to jump around, zoom, magnify, or annotate an exhibit on the fly. TrialPad is not really a competitor to PowerPoint or Keynote because it was designed to handle different situations; PowerPoint and Keynote are designed for more rehearsed linear presentations (opening and closing), where TrialPad works in more spontaneous situations like witness examination. Unlike PDF readers, it lets you create separate case folders, organize and sort important documents, and dynamically annotate and present documents via its flexible output options.

TrialPad cannot handle huge amounts of data as well as a PC can with TrialDirector, Sanction, or OnCue (or a Mac with TrialSmart), and its video editing tool is not as powerful, but it works very well for hearings and most cases with manageable volumes of records. Features include

- Organize and present evidence electronically (see Figure 24.12). Import process via Dropbox, Box, Citrix ShareFile, Transporter, WebDAV server, e-mail, or iTunes.
- No Internet connection is needed once files are loaded.
- Present wirelessly with Apple TV or AirServer (requires iPad 2 and above).
- Highlight, annotate, redact, and zoom in on your documents (see Figure 24.13).
- Make multiple callouts from documents or depositions.
- View documents side by side, comparing pages.
- Edit video clips or take snapshots of frames of surveillance video.

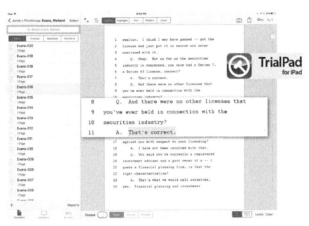

Figure 24.12. Presenting Evidence with TrialPad

- Create Key Docs with saved annotations, and then print or e-mail them with the annotations.
- Have your expert mark up an exhibit and save it as a Key Doc for closing.
- Use the whiteboard tool to draw freehand.
- Create separate case and witness folders.
- File formats supported: Adobe Acrobat PDF, JPG, PNG, TIFF, multipage TIFF, and TXT. (Also imports DOC, DOCX, XLS, XLSX, PPT, PPTX, Keynote, Pages, and Numbers. Note: Our best-practices recommendation is to convert these files to Adobe Acrobat to maintain the formatting and look of the original document.)
- Video formats supported: All formats supported by iPad, such as .m4v, .mp4, and .mov

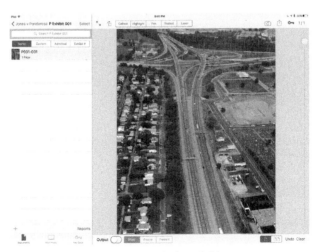

Figure 24.13. TrialPad Photo

Honorable Mentions

- **ExhibitView** ($89.99, http://bit.ly/1nLriZS). This app is a worthy competitor to TrialPad. It offers a "Witness View," where you can hand the witness your iPad to view an exhibit without showing any of your other case files.
- **TrialDirector** (Free, http://bit.ly/ZW8xb1). If you or your firm uses the PC version of TrialDirector, using the iPad version in court is a no-brainer. Even if you don't use the full desktop version, this is still a good evidence presentation tool, and you can't beat the price.

Legal Research

When you go to court, how many rulebooks do you bring with you? During trial or a hearing, it's important to have access to the case law, codes, and rules that are applicable in your case. Tools like the iPad now make it easy to have access to your entire law library, no matter where you happen to be. Here are a few of the tools we like:

- Fastcase (Free, http://bit.ly/ysOcTY) It's the companion to the legal research service.
- Westlaw (Free, http://bit.ly/z5pKRs; requires Westlaw subscription) A great tool for the courtroom, it allows you to conduct legal research, annotate the results, and e-mail case law to the judge or others.
- Lexis Advance HD (Free, http://bit.ly/vo7wzp; requires Lexis subscription) Similar to Westlaw, LexisAdvance provides most of the same features for accessing your Lexis account.
- RuleBook (Free with in-app purchases, http://bit.ly/1tgxNXf) Offers access to court rules and selected statutes of 23 states, which are available on an à la carte basis.
- Thomson Reuters ProView (Free, http://bit.ly/wVrUZc; requires purchase of rulebooks)—If you practice in a jurisdiction that has rules published by Thomson Reuters, you can access the full version of those rulebooks on your iPad with this app.

Courtroom Chatting

BT Chat HD

(Free, http://bit.ly/xE16tG)

If you have ever had the need to pass a note discreetly in the courtroom, you will completely understand the need for this app (see Figure 24.14).

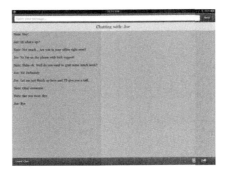

Figure 24.14. BT Chat HD

With BT Chat HD, you can chat with other iPad users via Bluetooth or Wi-Fi (Wi-Fi is better if sitting at a distance).

Other Must-Have iPad Apps

So many apps—which one is best? There are many incredible apps for the iPad. In fact, there are so many that you will probably be overwhelmed about which ones to select, especially if you are new to the iPad.

We have listed our picks below, and we also have some honorable mentions. Some of our honorable mentions may end up being your top picks. Don't let this overwhelm you. With so many fantastic apps out there, it is hard to go wrong. In deciding which apps are best for you, follow these guiding principles:

- There are probably a dozen apps that accomplish the same thing. Review legal app blogs, consumer reviews, and ask trusted people what they recommend.
- Your workplace may prefer one app over another. Consistency and uniformity at the office is typically a good thing.
- If your co-workers or friends use the app, they can provide you with a support network to better learn and use the app.
- If a new app is released from a competing software company, don't be too quick to switch! Your app will probably catch up fast and may have features the other app doesn't have yet. Remember your time invested in the app you already own.
- Apps are cheap; if you are curious, just buy it. Most apps are less than $10. The most expensive app cited in these materials is $129.99.
- If you want more recommendations, check out Tom's book, *iPad Apps in One Hour for Lawyers*—he lists more than 200 of his choices

for the best productivity, document creation and management, legal, travel, and leisure-time apps in the App Store. It's available from the ABA webstore.

Dropbox

(Free, http://bit.ly/z54Tpv; Free Dropbox account up to 2GB at www.dropbox.com)

Paul and Tom's Top Pick

If you have an iPad, Dropbox is almost mandatory. Setting aside debates about security, Dropbox has become the gold standard for storing files and getting them to the iPad. Most software developers build their apps to integrate with Dropbox because it has become so widely used.

Dropbox sets up a local folder on your computer that allows you to create any subfolder structure. These subfolders synchronize into the cloud and can be shared with other people (clients, co-counsel, co-workers, etc.), if desired. The iPad can also connect to your Dropbox account so it can see and access everything that you can see on your PC (see Figure 24.15).

If you can create a folder, copy and paste, and drag and drop, you can use Dropbox. If you need to edit a document, you can open it directly in Word, or leave comments for others on your team to see, all from within the app.

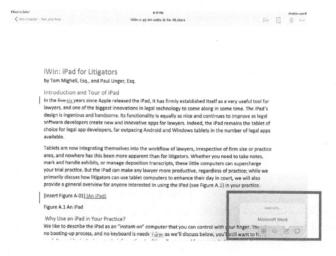

Figure 24.15. The iPad's View of a Dropbox Account

Dictate + Connect

($16.99, http://bit.ly/wuv1Mq)

Paul's Top Pick

Dictate + Connect is a dictation application for your iPhone or iPad (see Figure 24.16). Like a traditional digital recorder, it allows you to rewind, overwrite, and insert anywhere. Download recordings, send as e-mails, or upload to Dropbox, iCloud, FTP (File Transfer Protocol), or WebDAV.

GoodReader

($1.99, http://apple.co/2bajRLT)

Paul and Tom's Top Pick

Since documents are the lifeblood of the legal profession, it makes sense that one of the best uses of the iPad in a law practice is to read and annotate documents. GoodReader is best described as a universal document viewer, although it arguably works best with the PDF file format (see Figure 24.17).

It provides excellent annotation tools for PDF files, including the ability to highlight text, insert text boxes, post sticky notes, compose freehand

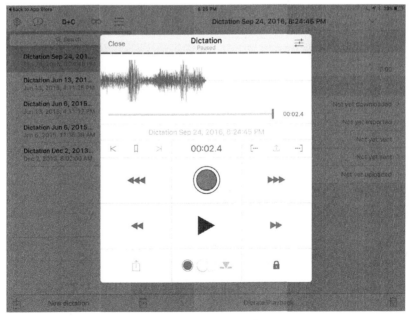

Figure 24.16. Dictate + Connect

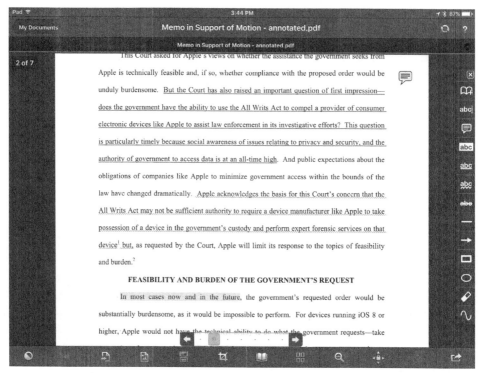

Figure 24.17. GoodReader

drawings, and add lines, arrows, rectangles, and so on (see Figure 24.18). These tools are extremely useful when you're reading a court opinion or law review article.

Figure 24.18. GoodReader Annotations

GoodReader also has a robust file manager and has the ability to sync directly with your accounts from Dropbox, Box.com, Google Drive, One-Drive, or even your own web-connected server (see Figure 24.19).

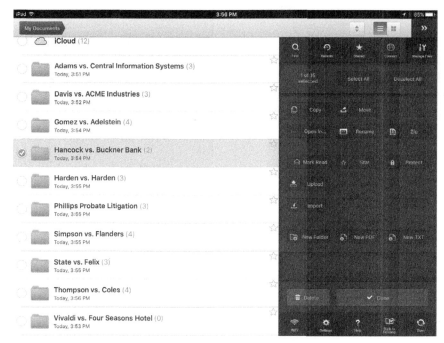

Figure 24.19. GoodReader File Management

PDF Expert

($9.99, http://bit.ly/1ra1wjz)

Paul and Tom's Top Pick

Many lawyers use PDF Expert because (1) clients can sign documents that can then be e-mailed back to the office and (2) form-fillable PDFs can now be "mobile" and filled out on the go (see Figure 24.20).

Similar to GoodReader, PDF Expert will let you read and annotate PDF files, and has just the right amount of annotation tools a lawyer would need. But PDF Expert offers a few additional features that appeal to legal professionals and are hard to find in other apps.

PDF Expert supports PDF forms and allows you to fill them in using text fields, check boxes, radio buttons, and other form elements. You can create a PDF form on your computer and transfer it to your iPad when you need to complete the form away from the office.

Figure 24.20. PDF Expert

Microsoft Office for iPad

(Free, http://bit.ly/1e17n4j (Word), http://bit.ly/1g8csnl (Excel), http://bit.ly/1jApmPu (PowerPoint)

Paul and Tom's Top Pick

Microsoft has finally brought its Office suite to the iPad, and for Office users, this is the recommended set of apps to use. Frankly, they are the work productivity apps *everyone* should be using on the iPad. Working in these apps is almost like working in the desktop versions of Word, Excel, and PowerPoint, although Microsoft modified the layout to better accommodate the tablet interface. The experience using these apps is the closest you'll get on the iPad to working with the real thing.

Even better, the apps are free to download for basic review and editing. For more advanced editing or creation of documents, however, you'll have to purchase a subscription to Microsoft's Office 365 product; this can range between $69 and $150 per year, depending on the version you purchase. This is actually a good deal—for this price, you get five licenses to Microsoft Office. Further, there's no need to wait for the next version to come out, then use CDs to install it on your computer. The Office 365 model is download-only, so as Microsoft releases new versions of the software, it is downloaded and your computer is automatically updated.

The Office apps also allow you to save documents to cloud storage, with connections available to OneDrive, OneDrive for Business, Dropbox, and SharePoint.

We highly recommend the use of Office apps on the iPad, especially if you plan to spend a lot of time on your tablet creating and revising documents, or presenting slideshows (see Figure 24.21).

Figure 24.21. PowerPoint for iPad

Honorable Mention

- **Documents To Go Premium** ($16.99, http://bit.ly/A5LPMq). If you don't want to pay for Microsoft Office, Documents To Go is currently your best low-cost option. While it does not come close to the functionality of Microsoft Word or Excel for iPad, Docs To Go provides basic editing tools for Word, Excel, and PowerPoint documents. It also connects to most major cloud services for easy sharing and syncing. Note: At the time of writing this app had not been updated in more than nine months, perhaps indicating the developer's recognition that Office apps are becoming the dominant option on the iPad.

Notability

($7.99, http://bit.ly/wZT4wD)

Paul and Tom's Top Pick

Very few note-taking apps perform all three functions of handwriting, typing, and audio. We have found that Notability provides a great writing experience. You can change the thickness of the pen and the width of lines and add lines and gridlines—all important to simulate an experience similar to writing on a piece of paper (see Figure 24.22).

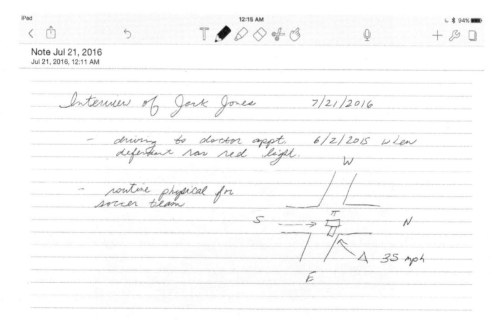

Figure 24.22. Notability

You can use your finger to write notes on the iPad, but we recommend investing in an Apple Pencil if you have the iPad Pro, or a traditional stylus for the earlier iPad models so the writing experience is as similar as possible to writing on paper with a pen.

The audio feature not only records your meetings, conferences, or other gatherings but also synchronizes the recording to your notes so that you can simply tap a word or picture and hear what was being said at that moment.

Paul finds the ability to record a meeting, lecture, and so on, to be immensely helpful in certain situations. He absolutely loves this feature and does not want to have a separate notes program to do this (like Auditorium), a separate typing program, and a separate audio recorder. Notability provides all three functions.

Noteshelf

($8.99, http://bit.ly/y73OZd)

Tom's Top Pick

For pure handwritten note-taking, Noteshelf is one of the highest-ranking and most popular apps. You can create notebooks for your clients, cases,

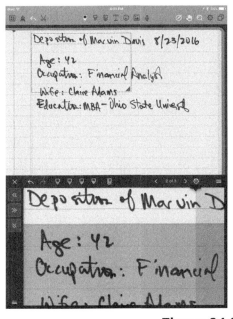

Figure 24.23. Noteshelf

or projects and see them at a glance on your Noteshelf bookshelf (see Figure 24.23). You can e-mail notebooks to yourself or others, or they can be exported to a PDF file and saved in Dropbox, Box, Google Drive, or Evernote. Tom recommends this app because it has just enough features that lawyers need to take notes without being overwhelming. It just works, and works well.

Keynote for iOS

($9.99, http://bit.ly/z6C1R9)

Paul's Top Pick

Keynote for the iPad or Mac is the equivalent of PowerPoint in the PC world. Keynote truly is an excellent presentation tool, and Apple has ported the software to the iPad iOS.

Keynote on the iPad can certainly be used to give presentations on a large screen with a projector. But many lawyers also use Keynote as a way to share a set of images and information with a small group, such as at a client meeting. Keynote is a beautiful app on the iPad, and you can easily manipulate the slides and images.

If you have an iPhone, you might want to enable the "Keynote Remote" feature, which turns your phone into a remote for the iPad's Keynote app. You can control your slides from the phone or another iOS device and even view any notes you might have included as part of the presentation.

OneNote

(Free, http://apple.co/2aNPonz)

Tom's Top Pick

OneNote has quickly become one of the more powerful note-taking apps for lawyers, because it's so versatile (see Figure 24.24). Litigators are creating trial notebooks in OneNote with separate sections for discovery, witnesses, and motions, and places for individual notes in each of these sections. You can type or use a stylus in OneNote, and the app will recognize your handwriting and make it searchable.

OneNote also has a web clipper that you can use to send websites or articles to OneNote for future reference. And you can share all of the notes you create in OneNote with others in your office, family, or friends.

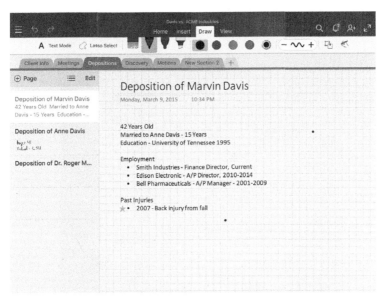

Figure 24.24. Microsoft OneNote

Scanning Apps

Scanner Pro

($3.99, http://bit.ly/1q9B3fT) and PDFPen Scan+ ($6.99, http://bit.ly/1vJyBEN)

Paul and Tom's Top Picks

As lawyers continue the move to a more paper-free work environment, we recommend these scanning apps for converting paper files to PDF format, when you receive documents from a client, opposing counsel, or in discovery. We like Scanner Pro because it is so simple to use, and does a great job of capturing and saving paper scans as PDF files. In its latest release, you can now create text-searchable PDFs. Just take a picture of the document, adjust the image to your preference, run the text recognition (if desired), and e-mail the document or save the PDF to your Dropbox, Google Drive, or Evernote account (see Scanner Pro in Figure 24.25).

Honorable Mention

- **Scannable** (Free, http://apple.co/1DcxhuT), Tom's Pick. Tom loves the simplicity of Scannable, an app published by the makers of Evernote. The best part of Scannable is that it works automatically. Just hold your iPad over a document, and the app finds the corners and

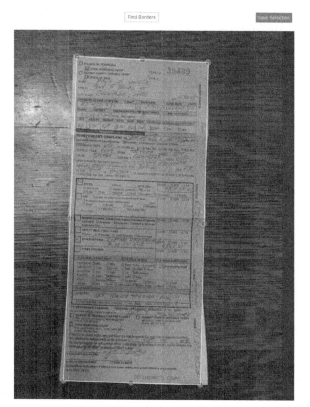

Figure 24.25. Scanner Pro

immediately scans it, without you having to do a thing. The images are good quality, and can be exported via e-mail or saved in other apps—including Evernote, of course.

LogMeIn

(Free, http://bit.ly/ws9m3y)

Paul's Top Pick

As much as the iPad can do, there will inevitably be a time when you need to work on your office computer or need to access a file that is only located on your home computer.

To access a computer from your iPad, you'll need to install the LogMeIn software client on the computer you want to access and that computer will need to be running. When you need to access the computer from the iPad,

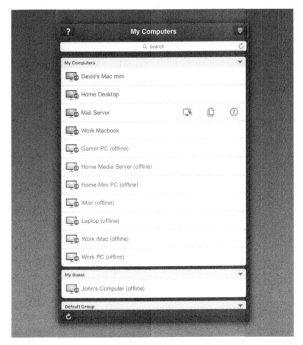

Figure 24.26. LogMeIn

you'll simply launch the LogMeIn app and put in your credentials (see Figure 24.26). Controlling and manipulating your computer from the iPad can be a little tricky due to the small(er) size of the iPad's screen. But when you need access to your office computer from the road, the LogMeIn app can be your saving grace.

To use LogMeIn on your computer, you'll need to purchase a subscription, which currently starts at $149/year for two computers.

Find My iPhone (for the iPad)

(Free, http://bit.ly/xbwDkm)

Paul and Tom's Top Pick

The Find My iPhone/Find My iPad service is part of the free iCloud service. Because there is so much personal information and confidential client data stored on iOS devices today, we urge every legal professional with an iPad to sign up for a free iCloud account and enable the Find My iPad service. When you misplace or lose your iPad, you are able to either use the Find My iPhone app installed on another iPhone or iPad, or log on to any computer

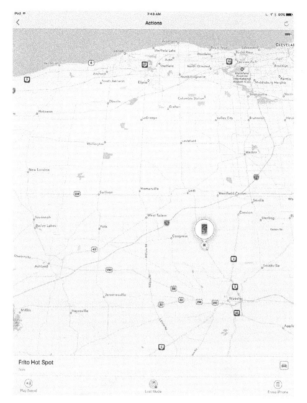

Figure 24.27. Find My iPhone Desktop Display

at icloud.com/find to geographically locate the iPad (see Figure 24.27). From there, you can lock your iPad, send a message to the person who might have it, or erase the data that's on it.

Since this service is free and the risk of losing so much information on an iPad is so high, many leading experts, like Brett Burney, argue that setting it up should be mandatory for any legal professional. See "Free Security for Your iPhone & iPad That Should Be Mandatory" at www.macsinlaw.com /find-my-iphone-free-security/.

Library of Other Favorite Apps

We couldn't mention all of the apps we like in detail here, so we've listed the names of some of our favorite apps in several categories. To find out more about them, go to the App Store in iTunes or on your iPad or simply type "[app name] iPad app" into your favorite search engine.

Browsers—Alternatives to the iPad's Safari Browser

- Google Chrome
- Opera Coast

Entertainment

- Fandango—great app for buying movie tickets
- HBO Go—subscribers can watch all HBO content for free
- Hulu—for watching television shows
- IMDb
- Netflix
- YouTube

File Management

- Box.com
- Dropbox—probably the best-known cloud-based file management tool
- GoodReader
- Google Drive
- OneDrive
- SpiderOak
- SugarSync
- Transporter

Finance

- Bank of America
- Chase Mobile

Food

- Food Truck Fiesta
- OpenTable—make reservations online
- Yelp

Games

- Angry Birds
- Crosswords
- Plants vs. Zombies (1 and 2)
- QuizUp!
- Scrabble
- Words with Friends

Legal-Specific

- All Law
- DocReviewPad
- Fastcase
- iJuror
- iTimekeep—timekeeping app that works with most major time and billing software products
- Jury Tracker
- TranscriptPad
- TrialPad

Meetings and Calendars

- Calvetica Calendar
- Syncronicity Pro for Exchange—see group calendars
- Fantastical
- Fuze Meeting
- GoToMeeting
- Join.me—easy-to-use screen-sharing app
- WebExZoom Web and Video Conferencing

News

- AP News
- CNN
- LinkedIn Pulse
- News 360
- NPR
- Nuzzel
- USA Today
- SmartNews

Photos and Video

- Google Photos
- Photogene—photo editor
- PhotoSync—transfer photos from iPhone to iPad
- Pro HDR—improved HDR photography
- Snapseed
- MoviePro
- Videoshop

Productivity

- Documents To Go—document creation/editing
- DocuSign—sign documents on the iPad
- Dragon Dictation—fantastic voice recognition/transcription tool
- Evernote—a fantastic repository for notes
- iThoughts HD—mind-mapping app
- iType2Go Pro—text editor and camera viewer
- JotNot Scanner+—document scanner
- Keynote
- Microsoft Excel for iPad
- Microsoft OneNote
- Microsoft PowerPoint for iPad
- Microsoft Word for iPad
- MindMeister—mind mapping
- Note Taker—note-taking
- Noted—note-taking
- Notes Plus—note-taking
- Outliner—organize your thoughts
- Pages—document creation/editing
- PDF Expert—document editor
- Penultimate—note-taking
- PlainText 2—text editor
- Prezi—great alternative app for conducting presentations
- Prizmo—scan and OCR
- SignMyPad—have clients sign documents on your iPad
- SmartNote—note-taking
- UPAD 3—note-taking
- WritePad—note-taking

Reading

- Feedly—probably the best news reader/RSS feed reader currently available
- Flipboard—creates magazine-style layout of Facebook/Twitter feeds
- GoodReader—best file reader, period
- iAnnotate PDF
- Instapaper—save articles to read later
- Kindle for iPad
- Mr. Reader—imports RSS feeds from just about anywhere

- Texture—"Netflix for Magazines"—for a low monthly price, subscribe to over 100 magazines
- Pocket—save articles to read later
- Reeder—another great choice for reading newsfeeds/RSS feeds

Social Networking and Communications

- Buffer—social media scheduling and management
- Facebook
- HootSuite—social media aggregator
- Skype—VoIP (voice over Internet protocol) calls and video
- TextNow—send texts for free from your iPad
- Tweetbot—the best Twitter client for iOS
- Twitter

Travel

- FlightBoard
- FlightTrack
- GateGuru—airport information
- Google Maps
- Google Translate
- Kayak—fantastic travel search engine
- Orbitz
- Curb
- TripAdvisor
- TripIt
- Uber
- xe Currency

Utilities

- Duet—create second monitor with your iPad (wired and rock solid)
- Air Display—create a second monitor with your iPad (wireless)
- Citrix Receiver—remote access
- Digits Calculator
- IFTTT—Create "recipes" to make the services you use work better with each other
- Eye Glass—magnifying glass
- Google Voice—phone service
- GoToMyPC—remote access
- Text Expander—macro utility

Navigation Tips and Settings

- **Add apps and folders to the iPad's dock.** Out of the box, the iPad features four apps on the Dock, which is the always-visible bar at the bottom of the screen (see Figure 24.28). You can add up to six apps in the Dock, and you can also add folders containing multiple apps in the Dock.

Figure 24.28. iPad Dock

- **Launch apps from the Spotlight Search screen.** While the Spotlight Search bar (accessed by swiping downward on any screen) can be used to search Notes, E-mail, Calendar Appointments, and more, you can also search for an app and tap to launch it (see Figure 24.29).

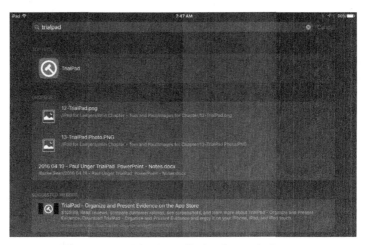

Figure 24.29. Spotlight Search Screen

- **Double-tap space bar to add a period and a space.** You can quickly add a period and a space to the end of a sentence by double-tapping the spacebar. You can turn this option off in the Settings menu if you prefer.

- **Lock orientation in the Control Center.** If you want to "lock" the orientation of your screen, so it permanently remains in either Portrait or Landscape mode, swipe up from the bottom of your screen to bring up the Control Center. Press the button with a rotating arrow and lock in the center.

- **Turn on battery percentage indicator.** While the iPad by default shows you a graphical representation of the battery level, you can also turn on the percentage indicator under Settings > Battery (see Figure 24.30).

- **Undo typing.** Many people aren't aware that there is an Undo option for the iPad. When you want to undo your most recent typing, you simply (and carefully!!) shake the iPad back and forth. A small window will appear, allowing you to undo your most recent typing.

- **Disable the clicking sound for typing and other sounds.** You can turn off the clicking sound for typing by going to Settings > Sounds.

Figure 24.30. Battery Usage Settings

- **Take a screenshot.** You can take a screenshot from your iPad by simply holding down the Home button (front-center of device) and Wake/Sleep button (top of the device) at the same time. You'll see the screen flash once and the image will be saved in your iPad's Photos app.
- **Use your iPad as a second monitor.** You can use apps such as Duet (Mac or PC), Air Display (Mac), and MaxiVista (Windows) to turn your iPad into a second monitor. This probably won't be your standard setup, but it can be helpful when you're traveling and need the convenience of a second monitor. Our favorite is Duet. It uses the Lighting or 30-pin cable to plug directly into your Mac or PC, eliminating latency that you may experience using Wi-Fi with Air Display or MaxiVista.
- **Save an image while browsing the web**. If you see a picture you want to save while browsing the web on your iPad, simply tap and hold your finger on the image, and you'll be prompted to save the image into your iPad's Photo app (see Figure 24.31).

Figure 24.31. Save Web Image

Passcode Lock

It is very important to become familiar with the security settings of the iPad so that you can keep information stored on your tablet safe.

You can access the security settings through Settings > Touch ID & Passcode. At a minimum, lawyers and their agents should assign a passcode lock in conjunction with the auto-lock function. This will auto-lock your iPad after a set number of minutes and require a passcode to regain access to the iPad (see Figure 24.32).

The iPad defaults to a "Simple Passcode," which is a six-digit number similar to your ATM PIN. We recommend that you turn "Simple Passcode" off and set a longer passcode—at least ten to 12 numbers, letters, and characters. You should also set a time for the iPad to be idle after which the iPad will then require the passcode. Lastly, you should enable the option that erases data after ten failed passcode attempts.

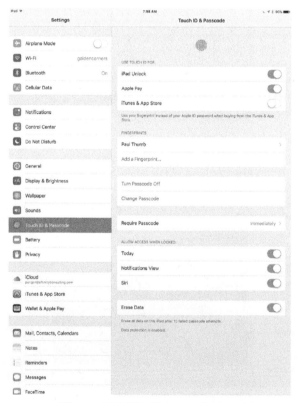

Figure 24.32. Passcode Lock

Resources

There are a number of good resources for lawyers using an iPad.

- iPad 4 Lawyers by Tom Mighell (http://ipad4lawyers.squarespace.com)
- iPhone J.D. by Jeff Richardson (www.iphonejd.com)
- Pad Notebook by Justin Kahn (http://ipadnotebook.wordpress.com)
- Two blogs from Brett Burney:
  - Macs in Law (www.macsinlaw.com)
  - Apps in Law (http://appsinlaw.com)
- The Mac Lawyer by Ben Stevens (www.themaclawyer.com)

Another fantastic website to use for app recommendations and information is App Advice. It provides access to hundreds of articles and reviews of new iPad apps.

About the Authors

Tom Mighell, Esq.

Contoural, Inc.
tmighell@gmail.com
Tom Mighell is Vice President of Delivery Services at Contoural, Inc., where he helps companies deal with their information governance, privacy, and litigation readiness issues. Before becoming a consultant, Tom was a litigator for 18 years in Dallas, Texas. He is a frequent speaker and writer on the Internet and legal technology and is the author of several books: *iPad in One Hour for Lawyers* (3rd edition), *iPad in One Hour for Litigators* (2nd Edition), *iPad Apps in One Hour for Lawyers,* and *The Lawyers' Guide to Collaboration Tools and Technologies: Smart Ways to Work Together* (with Dennis Kennedy). He has published Inter Alia (www.inter-alia.net, a legal technology blog, since 2002. He and Dennis Kennedy are the co-hosts of The Kennedy-Mighell Report, a legal technology podcast. Tom is a past Chair of ABA TECHSHOW 2008, as well as past Chair of the ABA Law Practice Division.

Paul J. Unger, Esq.

Affinity Consulting Group
punger@affinityconsulting.com
Paul J. Unger is a national speaker, writer, and thought-leader in the legal technology industry. He is an attorney and founding principal of Affinity

Consulting Group, a nationwide consulting company providing legal technology consulting, continuing legal education, and training.

He was the Chair of the ABA Legal Technology Resource Center (2013–14, 2014–15) (www.lawtechnology.org/), former Chair of ABA TECHSHOW (2011) (www.techshow.com), member of the American Bar Association, Columbus Bar Association, Ohio State Bar Association, Ohio Association for Justice, and Central Ohio Association for Justice. He is also the author of *PowerPoint in One Hour for Lawyers*. He specializes in trial presentation and litigation technology, document and case management, paperless office strategies, and legal-specific software training for law firms and legal departments throughout the Midwest. Mr. Unger has provided trial presentation consultation for over 400 cases. He is an Adjunct Professor for Capital University Law School's Paralegal Program. In his spare time, he likes to run and restore historic homes.

CHAPTER TWENTY-FIVE

Voice and Data Communications

The ability to make and receive phone calls is an absolute necessity for a law firm. In addition, some sort of data access is critical to the success of a firm these days. We are a very connected society, and any potential client expects to be able to contact you with relative ease, whether via voice or data transmission such as e-mail. In this chapter, we cover some of your technology options for voice and data communications.

Unified Messaging

Unified messaging is the delivery of traditional voice communications into your e-mail box, including the delivery of facsimile transmissions. Unified messaging systems have been around for some time now. Many clients expect you to be able to monitor your communications constantly in order to rapidly respond to their needs. Unified messaging is a stable technology that will make that happen.

The simplest way to implement unified messaging is to have it integrated with your phone system. Some small firms may not even have a phone system, and we'll address that issue in a moment. Many of the modern PBX (private branch exchange) systems can incorporate a voicemail card directly into the telephone system chassis. Stand-alone voicemail systems are also an alternative for larger office environments. You can even integrate unified messaging with your Exchange server or your VoIP (voice over Internet protocol) implementation. The latest versions of Exchange Server (2007, 2010, 2013, and 2016) include unified messaging capability at no additional charge. Some outsourced providers of VoIP solutions will provide unified messaging capabilities too, which means you don't have to have any physical equipment to gain the benefits of integrating all your communication streams.

Previously, unified messaging systems were specialized, proprietary implementations. File formats were all over the board and some needed specialized software just to access the data. The good news is those days are over. Modern unified messaging systems output the files in a standardized format that can be opened on a Windows or Mac computer. Just make sure that you choose a vendor that can provide the files in a format that works across all of your systems and with your applications. Our recommendation is to stick with well-known vendors of communication equipment. You really can't go wrong with suppliers such as Avaya, Cisco, NEC, Toshiba, and so on.

Some companies resell complete unified messaging solutions, thereby saving you the investment in hardware and software. These solutions are typically available for a monthly fee, and you may have to commit to a multiyear contract to obtain the service. One concern is that all of your communications may be going through a third party if it is not an on-premise solution. This means your phone calls actually route through the vendor's system before being delivered to your location. In that way, it can capture a voice-mail message or fax and repackage it for delivery to your e-mail address. We are generally not fans of having client data move through third-party providers and recommend that you first investigate systems you own and can control. As an alternative, make sure that any contract terms clearly state what data the vendor can access and what procedures are in place to protect the confidentiality of the communications.

We are beginning to see on-premise solutions for the small and medium-sized business market, which may reduce your cost and provide a more stable environment versus hosted solutions. Understand that the cost of an on-premise solution will vary based on the number of extensions, inbound line capacity and phone system features. The systems can cost just a few thousand or tens of thousands of dollars. The majority of the cost is for the base phone system and the unified messaging features should only add a few thousand to the total.

In this chapter, we cover some of the concerns and questions you should have when considering whether to implement a unified messaging solution. These issues are related to equipment that is provided as part of your telephone communication system. The first issue is what communications the system handles. Can it manage both voice messages and fax transmissions or just one? Even though most systems will handle both voicemail and fax, generally firms use only the voice capability and route the faxes to a dedicated fax machine, printer, or general e-mail box rather than to a specific person's inbox.

How do you want the voice messages delivered? Most firms will elect to send only an e-mail notification that a voicemail message has been received. This configuration saves bandwidth because the message itself is not transmitted to the e-mail client. It stays on the voicemail server until you retrieve it—hardly convenient if you are traveling. In fact, as a security measure, some telephone systems are configured not to allow remote connections, even for voicemail retrieval. A lot of lawyers use some type of smartphone, and sending a notification-only message saves on their data usage, but what hoops do they have to jump through to listen to the message? The other alternative is to deliver the actual message to your inbox. Obviously, this method uses much more bandwidth, especially if you are delivering it to a cell phone that also receives your e-mail. If you elect this configuration, you'd better have a data plan that can cover your traffic load. Make sure your portable device can play back the file format for your voicemail if you elect to deliver the message to your inbox.

Another question for your PBX provider is how it handles the message delivery itself. Is the message forwarded to your inbox and then deleted from the voicemail system? If so, there is only one copy of it and you'll never know you received a message if it gets trapped or trashed by your spam filter. If the original stays on the voicemail system and a copy gets delivered to your inbox, does the message light stay lit on your phone? You may not want this, but then again you may want a visual indication that a voice message was delivered.

How does the vendor identify the voice message in your inbox? Is the "From: address" something that is easily recognizable as the phone system, or does it come from you? What does the subject line contain? Showing the caller ID in the subject line is particularly helpful, but not all vendors package messages that way. How is the voice message delivered to your e-mail system? Do you have to have a user ID and password configured on your voicemail box that is consistent with your network credentials? If so, you have the issue of constantly synchronizing your logon credentials with the telephone system, assuming that your network passwords must be changed after a set number of days (shame on you if your password never expires). Many phone systems only accept numbers as a password, so you can't even use letters (forget capitals). This restriction may render your integration unacceptable.

Finally, how do you retrieve your messages? They should be delivered as standard audio attachments to e-mail messages. This is certainly preferred, since you don't need any special software to listen to the messages. Can you play the message on any device that you use, or will you need some conversion software or app on your mobile device? Another problem deals with specific software versions. You must make sure that any potential voicemail system is compatible with your firm's e-mail solution. If you have questions regarding what versions of Microsoft Exchange and Outlook the voicemail system is compatible with, make sure you ask your vendor before you make the investment.

If all of this has given you a headache, don't worry. Make sure your IT consultant reads this chapter—he or she can answer all the questions for you. But make no mistake about it: No one who has successfully implemented unified messaging has ever discarded it. The value of unified messaging is phenomenal—being able to access your voicemail on your cell phone is a remarkable enhancement. You need never worry again about being out of touch. If you prefer not to give clients your home or cell phone number, you'll still get their messages. We cannot count the number of times that having voicemail sent to our cell phones has been worth its weight in diamonds.

Google Voice

For those lawyers constantly on the road, a free service they might find useful is Google Voice. If you'd rather not give your personal cell phone number to your pesky clients, who always have emergencies regardless of the time, then this service might be for you. With Google Voice you get a Google number that forwards inbound phone calls to your other personal phone numbers. This service allows you to provide your clients with a phone number (not your personal number), screen incoming phone calls, and receive voicemails left on the Google Voice phone number in your e-mail inbox. You also have the option to transfer your current mobile number to Google, which will then become your Google number. There is $20 fee to transfer your number and your current cellphone will no longer have service (since the number is transferred). There may be early termination charges from your carrier if you opt to transfer your current number. We would recommend that you just start a new account and let Google assign you a phone number.

With Google Voice, you can specify which e-mail address you would like the voicemails forwarded to. By default, the notification is sent to the address linked to your Google account, but you can add additional e-mail addresses. Google Voice will even transcribe your voicemails to text and provide them in the body of the e-mail, allowing users to read the content before they choose to listen to the messages. The voicemail itself can be downloaded and is delivered as an MP3 file, not a WAV file as in most other voicemail systems. Google Voice also allows users to receive and record phone conversations (be mindful of the laws in your state if you do this), index and search voicemails, and set up conference calls.

If you are currently a Sprint customer, you can take advantage of the Google Voice features without changing your phone number. Be sure to review the Google Voice help section (http://support.google.com/voice/) to see exactly what features you get by integrating your Sprint account with Google Voice.

VoIP

In its most basic definition, VoIP is a family of technologies for delivery of voice communications over Internet protocol networks such as the Internet. VoIP systems are digital and can run voice and data systems over the same network, reducing investment in infrastructure. Corporate usage of VoIP phone systems is pretty much the default for any new installation, replacing the traditional analog copper wire telephone systems that we all used in the past.

VoIP systems are primarily aimed at providing users with unified communications, delivering all services (voice, fax, voicemail, and e-mail) to a single location. VoIP systems are generally more flexible and less costly to implement than your standard dedicated copper wire systems, and they can integrate easily with most existing data network infrastructures.

Security used to be a major concern for VoIP systems. That concern has pretty much been eliminated. It appears that vendors have finally overcome the performance hit associated with encrypting the voice traffic. You would be hard-pressed to find a current vendor that sends voice traffic in an unencrypted stream. This means that you'll sleep a little better knowing that your voice traffic travels in secure encrypted channels. That doesn't mean your VoIP traffic isn't subject to hacking. In fact, security guru Bruce Schneier has published several blog posts describing how to hack a VoIP data stream. One past post discusses how it is possible even to "identify the phrases spoken within encrypted VoIP calls when the audio is encoded using variable bit rate codecs." Sound scary? Given the ongoing news of the capabilities and actions of the National Security Agency, VoIP systems carry just as much risk of interception as traditional phone networks.

Because the underlying IP network that a VoIP system uses is unreliable, it's not uncommon to experience some level of latency or jitteriness when making a call using a VoIP phone system, especially to off-site destinations. Once your voice packet hits the already congested Internet, you are no longer in control of how fast your data gets to where it's going, and that's what causes the delays. Using a VoIP system on the same data network as your computer system might tremendously slow down how fast you can access your server and case management applications because of all the data traffic on your local network. Be sure your existing data network and Internet connection are capable of handling the increase in load before implementing a VoIP system that shares the network infrastructure. If you have to upgrade existing hardware or the speed of your Internet connection, those are hidden costs that you might not be aware of and that you will have to plan for.

Implementing an MPLS (Multiprotocol Label Switching) network gives you the option of configuring QoS (Quality of Service), where you can give the voice traffic a higher priority. MPLS networks are not cheap and tend to be used in larger firms with multiple office locations. Frankly, we think MPLS is overkill and too expensive for a solo or small firm considering VoIP. As an alternative, a large number of VoIP installations use the IP network on the local premises. They then route the external calls to the Internet and may even have some traditional phone circuits connected too. The reality is that the telephone carriers themselves are using VoIP between two IP gateways in order to reduce the long-haul bandwidth.

Finally, VoIP systems are susceptible to power failures and outages. Unlike analog phones that get their power directly from the copper phone lines, VoIP systems need electricity to operate, just like your computer system does. You'd better have an analog phone line as a backup, or at least a cell phone. However, a lot of metropolitan areas have abandoned copper analog technology, making it no longer available for purchase. We're still hanging on to our traditional copper wire analog lines, despite the telcos trying to force fiber and VoIP down our throats.

VoIP phone systems have their pros and cons when compared to other digital phone systems. Be sure to ask your vendor the right questions to determine which type of system is right for you. And be wary of those vendors and definitely check their references. We have seen a lot of VoIP installations that caused major-league heartburn for the law firms that undertook them.

Besides hidden costs pushing budgets far beyond the original numbers, vendors tend not to plan for redundancy or to warn of the potential downsides of VoIP. We have had both happy and unhappy VoIP clients, so we're not saying, "Don't do it," but be aware that VoIP may not be the right choice for everyone. As a side note, we have yet to hear of any clients who weren't happy with their Cisco VoIP installation. That has to tell you something about the quality and stability of Cisco products.

High-Speed Internet

None of our lawyers or other clients ever complain that their Internet connection is too fast. We have collectively almost forgotten how slow the Internet used to be and how patiently we had to wait for our screens to load. High-speed Internet is now a requirement for solo and small law firms. High-speed Internet has all but replaced dial-up Internet connections because of the low cost and fast connection speeds, although there are still some parts of the country where dial-up is the only option. Why continue to wait for web pages to load and attachments to open if you don't have to? Few creatures are more impatient than lawyers, so virtually all of them have jumped to high-speed Internet installations.

High-speed Internet connections are available from your local Internet service provider (ISP) and usually are provided over a cable, DSL, or fiber-optic connection. These high-speed connections offer download speeds in excess of 25 Mbps (some can reach 100 Mbps) and varying upload speeds, depending on the provider and the service tier to which you've subscribed. If your firm hosts its own services, such as e-mail or a website, you can obtain static IP addresses from your local provider for these types of connections. The ISP may charge more to issue your business a static IP address than if you just require a dynamically leased IP address. High-speed Internet access connectivity generally will cost $75 to $300 per month.

If your firm requires a larger amount of bandwidth due to the number of users sharing the Internet connection or to run web-based applications, your local ISP may be able to provide a connection type that meets your requirements. Historically, the ISPs and telco providers classified upgraded service connections as T1 or fractional T1 connections. While they may call them upgrades, they are much slower than alternative technologies and will cost hundreds of dollars more per month. These types of connections also require longer service agreements and usually include a large setup cost. They do have the advantage of a service level agreement (SLA), which means the connection must be repaired within a particular time and must be available a high percentage of the time. DSL or cable modem connections do not carry an SLA, so repair times could be several days during an outage. T1 circuits are becoming less and less popular, even though they are very reliable and guarantee bandwidth. A full T1 provides only 1.544 Mbps up and down and typically will cost $300–$500 per month. Compare this to other broadband services (cable or DSL), where you can get 30 Mbps download and 5 Mbps upload for less than $200 a month. Do the math: 30 is a *much* bigger number than 1.544. As a result, we have *no* clients that are using T1 services. A T1 circuit is just too slow for today's modern Internet usage patterns and bundling multiple T1s is just way too expensive. Broadband circuits are fairly reliable and installing two different broadband providers helps maintain reliable Internet service for the firm.

If available in your area, a speedy alternative to a T1 is fiber optics. Fiber to the curb, such as Verizon FiOS or Google Fiber, can offer business subscribers increasingly faster Internet connections at a much lower cost. Check with your local service providers to see if such a connection is currently available. In general, solo and small firms are well served by cable and DSL to meet their Internet connection needs.

Another option for Internet access is from your cellular provider. Mobile broadband Internet access has gained steam lately and is becoming a growing trend with mobile lawyers. Plus, it's a good way to avoid having to pay those outrageous prices for Internet access that some hotels charge. The good news is that more and more hotels are no longer charging for Internet access and wireless access is included in the room rate.

You may have heard the terms 3G, 4G, and so on, used to identify mobile broadband. Carriers are now charging for wireless broadband based on the amount of data consumed. The cost is approximately $20–$30 a month for 2 GB up to $60 a month for 10GB. Some will even sell you 100 GB for $450 a month. Most providers will throw in the broadband card for no cost when you sign up for their service. We have found that it is cheaper to activate the mobile hotspot feature on our smartphones instead of acquiring a separate mobile data plan. That way we use the data plan from our phone to create the Wi-Fi "cloud" for other devices to share. We can then use the Wi-Fi-only iPad (a lot cheaper) instead of one with the built-in 3G/4G capability.

CHAPTER TWENTY-SIX

Utilities and Apps

What we all need is Batman's belt, with a full repository of tricks that we can draw upon at any moment to perform the myriad tasks associated with the practice of law on our computers and mobile devices. Failing that, we must acknowledge that it is impossible to list all of the utilities that a solo or small firm might find useful. There are many great selections and just as many opinions as to what makes one utility more valuable than another. In this edition, we have included some of our favorite apps for mobile devices, in addition to those discussed in the iWin chapter.

The threshold question is, what constitutes a utility? For our purposes, we will consider a utility to be a software application that takes data and manipulates it for a specific purpose. That definition allows us a lot of latitude.

The challenge is to list utilities that offer a unique purpose for the solo and small firm lawyer. We have used many of these utilities ourselves and have had some great suggestions from our friends and colleagues. If you don't see your favorite utility here, just drop us a line and perhaps it will be listed in the next edition of the book.

Doodle

Doodle Mobile is a mobile app that lets you schedule events from anywhere. Using the app, you can propose different group scheduling times, invite a group of people, and get notified once the best time for everyone is found, so the endless back-and-forth communication days are over! This app is available for both iOS and Android mobile devices.

Using social scheduling, this app keeps responses in one organized place. The app connects directly to your calendar and only proposes time slots when you're actually available and saves you the time of having to sift through all of your calendar entries. You can even set up and configure notifications that will keep you up to date as users respond to the time polls. This app can be downloaded for free from your mobile device's app store.

It's also worth mentioning that there is a Premium version of Doodle that allows the sending of automatic reminders, shows who is missing and hasn't responded to your poll, and also will enforce end-to-end SSL encryption of the calendaring process. Doodle Premium costs $39 per year and is offered with a free 30-day trial.

FindTime

FindTime, a Doodle alternative by Microsoft, integrates directly with Microsoft Outlook. This free Outlook add-in allows users to create scheduling polls to send out to meeting attendees to determine the best time to schedule the meeting. Once the times are proposed and attendees vote, the meeting is scheduled and an automated Calendar invite is sent out. FindTime shows you what days and times work best for you and the attendees and will liberate you from the endless back-and-forth scheduling e-mails.

To work, other recipients do not need to have the FindTime add-in installed. They only need to have an e-mail address and Internet access for this product to work its magic. FindTime works with Outlook on both Windows and Mac-based computers, and even Outlook on the web and Office365. This product can be downloaded for free from Microsoft's FindTime website at http://findtime.microsoft.com.

DuckDuckGo

DuckDuckGo is an Internet search engine that emphasizes protecting searchers' privacy and avoiding the filter bubble of personalized search results. Since this search engine doesn't collect any personal information, it doesn't have anything to share with marketers—a nice change from Google.

In our experience, search results are just as good as they are with Google—and in some cases, even better. You can find and use the search engine at www.duckduckgo.com. Don't forget to configure your browser of choice to use DuckDuckGo as the default search engine.

Epic Privacy Browser

Taking privacy one step further, users can download and install the free Epic Privacy Browser on their Windows or Mac-based computer. To keep your data and location private, Epic restricts access to your IP address through the blocking of fingerprinting scripts and functions.

When using the Epic Browser with the encrypted proxy on, your data is encrypted and hidden from the government, the Internet service provider, and hundreds of other data collectors. When the Epic Browser is closed, there is no easily accessible record of your browsing history left on the computer system. The default configuring of Epic is "extreme privacy," through no web cache or DNS cache, no auto-fill or auto-suggest, and no password saving.

The Epic Privacy Browser can be downloaded from the vendor's website at www.epicbrowser.com.

Slack

The Slack app allows and stores your team communications in one place. It's a way to get more done and spend less time in meetings and drafting e-mails. Slack provides communication for teams through the organization of conversations into channels. Users can make a channel for a project, topic, a team, or practically anything. Private channels can be created for sensitive information and access can be restricted to only those individuals that you invite to join. Users can send direct messages to a colleague that are completely private and secure. Data is encrypted in both transit and at rest, which is a requirement if the legal community is going to take up using this app. Slack's security practices are very transparent (and impressive) and can be viewed here: https://slack.com/security-practices.

Besides messaging, users can drag, drop, and share files including images, PDFs, and other documents right into Slack. Users can add comments and references, all of which are completely searchable. Users can paste links to documents within Google Drive, Dropbox, or Box, and that document is immediately synched and made searchable within Slack. Collaboration is truly made easier with this application. Everything within Slack is truly searchable and is available everywhere you go, with fully native apps for iOS and Android devices.

There is a free version of Slack, which has some limitations but may be worth a try before purchasing a monthly Standard or Plus subscription. The difference in plans, as well as pricing, can be viewed on Slack's website at https://slack.com/pricing.

X1 Search

How often do you find yourself frantically searching your computer for a file only to discover that you have no clue where you saved it? It's happened to all of us, and the problem is compounded when you have copies of the same file saved in multiple locations. Which file is the right one? What a headache!

To relieve some of the stress, we recommend that lawyers use X1 Search, which is a piece of software that enables users to search for and instantly find information while keeping the resulting file in its native format. The product is marketed as a premium alternative to Windows Desktop and Outlook Search. No more messy conversions. X1 allows users to search for any file, whether located within their e-mail on the local computer, a network share, removable storage drive, or even within virtual desktops. This software currently supports more than 500 file types in their native format and layout, and it can even search for data within multiple Microsoft Outlook PST files and Lotus Notes without having to mount the files. It can even index files located within cloud storage providers like OneDrive and Box, making all of your data repositories searchable through a single interface.

The X1 program displays the search results as you type, similar to the Google Instant Search, which allows users to modify their search query in real time. The advanced searching options allow users to search multiple e-mail metadata fields such as From, To, and Subject and then sort the resulting files by any of the file properties.

The X1 program is a powerful search tool that includes a number of advanced features, such as support for searching inside compressed ZIP files and RSS feeds, as well as a number of export options, such as exporting the search results to a folder or Microsoft Outlook PST file. The product is even administrator-friendly, supporting integration with Active Directory and Group Policy, for ease of deployment and flexibility in its configuration.

Before installing, you will need to make sure that you have enough storage space for the search index this program will create, which is roughly 20 percent of the total volume of files indexed. X1 supports Microsoft Windows (32-bit or 64-bit) operating systems, Microsoft Outlook 2007 to 2016 (32-bit or 64-bit), and SharePoint 2007/2010/2013 and 365, Box, OneDrive, as well as all IMAP-based e-mail accounts. Support for Lotus Notes, Eudora, and Thunderbird e-mail clients has been dropped in X1 Search and can only be found in prior versions of the X1 Search Professional Client.

The X1 Search 8 software costs $49.95 per license and can be purchased with varying levels of support. If you want to try before you buy, a 14-day trial is available as well. To view or purchase this product, visit www.x1.com.

Outlook Send Assistant

Concerned about inadvertently sending an e-mail message to an unintended recipient? If so, we have the tool for you. This add-in warns or prevents accidental disclosure and sending of e-mails to unintended recipients. It is a must-have utility for every Microsoft Outlook user. Outlook Send Assistant (http://www.thepaynegroup.com/products/outlooksend/) is a small tool that packs a big punch.

Here are some of the features of this simple and elegant tool:

- Integrates with Microsoft Outlook 2007 to 2016
- Is compatible with Windows 10, Windows 8.x, Windows 7, and Windows Server platforms
- Available in both 32-bit and 64-bit versions
- Supports HTML and Plain Text formats
- Alerts users when the Reply All button is selected
- Warns users that the message has a blank subject line
- Prompts the user when external recipients are detected
- Confirms with e-mail senders if they'd like to continue sending the message
- Prompts when the e-mail is addressed to a Distribution List
- Alerts users when recipient(s) are detected in the BCC field
- Inserts BCC disclosure text into the recipients' message, thus notifying them of the BCC status
- Customizes warnings when specific recipient addresses are detected
- Automatically adds Marketing, Circular 230 Disclosure, SEC, SPAM warnings, and security disclaimers to e-mail messages
- Warns for missing attachments
- Alerts for specific e-mail attachment types, including document links attached to the e-mail from a document management system
- Warns when specific text is detected in the subject line

Outlook Send Assistant can be purchased from the PayneGroup website (www.thepaynegroup.com) at a cost of $45 per license. There is also a 30-day free trial should users wish to take the product for a test-drive first, and discounts are available if you need 20 or more licenses.

Winscribe for the Legal Profession

Winscribe, a leading developer of dictation software, has made a product specifically for the legal profession that allows dictations to be transcribed automatically, converting recorded words to text. Automating the process saves both time and money, increasing the efficiency of your employees. It marks the end of the "listen . . . type" era. Now your employees can spend their time doing something more productive and billable. Winscribe can even integrate with existing applications, such as your document management system, streamlining your workflow process.

As the creator of the dictations, you can manage and monitor the status of your work as well as retrieve jobs for review and editing. Another innovative feature of this software is that it supports a wide range of input from recordings made on telephones, PCs and laptops, digital handheld devices, BlackBerrys, Windows Phones, iPhones, and Androids. With the Winscribe Mobility Suite, the days of carrying around a digital recorder may be over. Now you can install mobile software on your smartphone to record dictations and transfer the files wirelessly to your firm's network. As always, client confidentiality is an extremely important issue. Winscribe protects dictations through the encryption of the files and through the implementation of a secure file transfer process. Winscribe has been vetted by the experts and found worthy. This product is available on Winscribe's website at www.winscribe.com and can be purchased as an in-house package or an on-demand software as a service (SaaS) over the web.

TinyURL

Have you ever wanted to give somebody a reference link only to discover that it is about 400 characters long and contains all kinds of goofy characters and nonword representations? Probably the biggest problem is the breaking up of the URL link, especially when the e-mail is viewed as formatted text. The last thing you want to do is have the recipient cut and paste the various parts of the URL back together. TinyURL stores the complete URL on its servers and provides a very small URL instead. The user selects the smaller TinyURL, which translates and redirects to the much larger one.

This is a free service to make the posting of long URLs easier—especially handy for Twitter. If you're a frequent user of TinyURL, there's even a toolbar for your browser that you can install to make the service more accessible. It is available at http://tinyurl.com.

Security issues arise when dealing with any shortened URL. The "bad guys" are sending malware links disguised as shortened URLs in phishing e-mails appearing to come from someone you know. As the recipient of the shortened URL, you have no idea where the URL will actually send you unless you decode it first. If you want to use any URL shortening service, make sure you trust the originator of the URL or use a service to decode it before you click on the link.

TinyURL has a preview feature to show you a preview of the URL before directly going to TinyURL. You can then get an idea of where the shortened URL is going to send you. It requires that cookies be enabled for your browser.

CheckShortURL

Since we're talking about the security risk of shortened URLs, CheckShortURL is a free service to expose the real URL destination. Just go to www.checkshorturl.com and enter the shortened URL. Besides determining the actual URL, a thumbnail image will help you determine the web page contents.

SimplyFile

Long ago, we realized how much time we were losing each day carefully dragging and dropping e-mail into the correct Outlook folder, often accidentally filing messages in a folder below or a folder above the intended destination. Maddening.

With the SimplyFile software, each e-mail will display the name of the folder SimplyFile believes it belongs in. After it initially indexes and "learns" your filing system, it is correct more than 90 percent of the time. If it has guessed incorrectly, there is a QuickPick feature. Open it, and you'll likely find that the correct folder is near the top of the list of possibilities presented. If not, you can just type in the first few letters of the folder and it will appear. Most of the time, you'll just be clicking "file" and it's done. It can also turn e-mail into a calendar or a task. Marvelous. Authors Nelson and Simek regarded this product as their "find of the year" from 2009 and don't know how they functioned without it. They remain passionately devoted to it today. The current version is compatible with Outlook 2016 (32-bit and 64-bit versions) and Windows 10. This product does not work with Outlook Express.

The latest version, SimplyFile 4 may be purchased (or there's a 30-day free trial) at www.techhit.com/SimplyFile/. The cost for a single license is $49.95.

File Shredder

Every lawyer should have a utility to delete files securely. One of those tools is the free file-wiping utility called File Shredder, available at http://www.fileshredder.org. The user interface is simple enough to understand, but the software author is a little lax with the consistency of the website. As an example, when you click the update menu option in the application, it sends you to a web page announcing a new version; however, the version being distributed is not the one announced. Even with the inconsistencies though, the product works as advertised. We've tested the product using our forensic tools, and it does securely delete the targeted files. You can select a file to "shred" or "wipe" by right-clicking on the filename. You can also drag and drop files into the application interface. There are several wiping methods available from the simple single pass (good enough to prevent recovery) to the totally paranoid 35 pass overwrites. Even though the product is free, you should donate (via PayPal) to the software developer if you use the software and find value in its use.

Snagit

No lawyer should be without a screen-capture program. Snagit 13 is a screen-capture utility that can capture anything on your desktop. You can capture a specific window, a defined area, a specific object (e.g., the title bar), or a multitude of other things. There are more than 40 ways to capture the information you want to preserve. A screen-capture application is a great tool to "grab" images to place in a motion or brief that show exactly what is shown on the computer screen. This is particularly handy when you want only a specific area of the screen. Snagit can output the "snagged" image to a multitude of formats as well. The latest version includes additional video capture options, new stamps, more zoom options, including features that make it easier to edit and resize captured images. Snagit costs $49.95 for a single license version, with discounts for multiple copies. A 30-day trial version is available, so you can see whether it fits your needs before purchase. It is available from https://www.techsmith.com/download/snagit/ and now works on all Windows 32-bit and 64-bit operating systems, including Windows 10. A Mac version is available as well. Each license purchased allows the user to install the software on up to two machines.

If you are using Windows, you should try the Snipping Tool before deciding to purchase a third-party application for your screen-grabbing needs. The Snipping Tool, Microsoft's version of a screen-grabbing utility, is included by default and allows you to save the captured data to a file or copy it to the Clipboard, which is handy when creating PowerPoint slides. On a Mac, you should try the Grab app, which is Apple's equivalent screen-grabbing utility.

Metadata Assistant

One of our favorite metadata analysis and removal tools is Metadata Assistant by Payne Group (www.thepaynegroup.com/products/metadata/). Metadata Assistant integrates with your Microsoft Office installation and is particularly valuable when sending file attachments. The product will display a dialogue box asking if you want to clean the attachment or just send it as is. As we mentioned previously, don't clean the metadata if you are collaborating on a document with another person, as it will remove the tracked changes. Metadata Assistant can also convert the attachment to PDF on the fly. The product is available in both 32-bit and 64-bit versions. Metadata Assistant 5 offers more file type handling than earlier versions and has also accelerated the cleaning process.

Metadata Assistant is extremely flexible and works with Microsoft Office 2007 to 2016; Lotus Notes 8.5 and 9.0; OpenText eDocs DM 10, 5.3 and 5.2; Worldox GX/GX2/GX3; iManage 8.5/9.0; FileSite 9.3/9.0/8.5; and NetDocuments 14.1. This product is also compatible with Windows 10. Users may purchase this product directly from Payne Group for $98 per license. Discounts are available for enterprise-level installations involving 20 or more licenses.

No lawyer should be without some sort of metadata scrubber to ensure removal of potentially confidential data. Some states are even addressing the removal of metadata in their ethics opinions. Whether you are required to scrub metadata or not, Metadata Assistant is a possible solution for your practice.

You can also remove metadata by converting the file to PDF. This does not remove all of the metadata, but it does remove a large portion of it and leaves only what are typically considered innocuous values. Microsoft also provides the ability to analyze and remove ("clean") a document's properties in Microsoft Office 2010 to 2016. However, some values that it leaves behind are still viewable by third-party products like Metadata Assistant.

Litera Metadact and Metadact-e

If you're looking for another possible solution for metadata analysis and scrubbing, we have become very fond of Litera's Metadact-e and Metadact programs. Metadact installs to the user's computer just like Metadata Assistant. Metadact identifies and removes all of the commonly known types of metadata, such as author and creation date, as well as many of the hidden metadata fields that are behind the scenes. Some of the product features include

- Outlook integration
- SharePoint integration
- DMS integration
- Removing Tracked Changes and Comments from documents
- Converting attachments to PDF and PDF/A
- Desktop batch cleaning
- Ability to choose which metadata stays and which goes
- Removing formulas in Excel files
- Obtaining a metadata risk estimate based on multiple variables, including metadata quantity, type, and location

This product integrates with iManage Work; OpenText, including DM5; DocsOpen; PowerDocs; Worldox; NetDocuments; Office 2001, 2010, 2013, and 2016; and Microsoft SharePoint.

The Metadact-e program, which is a server-based product, adds profile management to the list of features mentioned above. It has the ability to scrub metadata from documents in Outlook and Outlook Web Access on tablet, smartphone, and desktop-based documents. Whether it's a Microsoft Office, PDF, image, or ZIP file, this product will ensure that all metadata has been removed. We are not aware of any other product on the market that has the ability to enforce metadata policies on mobile devices such as smartphones. We are huge fans of Metadact-e.

Unlike stand-alone versions, Metadact-e is centrally managed and administered, and it's suggested that this application be installed on its own server, so your practice can enforce its metadata policies on employees without giving them the option to bypass your written policies and procedures. The benefits of a server-based solution include the ability to prevent the disclosure of confidential client information and other sensitive data, transparency for the users (no more waiting for a locally installed product to do the cleaning—you are immediately released to go to your next task while the server does the scrubbing), and compliance control through enforcement of your practice's policies and procedures.

Metadact can be purchased from Litera's website at www.litera.com for $55 per license per user (same as last year's price) and must be renewed on a yearly basis. Users must contact Litera directly for Metadact-e pricing. Even though this product is licensed with an annual subscription model, we highly recommend investigating its purchase. It is a very cost-effective tool that is extremely flexible to meet the specific needs of your firm. We'll also add that from personal experience, Litera's support staff is top-notch and totally committed to solving a user's problems.

Evernote

Have trouble remembering everything? We sure do. That's a reason to use Evernote. This program makes it easy to remember things big and small, allowing you to capture everything you see when using your computer, cell phone, or mobile device. Using the program, you can clip a web page, snap a photo, or grab a screenshot and upload it to Evernote. Once uploaded, everything you capture is automatically processed, indexed, and made searchable. Of course, you can add your own tags and labels to your notes. Evernote will even scan handwritten notes and make the content searchable. There are a limitless number of ways to use this program, whether for play or work. Since all of the data you capture and tag is uploaded to your Evernote account, these files are accessible from all of your devices. Evernote is available for free, but the Plus ($34.99 per year) and Premium ($69.99 per year) subscription levels offer the same features as Evernote Basic, with the addition of enhanced search features and collaboration, including additional storage capacity.

Evernote can integrate with your web browser, or you can install a small application on both Mac OS X and Windows-based computers or your mobile device. To sign up for a free account, visit Evernote's website at www.evernote.com.

The free Basic version is limited to two devices, which is far too few for most folks these days. Just think: if you need to synchronize across your smartphone, computer, and tablet, you're already over the limit. As a result of Evernote's change in pricing plans during the summer of 2016, users are jumping to alternative tools such as Microsoft's OneNote.

7-Zip

7-Zip is an application for compressing data. As an alternative to the built-in Windows ZIP feature, this product allows users to create encrypted, password-protected ZIP files.

7-Zip is compatible with Windows 10, offered in both 32-bit and 64-bit versions, and is available to download for free at www.7-zip.org.

eWallet

Do you have a hard time remembering all of your different passwords to your web-based accounts? We certainly do—especially since we should all be using a different password for each of our accounts. Whatever you do, do not use the same password over and over for your different accounts. This is basic security 101.

To help you remember your passwords without having to write them down, we recommend a product called eWallet. eWallet is an app that is available for iOS, Android, BlackBerry 10, Windows Store, and both Windows (including Windows 7, 8, RT, 8.1, and 10) and Mac OS X 10.7 or higher. It keeps your passwords safe by remembering them so you don't have to. The app stores the passwords in a vault using 256-bit AES encryption and allows you to synchronize your data across all of your devices on which the application is installed. eWallet can store website passwords, frequent flyer numbers, credit card information, membership data, and much more. This product can be purchased from your device's app store or eWallet's website at www.iliumsoft.com. The price varies, depending on the device for which you're purchasing the software, but runs between $9.99 and $19.99.

LastPass

Like eWallet, LastPass is another secure password management tool. LastPass allows you to save your passwords and form data in a secure database and access it when needed. You no longer have to remember another password, and filling out forms and password fields is as easy as a single click. This software works on Mac, Windows, and Linux-based computer systems, as well as all of the major smartphones.

There is a new security feature called LastPass Sentry that will alert you if your logon credentials are compromised. LastPass checks the PwnedList database (database of compromised accounts) to see if your e-mail address is on the list. If so, you receive an e-mail notifying you that your ID has been compromised. The new feature is available for all versions of LastPass.

LastPass also now supports two-factor authentication. Users can add a layer of protection to their LastPass account by requiring a second login step. LastPass supports integration with Google Authenticator, Duo Security, YubiKey, and more.

LastPass does offer a free version available for download, as well as a paid premium version that offers a few additional features. We recommend trying the free version to see if the software meets your needs before making any purchases. You can download and take this software for a test run from its website at www.lastpass.com.

WordRake for Microsoft Word

WordRake fundamentally consists of a set of rules designed to cut flabby verbiage from your writing. Even good authors (and we have a club ring!) clearly can use some editing. Even our editors missed most of what WordRake found. There is now also a version for Microsoft Outlook, which is sold separately from the Microsoft Word version.

To be sure, it's not perfect. The founders purposely do not include an "Accept All" button because they know we can never tame the infinite variety and positioning of words. You have to approve each edit. Because of that, we wouldn't use it for casual writing. But for articles or any other writing that is significant, we sure would.

WordRake's creator, Gary Kinder, is a lawyer himself, and he's taught over 1,000 writing programs to firms like Sidley and Jones Day. He's also a *New York Times* best-selling author. He must use his own program!

WordRake is a Word add-on that inserts itself into Word's ribbon. It works with Word 2007 to 2016 running on Windows 10. Support for Word 64-bit versions includes 2010 and 2013. Support for Windows 10 isn't currently listed on the vendor's website. The program is licensed on a subscription basis. The one-year cost is $129, two years is $229, and three years is $259. All of them can be purchased from the website at www.wordrake.com. We recommend that you try the free 30-day trial before committing.

It's been reported that the next version will have two separate functions, Clear and Concise—what WordRake does now—and a new function called Plain Writing. Plain Writing will tackle legalese, suggesting ways to eliminate extra legalese language from documents.

Users may opt to bundle the purchase of WordRake for Microsoft Word along with WordRake for Microsoft Outlook, saving you some money off the two subscriptions should you be in the market for both products.

Redact Assistant

Redact Assistant, another wonderful piece of software from Payne Group, provides an invaluable tool to assist users with removing sensitive content from documents. This product can be run against a single file or multiple files at the same time.

Some of the features of the redaction tool include

- Redact multiple terms in a single process
- Search and Replace multiple terms in a single process
- Create lists of terms for specific redaction and search/replace criteria
- Use Word's and Excel's native search options as well as Regular Expression to create your list of terms
- Save and share your lists with colleagues on projects for collaboration
- Process multiple files at once using the stand-alone component
- Manually select words for quick redaction using Word and add-ins
- View and save reports instantly

This product is compatible with Windows 10 and can be used to redact information present within Microsoft 2010 to 2016 and Microsoft Excel 2010 to 2016. Please note that it is only compatible with the 32-bit versions of these Office products, and it doesn't currently support Adobe Acrobat PDF files.

There is a free 30-day trial, which users should take advantage of. This product is sold on the vendor's website for $45 per license (www.thepayne group.com).

Redact-It

Redact-It Desktop version is another redaction tool that we want to inform our readers about. This product supports multiple file formats to redact sensitive content from. Unlike Redact Assistant, this product can remove sensitive content from Adobe Acrobat PDF files, but cannot be run against multiple files at the same time (the Enterprise version does this).

This product does not output redacted documents in their native formats. Instead, users may select the output file format as PDF, TIFF, or CSF (Content Sealed Format) files.

Finally, this redaction tool is a stand-alone product and doesn't integrate with the native applications. This requires the user to launch this software in order to redact sensitive content from a file the user selects. This software also provides the ability to redact Social Security numbers, telephone numbers, e-mail addresses, and dates of birth automatically.

The Redact-It desktop version starts at $295 per license (Premier version), but you are also required to purchase maintenance at a cost of $59. That makes the total cost $354 for the first year. Redact-It is available for purchase from the vendor's website at www.redact.com.

CHAPTER TWENTY-SEVEN

E-Mail Providers

Arguably, the most used technology for any attorney is e-mail. The default communication method is sending electronic messages instead of breaking out the typewriter and postage stamp. And most of the profession prefers e-mail to any other kind of electronic communication. That may change, but not yet.

What are some of the considerations when choosing an e-mail provider? Is the communication secure? What devices can access the messages? You'll also need to consider if there are any limitations for the e-mail such as attachment size, attachment type, fonts, color, and so on. Sending large attachments could be an issue for some attorneys. If your e-mail system has a low threshold for attachment size, you'll need some sort of file-sharing system to collaborate or distribute the information. You may want to consider investigating Citrix ShareFile for securely sharing files instead of sending them as attachments. Another alternative is to implement the Large File Send option in Mimecast, where you can set additional attachment options such as expiration time, printing restrictions, and so on.

Microsoft Exchange

By far, the most popular mechanism to handle e-mail is Microsoft Exchange. Many solo and small firm attorneys host Exchange on their own network while others use a hosted Exchange system with a third-party provider. Having your own Exchange server gives you a lot of flexibility. You have total control over the configuration of the Exchange server. As an example, you can increase the attachment size that is allowed, define distribution groups, and create rules that automatically take action with messages.

By default, Exchange will attempt to send messages using TLS (Transport Layer Security), which is an encrypted communications channel. You have the option of enforcing the TLS connection as well. This means that if you have a sensitive matter, you can configure Exchange to always use TLS when communicating with a particular domain or e-mail address. This would ensure that any message you send to that domain or e-mail address would be encrypted.

Exchange also includes some security controls for mobile devices. You would configure the Exchange ActiveSync Mailbox Policies to enforce certain requirements. You can require a password, which is an absolute must. When you require a password, other options become available such as alphanumeric password, require encryption, require encryption on storage card, number of failed attempts allowed, minimum password length, maximum inactivity timer, and password expiration. If you have Exchange Enterprise client access licenses (additional cost and add-on), you can then restrict the usage of certain features. You can allow or prevent the usage of removable storage, camera, Wi-Fi, Internet sharing from device, remote desktop from device, and so on. The base level security features (e.g., password policies) are included with Exchange for no additional cost.

Having your own Exchange server does mean hardware and software expense, although it can be very affordable when dealing with virtualized servers. Having control of your own Exchange instance does have the advantage and flexibility of integrating with other applications. As an example, having your own Exchange server tends to make it easier to integrate your e-mail with your practice management software.

Office 365

Each year we continue to see more and more solo and small firm attorneys moving to Office 365. There are a lot of different offerings for Office 365. If you are looking to abandon your local Exchange server, you can purchase a subscription that includes e-mail provided by Exchange. If you only want Exchange and not the Office products, take a look at the Exchange Online Plans. There are other online Exchange products as well such as Online Archiving, Online Protection, and Online Advanced Threat Protection. The bottom line is that Microsoft has a lot of options for the solo and small firm attorney from basic e-mail only to full-function office suites, analytics, advanced e-discovery tools, and much more.

Gmail

We see a lot of solo and small firm lawyers using Gmail as their e-mail address. While it is totally functional, it is not very professional looking. We believe that we are now at the time where every lawyer's e-mail address should be associated with a domain name. Forget about an e-mail address from Hotmail, Yahoo, AOL, and the like. Use of such addresses is a virtual billboard saying that you are not a modern attorney.

As we've mentioned elsewhere in this book, using the free Gmail from Google is not where you want to be since you've given Google the right to access your content. You should be using G Suite since it provides more reliable, secure communications in addition to productivity tools. With G Suite you can also have an e-mail address associated with your domain name even though Google is providing the service. This means you can have an e-mail address such as yourname@yourlawfirm.com. Now doesn't that look a lot more professional than a Gmail address?

Other E-Mail Providers

There are a lot of providers of e-mail services for the taking. Consider how you would access the e-mail. Is it a POP (Post Office Protocol) account, where you have to download the message to your local computer? POP accounts are a problem if you need to access your mailbox from multiple devices. The sent and received items aren't the same across the various computers and mobile devices. IMAP (Internet Message Access Protocol) is a better type of e-mail account and will maintain synchronized items across all devices.

Even better solutions are some sort of hosted Exchange where you use Outlook to access the mailbox that contains your e-mail, calendar entries, tasks, contacts, and so on. That way all the data stays on the provider's server, which you just access using the mail client from any device.

Additional E-Mail Considerations

Besides just e-mail, you should also address spam control, encryption capabilities, potential archiving, threat protection (e.g., viruses, malicious links, malware attachments), and metadata removal. You may be able to address these functions with the e-mail provider or it may steer you toward hosting your own Exchange server in order to control how each item is configured. Third-party vendors can also provide these some or all of these services.

If you have your own Exchange server, inbound e-mail is routed through a provider that scans the messages and attachments for any malicious code. The message is then delivered to your server or blocked if it is infected. Outbound messages are sent to the provider for processing as well. They may scan for malicious attachments or provide the ability to encrypt the e-mail.

Some systems have the ability to provide URL protection too. The URL in the message is changed to route through the provider's servers. The provider then inspects the URL to see if it is malicious or has the ability to deposit malware on your machine. Clicking the modified URL sends you to the third-party provider. If the URL is "clean," you will be rerouted to the original destination. If the URL is suspicious or determined to be malicious, a warning panel will be displayed before sending you to the original destination or access will be totally blocked for known malicious sites.

CHAPTER TWENTY-EIGHT

Backup Strategies

by Catherine Sanders Reach

The need for a firm to have adequate backup procedures in place is implied in ABA Model Rules of Professional Conduct 1.1, 1.3, and 1.4. How can you diligently and competently serve clients and provide timely communication if your files are lost or destroyed? What if your hard drive crashed, your cloud provider disappeared in a puff of smoke, a lengthy brief became corrupted, Google lost all your e-mail, you got to the office and your server was gone, you dumped your coffee on your laptop, or you left your iPhone in the back of a cab? Would your reaction be "no problem" or "oh NO"?

Five-Step Backup Strategy

Securing and protecting your firm's data is essential. Client files, important communications, and valuable work-product often exist exclusively in digital format today, and thus a major data loss could have catastrophic professional and ethical ramifications.

Whether you're revisiting an existing backup strategy or seriously implementing one for the first time, this five-step plan will help you make sure you're covering your bases.

Step 1: Analyze

The first step in developing a data backup strategy for your firm is to analyze your current data usage. What data do you store, where do you store it, how often do you access it, and what are the risks and costs associated with losing that data? This is a challenging endeavor in the current computing environment, as data may be spread across numerous devices and services: computers and smartphones, firm servers and cloud computing platforms, and so on.

Be sure to involve everyone in your firm in this exercise. You'll probably be surprised to learn where firm employees—lawyers and staff alike—are storing valuable data. Use the opportunity to review your firm's overall handling of sensitive data. If, for example, sensitive documents are being sent to personal e-mail addresses so employees can work from home over the weekend, you may be facing serious security problems that will need to be addressed along with the backup issues.

In the end, your backup analysis should establish

- What electronic data your firm currently uses
- Where that data resides, including the specific vendor/host if it's held outside of the office
- The approximate amount of data (e.g., 2 TB)
- The sensitivity of data, both in terms of time (i.e., urgent matters) and confidentiality

Step 2: Plan

Once you have a firm grasp of the size and scope of the data you need to back up, you should begin developing an actual backup plan. Your backup plan should provide at least two levels of redundancy, with both data redundancy (more than one backup of any given file) and geographic redundancy (backups housed in more than one geographic location).

The exact tools and software you use will vary widely depending on the size of your firm and the complexity of your electronic efforts. In general, you should:

- Focus on business-grade tools. Popular online backup tools geared toward consumers and less-sensitive consumer data may not be appropriate.
- Plan for where you'll be, not where you are. The quantity of data you need to back up is only going to increase as time goes by.
- Work with outside companies that hold your data. You should try to keep local copies of data you store with a third party, and you should be sure the third party has its own backup strategy.
- Keep security at the front of your mind. Data needs to be backed up, but it also needs to be kept secure.

Step 3: Implement

It may seem obvious to say that the next step is to implement your plan, but this is unfortunately where many well-intentioned backup strategies fall apart. Corners are cut both in cost and time, key efforts are entrusted to people who lack technology expertise, software and hardware is installed but never properly configured, and so forth.

Keep in mind that proper backup is critical to maintaining a healthy, stable, ethical law practice, and invest in its implementation appropriately. If your firm lacks the technology know-how to do this in-house, find an expert to help.

The keys to proper implementation:

- Don't cut corners—follow through on the plan you developed in Step 2.
- That said, stay flexible—you may discover during implementation that you missed something. This is the time to correct the error.
- If necessary, get expert help to implement your backup system correctly.

Step 4: Test

It's an all too common horror story: a business has a catastrophic data loss, turns to its backup system to recover the data, and only then discovers there's a serious flaw in its backup strategy. Maybe data was backing up monthly rather than daily, or key files were being left out of regular backups entirely, or perhaps the backup hard drive itself has failed. There can be many causes, but the results are the same: your backup efforts come to nothing because you've failed to test your system.

As a best practice, you should test your backup solution immediately after implementation and routinely thereafter. Simulate real-world disaster scenarios, from the major (total loss of a system) to the relatively minor (accidentally erasing a single file).

Not only does regular testing help identify problems in your backup setup, it also has the benefit of training your staff to quickly and efficiently recover files in the event that it's necessary to do so. This means that if you ever experience a real computer loss and need to restore from your backups, you'll be prepared to do so.

- Test your setup immediately to be sure it's working as intended.
- Periodically retest your systems to ensure they're functional and data is being backed up appropriately.

- Prepare to restore data quickly in the event of data loss to minimize impact on your firm.

Step 5: Review

Your data backup strategy will begin to be outdated almost as soon as you implement it. The reason is simple: technology advances at an incredibly rapid rate. New tools, new software, new data—each requires that you adjust your strategy.

- Conduct a full review of your strategy at least annually—more often if your setup is particularly complicated.
- Revisit your backup strategy anytime you make a significant technology investment.

The Cloud

Offline Access: When the Cloud Is Down

Sometimes you just don't have access to the Internet. Whether you're traveling in a plane without Wi-Fi, or in a remote (or sometimes not so remote) area that has no Wi-Fi, 3G, or 4G coverage, or simply because your cable or T1 line is down due to weather or some other outage, on occasion you will have some forced downtime because you can't access your cloud-based documents, send e-mails, or pull up a client's contact information from a cloud-based provider. In fact, it is likely to happen at the most inopportune moment. Fortunately, there are ways to access online information locally.

Google in the House

Gmail, Google Docs, and Google Calendar are all available in an offline mode. Of course, you can also set up IMAP or POP to maintain a local copy in the e-mail client of your choice. Likewise you can access a version of your calendar anytime. Alternatively, you can sync it with a local calendar application, like Mozilla's Lightning.

To set up Docs offline (https://support.google.com/docs/answer/6388102 ?hl=en&rd=2), go to the settings in Google Docs and click the link at the bottom to "set up Docs offline." You can set up offline Docs locally, though you will have read-only access to Google Docs, spreadsheets, presentations, and so on. For Microsoft Office or other document formats you uploaded to Google Docs, you will still be able to edit them if you have Office software installed. Offline access to Google Docs, mail, and the like only works in the Chrome browser. Google recommends that you do not use this option for shared computers, since the files will be available to anyone who has access to those computers. Google Apps administrators can use the Chrome browser for Business MSI (https://www.google.com/intl/en/chrome/business /browser/) to push out offline capabilities to the entire office.

Office 365, the subscription-based Microsoft Office suite, makes it easy to set up bidirectional sync for Outlook and Word (plus PowerPoint and Excel). Your contacts and e-mails can be local to a machine if the cloud is down.

Online file storage and sync services like Dropbox keep a local copy of your file, unless you take steps to remove it. Drive, Google's competitor to Dropbox, allows for offline access (https://support.google.com/drive /answer/2375012?hl=en) in the settings, through a few clicks and a Chrome Web Store install. Apple's iCloud, similar to Dropbox, maintains a cloud copy of your Apple content (http://www.apple.com/icloud/) and a local copy.

Tools like Evernote (https://evernote.com/?var=c) also make having a local copy of your data easy and available. A lightweight software version resides on the desktop, syncing with the cloud version and your apps. Offline or online, you have access to all the information stored in Evernote.

Legal Document Management Ease

Whether you're creating documents and e-mail in the cloud and maintaining a local copy, or generating content on your desktop and syncing to the cloud, offline access for the "simple" tools is pretty straightforward. What about offline access to more complex applications, like legal document management or practice management? In most cases there is not a complete replication of the software and data locally, although the growing development of HTML5 will be changing that in the near future. For now, many lawyers still have a few offline options.

Some practice management applications like MyCase, Clio, and Rocket Matter have various sync capabilities with Google Apps, as well as with Google Calendar and Gmail. Since Google makes these services available offline, you can access some of the stored data, though not the entire database. In all three cases the representatives for these products were enthusiastic that offline access was in the development calendar. Additionally, these providers have sync capabilities with Microsoft Outlook, which will also serve to create a local copy of some of the data (although you will need to sync Outlook with Google to sync with Rocket Matter).

While traditional document management software like Worldox now offers a web-accessible version (Worldox/Web Mobile—https://www.worldox.com /mobility-sharing/worldox-web/), the files are still available on the local server. Native software as a service (SaaS) document management provider NetDocuments offers to set up a local version of the NetDocuments repository, so that users can have access offline. This is the local document server (https://support.netdocuments.com/hc/en-us/articles/205219980-Local -Document-Server), which is an add-on for an additional fee.

Needless to say, the above is not comprehensive, but rather it provides a taste of some of the options. Check with your favorite cloud providers to see if and how you can access information offline. As we see business adoption of the cloud mature, we will likely see a rise in the number of offline options to address not only the concern for when Internet access is slow or impossible, but also for business continuity.

Cloud Due Diligence: Questions for SaaS Vendors

It's important to carefully examine all technology before buying, whether it's SaaS or traditional. Here are 20 questions you should be sure to ask any SaaS vendor before committing your data to their hands. Vendors that aren't willing or able to answer these questions should be treated with caution.

- How do you help with data migration from other products?
- What kind of documentation (e.g., knowledge base, product manual) is available for your product?
- How often are new features added to your product?
- How does your software integrate with other products on the market, especially products in the legal market?
- How many attorneys/firms are currently using your product?
- What hours is your tech support available?
- Do you offer a Service Level Agreement (SLA) and/or would you be willing to negotiate one?
- What types of guarantees and disclaimers of liability do you include in your terms of service?
- How do you safeguard the privacy/confidentiality of stored data?
- Who has access to my firm's data when it's stored on your servers?
- Have you (or your data center) ever had a data breach?
- How often, and in what manner, will my data be backed up?
- What is your company's history—for example, how long have you been in business and where do you derive your funding?
- Can I remove or copy my data from your servers in a nonproprietary format?

- Where does my data reside—inside or outside of the United States?
- What happens to my data if your company is sold or goes out of business?
- What happens to my data if I stop paying?
- Do you require a contractual agreement for a certain length of service (e.g., 12 months, 24 months)?
- What is the pricing history of your product? How often do you increase rates?
- Are there any incidental costs I should be aware of?

Backup: Disc Image

You have your computer backup strategy carefully planned. Your files are backed up in three locations, your servers are in a RAID array, you have all your installation disks and license numbers handy, and you have a test restore for your files scheduled on a regular basis. You are ready for the day that your hard drive fails. Or are you?

The best backup plans in the world often fail to recognize the time commitment involved in a ground-up hard drive recovery, including reinstalling the operating system, software, drivers, and files, plus customization and configuration. To speed things up, consider adding disk imaging to your backup arsenal. Disk imaging (or cloning) essentially takes a snapshot of your hard drive, including software, configuration, files, and so forth, so that you can get your computer back up and running faster.

- **For older operating systems or for networks** you will need to use a third-party software tool such as Acronis True Image (http://www.acronis.com/en-us/promo/update-your-browser/index.html), Norton Ghost (http://us.norton.com/), or ShadowProtect (https://www.storagecraft.com/products/shadowprotect) to create a disk image. Most of the third-party tools will cost $50 to $100; however, there are some free tools, like DriveImage XML(http://www.runtime .org/driveimage-xml.htm), that require a bit more technical skill. MS introduced drive imaging into the Vista operating system (Ultimate, Business, and Enterprise only), but most reports suggest it is difficult to use and not extremely effective. The third-party commercial tools are designed to make disk imaging easy to use, and effective.
- **Mac OS X 10.4 (Tiger).** Macintosh users still running Tiger will need to get third-party tools to create a disk image. These tools include shareware Carbon Copy Cloner (http://bombich.com/) and

Super Duper (http://www.shirt-pocket.com/SuperDuper/SuperDuper Description.html—$27.95 fully functional), and probably quite a few others.

- **Windows 7, 8, and 10.** Microsoft offers disk imaging as built-in functionality in all supported versions of the OS. It is reportedly easy to set up, and restore from, as detailed in these step-by-step instructions (http://www.groovypost.com/howto/microsoft/windows-7 /create-a-windows-7-system-image/).
- **Mac OS X 10.5 (Leopard) and up.** Mac users running current versions of the operating system have cloning built in through the Time Machine feature. Mac 101 has a nice set of instructions on how to setup Time Machine to create a disk image (https://support.apple.com /en-us/HT201250). This tutorial also includes instructions on how to restore your hard drive from Time Machine.

Although you will be given options with the third-party tools, and the built-in functionality of your OS, to clone your drive to a set of DVDs, this is not practical given the huge drive capacities on today's computers. Save the disk image to an external hard drive, and you won't have to worry about switching disks or space limitations. An external hard drive with a terabyte capacity costs around $100. These devices are available with USB and Firewire connectors, and are truly plug-and-play.

Imaging has long been used by IT departments, which are constantly deploying computers to new users or restoring crashed hard drives. But *anyone* who wants to keep a complete working copy of their hard drive on hand should consider adding disk imaging to their backup arsenal.

Backup: E-mail

Google's Gmail has made news in the past couple of years by "losing" users' e-mail[1]—often years' worth. While these outages have primarily affected the free Gmail service, even access to the paid Google Apps has occasionally been lost.[2] More egregiously, in 2008 Charter Communications (an ISP) accidently deleted 14,000 customers e-mail accounts—and all the e-mail

1. Sean Hollister, *Gmail Accidentally Resetting Accounts, Years of Correspondence Vanish into the Cloud?*, ENGADGET (Feb. 27, 2011), https://www.engadget.com/2011/02/27/gmail-accidentally -resetting-accounts-years-of-correspondence-v/.

2. Clint Boulton, *Google Gmail, Google Apps Outage in the Cloud*, EWEEK (Aug. 7, 2008), http:// www.eweek.com/c/a/Messaging-and-Collaboration/Google-Gmail-Google-Apps-Suffer-Outage-in -The-Cloud.

messages in them.[3] For lawyers who are using the free Gmail, or other web-mail services, as their primary e-mail tool for client communications, one must ask, "How are you backing that up?"

With Gmail, there are a number of options.

- You can run Gmail Offline Chrome App (https://support.google.com /mail/answer/1306847?hl=en) to maintain a local copy of Gmail. This is a pretty useful option, letting you choose which folders you want to maintain locally. Look in Gmail Settings under "offline" to set this up.
- Another option is to set up IMAP, which synchronizes your Gmail to a downloaded e-mail client (like the free and multi-OS compatible Thunderbird, https://www.mozilla.org/en-US/thunderbird/, or the open source Zimbra, http://www.zimbra.com/downloads/zimbra -desktop/) to keep on your server or hard drive. (Which you *do* back up, don't you?)
- Or you can set up POP to keep a copy of your e-mail local, but with no synchronization.

There is an extension for Thunderbird (http://webmail.mozdev.org/) to integrate with most major webmail providers, and Zimbra (http://www.zimbra .com/downloads/zimbra-desktop/) also has built-in aggregation. For other web-based e-mail services, including those provided by your ISP, you can hunt around for instructions or FAQs to see what your options are for creating a local backup.

To back up e-mail in MS Outlook if you are using hosted Exchange, make sure the provider keeps a backup copy. There is no easy way to archive a folder full of e-mails in MS Outlook. If you want to save e-mails from a stand-alone installation of MS Outlook you can save each e-mail as an HTML or text file, or all the folders as a .pst file. However, Adobe Acrobat has provided an Outlook plug-in in their professional line that lets you quickly and easily create a sortable, searchable PDF archive of e-mail messages. You can select a folder, and right (alternate) click to create a PDF portfolio of all the e-mail messages in the folder, which can be searched, sorted, and extracted. E-mail attachments are also saved, but they are not converted to PDF. For management of closed matters, simple e-discovery, and archiving, this is a really great feature of the Adobe Acrobat Pro version.

---

3. Marguerite Reardon, *Charter Accidently Deletes 14,000 E-Mail Accounts*, CNET (Jan. 24, 2008), http://www.cnet.com/news/charter-accidently-deletes-14000-e-mail-accounts/.

Really, there are lots of options. Don't let your record of client communication fly in the ether without a safety net.

Backup: Social Media

While there are many ways to get back into social media content, the information is vast and fleeting. You may have a need to capture and keep social media content, either for your firm or your client, as backup, as a record of interactions, or to ensure compliance with a social media policy. You may have heard of the Wayback Machine, also known as the Internet Archive, which records and archives certain web pages. The problem is that this site is inconsistent as to which sites it archives, and for how long. For lawyers who want to take control of monitoring and storing web page content, enter NextPoint's Preservation Cloud (http://www.nextpoint.com/), which crawls and archives specific web properties—blogs, social media sites, or web pages. You can tag, export, and search the data collected. This is a cloud tool, so the data is stored on external servers, which does introduce some risk in using the service, though it is easy to sign up and get going as there is no installation or configuration. Similarly, PageVault will help you capture copies of social media and web pages.

There are tools like Backupify (http://www.datto.com/backupify) that back up Google Apps and Office 365 and also Facebook pages and Twitter accounts. A personal account is free, but limits storage to 1GB and backs up only weekly. To archive your website, talk to your site host. For those running WordPress there are the Backup Buddy (https://ithemes.com/purchase /backupbuddy/) or BackWPup (https://wordpress.org/plugins/backwpup/) WordPress plugins to back up your posts.

Online Backup

With the growing availability of broadband Internet access, online storage for your critical data is also an option. Products like Mozy (www.mozy.com), Carbonite (www.carbonite.com), and CrashPlan (www.crashplan.com) provide a wide range of support and services.

The online backup services are cloud services, and should be well scrutinized. See the ABA Legal Technology Resource Center resource on cloud computing ethics opinion (http://www.americanbar.org/groups/departments _offices/legal_technology_resources/resources/charts_fyis/cloud-ethics-chart .html) that provide some useful information about evaluating the services.

Note that file synchronization tools such as SugarSync, OneDrive, and Dropbox are not online backups. Online backup services offer encryption in transit and storage, versioning, and process automation, as well as server backup and other sophisticated functions needed by businesses.

Backup: Hardware and Software

Numerous software options are available and often come bundled with the storage device. Forget the old disc and tape devices, and go to external hard drives like Maxtor or ABS. The software is more important than the hardware, because it has to work well for the user or the user won't use it! Too often lawyers buy the backup device but fail to use it because the software is cumbersome or does not have automatic settings. Consider Backup Now, BackupMyPC, Retrospect Backup, or CMS's Bounce Back. Whichever method you choose, your office computer should be backed up daily. That is where the competent person comes in! Unless the backup system is used, the technology is worthless. Make sure a competent person carries out this important security step in your firm. Also, do a periodic test to restore a file to make sure your backup system is working.

CHAPTER TWENTY-NINE

Social Media for Lawyers— An Overview

by Jennifer Ellis, Lowenthal & Abrams/
Jennifer Ellis, JD

Social media has become a crucial part of the average American's life. As a result, whether they want to or not, attorneys must, at the very least, appreciate the impact of social media on their clients. Failure to understand how social media can affect clients' cases could lead to serious damage to a case that might result in a malpractice complaint. Further, wise attorneys will take advantage of social media to develop their practices through the networking and marketing opportunities provided by both their own websites and the various social media sites and applications.

The best way to appreciate how important social media has become in people's day-to-day lives is to look at some statistics for popular sites:

- Facebook—1.71 billion monthly active users[1]
  - 167 million daily active users in North America[2]
  - 169.2 million users in the United States by 2018[3]
- LinkedIn—450 million users[4]
  - 128 million users in the United States[5]

---

1. As of July 27, 2016. http://expandedramblings.com/index.php/by-the-numbers-17 -amazing-facebook-stats/.
2. As of November 5, 2015. http://expandedramblings.com/index.php/by-the-numbers-17 -amazing-facebook-stats/2/.
3. As of March 4, 2015. http://expandedramblings.com/index.php/by-the-numbers-17 -amazing-facebook-stats/2/.
4. As of August 4, 2016. http://expandedramblings.com/index.php/by-the-numbers-a-few -important-linkedin-stats/.
5. As of April 30, 2016. http://expandedramblings.com/index.php/by-the-numbers-a-few -important-linkedin-stats/.

- Snapchat—over 100 million daily active users
  - "On any given day, Snapchat reaches 41% of all 18-34 year-olds in the United States"[6]
- YouTube—Over 1 billion users
  - "[A]lmost one-third of people on the Internet"[7]
- Instagram—500 million monthly active users
  - 20 percent inside the United States[8]
- Twitter—313 million monthly active users[9]
  - Twitter numbers dropped from 316 million a year ago to 313 million in 2016
  - Of the sites reported, only Twitter has decreased

A Pew study from 2015 showed that 74 percent of all Internet users use social media.[10] According to Statista.com, that number has increased to 78 percent.[11] Mobile use of cell phones is high and continues to increase. In 2015, "40% of cell phone owners use a social networking site on their phone and 27% do so on a typical day."[12] This ease of access means people use social media on the go as a method to locate businesses they plan to hire. It also means people have a tendency to use social media to quickly share intimate details about their lives and activities. The former shows the value of social media as a marketing tool. The latter shows the amount of information people are sharing, which can be harmful to their cases.

Attorneys who plan to use social media should keep in mind that the ethical risks involved, both in terms of evidence collection and marketing, are very real. Therefore, a proper understanding of appropriate and ethical behavior is extremely important.

It is also important to understand that in certain areas of practice, it is now verging on malpractice, and the author would argue it *is* malpractice, to fail to communicate with clients about whether and how they use social media. Failing to warn the client to halt or at least limit social media use could result in that client posting materials that will harm his case. Failure to warn a client about evidence preservation could result in substantial sanctions for spoliation.[13] In addition, it is quite conceivable that the opposing party will

---

6. https://www.snapchat.com/ads/.
7. https://www.youtube.com/yt/press/statistics.html.
8. https://instagram.com/press/.
9. https://about.twitter.com/company.
10. http://www.pewinternet.org/fact-sheets/social-networking-fact-sheet/.
11. http://www.statista.com/statistics/273476/percentage-of-us-population-with-a-social-network-profile/.
12. *Id.*
13. *See* Lester v. Allied Concrete Co. (order dated Sept. 1, 2011).

post information harmful to his case and failure on the part of the attorney to seek out possible harmful posts can result in loss of a substantially better bargaining position, or even loss of a case that might have been won.

Specific Sites and Applications

Social media essentially includes sites and applications that enable people to share information, pictures, videos, and the like at a rapid rate, and, in return, allows other people to respond to the shared content. In some cases, social media is referred to as Web 2.0. Web 1.0 refers to sites that serve to provide one-way communication, much like a newsletter or a book. Traditional websites are Web 1.0.

Currently, some of the most popular social media sites and applications in the United States include Facebook, Twitter, LinkedIn, Pinterest, YouTube, WhatsApp, and Instagram.[14] Further, blogs are sometimes considered part of social media and so will be included in this discussion. At this point, there are over 150 million blogs on the web and almost 50 percent of Internet users read blogs.

Marketing and Networking

It is not always easy to understand how social media can increase the potential for bringing in new clients. It is therefore important to think of social media as having uses for practice building.

Advertising

Social media includes straightforward advertising. Sites such as Facebook, YouTube, and LinkedIn provide the opportunity to purchase small ads that appear on the top or side of the page. These ads are managed through varying means, demographics, keywords, areas of interest, and so on. Generally, the cost of the ads is controlled through a bidding process known as pay-per-click. The site provides a suggested fee that its algorithm suggests will be successful. The purchaser identifies the amount he is willing to pay and competes against those who are seeking to advertise to the same individuals. Normally, the purchaser pays only when someone clicks on an ad. Some sites allow advertisers to pay per impression. This means that the purchaser pays when the ad is shown.

---

14. While Google+ has not served Google well as a social media site, Google Business remains an important part of being found on the web.

Networking

Social media provides substantial opportunities for networking. It simply moves the networking from the bar association or educational program, to networking online. Providing information about interests, sharing day-to-day activities, responding to the posts of others—each of these behaviors is simply a way to connect with other people. Those people, in turn, may need an attorney or may need to refer someone else to an attorney—just as in the offline world. Further, people tend to recommend individuals who they know, or feel they know, and social media allows the formation of that kind of relationship.

Content

Sharing useful content is a crucial part of social media for attorneys. Providing high-quality content that informs users about the areas of law in which an attorney practices is an excellent way to bring attention to that attorney. The content can be as simple as commenting on a case on Facebook, sharing a useful link on Twitter, or providing a detailed analysis of a specific issue on a blog. This content shows potential clients that the attorney is knowledgeable in her area(s) of practice. Further, well-written content, related to the work the attorney performs, provides a substantial boost to search engine optimization and online reputation.

Specific Sites

Different social media sites provide different tools. Further, some sites are better utilized by attorneys who tend to represent businesses, while others are better utilized by attorneys who represent individuals. It is important to target the correct site or mixture of sites for the best return on investment of time and/or money. Research the type of people and/or businesses that use a site before you make up your mind about where to extend your efforts.

Content of Posts

When you post on social media, you need to consider whether you are causing any ethical problems for yourself. Given the open nature of social media, a number of issues can arise when lawyers post. Two important ones: Is social media advertising and are you forming an attorney/client relationship by answering questions?

Is Social Media Advertising?

When choosing what to write on social media, it is important to determine whether your post is advertising under Model Rule 7.2 (or whatever rule applies in your jurisdiction). If your account is completely private and you share only with friends and family, chances are very good that your posts would not be considered advertising. However, the question becomes cloudier when you open up your account to a larger group. The author's view is that if you are not certain whether your post is advertising, assume it is and act in accordance with your jurisdiction's rules. Some jurisdictions define advertising very clearly. Others do not.

As noted previously, Twitter is a site that is problematic for states such as Florida, where any posting might be considered advertising. In its guidelines on social media, Florida's advertising standing committee states about Twitter that pages of individual lawyers on social networking sites that are used solely for social purposes, to maintain social contact with family and close friends, are not subject to the lawyer advertising rules." Pages appearing on networking sites that are used to promote the lawyer or law firm's practice are subject to the lawyer advertising rules. These pages must therefore comply with all of the general regulations set forth in Rules 4-7.11 through 4-7.18 and 4-7.21." [15] This language means that many posts on Twitter would be considered advertising, simply because most people have their accounts entirely open and it is common for users to discuss a cross-section of personal and work-related details of their lives.

Most problematic, given Twitter's 140-character limit, is that, in Florida, the tweet must include geographic information as well as "the name of at least one lawyer in the firm." The attorney may use appropriate abbreviations for the geographic requirements, which helps, to a degree. However, as soon as the poster puts both the full name of a lawyer and a geographic location, most of the allotted characters will be used up, substantially limiting the value of any tweet.

Florida amended its guidelines in 2016 to allow lawyers to create a restricted account. When the account is restricted, then the rules change, because of the fact that the audience sought the communication.

> If access to a lawyer's Twitter postings is restricted to the followers of
> the particular lawyer, the information posted there is information at

---

15. Fla. Bar Standing Comm. on Advertising Guidelines for Networking Sites (rev. May 9, 2016), https://www.floridabar.org/TFB/TFBResources.nsf/Attachments/18BC39758BB54A598525 7B590063EDA8/$FILE/Guidelines%20-%20Social%20Networking%20Sites.pdf?OpenElement.

the request of a prospective client and is subject to the lawyer advertising rules, but is exempt from the filing requirement under Rule 4-7.20(e). Any communications that a lawyer makes on an unsolicited basis to prospective clients to obtain "followers" is subject to the lawyer advertising rules, as with any other social media . . .

Florida is not the only jurisdiction with special requirements for Twitter, so be certain to check your state's rules before you tweet. That said, many jurisdictions have not placed onerous requirements on lawyer's abilities to use Twitter, and a well-written tweet can be an excellent way to drive traffic to your website or share useful information. Fortunately, Twitter will very shortly do away with its 140-character limitation, which will make many of these issues a moot point.

Pennsylvania's Analysis

In Formal Opinion 2014-300 (Ethical Obligations for Attorneys Using Social Media), the Pennsylvania Bar Association provides a detailed guidance opinion on social media use by attorneys. This includes analysis of what is acceptable for marketing purposes.

As related to advertising, and connecting with others on social media, the opinion offers the following:

1. Attorneys may advertise using social media.

There is nothing in the rules that prevents attorneys from utilizing social media for advertising purposes. In doing so, the attorney must follow all relevant ethical rules.

2. Attorneys may endorse other attorneys on social media.

It is acceptable to endorse other lawyers; however, the endorsements must be accurate. If you choose to endorse a lawyer, it would be wise to make certain you actually know the lawyer and his or her skillset and abilities. Many attorneys on sites such as Avvo and LinkedIn provide endorsements when they are complete strangers to the lawyer they are endorsing.

3. Attorneys may respond to endorsements and reviews and may solicit them.

In Pennsylvania, under Rule 7.2, "no advertisement or public communication shall contain an endorsement by a celebrity or public figure." In addition, if an endorsement is paid, this must be revealed. Both of these rules apply to social media use in Pennsylvania. The latter rule, involving paid endorsements, is common in most states.

Regardless of who provides the review or endorsement, it must be honest. It is the job of the attorney to correct the review if it contains improper information, is dishonest, or is false or misleading. "If the lawyer is unable to correct or remove the listing, he or she should contact the person posting the information and request that the person remove or correct the item."[16] Attorneys in Pennsylvania may not pay for or offer anything of value in exchange for a review.

It is appropriate for an attorney to respond to a review, but he must be careful how he responds to a negative review. "[L]awyers may not reveal client confidential information in response to a negative online review."[17] Interpret the concept of confidential client information broadly. In the author's experience, the best way to respond to a negative review is (1) no response at all, (2) a polite response asking for the person to phone or e-mail so you can see if you can resolve the problem, (3) a general response stating that you are sorry the person was displeased. An attorney in Illinois was reprimanded due to sharing confidential information in response to a negative review. She was suspended when she revealed that the client had engaged in a physical altercation and other confidential information, and that was why the client lost the case.[18]

California's Analysis

California is a bit unique in the fact that it provides a rather bright line rule about what is and is not advertising. In California, if something is considered advertising based on the 1-400 Rule of Professional Conduct and 6157–6159.2 Business and Professional Code, then it is controlled by those rules. If it does not, it is not controlled by the rules of advertising, though it could potentially be controlled by some other rule.

In Opinion 2012-176, the State Bar of California provides an excellent and detailed analysis that helps its attorneys determine whether something constitutes advertising.[19]

---

16. Pa. Bar Ass'n Comm. on Legal Ethics and Prof'l Responsibility Formal Op. 2014-300.

17. Formal Op. 2014-300, *citing* Formal Op. 2014-200.

18. *In re* Tsamis, Comm. File No 2013PR00095 (Ill. 2013), http://www.iardc.org/13PR00 95CM.html.

19. Cal. R. 1-400 (Advertising and Solicitation,) Cal. Art. 9.5 (Legal Advertising).

In California, a communication is considered to be "any message or offer made by or on behalf of a member concerning the availability for professional employment of a member or a law firm directed to any former, present or prospective client." Under the rules and articles of California:

Any communication or solicitation shall not:

1. Contain any untrue statement; or
2. Contain any matter, or present or arrange any matter in a manner or format which is false, deceptive or which trends to confuse, deceive, or mislead the public; or
3. Omit to state any fact necessary to make the statements made, in the light of circumstances under which they are made, nor misleading to the public or
4. Fail to indicate clearly, expressly, or by context, that it is a communication or solicitation as the case may be; or
5. Be transmitted in any manner which involves intrusion, coercion, duress, compulsion, intimidation, threats or vexatious or harassing conduct.

The bar, using its rule and article as a basis for analysis, next examines several hypothetical posts. They are

1. "Case finally over. Unanimous verdict! Celebrating tonight."
2. "Another great victory in court today! My client is delighted. Who wants to be next?"
3. "Won another personal injury case. Call me for a free consultation."
4. "Just published an article on wage and hour breaks. Let me know if you would like a copy."

In its analysis, the bar found posts 1 and 4 were not communications (i.e., advertising), but 2 and 3 did meet the requirements constituting a communication and therefore needed certain information that they lacked.

Post 1 was not considered a communication because it did not contain an offer concerning the availability for professional employment. Had the post used "Who wants to be next" as in hypothetical 2, the posting would have become advertising based on the attorney stating that he is seeking additional clients. Post 4 was not advertising because, again, it did not state that he was seeking clients—it was simply providing useful information.

Post 2 is a communication because it makes it clear that the lawyer is available for employment. Since the post is advertising, it now has several problems under California's rules. First, it does not contain a disclaimer. Second, it does not state it is an advertisement. Third, it offers a guarantee or prediction of winning. In order to make this particular post appropriate, a lawyer in California would need to add the required language. Such a post would become quite lengthy however, so a question would arise as to whether it would be worth it to share such information in the first place. It also would not be possible to share this particular post on Twitter in California. Post 3 is considered communication/advertising for the same reason post 2 is. Asking for readers to call for a free consultation is clearly seeking employment from potential clients.

Remember, the rules in your jurisdiction(s) might be very different from California. However, the broad analysis in the bar opinion is one that you can apply to your posts. The first question is always going to be, is it advertising? The second question will be, if it is, does the post meet the ethical requirements? Be certain to give your posts the appropriate consideration.

Other States

Many other states have provided opinions on the subject of whether social media is advertising and ethical issues surrounding its use. The states have generally handled the issues much the same way Pennsylvania has. However, there are some unique opinions. New York, for example, released an opinion to analyze LinkedIn, in particular, in March 2015.[20] In its opinion, the Ethics Committee found that a general LinkedIn profile listing education and employment experience is not enough to make the profile advertising. But, adding "a description of areas of practice or certain skills or endorsement" may make the profile advertising. Regardless, all content on the profile should be accurate.[21]

Is Blogging Advertising?

If you search "is blogging attorney advertising" online, you will find many different opinions. As with social media, California has established a bright line test for whether a blog is advertising. In California, a blog is advertising

---

20. N.Y. Cnty. Laws. Ass'n Prof'l Ethics Comm., Formal Op. 748, Mar. 10, 2015.

21. Opinion 748 references the Social Media Ethics Guidelines of the Commercial and Federal Litigation Section of the New York State Bar Association. As of this writing, the guide was updated in June 2015 and provides a solid overview of social media ethics in New York. *See* http://www.nysba.org/workarea/DownloadAsset.aspx?id=47547.

if it addresses the availability of a lawyer for employment.[22] In that state, if a lawyer wants his blog to fall outside of attorney advertising, he would need to have a stand-alone blog, separate from his website, which does not, in *any* way, including by implication, express his availability for professional employment. Such a stand-alone blog would need to avoid discussing the qualifications and history of the lawyer as well.

The seminal case on attorney blogs is *Hunter v. Virginia State Bar*. The rather convoluted history of this case involved an attorney who reported the results of cases with favorable results. He also posted about other issues. He did not, however, have a disclaimer on that blog. The Virginia State Bar found ethical violations under rules 1.6, 7.1, and 7.2. 1.6 involved "disclosure of client information" and the latter two rules involve attorney advertising. On appeal, the circuit court found no violation of the rules and determined that the blog was protected under the First Amendment. However, it also required that Hunter put a disclaimer on his blog. The Supreme Court of Virginia ruled that a blog is unprotected commercial speech and that Hunter did not violate rule 1.6. The court felt that the blog was commercial speech for several reasons:

1. Motivation was, at least partly, economic.
2. The majority of posts discussed favorable case results to show attorney's skills.
3. The blog was part of the firm's website as opposed to a stand-alone website.
4. There was no ability to interact with the blog. This suggests that Hunter's blog did not allow for comments. It is important to note that most blogging software provides the ability to allow communication via a comments feature that may be turned on or off.[23]

Are Blogs Advertising?

So, are blogs advertising? The answer is, it depends on how your blog is set up and what you post about. The safest answer is to treat blogging as if it is advertising. For this purpose, it is wise to include an appropriate disclaimer on your blog. The disclaimer should be much the same as the disclaimer you put on the rest of your website.

---

22. State Bar of Cal. Standing Comm. on Prof'l Responsibility and Conduct Formal Op. Interim No. 12-006.

23. Renee Choy Ohlendorf, *Attorney Blogger Runs Afoul of Ethics Rules on Advertising*, A.B.A. Litig. News (May 30, 2013), https://apps.americanbar.org/litigation/litigationnews/top_stories/053013-blog-ethics-advertising.html.

Is a Social Media Post Legal Advice?

The line for what is and what is not legal advice is a bit blurry. Given this, it is important that you stay on the right side of the line to make certain you are not inadvertently creating an attorney/client relationship. An attorney/client relationship is formed when a client has reason to believe that the attorney is handling his legal interests. The relationship can be formed expressly or it can be implied. The implied relationship is the one that can cause trouble online. The standard in determining whether an attorney/client relationship has been formed is based on what the objectively reasonable belief on the part of the client is. If you answer questions online, make certain there is an appropriate disclaimer, such as can be found on sites like Avvo and Quora. In addition, limit yourself to providing broad answers that are educational in nature as opposed to providing specific advice that directly answers the asker's question. At this point, there have been no lawsuits involving attempts to claim a lawyer has formed an attorney/client relationship through an ask/answer site. Keep in mind, not only could you inadvertently form an attorney/client relationship, but if you provide legal advice in a state in which you are not licensed, you could be engaging in the unauthorized practice of law.

Recommendations/Testimonials

The rules around recommendations and testimonials vary greatly across the United States. As a result, it is difficult to provide specific guidelines. Given this, it is crucial that you refer to the state(s) in which you are licensed to make certain you follow the rules. In most states, it is perfectly acceptable to ask for testimonials. However, those testimonials must follow all relevant rules. When clients write recommendations, those recommendations must not create false expectations and they must be correct. If a client writes a recommendation that violates the rules, it is the attorney's obligation to correct it. In some cases, for example LinkedIn, the attorney will be able to control whether an improper testimonial is posted. In other cases, for example Google+, Avvo and Facebook, the attorney is not able to approve the testimonial. In such cases the attorney must ask the client to remove the recommendation, or provide a correction in the comments.

Dealing with Negative Reviews

Negative reviews are a serious problem on social media and on the web in general. A negative review can be very harmful to a law firm. That said, no matter how negative the review, it is crucial that lawyers respond appropriately if a past client attacks them online. Most importantly, attorneys may not share confidential information about the client in a response to a negative review. For example, a lawyer from Illinois responded to a negative review on Avvo by providing confidential information about her client. The hearing board found that she engaged in misconduct that included

1. [R]evealing information relating to the representation of a client without the client's informed consent, in violation of Rule 1.6(a) of the Illinois Rules of Professional Conduct (2010);
2. [U]sing means in representing a client that have no substantial purpose other than to embarrass, delay, or burden a third person, in violation of Rule 4.4 of the Illinois Rules of Professional Conduct (2010); and
3. [C]onduct which is prejudicial to the administration of justice or which tends to defeat the administration of justice or to bring the courts or the legal profession into disrepute.[24]

The complaint against the attorney also involved a bounced check. For both the check and the comment on Avvo, the attorney was reprimanded by the disciplinary commission.[25]

Keep in mind, an online review does not trigger the necessary controversy allowing the lawyer to reveal confidential information. The author has heard other ethics attorneys disagree with this concept, and feels that the attorney should be able to respond fully. But clearly, based on the sanctions and guidance opinions being handed out, the various disciplinary boards are falling on the side of confidentiality.[26] Therefore, it is critical to be careful about how you respond to reviews.

Should You Sue Over a Bad Review?

For the most part, suing over a bad review is a bad idea. There are a number of reasons for this. The first reason it is bad to sue is due to the Streisand Effect. The Streisand Effect is so named because of the efforts on behalf of Barbra Streisand to remove images of the California coastline that included pictures of Streisand's home. Once the lawsuit was filed, the picture that Streisand's attorneys had sought to suppress became very popular online. Prior to the suit, the image had been downloaded six times. After the suit, the image went viral and now is used as an example of the unintended

---

24. *In re Tsamis, supra* note 18.
25. http://www.iardc.org/HB_RB_Disp_Html.asp?id=11221.
26. Bar Ass'n of S.F., Legal Ethics Op. 2014-1 (Jan. 2014) ("The duty of confidentiality prevents the attorney from disclosing confidential information about the prior representation absent the former client's informed consent or waiver of confidentiality."), http://www.sfbar .org/ethics/opinion_2014-1.aspx.

consequences of intense publication that can result from trying to remove information from the web.[27] The second reason it is unwise to sue is because if potential clients learn about the suit, which they might well do because of the Streisand Effect, they may be concerned about retaining a firm that will sue its clients. However, it is also clear that filing a suit does trigger the controversy necessary to reveal confidential information as part of the suit.

Examples of Suits over Negative Reviews

Over the past few years, a number of lawyers have sued over bad reviews, to mixed results as far as publicity.

Negative or Mixed Results from Suing

A suit from 2014 involved a Texas firm that sued over a negative review on Yelp.[28] The former client wrote, "[T]his firm not only won't help you—they intend to do you harm if they can't extract enough money of you[.] They are disorganized, deceptive, manipulative and largely disrespected. . . ."

The defamation suit was successful, resulting in a $100,000 verdict against the defendant. This was after the firm successfully sued its client for unpaid fees. However, when researching the firm online, readers will find a great deal of information about the suit. In fact, at the time of this writing, the first link on Google when searching the firm's name is about the suit. In addition, for a brief period, there was another review on Yelp stating that the defendant's review was correct, further attacking the firm. That review has since been removed. It is likely that some of the attention this particular suit received comes from the fact that it was, at that time, still relatively novel to sue over a negative online review. Therefore, although the suit was successful, the author wonders if the resulting negative online information has caused more damage than the original, negative review.

A more recent suit is likely causing substantial damage to the reputation of the firm involved. In this case the firm is based in Houston, Texas. The client, who fired the firm prior to writing the review, wrote comments on Yelp such as, "I wouldn't even give this law firm a star. . . . When I first start [sic] talking to them they were very pushy. When I try to reach them, no one would answer my call or email. Please, don't waste your time here.'"[29]

27. Streisand Effect, http://knowyourmeme.com/memes/streisand-effect.
28. Grissom & Thompson, LLP v. Browning, http://pdfserver.amlaw.com/tx/Grissom-ThompsonVBrowning-petition.pdf.
29. http://www.chron.com/neighborhood/fortbend/crime-courts/article/Law-firm-sues-woman-after-she-writes-bad-reviews-8468178.php.

She also accused the attorneys of bursting into her bedroom when she was in bed and not fully dressed. (The firm responded that it was directed to enter her room by the woman's mother.) It is also alleged that after the firm requested that the woman adjust her review to be more accurate, she wrote more negative reviews or added more negative information to her original reviews. After the suit was filed, the defendant amended her reviews to note that she was being sued. The result has been catastrophic in terms of the responses from the web. Negative reviews on Yelp, Google, and Facebook now proliferate. Numerous articles have been written.[30] The firm's website was even inaccessible for a time. (It is back up as of this writing.)

Generally Successful Results

There are at least two cases where there has been very little attention paid to the lawsuits by the general public. In addition, the verdicts have been substantial.

In *Blake v. Ann-Marie Giustibelli, P.A.*,[31] the client and her husband wrote negative reviews about Giustibelli. The reviews included language such as:

- "No integrity. Will say one thing and do another. Her fees outweigh the truth."
- "Altered her charges to four times the original quote with no explanation."

The case was successful, resulting in a $350,000 verdict, which was upheld on appeal. The husband settled with the firm. The client set up a website attacking the firm, though as of this writing it appears to have been taken down. The bulk, if not all, of the commentary online has come from law-related websites and there has been no response from the general public. The first site found in a Google search is the site belonging to the law firm.

The case of *Pampattiwar v. Hinson*[32] had similar results and a larger verdict of over $400,000. This case was also upheld on appeal. The attack on Hinson called her a "crook lawyer" and an "extremely fraudulent lady." As with *Giustibelli*, there seems to have been no public fall-out; most attention has come from legal websites. The first result on Google is Hinson's website. The second and third, though, involve the lawsuit, so even in suits where the general public fails to pay attention, the damage on Google can remain for a long period of time. This particular suit was filed in 2014.

---

30. http://www.houstonpress.com/news/student-sued-by-law-firm-for-bad-facebook-review-asks-judge-to-dismiss-case-8614075.
31. Blake v. Ann-Marie Giustibelli, P.A., 182 So. 3d 881 (2016).
32. Pampattiwar v. Hinson, 756 S.E.2d 246 (2014).

Before you make the decision to sue, it is best to evaluate the amount of damage one negative review will actually cause to your firm versus the potential negativity that *could* result as the news of your suit is brought to the public's attention. In some cases, a suit may well be necessary. But in others, in the majority, a better response may be to (appropriately) seek out positive reviews to minimize the potential damage of a negative one.

The Best Way to Handle a Negative Review

Unfortunately, in many cases, it is not possible to get a review removed from the web. On sites such as Avvo, if you believe the review is from someone who was not actually a client, you can ask Avvo to look into the situation. Avvo will ask the reviewer to confirm the review.[33] This, at least, should mean that if the person does not provide a real e-mail address that Avvo will remove the review. The author can confirm that reviews from nonclients have been removed on Avvo.

In the end, the best way to deal with a negative review is to provide a polite response. If you are too angry to give a polite response, the best response is none at all or to wait until you are calm. Remember, it is very unlikely that one negative review will have a huge impact on your practice. As noted, the best way to deal with reviews is to consistently ask for them from satisfied clients at the end of representation—assuming, of course, that it is acceptable for you to do so in your jurisdiction(s). Never offer your clients anything in return for the review.

Specific Rules

Honest Communication and 8.x Integrity

The first two rules for online behavior should be considered an umbrella under which all behavior is judged. First, attorneys should never be misleading in their communications in relation to their services. No communication should contain a material misrepresentation of either fact or law, nor should any statement omit facts necessary to make the statement appropriate under rule 7.1. This concept flows throughout all communications by attorneys when discussing their services. The second set of rules, 8.x, involve maintaining the integrity of the profession; in other words, not holding the profession up to ridicule through one's behavior.

---

33. http://www.avvo.com/support/What_if_I_get_a_negative_Client_Review.

Advertising

The first rule of which attorneys need to be aware is Model Rule 7.2, which relates directly to advertising. One of the issues that can be a problem under Rule 7.2 is that various states require attorneys to keep all ads for a certain period of time. In Pennsylvania, for example, attorneys must keep copies of ads for two years. Other states have longer requirements. It is also important to note that a specific attorney must take responsibility for the ad and its placement, so make certain that a specific attorney is responsible for every action, even if performed by a nonattorney. Fortunately, the various accounts are meant to stay intact, so it is easy to keep records. If a post needs to be deleted, grab a screenshot of it and store it where it will be easily located. Make certain to identify the attorney responsible for the item.

Various states have other requirements, so attorneys should check Rule 7.2 in every state in which they are licensed.

Solicitation of Clients

Also implicated by use of social media for communication with potential clients is Model Rule 7.3. Attorneys may not solicit potential clients through real-time communication. This aspect of the rule does not apply to family members, current clients or other attorneys. Real-time communication includes telephone, in person and real-time electronic chat. There is disagreement as to whether attorneys may solicit new clients through chat rooms, in which a large number of people are present, versus instant messages, which are more personal and direct. Given this, it is safe to assume that starting a chat on Facebook is real-time communication and should be avoided. E-mail is considered written communication. To obey the rule, at a minimum, attorneys must label advertising as such and comply with Rule 7.1.

Attorneys may not solicit a client who has already made it clear he does not wish to be contacted, or if "the solicitation involves coercion, duress or harassment." This means if someone has made it clear through social media that he desires not to be contacted, it would be a violation of the rule to contact him. The tone of writing matters as well. If the content is seen as inappropriate, it violates the rule.

In most states, it is also improper to seek to communicate with a potential client who the "lawyer knows or reasonably should know that the physical, emotional or mental state of the person is such that the person could not exercise reasonable judgment in employing a lawyer." Given this, it is inappropriate to seek to directly communicate via social media with someone the lawyer knows or should know is in the midst of a crisis. For example, tweeting at someone who just lost a loved one or sending a direct message to such a person. Also, tagging someone in a Facebook post when you know the person just suffered a loss would be inappropriate in the author's opinion.

Multistate Practice

An area in which it is easy to get in trouble, due to the vast and multi-jurisdictional nature of the Internet, is multistate practice. Attorneys must comply with their home state rules in relation to:

- Where the office is located
- Where the attorneys are admitted
- How they are seeking clients
- How they engage in advertising
- All states' rules in which they market

Additional Ethical Issues

Aside from advertising, communication with potential clients, and inappropriate use of social media in discovery, there are other ways in which legal professionals have gotten themselves in trouble using social media.

Confidentiality and Honesty

One potential area of trouble involves confidentiality, Rule 1.6. An attorney got herself in trouble by sharing confidential information about a case in such a way as to make it possible to identify her client. She also provided information that suggested she knew her client had lied on the stand and did nothing about it. In addition to Rule 1.6, the attorney was accused of violating other rules involving honesty, fraud, and more.[34] In the end, the attorney lost her job of 19 years[35] and was suspended for 90 days by two different jurisdictions.[36]

---

34. *In re* Peshek, Comm'n No. 09 CH 89, Ill. Att'y Registration and Disciplinary Comm'n (2009).

35. Debra Cassens Weiss, *Blogging Assistant PD Accused of Revealing Secrets of Little-Disguised Clients*, A.B.A. J. (2009), http://www.abajournal.com/news/article/blogging_assistant_pdaccused_of_revealing_secrets_of_little-disguised_clie/.

36. Office of Law. Regulation v. Peshek, 2011 WI 47 (2011); Chris Bonjean, *Illinois Supreme Court Disbars 12, Suspends 26*, Ill. State Bar Ass'n (May 18, 2010), http://iln.isba.org/2010/05/18/illinois-supreme-court-disbars-12-suspends-26.

Another serious consequence the attorney suffered is that when searching her name online; page after page of results show her disciplinary problems. Though she has since opened her own firm, it is difficult to find anything positive about her on the web in a Google search. A check in August 2016 shows that the majority of information about the attorney still involves her disciplinary proceedings.

While it is perfectly acceptable to discuss one's life, and even one's professional activities, it is important to obey the ethical rules while doing so. Discussing a case on a blog while it is going on, outside of appropriate public relations, is a bad idea. Failing to protect a client's confidentiality is even worse. And, of course, failing to properly inform the court of inappropriate conduct by the client was a serious mistake. Judgment is a critical part of both practicing law and posting online.

Jokes and Satire

Jokes can also be a serious problem online. It is impossible to see body language or hear the tone in a person's voice. Something one person might find amusing might not be so funny to another. As a result, joking through social media can be problematic, especially on a politically charged topic. An Indiana deputy attorney general learned this the hard way when he tweeted an unfortunate joke surrounding protests in Wisconsin in 2011. His tweet led to an argument with the editor of *Mother Jones* magazine. In turn, the magazine researched the attorney and found similar comments on his blog. In the end, the price of the attorney's online behavior was his job.[37] The attorney general's office stated that it chose to fire the attorney after a "thorough and expeditious review," noting that it respects First Amendment rights but expects civility from its public servants.

Seeking Attention for a Client or Friend

There are rules about how members of the bar may use the press. Similar rules apply to using social media to advocate for a client, or even for a friend. As an example, a lawyer in Louisiana was disbarred due to a Twitter and blog campaign in which she created a petition and encouraged the public to directly contact two judges in a custody case involving a friend.[38] To facilitate communication with the judges, she provided their contact information. She also revealed confidential information, including linking to an audio recording of the children talking about the alleged sexual

---

37. *Indiana State Prosecutor Fired over Remarks about Wisconsin Protests*, CNN.com (Feb. 23, 2011), http://www.cnn.com/2011/US/02/23/indiana.ammo.tweet/.

38. *In re* McCool, Att'y Disciplinary Proceeding, http://www.lasc.org/opinions/2015/15B0284 .opn.pdf.

abuse they suffered. The attorney was not admitted in Mississippi, the state where the case was located. A judge involved in the custody case filed a complaint with Louisiana. The attorney felt that she was protected by the First Amendment and that she did not engage in any ethical misconduct.

The hearing committee determined that the lawyer violated Rules 3.5(a) and (b) as well as 8.4(a), (c), and (d). The committee determined that, among other violations, the attorney disseminated false, misleading, and inflammatory information about how the judges handled the case and encouraged ex parte contact with the judges in an effort to influence rulings. The committee felt that the attorney "acted knowingly, if not intentionally" and "caused actual and potential harm by threatening the independence and integrity of the judicial system and caused the judges concern for their personal safety and well-being." The end result is that the attorney was, as previously noted, disbarred.

Given the opportunity for easy sharing of information on social media, it is critical that attorneys think carefully before using the web to seek to encourage action on behalf of their clients. They would do well to advise their clients to use the same level of caution.

Personal versus Private

Sometimes attorneys will develop both a private and public persona on the web, believing the two will remain separate. Unfortunately, this is simply not the case. It takes very little effort to perform research on the web and to connect the public and private behaviors of someone who has written something offensive or upsetting. In an infamous case, an assistant Michigan attorney general was fired due to his online (and perhaps offline) behavior surrounding the student body president of the University of Michigan. The attorney argued that his speech was political and also had nothing to do with his work as an assistant attorney general. But in the end, the public and private became much too intertwined, and the attorney general was left with no choice but to fire him. Recently the student won a verdict of $4.5 million for invasion of privacy, defamation, abuse of process, and intentional infliction of emotional distress.[39]

The attorney in this case did not hide who he was, but he did try to argue that his actions had nothing to do with his work. However, as a public

---

39. Kevin Dolak, *Attorney Andrew Shirvell Ordered to Pay 4.5 Million for Attacks on Gay Student*, ABCNEWS.GO (Aug. 17, 2012), http://abcnews.go.com/US/attorney-andrew-shirvell-ordered-pay -45-million-attacks/story?id=17028621.

servant and as an attorney, it was simply impossible to separate the public employee from the (not so) private behavior, and that cost him his job. He was fired for "violat[ing] office policies, engag[ing] in borderline stalking behavior," and more. The attorney sometimes posted his online attacks while at work, and engaged in behavior that was "not protected by the First Amendment."[40] Much of his behavior was offline, but it was his online behavior that brought an incredible amount of attention to what he was doing, so much so that he ended up on TV shows including *Anderson Cooper* on CNN.[41]

More recently, a bankruptcy attorney who posted angry statements about a car crash in which a corrections officer was killed ended up creating a huge mess for himself on Facebook. In the end he posted an apology and resigned from the law firm at which he worked.[42]

It is unwise to believe that anyone can live two separate lives online. If one engages in controversial behavior, the result will be a magnifying glass of attention. In turn, it is virtually impossible for the individual to keep his private and public online lives from colliding.

Discovery of Social Media

Given the value of the information contained within social media accounts, it is no surprise that attorneys desire to obtain access to the information. It is not at all uncommon, for example, for an individual to say one thing in person to her attorney or a judge and to post completely contradictory information on Facebook. An individual might claim in court or interrogatories that she cannot leave her home due to emotional harm from an injury, but in turn post a video on Facebook showing her dancing at a party. In the past, it was necessary to hire a private investigator to prove someone was lying about his injury for a workers' compensation claim; now the plaintiff frequently posts a picture of himself chopping wood or carrying a heavy couch, the exact evidence the defense attorney needs to prove her case.

---

40. David Jesse, *Andrew Shirvell Fired from Job at Michigan Attorney General's Office*, Ann Arbor News (Nov. 8, 2010), http://www.annarbor.com/news/andrew-shirvell-fired-from-job-at-attorney -generals-office/#.UFQIPVEQd60.

41. *Anderson Cooper: Andrew Shirvell Responsible for His Firing, Not "Liberal Media,"* Huffington Post (Nov. 9, 2010), http://www.huffingtonpost.com/2010/11/09/anderson-cooper -andrew-sh_n_780874.html.

42. Len Wells, *A Bankruptcy Attorney's Facebook Mess*, Courier & Press (Jan. 23, 2016), http:// www.courierpress.com/columnists/len-wells/len-wells-a-bankruptcy-attorneys-facebook -mess-29a20fb1-8d56-3de0-e053-0100007fc312-366304311.html.

Privacy Settings Are Important

Privacy settings control what an individual shares on social media sites. However, many users never change their privacy settings, or simply find the settings too complicated to alter. Many social media sites barely have any privacy settings at all. Twitter, for example, is either open, limited, or private.[43] Facebook's settings are extremely complicated and confusing.[44] Blogs are meant to be open, and people frequently believe they are private when they are not.[45] Since many people do not change their settings, attorneys should and do look through the social media sites in an ethical manner and view and preserve the information they can find.[46] Keep in mind, if the attorney does the preservation, and authentication becomes an issue, the attorney could be forced to become a witness in her own case. It is best to have someone else in the firm do the preservation, or to hired an outside expert, which is generally fairly expensive.

The Client's Social Media

The first step when a new client walks through the door is to ask if he uses any social media. The next step, in some cases, is to inform the client that he must stop posting immediately. Unfortunately, the addiction to and use of social media can be so great that the client will be unwilling to stop. As a result, the attorney should also advise her client that if he does post, he should not post anything that deals with the case. The attorney must be clear about what "deals with the case" means, since many clients will simply think it means specifics about how the case is going, as opposed to comments about giving money to his mistress, lifting a heavy couch, attending a party, and so on. Make certain to ask the client not only about his own accounts, but his comments on blogs and websites that might be relevant to the case. Social media and other online surprises can be very

---

43. https://support.twitter.com/entries/14016#.

44. Approximately 13 million U.S. users never change their Facebook privacy settings. Of those that do, the majority are unaware that their privacy settings can be compromised by allowing additional applications access to their accounts and do not take the steps necessary to further protect their data. Emil Protalinski, *13 Million U.S. Facebook Users Don't Change Privacy Settings*, ZDNET (May 3, 2012), http://www.zdnet.com/blog/facebook/13-million-us-facebook-users-dont-change-privacy-settings/12398.

45. Natalie Munroe was a teacher in Pennsylvania who blogged about her students. She believed her blog was only being read by a few people, apparently unaware that it could be widely read. *See* Douglas Stanglin, *Blogging High School Teacher Has No Job—And No Regrets*, USA TODAY (Feb. 15, 2011), http://tinyurl.com/8hx95c6. Munroe was suspended, reinstated, and eventually fired. She claims she was fired due to the blog. The district claims she was fired for incompetence. Munroe has since brought a lawsuit against the district. *Blogging Central Bucks Teacher Is Fired*, PHILA. INQUIRER (June 26, 2012), http://www.philly.com/philly/blogs/bucksinq/160413996.html.

46. N.Y. State Bar Ass'n, Comm. on Prof'l Ethics, Op. 843, (Sept. 10, 2010).

harmful. It is also important to remind the client that he may not delete any content from his account, even if it is potentially harmful to his case.

The first meeting with a client is also the time to speak with him about changing his privacy settings to make certain that his account is secure. Providing instructions on how to change privacy settings in written form or a video can be very helpful. It is also a good idea to have the client sign a document making it clear that he was told not to delete any content. This will protect the attorney from accusations of spoliation later on. In some cases, it might be wise to ask for access to the account(s). Asking to friend the client is not enough, the password is necessary for a complete review of the client's online conduct. You will have to make a decision as to whether connecting with the client and reviewing his account is wise. Remember, if you become aware of any content that shows the client is lying or will lie before the court, you will be in an ethical quandary.

Also, if the client has a personal relationship with the opposing party, ask about whether he is connected to the other side's social media, for example as a friend on Facebook. In addition, ask the client if any potential witnesses are using social media. Find out if the client is connected to those witnesses and therefore has access to private areas of the accounts. Of course, if your client has access to the opposing party's account, then the opposing party has access to your client's. In some cases, it is possible to limit what specific individuals can see to protect your client from this problem, while still providing access to the opposing client.[47] In others, this possibility does not exist.

Last, it is important that attorneys speak with not only with their clients but also other relevant individuals about their online conduct. In a recent case, the daughter of the plaintiff caused an $80,000 settlement to be overturned because she posted about the result on Facebook (contrary to the settlement terms).[48, 49] As a result, it is important to make certain that the settlement agreement contains the correct language.

In the end, what matters most is proper communication with the client in order to protect both the client's case and your ethical obligations.

---

47. http://www.pcadvisor.co.uk/how-to/social-networks/limit-what-friends-can-see-on-facebook-3637262/.

48. Matthew Stucker, *Girl Costs Father $80,000 with "SUCK IT' Facebook Post*, CNN.com (Mar. 2, 2014), http://www.cnn.com/2014/03/02/us/facebook-post-costs-father/; Gulliver Sch., Inc. v. Snay, 137 So. 3d 1045, 2014 Fla. App. LEXIS 2595 (Fla. Dist. Ct. App. 3d Dist. 2014).

49. Alternatively, an agreement that provided only that the terms of the settlement were to remain confidential was not enough to prevent the defendant from bragging that he defeated the plaintiff. Coupons, Inc. v. Stottlemire, 2009 U.S. Dist. LEXIS 35110 (N.D. Cal. Apr. 9, 2009).

Opposing Party and Witnesses

Immediately view the opposing party's accounts and witness accounts if they are freely accessible. It is permissible to view the accounts if the client has access. It is also permissible to ask witnesses to provide access to their accounts, though the attorney or other individual asking for access must be honest about her relationship to the case.

Also send a notice of preservation to opposing counsel. Fortunately, the amendments to the federal discovery rules from 2006 allow for discovery of electronic data to begin very early in the litigation process. Make it clear to opposing counsel that all data must be preserved. Do not just name specific social media sites, but be clear in the preservation letter that it means all sites and all accounts. Unfortunately, exactly what preservation is required is not yet clear. Does preservation mean keeping the privacy settings as is, so if an account was open it remains such? Does it simply mean that data may not be deleted? Be clear about expectations and do not be surprised if the matter ends up before a judge.[50]

Send out the interrogatories relating to social media as quickly as possible and ask the right questions. Again, do not give the opposing client a chance to wiggle out by asking simply for Facebook when the client might have a Plaxo account. Ask for everything. Ask for all e-mail addresses as well, because the opposing party might have several accounts under various e-mail addresses. Further, keep in mind that with strict privacy settings the opposing party can all but hide the existence of his account(s).

Trouble for Failure to Preserve

In the past, some have believed that it is acceptable to delete posts from social media accounts. A Virginia decision from 2011 puts the debate to rest. It is spoliation to delete relevant posts without preserving them and providing them when properly requested through discovery. In the case, the attorney instructed his client to "clean up" his Facebook because "we don't want blowups of this stuff at trial." The attorney further instructed the client to delete or deactivate the account, and then responded to discovery requests by informing opposing counsel that his client had no Facebook

---

50. In a recent opinion, the Philadelphia Bar Association made it clear that not only is it acceptable to change privacy settings, but also to delete content, as long as that content is properly preserved prior to deletion. In addition, the lawyer must "make reasonable efforts to obtain a photograph, link or other content about which the lawyer is aware if the lawyer knows or reasonably believes it has not been produced by the client." Phila. Bar Association Prof'l Guidance Comm., Op. 2014-5 (July 2014). A Pennsylvania Bar Association Formal Opinion provides the same advice, 2014-300.

account. The client deactivated the account instead of deleting it. Upon reactivating the account, the client deleted 16 photographs, following his attorney's instructions. Based on the spoliation, the court held that sanctions should be granted against both the attorney and the client. The sanctions amounted to $722,000 in legal fees, over $500,000 of which was payable by the attorney. In addition, the judge in the case reported the attorney to the Virginia State Bar.[51] In the end, the attorney agreed to a five-year suspension of his license and ultimately left the practice of law.[52]

A recent New Jersey case shows the serious consequences of deleting (without preserving) content from Facebook. In that case the plaintiff claimed that he deactivated his Facebook account and did not restore it quickly enough, resulting in deletion of his account. Leaving aside that this is not how Facebook deactivations and deletions actually work,[53] the end result was that the court found that deletion of the account was spoliation of evidence and granted an adverse inference against.[54] Given the cases and the trend, it seems to be straightforward that deleting posts, pictures, or videos without preservation is unacceptable and likely to lead to serious sanctions.

Ethical Pitfalls in Research, Discovery, and Communications

There are a number of relevant guidance opinions from the bar associations of New York City and State,[55] Pennsylvania,[56] Philadelphia,[57] and San Diego County[58] surrounding issues related to performing research utilizing social media.

General Research

First, as already noted, it is perfectly acceptable to search and access social media sites that are freely accessible. The New York State guidance opinion

---

51. *See* Lester v. Allied Concrete Co. (order dated Sept. 1, 2011).
52. "On July 17, 2013, the Virginia State Bar Disciplinary Board suspended Matthew B. Murray's license to practice law for five years for violating professional rules that govern candor toward the tribunal, fairness to opposing party and counsel, and misconduct. This was an agreed disposition of misconduct charges." VSB Docket Nos. 11-070-088405,11-070-0884222.
53. In the author's experience, when a Facebook account is deactivated it is not deleted. When the owner logs into his account again, it is restored. In order for a Facebook account to be deleted, specific actions requesting deletion must be taken on the part of the account owner.
54. Gatto v. United Air Lines, Inc., Case No. 10-cv-1090-ES-SCM (D.N.J. Mar. 25, 2013).
55. N.Y. State Bar Ass'n Guidance Op. 843 (2010).
56. Pa. Bar Ass'n Formal Op. 2014-300 (2014).
57. Phila. Bar Ass'n Guidance Op. 2009-02 (2009).
58. SDCBA Ethics Op. 2011-2 (May 24, 2011).

states, "[An attorney] may access the public pages of another party's social networking website (such as Facebook or MySpace) for the purpose of obtaining possible impeachment material for use in the litigation."[59] On the other hand, the 2009 Philadelphia opinion makes it clear that an effort to obtain access to the account through deceptive or illegal means is unacceptable.[60]

Friending a Witness

In the 2009 Philadelphia opinion, the attorney asked whether it would be acceptable for the attorney to have a third party request a witness to "friend"[61] the opposing client. The third party did not intend to lie, but neither did he intend to reveal his relationship to the attorney.

The opinion noted that such behavior would violate several rules of ethical conduct. The lawyer would be "procuring conduct [and be] responsible for [that] conduct" in violation of Pennsylvania Rule 5.3 (Responsibilities Regarding Nonlawyer Assistants). Also, the lawyer would be violating rule 8.4 (Misconduct) by engaging in "deceptive" conduct. In addition, the attorney would be encouraging a third party to violate Rule 4.1 (Truthfulness in Statements to Others) by having the third party "omit a highly material fact."[62] Based upon the Philadelphia Bar Association's 2009 guidance opinion, it is very clear that having a third party (or the attorney herself) friend a witness without revealing her relationship to the case would be highly inappropriate.

A real-world example of what can happen when an attorney lies to potential witnesses comes from a lawyer who is learning a hard lesson in negative publicity. This attorney, a prosecutor in Ohio, posed as the ex-girlfriend of a murder defendant on Facebook. The attorney's stated goal was to convince the two female alibi witnesses to change their stories. In the end, the prosecutor was fired and has seen numerous stories written about this conduct online.[63] The lesson from this case is that lawyers may

---

59. N.Y. State Bar Ass'n Guidance Op. 843.

60. Phila. Bar Ass'n Guidance Op. 2009-02.

61. "Friend" is Facebook's term for two people who are connected to each other on the service. Different social media providers use different terms. For example, LinkedIn uses "contact" and "connection." Friending someone requires the affirmative action of a request on the part of the individual seeking the connection and an affirmative action on the part of the individual accepting the connection. *See* Facebook, How Do I Add a Friend?, http://www.facebook.com/help/?faq=12062.

62. Phila. Bar Ass'n Guidance Op. 2009-02 (2009) and Pa. Bar Ass'n Formal Op. 2014-300.

63. Martha Neil, *Prosecutor Fired after Posing as Ex-Girlfriend in Facebook Chat with Defendant's Alibi Witnesses*, A.B.A. J. (June 2013), http://www.abajournal.com/news/article/prosecutor_is _fired_after_posing_as_woman_in_facebook_chat_with_murder_defe/.

not lie when communicating with anyone through social media, including witnesses.

Communicating with a Represented Party

The San Diego County Bar Association took on the issue of communicating with a represented party. In short, as is the case offline, it is inappropriate to communicate with a represented party online. In the instant case, the attorney did not identify himself as the attorney, which made the effort to communicate all the more grievous. An additional issue, of concern for those involved in employee cases, includes an analysis of whether the contacted employees were represented parties.[64]

In 2012, the issue of friending represented parties came up in New Jersey where two attorneys are likely to face sanctions due to their paralegal friending the opposing party in a case.[65] The issue came to light during a deposition when it became clear that the attorneys had access to the private areas of the plaintiff's Facebook account. The attorneys denied responsibility because they asked the paralegal simply to perform a general search of the web. The issue with this defense is that attorneys are responsible for the behavior of their staff. The attorneys are charged with violating New Jersey rules 4.2 (communications with represented parties), 5.3(a), (b), and (c) (failure to supervise a nonlawyer assistant), 8.4(c) (conduct involving dishonesty and violation of ethics rules through someone else's actions or inducing those violations), and 8.4(d) (conduct prejudicial to the administration of justice). In addition, the more senior of the two attorneys is charged with Rule of Professional Conduct 5.1(b) and (c) (ethical obligation in relation to supervising another attorney). In April of 2016, the Supreme Court of New Jersey found that the case will continue.[66] These are all very serious charges, and regardless of the outcome, the publicity, which will spread rapidly through social media, will no doubt be very harmful to the two attorneys in question.

At this point it seems well settled that the action of friending someone or seeking to access their accounts through some form of communication, is contact. Therefore attorneys should never seek to friend or obtain access to the account of an opposing party through any form of communication with

---

64. SDCBA Ethics Op. 2011-2, May 24, 2011.

65. Eric Meyer, *Ethics Charges for Two Lawyers over Facebook Friending a Litigant*, LexisNexis Legal Newsroom (Sept. 13, 2012), http://www.lexisnexis.com/community/labor-employment -law/blogs/labor-employment-commentary/archive/2012/09/13/ethics-charges-for-two-lawyers -over-facebook-friending-a-litigant.aspx.

66. http://njlaw.rutgers.edu/collections/courts/supreme/a-62-14.opn.html.

a represented party. If seeking to friend a witness, the attorney or individual assisting the attorney must make clear her relationship to the case.

How to Properly Obtain Access

If an attorney believes that there is useful information contained within a social media account, she should seek to obtain access to the information hidden therein. There are a number of ethical ways to do so, aside from just looking to see what is freely available.

See if the Client or a Friendly Witness Has Access

In family law cases especially, the parties or witnesses might have access to each other's accounts. It is perfectly acceptable to view and use any information that is freely available through this method. Be cautious though where it looks like a witness might be sharing the information under duress. For example, in an employer/employee case, if another employee is friends with a plaintiff on Facebook, he might feel he has no choice but to share the information. If that employee complains later and says he was forced to share the access, it is uncertain how a court will look upon it.

Ask for Access to the Account

During the discovery process, unless there is a reason not to do so, ask for access to any and all social media accounts. In terms of Facebook, it is possible to download an entire account, so request that the opposing party do so and provide a copy.[67] Be sure to ask for continuing access as well. The opposing party will likely refuse this request, and wisely so. Social media postings can provide a plethora of private information, some of which may be harmful to a case. It is possible to simply ask the opposing party to adjust privacy settings so the account is viewable, but again, it is likely this request will be refused. It is always best to ask though because during the discovery process the judge will certainly ask if the request was made.

Send a Subpoena to the Site

Though generally the social media sites will not cooperate with a civil subpoena, from time to time they will be surprisingly helpful.[68] As a result, it never hurts to send the subpoena. Even if the site won't provide

---

67. Facebook's Download Your Information tool is located under Account Settings.
68. *See* Won't the Social Media Provider Help, *infra*.

content, citing the Stored Communications Act, it will normally provide assistance in connecting an account with an e-mail address or giving other information that does not involve actual content. This can be helpful if ownership of the account will be in issue. For example, in a criminal case the prosecution's verdict was overturned when it was shown that prosecution had failed to tie the account in question to the defendant's girlfriend.[69] Proof of ownership could have been shown with MySpace's assistance.

Compel Discovery

This is where things get tricky. Different judges tend to have different responses to the request to compel discovery of a social media account. The best approach, and the one that has shown the most results, is to capture what is already viewable (through appropriate ethical means) and to show it to the judge. If the judge can see that the account has relevant and contradictory information, she is likely to provide access to the account. If the judge has concerns about the privacy of those other than the account holder, request that the court review the data first to help resolve the issue. Some judges, though a minority, do not feel that there are any privacy rights in social media content.[70]

Case Law

It is clear from the case law developing across the United States that social media is not, in and of itself, privileged or confidential. However, judges will not allow fishing expeditions. At this time the trend in such cases is to provide access to social media accounts only when the opposing party can show that there is relevant and/or contradictory information contained therein and when the request is narrowly tailored.

Contradictory Information

In *McMillen v. Hummingbird Speedway, Inc.*,[71] a review of the public areas of McMillen's Facebook page revealed information contradictory to what he was claiming in terms of his injuries. The judge provided access, noting specifically that the Facebook information was not privileged.

---

69. Kashmir Hill, *Bad MySpace Detective Work Results in Overturned Murder Conviction*, Forbes-Blogs (May 10, 2011), http://blogs.forbes.com/kashmirhill/2011/05/10/bad-myspace-detective-work-results-in-overturned-murder-conviction.

70. State v. Harris, 2012 NY Slip Op 22175 (June 30, 2012).

71. McMillen v. Hummingbird Speedway, Inc., No. 113-2010 CD (C.P. Jefferson, Sept. 9, 2010).

Another case is simply the paragraph-long *Piccolo v. Paterson.*[72] The judge denied access to the Facebook pages the defense desired. The judge noted that the defense already had many pictures, and that no pictures or other data were freely available that showed contradictory information to what the plaintiff was claiming. It is interesting to note that the plaintiff actually changed her privacy settings early in the case, to preclude anyone other than a friend from viewing her pictures.

In *Zimmerman v. Weis Markets Inc.,*[73] the judge granted discovery due to the public availability of pictures that contradicted the plaintiff's claim that he did not wear shorts due to his embarrassment about a scar. The plaintiff posted pictures on his MySpace profile that clearly showed him wearing shorts after his injury (the scar was visible). Due to the public availability of this contradictory information, the judge found that there was clearly relevant data to be found within the MySpace account and therefore access to the account was properly compelled.

Another important case comes from Judge R. Stanton Wettick. Judge Wettick is known as a discovery judge in Pennsylvania, so his view on the discovery of social media was quite welcome. Judge Wettick denied mutual requests for access to Facebook accounts in the case of *Trail v. Lesko* because he was not going to allow a fishing expedition when there was no evidence that contradictory or useful information could be found in either Facebook account.[74] Therefore Judge Wettick used the same reasoning as did many of the other courts on this issue.

Define the Request

It is important that, in defining its request for social media access, the proponent show that the request is narrowly tailored and likely to elicit relevant information. In a Florida case, the judge granted in part and denied in part the request by defense in a personal injury case for complete access to the plaintiff's social media network. He held that the plaintiff must provide copies of all pictures depicting her since her injury, rather than provide access to the entire social media account in question. He further held that in requesting that the plaintiff provides every device on which she accessed her social media accounts, the defense had overreached.[75] In reaching his

---

72. Gina Passerella, *Facebook Postings Barred from Discovery in Accident Case*, Legal Intelligencer (updated Apr. 8, 2013), http://www.thelegalintelligencer.com/id=1202493920630/Facebook-Postings-Barred-From-Discovery-in-Accident-Case#ixzz3COUstMur.

73. Zimmerman v. Weis Mkts., Inc., No. CV-09-1535 (2011).

74. Trail v. Lesko, No GD-10-017249.

75. Davenport v. State Farm Mut. Auto. Ins. Co., Case No. 3:110-cv-632-J-JBT (M.D. Fla. 2012).

decision the judge noted that social media sites are "neither privileged nor protected by any right of privacy." He also noted that the discovery request must be properly tailored. To support both assertions, the judge cited the decision in *Tompkins v. Detroit Metropolitan Airport.*

In *Tompkins,*[76] the court found that while social media is discoverable, and "generally not privileged," the opposing party still may not "have a generalized right to rummage through information that Plaintiff has limited from public view." The court required a "threshold showing that the requested information is reasonably calculated to lead to the discovery of admissible evidence." As in the other cited cases, the court wanted to see some evidence that justified the defendant's "delving into the non-public section of [plaintiff's] account." The court noted specifically that if the public segment of plaintiff's account had "contained pictures of her playing golf or riding horseback," that the defendant would have had a better case to access the private portions of her account.[77]

The most recent case on overly broad requests for social media comes to us from Kansas.[78] The plaintiff argued that the defendant's motion to compel was overbroad. Initially, the plaintiff and defendant worked together to narrow the request, but plaintiff still felt it was too broad and sought relief from the court. The judge disagreed that the request was too broad and agreed with the defendant that plaintiff was required to produce access to certain information.

The case involved a plaintiff who slipped on water at property owned by defendant and claimed an ankle injury. Defendant wanted information including "names/account names 'associated with [his] Facebook and Twitter accounts.'"[79] In addition, defendant sought "'all social network postings, messages, and photographs that he sent or received on the work dates he claims he missed as a result of his injuries.'"[80] Defendant also requested any social media postings related to "(a) the subject incident, (b) the condition of the subject locomotive, (c) his alleged injuries, (d) the work conditions he claims caused or contributed to cause his

---

76. Tompkins v. Detroit Metro. Airport, Case No. 10-10413, 2012 WL 179320 (E.D. Mich. 2012).

77. Kennedy v. Contract Pharm. Corp., U.S. Dist. LEXIS 67839 (E.D.N.Y. May 13, 2013) (noting that an "expression of an emotional feeling while utilizing a social networking site" is too vague for discovery purposes).

78. Waters v. Union Pac. R.R. Co., https://scholar.google.com/scholar_case?case=3863999 228956124609&q=Waters+v.+Union+Pacific+Railroad+Co&hl=en&as_sdt=6,44.

79. *Id.*

80. *Id.*

alleged injuries, and (e) the postings that reflect his physical activities during that time frame."[81]

In granting the defendant's request, the court noted that while "the scope of discovery is broad [but] . . . not unlimited," defendant had both properly narrowed and shown the relevance of its request. The court felt that the temporal limitations and the fact that defendant sought only "evidence which could be germane to the extent of Plaintiff's injuries and damages and state of mind," made the request appropriate.[82] It is the job of the party fighting the request, in this case plaintiff, to show why the information requested is overbroad. The court felt the plaintiff failed to do so.

Outlier

There are some judges who do not follow the trend that has established itself across the country. In one, *Peronne v. Rose City HMA*,[83] the judge determined to allow a forensic expert to review the content in question. However, it is important to note that there was conceivably contradictory information to be found in the account. In this case, there was a picture showing the plaintiff acting in a way other than she claimed she could act. The plaintiff argued that the photo was prior to her injuries. The defendant argued that the color of the inspection sticker on cars viewable in the photo revealed that the time period in question was after the injuries the plaintiff was claiming she suffered. It is the use of a neutral expert witness that is unique in this case. Note, though, how closely the defense reviewed the social media account in question. From this case it is clear that the use of social media accounts as evidence is only increasing and any opportunity to use them as evidence will be rightfully analyzed.

Conclusion about Access to Social Media Accounts

The conclusion to be drawn thus far about the majority of social media discovery decisions is that although courts are willing to provide access to private sections of social media accounts, they are not willing to allow fishing expeditions simply based on the view that the accounts *might* have useful information. Some evidence showing that relevant information can be found in the account must be offered before discovery will be granted.

---

81. *Id.*
82. *Id.*
83. http://www.americanbar.org/content/dam/aba/publishing/litigation_news/top_stories /docs/Perrone.authcheckdam.pdf

In addition, the request must be properly tailored and show relevance to the case.

Won't the Social Media Provider Help?

Social media providers will not provide content from a social media account in civil cases. As recently as 2007, some providers did respond to civil subpoenas with content, but now the providers state unequivocally that due to the Stored Communications Act, 18 U.S.C. §§ 2701 *et seq.*, they may not provide content.[84] The providers will respond to a subpoena only with information about who owns the account, perhaps dates and times of connections, IP addresses, and the like.[85] This means the only way to get the data is to have the owner of the account cooperate. In criminal cases, most social media providers will assist when provided with an appropriate subpoena or warrant. On occasion a social media site will be surprising, go against its stated rules, and provide the evidence. Therefore, it never hurts to ask with a subpoena in a civil case. Just be prepared (and make sure your client is prepared) for a no.[86]

The various social media sites generally have details on the subpoena process, and what they will provide. Review each site to learn the appropriate steps.

What Happens if the Owner of the Account Deletes the Data?

Most social media providers claim that when a user deletes information from his account, it is gone forever. Facebook, for example, explains that its deletion system works much like a recycling bin. In essence, when a user deletes data, that data is stored on Facebook's server briefly until the system writes over it; this means, unfortunately, if someone is savvy and starts deleting harmful data, there is nothing that can be done to bring it back, once it is overwritten. Facebook does state, "If a user cannot access content because he or she disables or deleted his or her account, Facebook will, to the extent possible, restore access to allow the user to collect and produce the account's content. Facebook preserves user content only in response

---

84. Facebook states, "Federal law prohibits Facebook from disclosing user content (such as messages, wall posts, photos, etc.) in response to a civil subpoena." http://www.facebook.com/help/?faq=17158.

85. For Facebook this requires the e-mail address that the attorney desires to connect to the account. https://www.facebook.com/help/?page=211462112226850.

86. *See* Send a Subpoena to the Site, *supra.*

to a valid law enforcement request."[87] Of course, if there is nothing to find because it has been deleted and destroyed, then the site cannot restore the data. And outside of criminal cases, it must be the account's owner who requests the data be restored.

Authentication

Authentication is another troubling issue when it comes to social media. Facebook states that the owner or someone familiar with the account can authenticate it. The issue is that it is impossible to know whether the user deleted something in the account, leaving only helpful items. This is why it is extremely important to perform research early in the process, and to take screen shots of any evidence discovered immediately. Be certain to keep records as to how the evidence was preserved.

In terms of proving who owns the account, remember, it is very easy to create a fake social media account. Just because an account looks like it belongs to someone does not mean that it does. That is why it might be important to at least subpoena the account identifying information from the social media site, if there is any question as to ability to prove ownership of an account.

The case law on authentication and admissibility of social media sites is contradictory. In *State v. Bell*, the court found that the level of admissibility is low and accepted as good enough testimony from a witness familiar with the MySpace account and e-mail address of the party the information was to be used against. The evidence also showed that the defendant used certain code words and that those words were contained within the account. The court also noted that the witness agreed that the provided print-outs seemed to be an accurate reflection of the MySpace account in question.[88]

On the other side, in *Griffin v. State*, the court was concerned about how easy it is to create a fake account and noted that information such as birthdate, picture, and residence were not enough to prove ownership.[89]

However, a new opinion from the Third Circuit Appellate court has followed along the lines of *Bell*. In *United States v. Browne*,[90] the court

---

87. *See* Information on a Civil Summons, https://www.facebook.com/help/?page=211462112226850.

88. State v. Bell, 882 N.E.2e (2008).

89. Griffin v. State, 2011 Md. LEXIS 226, 27-28 (Md. Apr. 28, 2011).

90. Opinion filed Aug. 25, 2016, http://www2.ca3.uscourts.gov/opinarch/141798p.pdf.

held that the standard for authentication was preponderance of the evidence based on extrinsic evidence. The court also made it clear that social media evidence such as chat logs, even when provided by the social media site itself, is not self-authenticating. In *Browne*, there were two federal agents and several other witnesses who were able to speak to and identify the content of the chats and the likelihood that Browne authored them. A certificate of authenticity from Facebook just served as further evidence that the chat logs were likely to be correct. In and of itself, however, a certificate of authenticity from the provider is not enough to support the conclusion that the alleged author of a post was actually the author.

The Other Side—Responding to Social Media Requests

It is important to be prepared to respond appropriately to requests for social media content. All businesses (including law firms) should have a social media policy that controls who may (and may not) speak on behalf of the company. The policy should also consider addressing whether supervisors may be connected to employees on the more social sites (as opposed to professional sites like LinkedIn), and remind employees about the fact that policies online are the same as policies off line; specifically, in relation to sexual harassment and other such issues. Employees should also be reminded not to discuss private information and/or litigation on their social media accounts. Employers should train employees on social media privacy settings to assist in security. As already explained, individuals should be warned not to post anything that can be harmful to their cases on social media.

Social media evidence needs to be preserved appropriately. For a business with a great deal of social media evidence to preserve, it is wise to involve a company that can help in the preservation process during litigation. An individual can simply print out the pages or download the account. If the account is large (and is not on Facebook where it can be downloaded) and it is likely the history of the account will enter into the lawsuit, it might be wise to arrange for preservation of the account through a third party, to avoid any accusations of spoliation later on.

In the end, it is crucial for clients, indeed for everyone, to remember that any content posted on a social media site, even back in 2004 when Facebook was first created and the client might have been in college, could come up later during litigation. Therefore, everyone needs to be careful to think before they post. This does not mean that people should go back and clean up their accounts just because some day they might, by chance, be sued. But it does mean they might want to give some thought to their online reputations due to their past and current postings.

Other Issues: Judges and Juries

Judges

Many judges enjoy having an online presence as well. This has led to questions over whether judges should be friends with attorneys, and what happens if a judge is a friend with a defendant.

In attempting to resolve the first issue, the Florida Supreme Court Judicial Ethics Advisory Committee determined that judges may not be friends on Facebook with attorneys who appear before them.[91] In turn, a defendant sought to disqualify a judge based on his Facebook friendship with the prosecutor. The trial judge denied the request, but upon appeal the motion was granted. The court held that the Facebook friendship "conveys the impression that the lawyer is in a position to influence the judge."[92] Ohio came down on the other side, noting that it is acceptable for judges to friend lawyers who appear before them. However the judges must comport themselves properly, follow all ethical rules, and must be careful to disqualify themselves should the online friendship cause a bias.[93]

Other states have seen issues arise when the judge learns he is Facebook friends with a defendant. Two cases occurred in Pennsylvania. In the first, the judge was asked to recuse himself, and eventually did so when it turned out he knew the defendant's father. He was, however, unaware of the Facebook friendship prior to being alerted to it. Like many people, the judge simply friended anyone who asked and thought nothing of it.[94] Another controversy arose when a judge suppressed evidence against a defendant, resulting in dismissal of the case. After the fact, the prosecution realized that the judge was Facebook friends with the defendant, though the defendant and the judge did not know each other. The prosecutor asked the judge to

---

91. Fla. Supreme Court Judicial Ethics Advisory Comm., Op. No. 2009-20 (Nov. 17, 2009).

92. Domville v. State, No. 4D12-556 (Fla. 4th Dist. Ct. App. 2012).

93. Supreme Court of Ohio Disciplinary Bd., Advisory Op.: Judges May "Friend," "Tweet" if Proper Caution Exercised. (Dec. 8, 2010).

94. Sara Ganim, *Cumberland County Judge Thomas A. Placey under Fire for Having Too Many Facebook Friends* (Sept. 2011), http://www.pennlive.com/midstate/index.ssf/2011/09/judges_facebook_friend_has_som.html.

reverse the suppression and recuse himself. The judge decided not to recuse himself due to concern about setting a dangerous precedent.[95] Pennsylvania Bar Association Formal Opinion 2014-300 made it clear that it is acceptable for lawyers to friend judges, and vice versa, as long as there is no intent to improperly influence the judge.

On February 21, 2013, the American Bar Association released Formal Opinion 462, Judge's Use of Electronic Social Networking Media. It offers an acronym, ESM, meaning electronic social media. Judges are allowed to participate in ESM so long as they "comply with the relevant provisions of the Code of Judicial Conduct and avoid any conduct that would undermine the judge's independence, integrity or impartiality, or create an appearance of impropriety."

In the end, the best advice for judges is that they be careful who they friend. Friending everyone is not a good idea for a judge, since it is easy enough, as shown above, for the judge to end up being friends with a defendant while being completely unaware of their online relationship. Judges who have many friends on social media sites might want to take a look at who those friends are, and determine whether they should remain friends. On the other hand, judges who prefer to have many friends online might find it wise to be certain they know who those friends are and at the least make both sides aware of the Facebook friendship prior to the trial beginning. If necessary, perhaps the judge could have a clerk make a quick check of his account to make certain that he is not friends with defendants who appear before him.

Jurors

These days it is extremely common to look over to the seats behind the prosecution, plaintiff, or defense and see individuals hard at work on their computers during the voir dire process.[96] This is because jurors, like almost everyone else, provide an immense amount of information about themselves online. Some of this information might well disqualify an individual from serving on a jury, or simply show a particular side that it would be unwise to seat a potential juror.

---

95. Aaron Moselle, *Judge Refuses to Recuse Himself from Parker DUI Case; State Plans an Appeal*, NewsWorks (Nov. 22, 2011), http://www.newsworks.org/index.php/neighborhoods /mt-airychestnut-hill-/item/30248-hayden-denial-story-.

96. Michael Cary, *Lawyers in Murray Trial Using Facebook, Twitter to Screen Jurors*, CNN.com (Sept. 20, 2011), http://articles. /2011-09-20/tech/tech_social-media_social-media-jurors -murray_1_prospective-jurors-potential-jurors-jury-selection?_s=PM:TECH.

While there are currently no conclusive decisions on the issue of research-ing jurors via social media, there is guidance on the subject.[97] A New York opinion, quite reasonably, makes it clear that it is acceptable to research jurors online, including viewing their social media accounts under several conditions. First, the accounts must be accessed appropriately, i.e., only looking at accounts and information that have been left freely accessible by the jurors. Also, it remains impermissible to communicate with the jurors in any fashion. That means no friending (or having a third-party friend) of a juror in order to obtain access to the private sections of an account.[98] How-ever, the American Bar Association does not bar visiting the public portions of a site even if it makes the juror aware that an attorney looked at a pro-file. Such contact might include using LinkedIn to look at a juror's profile. Unless set properly, LinkedIn will show the name of a person who looks at a profile, under certain circumstances. Pennsylvania's social media guidance opinion supports the opinions of other states related to researching jurors on social media. The Pennsylvania Bar Association deems such conduct acceptable.[99]

Of late, jurors have been engaging in social media or other Internet use that has caused serious trouble for the court system. Judges, prosecutors, and defense attorneys frequently find themselves throwing their hands up in the air due to the frustration caused by jurors who refuse to follow the instruc-tions. While it might seem beyond belief that a juror would choose to engage in social media discussion or Internet research after being specifically told not to do so, the reality is that they do.[100] In response to juror behavior, many judges and court systems are developing instructions to provide to jurors to warn them away from social media use. For example, the Judicial Conference Committee on Court Administration and Case Management recently created Proposed Model Jury Instructions [on] The Use of Electronic Technology to Conduct Research on or Communicate about a Case.[101] Regardless of the language, it is crucial that judges warn the jury right at the outset of a case of the serious ramifications, and potential punishments, for violating court orders on use of social media during a trial.

---

97. NYCLA Comm. on Prof'l Ethics, Formal Op. 743 (May 18, 2011).

98. The American Bar Association Standing Committee on Ethics and Professional Respon-sibility released an opinion, Lawyer Reviewing Jurors' Internet Presence, Formal Op. 466, 2014, which agrees with previously stated guidelines from other states.

99. Formal Op. 2014-300.

100. *Social Media's Clout Worries Legal System* (2012), http://archive.azcentral.com/news /articles/20120831social-media-clout-worries-legal-system.html.

101. Proposed Model Jury Instructions [on] The Use of Electronic Technology to Conduct Research or Communicate about a Case (2012), http://www.uscourts.gov/sites/default/files/jury -instructions.pdf.

Conclusion

Attorneys need to understand how the public uses social media so they can reach potential clients, but also so they can protect their clients during litigation. Failure to properly research your clients, the opposing party, lay witnesses, and expert witnesses may well violate both the ethical rules and the legal standard of care.

CHAPTER THIRTY

Taking Your Firm Paperless

by David J. Bilinsky, BSc, LLB, MBA

Introduction

"Tame the wild paper beast and transition to paperless with ease." Well, at least that is the plan—but this lofty and somewhat innocent statement brings back the saying that it is hard to remember that your objective was to drain the swamp when you are surrounded by snapping alligators or at least lawyers waving around their paper files saying something about only being able to pull them out from their cold dead hands. . . .

But the transition to paperless does not have to be a troubled and drama-filled exercise either. You can shift to paperless—indeed many law offices already have—with a minimum of fuss and disruption. With most technology projects—moving to paperless being no exception—the greatest hurdles are not technological at all. They are the human-based—getting everyone on board, dealing with the passive-resistors, dealing with those who feel threatened by the introduction of new ways of doing things, and the like. As I say in my presentations, it is the carbon-based units that pose the greatest hurdles—not the silicone-based ones. . . .

This highlights that there are several aspects to going paperless. Certainly part of the process is examining your technology and putting into place a well-thought-out strategic technology plan that will ensure that all parts of the system are robust and can handle the load—and the lofty expectations—that will be placed on them.

So in this chapter we—you and I—will focus on how best to manage your shift to paperless and ensure you have considered all aspects of your new paperless office before making the jump. I think it is important to put in as much time to planning as you can—as anticipating problems and knowing how to deal with them is much better than having them land on your desk—unexpectedly—in the midst of the change.

We will also discuss the various procedures you will want to introduce such as scanning, OCR (optical character recognition), document management, and the emerging mobile and cloud-based practice of law. Security and having good off-site backups are essential. Before you start, you need to evaluate your hardware and software and in so doing, determine what needs upgrading. You need to make all necessary upgrades to your hardware, install all software, and test the systems before starting to go paperless.

Then . . . taking that first deep breath . . . begin with your most receptive lawyer and legal assistant . . . and have them pilot the system. Having done all your homework, planning, upgrading, and piloting, you will soon see that flying paperless is not half the challenge you thought it might be . . . and soon the whole office will be there. . . .

So let's take that first step toward your future. . . .

Transitioning to Paperless: It Isn't (All) about the Technology (Really!)

I have spoken and consulted with many lawyers and law firms who have called about taking their law firm paperless. Certainly there is much anxiety exhibited about giving up on paper and practicing in a paperless world (there will probably never be a situation where we fully abandon paper). Yet lawyers (and staff) express many misapprehensions in going paperless, part of which is rooted in a concern that *somewhere* the regulations of practice *require* firms to keep paper files. There is, of course, no such specific requirement—information is information and the medium that it is stored on is largely irrelevant so long as you can meet the requirements of practice (there are exceptions such as original wills and such but even these are changing as new enabling legislation comes into effect).

The typical concerns that I hear can be summed up as follows:

- There is no paper trail.
- Computers can go down.
- No backup exists.
- You can be hacked.
- Data obsolescence is a factor.
- Media degradation is a factor.
- You can lose an e-document.
- There is no structure to the documents on the system.
- Documents can be sent outside the office easily.
- Changes are required to policies, procedures, and work routines.
- There will be increased time costs, including costs of running dual systems.
- There is the possibility of job elimination or reassignment.
- A lack of training could lead to a loss of face in not knowing how to work the new system.
- The firm would face increased costs of transferring a file.
- What about all the transition issues?
- How do we go from here to there?
- What about increased hardware and software costs?
- What do we do with the original documents?

The requirement in any paperless office would be that the office could produce a full and complete record of the client's file (and render this to paper, CD-ROM, DVD or flash drive or upload to a cloud service if required). So long as you have a *complete* record of the file (which is organized in a manner that the whole file could be reviewed and produced if necessary), which would necessarily include documenting all transactions and the client instructions in relation thereto, it should not matter on what type of media that file is stored. (Indeed ethics rulings have been consistent in holding that transferring a file electronically is acceptable in many jurisdictions and in fact may offer greater utility than printing up and transferring a paper file). The important considerations are that the file is well organized; that it is in a common format that if necessary, someone could review; and that it reflects the level of documentation expected in a well-run law office. If these are met, I submit that it should not matter on what media—paper or electronic—the file is stored or transferred.

Of course, there are also many benefits of going paperless:

- You can search one file—or the entire network—easily and fast, particularly compared to paper files.

- You can reuse documents easily—and thereby craft a precedent library (and build on the knowledge transfer within the firm).
- Document management software imposes greater organization as compared to a paper-based office where documents can be left in piles on desks, cabinets, and floors.
- The cost of electronic storage is much less than paper storage.
- Paperless offices enable remote access/telecommuting for full and part-time lawyers and staff.
- Paperless offices are greener.
- Paperless systems can integrate and share data—thereby saving time and money.
- The cost of handling files can be faster, cheaper, and easier.
- Paperless offices are neater.
- There is an increased ability to meet new client needs (via Share-Point and other extranet portals for example). At a recent Corporate Counsel meeting, counsel stated that they *preferred* electronic war and closing rooms or portals over e-mailing documents around. You can control access, distribution, and versioning and more importantly, these documents do not travel on (unsecured) e-mail systems.
- There is usually a decrease in photocopy/printing costs.
- Courts, land title offices, and other organizations and tribunals are increasingly accepting paperless filings in many jurisdictions.
- It is harder to forge or alter a properly secured electronic document. Moreover, metadata associated with an e-document records a great deal of information about who created it, when it was modified and by whom, and so forth—information that is not typically accessible in a paper file.
- Your clients' systems are electronic and they expect lawyers to be able to accept and use e-discovery documents electronically.
- Having a paperless office requires the firm to at least consider a file retention and destruction policy that is consistently applied in accordance with the Sedona (Canada or USA) Principles and current case law and ethics rulings to avoid any suggestion that files were destroyed in order to eliminate evidence.
- The courts are calling on lawyers to be paperless in court (see Justices Turnbull's and Granger's November 2009 posts to this effect at www.slaw.ca).

Of course there are many other reasons to go paperless (as well as arguments against it). However, there is no denying that the world is moving in a paperless direction: Barker, Cobb, and Karcher, back in a 2008 publication titled *The Legal Implications of Electronic Document Retention: Changing the Rules*, stated that 99 percent of business documents are currently being produced electronically. At this juncture, it is pointless going against the tide; lawyers need to adjust to the new reality, embrace the possibilities, and examine the risks and benefits in moving to a paperless world. We are headed for a new horizon.

How Will You Transition to Paperless?

There are two recognized ways of bringing existing paper files into the paperless system. One could be called the brute force method; the other could be called the accretion method. Which one you adopt depends on the size of your office and the willingness of your staff to pitch in and do the conversion all at once.

The brute force method typically involves the availability of a long weekend. On Friday the office closes; from that point onward the sole task of everyone is to use as many scanners to scan and OCR the contents of every open file and bring them into the DMS system. You can see that you need a dedicated team to throw everything that they have at the conversion of the files so when you open again for business, every file is now in paperless form.

The accretion method takes a different approach. Here, the first time you need to touch a file on or after the stated conversion date, then you stop everything and scan and OCR the contents to bring it into the DMS. In this approach, the most active files are brought in first—with the least active files last. The disadvantage is that the time to convert files may take a while, and laggards have the opportunity to drag their feet.

Also consider if you have legacy servers and data and how you will bring that data into your DMS. Some firms adopt a policy that the legacy servers can continue to be accessed but you cannot save any new information into them—all document saves must take place within the DMS. This way the important information on the legacy servers can be brought into the DMS when needed.

Which approach you take depends on the culture of the firm, the commitment of your staff to take a long weekend for work purposes, and the ability of everyone to pitch in.

Begin with the End in Mind: Defining the Goal(s)

Stephen Covey, the esteemed author of *The 7 Habits of Highly Effective People*, has stated that one should "Begin with the End in Mind." So how do you build your plan to take yourself paperless? What are the goal(s) of the move to paperless? Here are some of the components to consider:

1. **Decide what your paperless office will look and feel like (the Vision).** It is important to work out your vision for how the system will look and work before you start building it. Will you aim to eliminate paper as much as possible? Will everyone be working on workstations with dual monitors, and with a central document repository (using a document management system or DMS) with remote access capability and client portals? By writing down your goals (as many as possible) you can make the transition "real" and decide how to stage the transition to paperless over time. Moreover, you can visualize your system and thereby make the cost/benefit decisions that are so important in any system design and change management process.

2. **Commit to going paperless.** Call your staff to a meeting and explain the advantages for each of them individually and as a group. Fully involve them in the process, particularly in drafting the Vision and invite them to raise their concerns now while you are at a planning stage. Ask for their support and commitment to a successful transition. It will be your job as team leader to communicate the Vision, the benefits of the paperless system, and why the cooperation of everyone is central to realizing the benefits of the new paperless system.

3. **Call in your IT support as early as possible and involve them in the plan from the get-go.** They will have to check your existing computer hardware including your server, backup, and RAID systems to make sure they can handle the increased load from all paperless applications (hardware and software requirements). They will have to ensure that you have a reliable backup system (including storage off-site). They will need to make sure the software and hardware will run quickly and effectively, and to do this, there are many things for them to check: that your Internet connection has adequate bandwidth in order that people are not (frustratingly) waiting for the system, that you have effective security in place, and so on. There are many technical issues that will need to be thought about and addressed and having your IT team think these through in advance will save you countless hours down the road. Listen to them carefully when they raise potential issues.

4. **Analyze your needs—now and in the future.** Think about what you're likely to need in the future as your business grows as well as your current needs. Think about which documents need to be accessed often or quickly, which may need extra security or encryption, and which could be weeded out after a certain time.

After all, you don't want to be storing all documents *forever*, but you do have requirements for document storage and retention times from your ethics regulator or insurer (or both). For example, you may need the ability to build an electronic "ethical wall" to isolate lawyers and staff from certain files; you will want that ability before the need for such a wall arises where the absence of same could potentially jeopardizes your ability to keep a client.

5. **Develop a paperless transition plan and a timetable.** The timetable should be tight enough to keep everyone on line but not so tight so that it doesn't allow for reasonable adjustments and setbacks. Plan to be flexible! Writing down the plan allows for everyone to read, think about, and provide feedback on the process, the goals, and the methods. You wish to make this as painless for everyone as possible and listening to their feedback will make everyone feel part of the process and help them feel like they have a part in the plan.

6. **Start small.** Use a single lawyer and legal assistant who are both keen on the project to start. Learn from the pilot project so you can address any problems before broadening your scope. It is easy to correct small things at the pilot stage before they become much bigger things in a firm-wide rollout. Try, listen, and learn from the experience of your most enthusiastic adopters as you expand your scope to remove or reduce any difficulties. Your detractors (and there will be those) will seize on any setbacks as an example that the system is bound to fail so try to reduce the chances of these happening.

7. **Research**. Do a thorough investigation of the available tools to help you (document management systems, electronic faxing, scanners, data backup systems, security systems, document conversion companies, process consultants, storage formats, storage devices, remote access devices, etc.). Knowledgeable consultants can help you out a lot here!! Get references of other law firms who have adapted each recommended product and do your due diligence!

8. **Budget**. This is required!!! Select your needs in advance (hardware, software, training, installation, consultants) and arrange to incorporate these into your budget and into your business plans. You may have to spread things out a bit to accommodate everything in the budget, perhaps over a couple of years. For software, consider what will fit with your needs, including ease of use and implementation, cost, and integration with your existing systems. Don't neglect backup needs to keep electronic data from being lost! Also consider both present and forecast needs; you don't want to find yourself constrained as you grow!

9. **Do a small test project**. Make any needed changes; and then move to the transition into the rest of the practice, using your early adopters as change agents. This is most important.
10. **Develop a plan for ongoing practice-wide use.** Include a document storage plan for employees with specific guidelines or clients with specific needs.
11. **Consider creating a client portal** where clients can view their file documents online without using e-mail. This is one of the benefits of going paperless!
12. **Do a celebration followed by a post mortem.** Learn from the experience!

Assessing Your Office Procedures and People: How Suited Are They to Going Paperless?

Moving to paperless means having to examine the workflows in the office and how they should be changed to maximize the investment that you are making in the paperless world. Your handling of paper must change, as does how you save, store, find, and archive documents. Furthermore, you now must put an increasing amount of attention to security and backup procedures and the like. The one thing that you want to avoid is carrying the costs of dual systems—this provides you with no advantages and only additional costs. Before you embark on going paperless you should consider your staff—lawyers and others—to determine if you anticipate difficulties with those who will resist the change and cling to the old systems. This aspect of change management will be dealt with in greater depth herein, but being frank in your analysis and being prepared to deal with these difficulties early in the process will be a key consideration in your transition to paperless.

Here are some of the considerations with regard to office policies and procedures.

Converting Paper Documents to PDF

Paper is not going to go away any time soon. Accordingly, all paperless firms need a policy on how paper documents are to be converted into electronic files and in what format. The most common format is Adobe Acrobat's PDF (or PDF/A for archive) formats.

I know that many firms like the PDF/A format as it is an ISO standard and this should ensure that the files can be opened and read years into the future. However, I dislike how PDF/A removes data from the document such as images and the like. Personally I prefer to use the ordinary PDF format and keep all the data in the document—and hope for the best in terms of being able to open and read documents into the foreseeable future.

This raises another issue and that is whether to use Adobe Acrobat or some other application to convert your documents to the PDF format for storage purposes. Top 10 Reviews has evaluated the top PDF applications for 2016; their analysis—and suggestions on selecting a PDF application—can be found here: http://convert-pdf-software-review.toptenreviews.com.

Typically, firms go one of two routes when handling paper in a paperless firm. Either they have tasked specific people with the job of taking all incoming paper and scanning it (centralized scanning on a large networked scanner/printer) . . . or it is left to each person in the firm (distributed scanning on smaller scanners). There are advantages and disadvantages to both.

Centralized scanning ensures that documents are handled in a business-like and consistent manner and that there is a degree of quality control to ensure that the scans were done correctly. For example, scans should always be dual layer—incorporating the image of the document along with OCR of the text in the image—which allows the computer to search the words in the document. Distributed scanning means that you have smaller scanners scattered across the office and that everyone is responsible for ensuring that the scans were done correctly.

Document Retention

You will also need a policy for how long to keep the original documents before shredding. (A story from one firm that went paperless had a legal secretary come to the principal of the firm and confess she had taken home and stored every single document for the last three years as she was convinced the system would fail and she would have to recreate all the files. Her basement became stuffed with documents and the originals were never needed.)

Typically three to six months should be sufficient time to catch any scanning errors before the documents are shredded.

Of course you will need a storage policy for documents that should never be shredded such as original wills, government documents, and so on. These can be scanned (of course!) but the originals need to be retained for evidentiary or other purposes.

Backups and Archives

If you put all your eggs in one electronic basket there is a consequential rule that you should watch that basket very, very carefully. Accordingly, making copies of your electronic data and ensuring that this data is stored in at least two locations, one a hardened hard drive (such as the ioSafe line of hard drives that are designed to withstand fire, flood, temperatures, immersion, and so on for extended periods of time) and the second a cloud storage system, is not only prudent but well advised.

Many firms that the author has spoken to have been hit with the Crypto-Locker malware. This application encrypts everything it can find on your network and demands a ransom to be paid—otherwise it disappears, taking the decryption algorithm with it . . . leaving your data useless. In one case, fortunately, the firm's cloud backup—which only backed up on a schedule and was not continually connected to the network—was left untouched by the malware and they were able restore their data without paying the ransom. This is perhaps one of the best arguments for backing your data up into a secure cloud backup that can remain isolated from a malware attack such as the CryptoLocker and CryptoWall ransomware and their unending progeny.

It is important that you have a multiple layer redundant backup system. Don't depend on a sole backup system . . . if that backup fails, you are left totally vulnerable. It is important to test your backup system and ensure that it is operating properly so that you can restore your data as needed. I have seen situations where the sole backup system seemed to be functioning fine until the time came when it was needed—and then the realization hit that the backup was corrupted and useless. In one such case, what had been backed up to Dropbox was recovered . . . all other data was lost.

The benefit of having a local hardened hard drive backup is that you can restore your data quickly in the event of a loss. Cloud backups—while wonderful for preserving your data in a safe location—will take considerable time to restore onto your network since you are limited by your download speeds. However, if your system is hit with a system-wide problem, such as CryptoLocker malware, a flood, fire or other disaster or a failure of your primary backup, you will be thanking your lucky stars for having a complete cloud backup no matter how long it takes to do the restore. Believe me, I have had to restore data from the cloud after a system-wide failure. A fast Internet connection can never be fast enough when time is money. But ultimately, having a cloud backup made the difference between sheer inconvenience and absolute disaster.

File Retention and Destruction

You should check with your local bar association and/or insurer to see what requirements and/or recommendations they put forward for file retention and eventual destruction of closed files. Certainly follow their guidelines when setting up your retention and destruction policies. You should also ensure that you follow these policies to be able to demonstrate that you destroyed data pursuant to a written office policy that was consistently and clearly followed to avoid any allegations of spoliation of data.

Knowledge Management

The ability to start developing a consistent set of precedents, library of research memos and resources is one of the benefits of a paperless office, particularly if you incorporate a DMS that can search system-wide for work-product that you can reuse. Whether you adopt a DMS or not, give some thought to how you can take documents from files and convert them to office precedents or templates (by removing names and other identifying information) and storing them in an organized template (or research) collection. Once you start along this path you will quickly see how you can add in articles, books, and other resources to create your own library that supports your area(s) of practice. Consider acquiring one of the numerous systems such as Pathagoras, HotDocs, TheFormTool, or other document automation systems to systematize and speed up your ability to convert existing documents into precedents or templates.

A Bit about the Hardware that You Will Need

When there was no alternative to paper, the costs of building and maintaining a paper-based filing system were simply taken for granted. Rows of filing cabinets along with physical storage, associated filing clerks, photocopiers, and fax machines all had to be purchased and maintained and took up (expensive) rented floor space. The environmental effects of having to manufacture all that paper had a cost as well . . . from deforestation to consumption of fossil fuels and electricity to taking up space in land fill sites for unwanted documents.

According to IBM, as of 2012, every day 2.5 exabytes (2.5×10^{18}) of data were created.[1] One exabyte is 1 billion gigabytes. To put this in perspective,

---

1. IBM, *What Is Big Data?—Bringing Big Data to the Enterprise,* www.ibm.com.

according to Wikipedia: "Earlier studies from the University of California, Berkeley, estimated that by the end of 1999, the sum of human-produced information (including all audio, video recordings, and text/books) was about 12 exabytes of data."[2]

With that volume of information being created electronically, it is apparent that new ways of storing, searching, sharing, annotating, signing, retrieving, and eventually destroying information had to be found. In the context of a law office, we will be increasingly under pressure to deal with all kinds of electronic records (such as for litigation discovery requirements and the results of forensic audits of hard drives, smartphones, and other devices, for example). This is where the paperless office reaches its potential since we will be building systems and procedures to move us into the paperless world and help us deal with the ever-increasing amount of digital information.

There is another consideration in moving to paperless, at least in a litigation context. Being able to handle digital discovery means that you will have the capacity to examine the metadata that should come with e-discovery. Oftentimes is the metadata about data that is vitally important. For example, in a murder investigation, knowing from what narrow geographic location a text or e-mail message was sent may be important in being able to tie someone to a specific location at a specific time. Without the metadata associated with that text or e-mail, this bit of evidence would not be available.

So with this as background, what do we need in terms of software and hardware to implement a paperless office?

Hardware

While it is always fortunate to find that an office's hardware infrastructure is sufficient to implement a paperless system, in most instances that is not the case. If you host your own servers and network switches, chances are that they will require an upgrade to handle the increased load that a paperless office will place on them. If you have implemented a hosted office (where you use remote file servers that are on a third party's platform) then you may need to increase your storage and Internet bandwidth capacity to handle the load.

Furthermore you will have to ensure that the network cards in workstations are sufficiently fast (1000BASE-T would be the preferred speed). Switches should be capable of handling gigabyte speeds, as should the cabling

---

2. Wikipedia, Exabyte, https://en.wikipedia.org/wiki/Exabyte (citing Juan Enriquez, *The Data That Defines Us*, CIO Magazine (Fall–Winter 2003)).

connecting all parts of the system. Existing processors may not have the capacity to realistically run the increased load of being paperless or be capable of being upgraded to current standards. For example, there are lawyers who are still running Windows XP machines notwithstanding that Microsoft has withdrawn support for XP and these machines are increasingly vulnerable to malware in addition to being outdated and slow.

Basically, upgrading to paperless should not be undertaken without budgeting for an upgrade of your hardware, particularly if you have not refreshed your computers within the last three years (at a minimum, at least in the author's experience).

Servers

You will need, at a minimum, a dedicated server running up-to-date server software (such as a Windows Server operating system or a Mac server if you are in an Apple environment). A server will allow all your files to be kept and indexed in one place and allow your documents to be organized and efficient. A server can manage which users can access what resources. Your server setup should be sufficient to handle your DMS—your document management system—as well as host your website, e-mail system, print server software, databases, accounting software, and more, plus allow remote access. You can see that you are placing a large load on your server infrastructure and as such it is essential to check that your server setup will be able to handle the load of going to paperless. This is why you involve your IT support at an early stage as they should be able to advise you on any necessary upgrades to your server infrastructure to support your desired paperless system.

According to Techradar, the top rated servers as of June 2016 were as follows:[3]

- Dell PowerEdge T20 (barebones)
- Dell PowerEdge T20 (Xeon)
- Lenovo ThinkServer TS140
- Supermicro SuperWorkstation 5039A-IL
- Fujitsu Primergy TX1310 M1
- HP Proliant MicroServer Gen8
- Lenovo ThinkServer TS440
- HP Proliant ML350 Gen 9
- Scan 3XS SER-T20
- Asus TS500

---

3. Desire Athow, *Top 10 Best Servers of 2016 for SMBs*, TECHRADAR (June 27, 2016), www.techradar.com/us/news/computing/servers/the-top-10-servers-for-business-1100986.

CRN's Test Center lists the following as the "10 Coolest Servers of 2016 So Far" (note that some of these would be overkill for most smaller law firms):[4]

- Dell FX
- Dell PowerEdge R730
- Lenovo X-Series (E7-4800 and E7-8800 v4)
- Lenovo ThinkServer sd350
- HPE ProLiant DL360
- HPE ProLiant Easy Connect EC200a
- Cisco HyperFlex
- Skyport Systems Ultra Secure Servers
- Dell DSS 7000
- Oracle VM Server for Sparc

Just to add a bit of spice to the mix, there is the just announced ioSafe Server 5. This server is perhaps the most disaster-tolerant server appliance available. This is a server wrapped in a fireproof/waterproof enclosure to protect your data against local disasters. It protects data from fire up to 1550°F, 30 minutes per ASTM E-119, and protects data from floods up to 10 foot depth, three days, complete submersion.

Capacities: 5TB to 40TB

- Processor: Intel Xeon processor D-1520/1521, 4-Core, 8 Threads, 45W
- Memory: 16GB DDR4 RAM (up to 128GB)
- Five hot-swappable drive bays for simple upgrades/replacement
- Hardware RAID controller
- Dual Gigabit Ethernet Ports with Dual 10 Gigabit Ethernet Ports for failover with Link Aggregation Support

What should you look for when purchasing a server?

Scalability/price. Needless to say, you get what you pay for. A lower-end server may be fine for current needs, but if your needs grow (you add additional people and/or your volume of information grows) then you may exceed the storage capacity of the server (which is supposed to store all the paperless documents on your system). Accordingly, look for a server that can have additional drives installed and that has fault tolerance built in (RAID is the measure of fault tolerance—"redundant array of independent

---

4. Matt Brown, *The 10 Coolest Servers of 2016 (So Far)*, CRN (July 20, 2016), www.crn.com /slide-shows/data-center/300081393/the-10-coolest-servers-of-2016-so-far.htm.

disks"—meaning that if one drive fails, the other drives have copies of the data that was stored on the failed drive and can take over handling the load until you replace the failed drive). If possible, look for a server that has at least a RAID 5 (or even better, RAID 6 level, which has tolerance for up to two failed drives).

Degree of use: Servers typically come in different configurations. Try to anticipate the volume of transactions that you will process in any day and purchase a server that can easily handle that volume so you avoid delays in waiting for information. Your IT person should be able to assist you with deciding which configuration would be best for you.

Scalability. Look for the ability to add memory upgrades and hard drive upgrades and a server that has a sufficiently fast processor that can handle the increased load.

Virtualization. Many organizations have moved to running virtual machines housed in one physical server. There are many advantages to this, not the least of which are energy savings, smaller data centers, almost instant capacity increases, increased uptime, improved disaster recovery, isolated applications, the ability to run legacy applications, and not least of all, the capacity to prepare your office to move things into the cloud. If possible, look to build your paperless system in a virtualized server environment.

IT support. If you have an experienced IT person to manage your network—great. But if you largely have to go it alone, then at least get a server that is easy to administer. Also ensure that you have reliable and competent IT support that can respond to problems quickly in order that you don't end up with downtime, which only costs you money and potentially places you at risk for missing important dates and filing deadlines.

A match with your environment. If you run Windows machines, then acquire a Windows server and software. While you can marry Macs to Windows networks, you will be increasing the complexity of your system. Similarly with Mac-based networks. Make life easy for yourself!

Form factor. If at all possible, look for a rack-mounted server with a large number of drive bays that is expandable. Consider air flow, temperature, noise level, and fan quality (overheating is a common factor in crashes) in the location that will house your server setup.

Memory. Again the ability to add memory (RAM) is important as needs increase.

Network Speed. You will need multiple ports on the server as well as a GigE network switch or switches. The slower your network, the greater the time spent waiting. Accordingly, have network switches connect all your devices together that support GigE speeds.

Cabling. Ensure that all devices on your network are connected with Cat 5 or preferably Cat 6 network cabling and that all devices have gigabyte networking cards installed.

Operating System. Is it included in the price of the server? Is it a standard server system? Look for an up-to-date Mac or Windows operating system.

Power. You will need a UPS—an uninterruptable power supply—that will allow for the orderly shutdown of your system in the event of a power failure to avoid data loss and corruption.

Drives. Your server should have a drive (CD/DVD/Blu-ray) to allow you to install software. Of course these days, you only really need a USB drive since less and less software is being provided on optical disks.

Hard Drive Storage

Today you can have solid-state storage or traditional hard drives. Traditional hard drives have higher capacity but solid-state drives (SSDs) are typically much faster. The downside to SSDs is that they fail without warning, taking your data with them. Whichever media you choose, buy as much as you can afford—you will not regret having large storage capacity! Always ensure that your networked drives and networked devices have a robust backup system to avoid any data loss when, not if, a hard drive crashes.

Scanners

There are two camps when it comes to scanners. A scanner (or multiple scanners) are necessary to take paper documents and transform them into electronic documents that can be brought into MS Word or converted to PDF formats (preferably both). On one hand, there are firms that have one large networked printer/scanner with a good sheet feeder than can handle large print/scan jobs. Other firms have gone to small individual scanners such as the Fujitsu ScanSnap iX1500s or the older S1500s that are scattered around the office.

Which route you go depends on the size of your office, the volume of paper that you will need to scan, whether you will have dedicated staff for scanning or not, how your office is laid out and configured, and whether it will be a trek to get up and go to find a scanner. The latest iX1500s can work with both Macs and PCs and have some significant improvements over prior versions such as Wi-Fi scanning. They also come bundled with software that make them very cost effective, such as Adobe X Standard for PCs (see: http://solutions.ca.fujitsu.com/products/scansnap/ix500/).

Features to look for:

- Reliability (the Fujitsu's reputation is awesome), whether there is a sheet feeder or not and whether it can take legal sized documents as well as business cards.
- Flatbed scanners can be slower but can take various sized documents.
- Output: It is most desirable if you can directly select OCR'd PDF format (which scans the document into a dual-layer PDF and allows you to search the document as it recognizes words in a separate layer as opposed to a single-layer PDF, which is equivalent to a photograph image only).
- TWAIN compliance is often cited as an important consideration as you can then open a scanned document in any software application that supports TWAIN. If the scanner is not TWAIN compliant, you may have to save the document separately before opening it in your application of choice (personally I have never really found this to be a barrier, but some feel otherwise).
- Resolution is important as is black and white and color capability. In most cases black and white is fine, but you may want to scan some documents in color to preserve the ability to differentiate data that may be in different color inks that would be lost in black and white. Resolution is important, as low resolution may lead to being unable to OCR the document or increased OCR errors. I would use a minimum of 300 dots black and white per inch.
- The ability to connect wirelessly is a nice feature as is full duplex scanning (both sides at the same time) Consider size, weight, and whether you have an Ethernet port to connect it to the network.

Backup Systems

For anyone who has faced the "blue screen of death," or, in haiku:

A crash reduces
your expensive computer
to a simple stone

You know the angst and frustration caused by data loss. Moreover, the implications can be long-reaching: many businesses that have been hit by environmental calamities, fires, and even terrorist activities failed when they could not resurrect their lost data. Moreover, don't underestimate the effect that ransomware such as CryptoLocker can have on a law firm. Waking up and finding that all your data has been encrypted and you are facing paying the ransom in order to be back in business is a terrible situation to be in.

Accordingly, it is important that you match your expensive computer system with a good and robust backup system that will preserve your data and allow you to be up and running as quickly as possible. Fortunately, electronic data can be backed up and stored in multiple locations easily once the system is configured and set up. Contrast that with an office with paper files in a single location: if it is hit by fire or flood the files would be destroyed with no backups. . . .

I recommend that you back up your system to a rugged external hard drive that is resistant to fire and flood (such as the ioSafe SoloPRO, or for larger firms, its NAS storage devices) as well as to a cloud-based back up service.

The reasons are manifold. Your rugged hard drive can be used to restore your network quickly, provided that the hard drive survives (and there is a good chance that it will). However, if the calamity is such that your entire office is destroyed, then the cloud-based backup will be your "fail safe" method of preserving your data . . . cheap insurance versus going out of business (or even facing a malpractice claim).

TopTenReviews has rated the best backup software for Windows in 2016.[5] The top four products were

- NovaBACKUP
- Acronis True Image
- EaseUS
- AOME! Backupper

Note that this software is not expensive. It ranges from $29.95 (Nova) to $49.99 (Acronis)

Monitors

Like scanners, there are two camps when it comes to monitors in a paperless office. The benefits of having two (or even more!) monitors on your desk are easily demonstrated . . . you can have your reference information on one screen (or on one half of a very large screen) while you craft documents on

---

5. Jeph Preece, *The Best Data Backup Software of 2016*, TopTenReviews (updated Sept. 9, 2016), www.toptenreviews.com/software/backup-recovery/best-data-backup-software/.

another. Personally I always prefer to work on two large monitors as I find the time saved in not having to repeatedly open windows adds up quickly!

Consulting with an ergonomic consultant can help you design workspaces that are comfortable as well as functional (the author has done this and can say it was well worth it!) as improper placement can lead to neck, shoulder, and back issues.

Flat-panel displays are now the current state of the art.

Features to look for in a good monitor:

- **Definition.** While most people think that higher resolution is a good thing, it may not be depending on the age of your eyes because increasing the resolution, while it makes thing sharper, also makes things smaller. Most flat-panel displays have a recommended resolution. (In Windows click on Start, then Control Panel, then Appearance and Personalization, then Adjust Screen Resolution —the recommended display resolution should be shown. On a Mac, click System Preferences, then Displays, and select Resolution: Best for Display.) Microsoft has a listing of recommended resolutions based on monitor size as well as how to set the best resolution for your monitor at: http://windows.microsoft.com/en-ca/windows/getting-best-display-monitor#getting-best-display-monitor=windows-7

- **Dot pitch.** This is the spacing between different pixels on the monitor. It can range from .30mm to .15mm. Generally speaking, the smaller the distance, the better.

- **Brightness and contrast.** Most monitors have their own controls to set the contrast and brightness of the displays. Windows has a feature called Adaptive Brightness that will adjust the monitor display if your computer has a light sensor installed and enabled. Check for this by going to Power Options in System and Security settings and enabling adaptive brightness. Apple computers have a setting under Displays in System Preferences that allows the automatic adjustment of brightness. You can adjust contrast on external displays if you find that helps. Windows has a feature called ClearType that makes fonts easier to read and this should be turned on and adjusted to your monitor to ease your eyes.

- **Size.** Monitors now come in sizes up to 98 inches (NEC X981UHD for $29,999.00 USD (at Amazon), which is 14 inches bigger and $10,000 cheaper than last year's biggest monitor) but most users will want between a 24-inch and 34-inch monitor (or two)! Accordingly, you should be able to find a monitor to match your space and size requirements.

- **Ports.** Look for multiple ports to match the ones on your computer. Common formats are VGA, DVI (digital display), and HDMI. You don't want to end up with a monitor that will only accept a DVI cable when your computer only has a VGA port (I saw that in an office where the poor lawyer was given a brand new monitor only to find out it wasn't compatible with her computer system).
- **Warranty/reviews.** Check both the applicable warranty (two to three years is good) that comes with the display as well as online reviews from actual users. Common problems to watch for are backlight failure and multiple pixel defects. Also check whether there is a restocking fee if you return the unit.

Techradar.pro rates the top monitors for 2016 here: http://www.techradar .com/us/news/computing-components/peripherals/best-monitor-9-reviewed -and-rated-1058662.

A Bit about the Software You Will Need[6]

Below are a number of techniques to harness and control digital information to suit any law firm. With diligence, planning, and a few add-ons, any law office, regardless of budget constraints, can implement an efficient document management system. The time spent up front to determine the best system for a particular office will be well worth the immensely improved management and control of office documents.

DIY—Do It Yourself File Naming Conventions

The least expensive method of sharing and storing electronic documents is to use network drives or shared drive, a series of folders, and file naming conventions. It starts with a strategy that includes all lawyers and staff in the office. A small group of end users, representing everyone who creates, edits, or locates documents for the office, must sit down and create a standard naming convention for folders, subfolders, and file names. This should be easy to follow, logical even to outsiders, and checked for quality control on occasion. A "quick guide" to the structure should be created and shared with everyone who uses the system. For this method to work effectively all documents must be saved in a shared folder on the network.

While folder and subfolder names will vary depending on the type of law office in which you are working, there should be a logical basis for its

---

6. This section was written by Catherine Sanders Reach.

continued expansion. For example, if your office identifies work by "client" then that is one logical structure that will grow and expand nicely. Create a folder by client, then by matter. Then create subfolders for the types of documents in the matter folder. If a top-level folder is "client," then what is the naming standard—last name, first name? Take a look at your paper-based filing system. Can it be effectively replicated electronically? By scanning incoming paper and filing it electronically in your "file cabinet" you may be able to eliminate the paper and reduce filing things twice.

There are a few pointers to keep in mind when naming files. While a computer knows a lot about an electronic file—file name (sampledocument.doc), date created, date last modified, file location (C:/mydocuments/articles/xxx .docx), and much more—this information is created by the computer, and it can be automatically changed by the computer, depending on a variety of factors. Thus, the user should counter those automated fields by applying some consistent and human logic. One suggested convention is to start all file names with a year/month/day number, so that files within a folder can be sorted by oldest to newest (or vice versa) without being dependent on the automated date field. Also add the document author name, which may differ from the system applied document author field. For instance, a file could be named "20110621_jones_lettertojsmithre:foreclosure," which identifies the date the file was created, the author, and the subject of the document. Ostensibly this file would be in a client folder, under a matter subfolder.

Also note that different operating systems deal with symbols, spaces, and uppercase letters differently. To avoid problems, use an underscore for a space and avoid uppercase letters.

For smaller offices, this document management system may work. However, since it depends on users consistently and properly employing the conventions, human error sometimes intervenes to prevent it from working efficiently.

Full-Text Search Engines

A full-text search engine will increase the efficiency of a simple DIY system and there are a number of fairly low-cost tools available. Those with Windows 7, 8, and 10 operating systems will find an effective search tool built into the system. Indexing and searching network folders can be done and the user has the ability to search locally (on the laptop or desktop) and on network shared folders. The search is fast and efficient, but somewhat limited in the types of files it will index. For instance, it will not create a full-text index of WordPerfect document files. Mac users have Spotlight built in for search, though other search tools like QuickSilver or Found add functionality.

If you aren't using a desktop search engine, look at Copernic Desktop Search or X1. These programs can search within multiple file formats at the speed of light. Of course, the added bonus is that these desktop search tools not only search the research folder, but also your entire hard drive or specified network drives. You will have a fighting chance at finding files, e-mails, and more on your desktop, even if you haven't been very organized.

X1 and Copernic are two sophisticated desktop search engines that make finding content on your local machine, networked drives, or external drives a snap. Superfast, imbued with bells and whistles, and reasonably priced, these tools have been around for some time. But the developers have not rested on their laurels. Both of these superpowered search tools now offer mobile apps, to let you search your data on the go. With myCopernic On the Go! you can search your computer remotely from your smartphone, iPad, or remote PC (sorry, Windows only). You will need to install the myCopernic Connector for it to work. Then from your device you can login to myCoperic On the Go! to access search for your files. You will need Internet access, and functionality is delivered through a web-based app, not a native app. Because of that it works on just about any device with a browser, including BlackBerry. This service costs $9.95 annually, in addition to the $50 for Copernic Professional Desktop Search (though it is not necessary to have Copernic Professional Desktop installed).

X1 offers X1 Mobile Search. A native app for iPhone or iPad, this free app will let users search their Macs or Windows PC with or without having X1 Professional Client installed (although the manufacturer does mention it works best with X1 Search). X1 Mobile Search also lets you view and display files, share files, and download files for offline use. Setup includes downloading the X1 Mobile Search app from the iTunes store and installing the Windows or Mac version of X1 Mobile Connect. Et voila. Connections are protected by x.509 PKI-based two-factor authentication and RSA-powered SSL/TLS.

Another option is Otixo (http://otixo.com), which lets you connect your cloud services, such as document storage service, Evernote, and even your desktop and mobile devices to search, sync, share, and move. It creates a dashboard for your files, no matter where they happen to be. The free version provides search and connections, premium plans add sharing files, drag and drop between clouds, and more!

Finally, for really super search, there are two new tools on the market for lawyers. One, MetaJure, is more appropriate for a law firm with a network and shared file storage, document management system and other on-premise information repositories. The tool can search across all places a firm saves information, with many ways to slice and dice the search and the search results. SearchMyCloud will search network files, local hard drives, and the Microsoft Exchange Server as well, plus it adds the ability to search cloud repositories stored on third-party sites like Dropbox. SearchMyCloud will also index and encrypt files before they are sent to cloud storage.

E-mail

E-mail itself is often a record, and often documents and their versions attached to the e-mail may never be saved to even the most carefully con-structed DIY document management system. While manual in most cases, there are a number of ways to save important e-mails into a shared doc-ument repository. One way would be to have the IT administrator create group folders in Outlook or LotusNotes so that the users can drag/drop e-mails that need to be shared to one folder. Users can also save individual e-mails as a .msg or .html and save it in the appropriate folder in the file/folder structure on the network. For users with the full version of Adobe Acrobat, or similar "convert to PDF" functionality, you can save the e-mails to a PDF format.

But what about the attachments? Avoid attachment problems by sending internal e-mail recipients a file path instead of an attachment. The file path will take the recipient directly to the document on the server, without cre-ating a new version. This helps with version control *and* helps ensure that the document location and file name conform to the standards. When you receive a document attached to an e-mail make it a habit of "right" (alter-nate) clicking on the document and choosing "save as" to save it with the appropriate name and folder right away. A simple add-on for MS Outlook called EZDetach[7] from TechHit automates the process of saving and catego-rizing attachments. The product is $49.95 per user, though bulk licensing and site licensing is available.

Another method of dealing with e-mail is to keep it in a folder structure that mimics the network folder structure and use Adobe Acrobat to save the entire folder at close of the matter. Each e-mail in the folder will be con-verted to PDF, and can be sorted, searched, and extracted as needed. The attachments to the e-mails are stored within this PDF repository as well,

---

7. http://www.techhit.com/ezdetach/outlook_attachments.html

though they are not converted to PDF. Nuance PDF Converter Pro also provides this option, but you can also save attachments as PDF as well.

Case/Practice Management Systems

A class of software specifically designed for lawyers is commonly referred to as practice management software. This software helps manage all aspects of a law practice, and is often divided functionally between "front office" and "back office." Front office functions include document assembly, docket and calendaring, e-mail management, document management, conflicts checks, contacts management, time tracking/billing, and task management. Back office functionality includes trust accounting, general ledger, and accounting. The document management in most practice management software allows the user to save a document or e-mail into the centralized database. Users assign a case/client and matter to the document, which is stored with all the work regarding that matter. The software often installs add-ons to common office suite software, making the process of saving the documents directly to the system easier. Likewise the workflow can be initiated from the case/practice management software itself.

Choices abound for practice management software. Many applications, such as TimeMatters,[8] Amicus Attorney,[9] and Abacus Law,[10] are standard installed desktop software available on a licensed model. Newer entries to the field are the so-called cloud-based or web-accessible programs such as Rocket-Matter,[11] MyCase,[12] and Clio.[13] The principle behind the cloud is leveraging the Internet to provide access to computing power and storage. Users can access files on a remote server rather than requiring an on-site physical storage medium. Many users of the Internet may be using a form of cloud computing without realizing it. Those who use web-based e-mail such as Gmail, Hotmail, or Yahoo or online backup such as Mozy or Carbonite are using "the cloud." Cloud-based applications require no installation or IT support, and are available as long as the user has access to the Internet. These applications charge per user, per month. Most of these applications have a trial period. In many law offices this type of software may have its uses, but if the primary focus is document management, then the extended functionality may be overkill, and you will not see the return on investment for the product. However, if this type of software seems like a possible option, first

---

8. http://www.lexisnexis.com/business-of-law/products/practice-management/time-matters.
9. http://www.amicusattorney.com/.
10. http://www.abacuslaw.com/.
11. http://www.rocketmatter.com/.
12. https://www.mycase.com/.
13. http://www.goclio.com/.

request a demo, follow up with questions, then request a trial period and let representative users test the features and functions.

Document Management Systems

Document management software is designed to save all documents, including e-mail, into a central storage space on a server. In many cases the system "forces" the user to save documents to the system, though the user can mark certain documents private. When the user saves the document, the software invokes a screen that requests information about the document, for example, client and matter number, keywords, folder structure, and other information designated by the administrator at setup. This structure ensures that all documents are organized, categorized, and available for full-text searching. The system also provides for version control and check-in/check-out of documents, and is fully integrated with your primary office suite. Some additional functionality may include records management, which offers automated file destruction based on rules set up by the administrator.

The document management software programs commonly used by the legal profession include Worldox,[14] iManage Work,[15] and OpenText's eDOCS[16] (formerly DocsOpen). Of these, Worldox is by far the most appropriate for a smaller office environment, and provides concurrent licensing (concurrent licenses are shared by all users of the system, in contrast to individually licensed software requiring each user to have a license). An alternative option is NetDocuments,[17] another web-based application that has been in the market for over a decade. Like other web-based applications, this is priced per user, and has the benefits of being available anywhere you have an Internet connection. NetDocuments also provides a "local" copy, so that if the Internet is down, the product still works.

Document management systems are remarkable tools for managing, collecting, and searching documents and e-mail for an entire office, or a group within an office. It is robust, and often relatively expensive, software. However, considering the benefits it provides, the cost may be justified.

---

14. http://www.worldox.com/.

15. https://imanage.com/product/imanage-work/.

16. https://www.opentext.com/what-we-do/industries/legal/legal-content-management -edocs.

17. http://www.netdocuments.com/.

Project Management Systems

For some law offices, project management software may be the best solution. Traditional project management software, like Microsoft Project, will not necessarily solve the problems of lost documents, version control, and other problems associated with poor management of electronic documents. However, web-based applications such as Base Camp[18] and Zoho Projects[19] add structure to ensure effective completion of a project, aiding in task assignment, deadline enforcement, and collaboration. A project is assigned a date for completion, and split into milestones. Each milestone is then separated into tasks, and assignments are doled out to different individuals. Documents can be uploaded into the system for review, provides versioning, and can be checked in and out for updates. Users can track time in the system as well.

The best way to determine if project management software would work for a particular office is to try it out on a small project. Although this will require some forethought about the project itself—what are the milestones, tasks, participants, and so on—it will be worth the effort to test the effectiveness of the system before purchasing it. After logging in, users are presented with a "dashboard," a common interface used now by many applications, which shows recent updates, other projects the user is working on, and additional information. There is a system-wide search, as well as "white-boards" for loose notes and brainstorming and a messaging system to keep threaded discussions specific to the project. Users can set up e-mail alerts to be notified when there are changes to the project that affect them, such as a new document or new task.

Most web-based project management tools are relatively low cost. For instance, Base Camp's most expensive package is $149 per month for unlimited users and unlimited projects with 75GB of storage. For $200 per year, Zoho Projects offers unlimited users, unlimited projects, and 15GB of storage.

Collaboration Challenges

While all of the above methods will help provide a central storage of electronic documents, a few problems exist that have yet to be completely and effectively solved. One is real-time collaboration on a document. To retain the look and feel of a formatted document, and allow multiple people to do real-time editing, the only tool this author has found that actually works is

---

18. http://basecamphq.com/.
19. http://www.zoho.com/projects/.

Google Docs.[20] Because of the terms of service of the free Google Docs, some lawyers have determined that it is inappropriate for confidential information. However, if the information is not confidential, this is an excellent tool to share a document and allow multiple authors to edit, at their leisure or simultaneously. There are many tools that purport to provide multi-user collaboration on a shared document, but after testing, many did not work as advertised. However, there is hope that this type of functionality will continue to improve.

Cloud versus On-Premise Software

In the above examples of case/practice management and document management, distinctions were made between cloud or web-based applications and downloaded or "traditional" software. Lawyers should understand the benefits and potential risks of software in the cloud. The benefits of the cloud model include reductions on reliance on information systems staff, and a significant reduction to the time and complexity to install and configure new software. The cloud model also reduces the need to purchase, maintain, and back up expensive servers and other peripherals, as well as provides remote access to users. Expenses for cloud applications are generally annualized (monthly fee), versus a large capital outlay for new systems. The potential risks with the cloud model include saving confidential information with a third party, subpoenas issued to the cloud provider for data without notification to the data owner, consequences of data retrieval if the cloud application provider goes out of business, and ownership versus access issues. In many cases these risks can seriously be mitigated by asking the right questions, and taking steps to maintain a duplicate copy of the data locally.

Think about the Role of Cloud-based Services

The Law Society of British Columbia has released a report on cloud computing for lawyers along with a checklist when looking at the cloud.

Cloud computing due diligence guidelines: http://www.lawsociety.bc.ca /docs/practice/resources/guidelines-cloud.pdf

Cloud computing checklist: http://www.lawsociety.bc.ca/docs/practice /resources/checklist-cloud.pdf

---

20. https://docs.google.com/.

There are ethical decisions and guidance from numerous bar associations as well as from the ABA here: http://www.americanbar.org/groups/ departments_offices/legal_technology_resources/resources/charts_fyis/ cloud-ethics-chart.html

Before you move to the cloud, research what may be published in your jurisdiction and what steps you have to take before you jump into the cloud.

The cloud offers many benefits to lawyers in terms of the paperless practice of law and the ability to recover from a natural or man-made disaster, but these have to be balanced against possible privacy, security, ethical, and client concerns. There is no right answer; rather each firm has to determine the appropriate protections and such to meet the firm's and its client's needs (such as using encryption with cloud applications such as Dropbox).

Think about Mobile Computing, Remote Access and Apps

Mobile computing and apps are dealt with in a different chapter in this book. However, it is worth noting that the mobile practice of law does go hand-in-glove with the paperless practice of law since all your office files are already in digital form. You need to consider how to grant access to your staff and whether this takes place using smartphones, laptops, tablets, or other devices. Consider the policies that you should put into place (such as not using any insecure public Wi-Fi hotspots, as these are inherently vulnerable to a number of security risks such as man-in-the-middle attacks that steal user names and passwords) and how you will enforce them. Particularly consider policies that will prevent what is termed the "rogue cloud"—namely, staff sending documents between their home and work computers using e-mail or file transfer services that have not been approved by the firm and that place the integrity and the safety of the office network at risk. Consider for example if the home computer in question is also used by other persons (possible loss of confidentiality), if it is infected with any malware (placing the office at risk if that document is then subsequently brought back into the office network), or if the document is transferred using a file transfer service that is insecure.

There are any number of applications for the iPhone, Android, and Black-Berry smartphones (such as DocsToGo) that allow you to read, annotate, and in some cases work on documents on the road. With Microsoft Office now available for the iPad along with Office 365 for virtually any device that hosts a browser, the ability to work remotely has never been better. The enhanced ability to work remotely on virtually any device, wherever you can access an Internet connection, is definitely one of the strongest reasons for fully implementing the paperless office.

The Change Management Process in Taking your Firm Paperless

The authors have stated many times that the biggest hurdles in taking your firm paperless do not lie in the technology area. Indeed, they lie in dealing with the carbon-based units who must deal with, be persuaded to use, and will ultimately benefit from the paperless technology.

Many lawyers believe that implementing a paperless system is as straight-forward as implementing a management decision that all staff should now start using the new system from date X. Perhaps this is due to their experience dealing with government-mandated changes in the law that must be implemented as of a given date.

But leading the change to a paperless system is not just a management decision. It is not a top-down-driven decision. Yes, management is all about making a system work. But when you are taking a firm from one system (a paper one) to a different one (a paperless on) then you are exercising the strategies of leadership.

Leadership is all about leading or transforming an organization from one system to another. Management is making sure that that system continues to work properly once implemented. Leadership takes your firm into new and uncharted territory. In a fast-moving, high-pressure, and results-oriented business such as a law practice, this difference has huge implications. We believe that careful study should be given to the leadership and change management processes within a law firm before deciding to go paperless. Computing machines will run whatever software application you install on them. Humans, however, have many ways of trying to find ways around using systems that they choose not to learn. Your role as change agent and leader in your law firm is to ensure that your paperless system achieves the greatest benefit possible for your firm. This means that you must give careful consideration to how you will go about bringing about the change in your law firm that you wish to see. Leadership is a different skill set from lawyering. Indeed, some very, very smart people have failed to appreciate this distinction with the consequence that the change management initiatives that they have undertaken in their firm failed to live up to their potential and have not generated the benefits that were promised at the outset of the projects. Our goal in this chapter is to give you the greatest leg up that we can to achieve a successful paperless transformation in your practice.

Essential Conditions to Create Change

In moving to paperless, it has been generally recognized that you need to create the right conditions inside the firm before introducing the change. Think of this as being similar to doing your homework and preparation that must be done before you go to court.

Urgency

The first condition that you must instill is that there is a sense of urgency in moving to paperless. People don't respond to a complacent movement toward change. You need to bring about big change and you need to do it within a short time frame. This means that you must communicate the right message that produces a sense of urgency in bringing about the change.

Accordingly, think carefully about how you are going to frame this change to the firm. You and your team must launch the effort with a sense of urgency to generate the momentum to overcome the inertia in the firm. Lay out the business case for the benefits of the change to paperless. Don't forget to emphasize how the current model leaves the firm vulnerable (paper documents exist in only one place; electronic ones can be backed up in many places), how you can work from anywhere if your files are electronic, and the like. Remember to show hard data (such as from the ABA—LTRC annual tech survey) on how firms are moving to the different technologies inherent to going paperless.

The Team

A change such as moving to paperless can't be done by one person alone. You will need the support of the highest level of management as well as the right mix of team members at all levels in the organization that are willing to put their shoulder to the wheel to help bring about the change. Remember that not everyone will buy in to the idea at the outset. You need to give careful thought to who will be on the team to lead the change. But the people on the team should be seen as some of the most powerful individuals in the firm (and ensuring that you have their full support). Don't make the mistake of failing to realize how powerful a force a good change team can make. You need to overcome that most powerful force called inertia, and to achieve this, you will need an equally powerful team.

Divide the team into working groups that have a focus on each specific part of the overall goal. One team's role could be to focus on the DMS that you will adopt and to present their recommendations to the group—pros and cons. Another would be to determine the system upgrades that will be necessary to run the new hardware and software and ensure that there will not be "bottlenecks" that will drag the performance down to an unacceptable level.

Schedule regular meetings (say the first and third Tuesdays of every month) with a rolling agenda that calls for reports on accomplishment of goals by each working group of the team. There is an old expression, "what gets watched, gets done." By holding people responsible for task accomplishment, you keep the entire team on track, energized and focused on the goal.

Vision

Your role as leader is to communicate the ultimate benefits of the new procedures and systems. The importance of having someone act as a transformative visionary cannot be underestimated. This leader will serve as the compass point pointing the way forward when people get sidetracked or lose sight of the eventual goal when they are immersed in projects, goals, educational sessions, and other components of the change process along with accomplishing their daily tasks.

Don't underestimate the uphill battle in producing change. The role of the transformative visionary is key. Everyone will be watching the leader and looking for inspiration, direction, and alignment of the various parts. The visionary's role is to generate the energy necessary to overcome the inertia in your law firm working against change.

Acid test: Can you describe in five minutes or less where the paperless transformation will take the firm and achieve understanding, comprehension, and initial buy-in from the person or people to whom you are speaking? If not, then go back and rewrite your elevator speech on moving to paperless. Archimedes said: "Give me a lever long enough and a fulcrum on which to place it, and I shall move the world." Your visionary paperless change management speech will be the lever to change your firm. The fulcrum will be your change management team.

Action Speaks Louder than Words

At one time I was called into a law firm to assist in bringing about change in their firm. The firm was in disarray; there wasn't even one consistent letterhead template being used by the different firm members. Everyone kept all their information to themselves; the firm's accounting was still being kept on a paper system and the firm didn't even have a server or a network. Everyone, literally, was doing their own thing.

The managing partner warmly met me in the reception area and escorted me into his wood-paneled office with his arm over my shoulders. He sat me down in one of the deep client chairs and proceeded to sit behind his formidable wood desk. He looked at me over his tented fingers and said: "Let's make one thing perfectly clear. You can change anything about this firm; just don't change the way that I work."

Anyone with any interest in producing change knows that this was essentially a fatal blow. Without the support of the top members in the firm who are willing to "walk the talk," any serious change management initiatives were dead in their tracks. In any firm, the change initiative must receive the unconditional support of those at the top; otherwise their nonverbal communication that essentially says that they are not going to adopt the change sends the message to everyone in the firm that they too can comfortably ignore the initiative. You will be essentially flogging a dead horse and getting about the expected result.

Work carefully to ensure that all upper management are not only committed to the goal, but willing to be the early adopters of the new systems to demonstrate the firm's commitment to the new way of doing business. This is key.

Look for the Disruptors

Beware of those in all positions who may pay lip service to change but who really work against it. There are many categories that these individuals may fall into, from passive-aggressive individuals, to those who are afraid of losing status, income, or power as a result of the change, to those who are afraid that they will not be able to adapt to the new systems and are fearful of loss of face as a result. Technology is one of those areas that tends to make individuals fearful of change. Your role as a paperless change management visionary is to identify these individuals early in the process and develop strategies that deal with each person's particular fears and concerns. This is of vital importance. If you can turn around someone who would otherwise be an elephant standing in the middle of the road to change and convert them into either a supporter or at least someone who is at least willing to go along with the change, then you will have achieved a significant win. This will pay dividends all along the road to change.

Accordingly, the task of working group will be to look at the possible disruptors and come up with tactics to bring them on board. There will be different considerations for different individuals, depending on whether they are passive-aggressive, opposed to technology (technophobes), or simply "too busy to learn something new."

Look for the Wins and Celebrate Them!

Change is an elusive target. You have to communicate to everyone when you have crossed a hurdle and achieved a milestone on the path to change. Accordingly, look for short-term wins early in the process and celebrate them! Those that support the change initiative will be looking for early signs of success; those who are contrary to the change process will have to grudgingly acknowledge that you are making positive process. There is also a downside; without short-term wins, those opposed to the process will promote the lack of good news as vindication and justification of their opposition. Your job is to keep the good news coming and to demonstrate that positive progress that is being achieved.

Create a "paperless news area" on your firm intranet and post news about the project, timelines for committee meetings, and ways for interested people to work with on the project. Use this to post news on "wins" and the ways they are being celebrated, and about the individuals who have helped create the win. Keep the good news coming to help counter the naysayers.

Don't Declare Success Too Soon!

Celebrating wins is necessary. But those watching the project will be looking for the signs that you have actually reached the promised land. If the project seems to be taking a while, resist the temptation to simply accept what you have achieved, declare success, and end the project. Unfortunately, all too many organizations do this and this only poisons any future change management efforts in the firm. Keep the energy going and avoid feeding the resisters who will be looking for the evidence that their positions against the change were valid after all. Better to be honest and acknowledge that the promised land is still the goal and still achievable but taking a bit longer than expected than to give in and give up.

Be honest in your reporting on the progress of the project. People can see through a smokescreen; if you are honest in your news then people will recognize that accomplishing any change requires time and effort and any project will suffer setbacks from time to time. You will accomplish more by being forthright rather than by sugarcoating setbacks and alienating those who would otherwise jump on board.

Become an Organization that Adopts Change as a Way of Life

In business, there is a concept known as a "learning organization." A learning organization is one that has embraced change as a way of life in the same way that lawyers have embraced the need for continued professional development as being necessary to be a learned and effective lawyer.

Leading the successful push to adopt a paperless orientation will help bring about the transformation of your law firm to adopt change as being necessary to carry on in today's business environment. You have helped the organization move forward; be sure to take the time to capture how this was done (knowledge capture) to ensure that you are better equipped to bring about the next change initiative (tacit knowledge management).

Accordingly, after each goal accomplishment, hold a short meeting whose focus is to learn from the prior work. What worked? What didn't? Why? How can we do it better next time? Setbacks offer lessons too. Learn from your mistakes to avoid repeating them.

Conclusions

In terms of bringing about change, it will be worth your time to focus on each of the factors noted above. Failure to consider any one of them may not be necessarily fatal; but failure to consider all of them before starting your change management process most certainly will be.

Look for ways to always connect with firm members and have the system support them in what they do. As each team member converts over to the new system, you have lessened the inertia working against the change and increased your momentum.

Getting Buy-In from Your Team Members (Leading the Change!)

The one factor that will determine the success of your paperless project will be the buy-in from your organization. Accordingly give careful consideration to the choice of the people who will be the innermost team leading the change.

Invite them into an initial meeting. Communicate the vision. Listen to their concerns. Have them pitch ideas in a brainstorming session on how to bridge the gap from where you are now to where you want to be. Energize and empower them. Have them draw the brainstorming ideas into an initial plan to move forward with milestones and SMART goals.

SMART goals have the following attributes:

- **Specific**
  - Who: Who is involved?
  - What: What do we want to accomplish?
  - Where: Identify a location.
  - When: Establish a time frame.
  - Which: Identify requirements and constraints.
  - Why: Specific reasons, purpose or benefits of accomplishing the goal.
- **Measurable**
  - How will we know when the goal is accomplished?
- **Attainable**
  - How can we make this goal happen within the established time frame?
- **Relevant**
  - Our goals must represent an objective toward which we are both *willing* and *able* to work.
- **Timely**
  - When will these goal(s) be achieved? What are the milestones?

You may wish to bring in a consultant to lead this initial meeting who is skilled at chairing such a meeting and building consensus among the team. This allows you to concentrate on the management aspects of where all this is going.

This initial meeting will set the direction and the time frame for the rest of the project. That isn't to say that everything is set in stone; rather, you have consensus on the scope of change and what success will look like at the conclusion of the process. There will be setbacks and such but the team can help overcome these by the momentum that you have built. Your job from here on in is to keep that momentum going to overcome the inertia in the organization.

Let us discuss further change management details of what you are contemplating in going paperless.

Awareness about the Nature of Change

Before you start, think about and come to an understanding of the scope or magnitude of this change toward paperless that is being introduced. How many people, structures, systems, and so on will be affected by the introduction of change? Will people in the firm regard this change a voluntary one or not? How do you deal with people who feel that this change is being thrust upon them rather than change being led from within? Notice that in most cases, law firms deal with change from outside the organization—now, however, you are being a catalyst of change from within and you need to make your staff and lawyers appreciate that this will result in a better and more efficient and effective organization once the change is implemented!

The Three Levels of Change

There are three levels of change that you will deal with: procedural, structural, and cultural. What are the implications of each in your change to paperless?

Procedural change means the rules or policies around handling, storing, searching, and retrieving documents will change. Structural change means that the office will no longer look or feel the same . . . paper will disappear, documents will be scanned and stored, files will be only electronic, and the like. Cultural change means that people will have to adapt to living and working in a paperless world and that new entrants will have to learn and become part of the new system.

Management of Change

The old expression states that you never get a second chance to make a first impression. Accordingly, it is vitally important to give considerable thought to the plans for the introduction of the change as well as for people and organizations' first exposure to the new system. Identify the roadblocks and strategies to cope with them well ahead of time. Identify tactics to deal with issues before they appear. Bring people into the process early on and let them shape the eventual systems, policies, and procedures. Listen to their concerns and respond accordingly.

Focus on Who Matters Most

The third step recognizes that if everyone openly adopted change, there would never be any need to be concerned with implementing change. However, there will always be three groupings of people and organizations when change is involved:

- Enthusiasts: those who recognize the benefits of the new system and line up to help spread and support the new system
- Backbones: the great majority of people and organizations who are solid performers and who will support the change since they are reliable workers
- Resisters: those who oppose change either due to a perceived loss of power, status, money, or other attribute or who simply do not wish to expend the time and/or energy to change

Obviously you need as many people in the first two camps and as few in the last one as possible. You may have some hard decisions to make—if someone who stands in the way of the change consistently opposes you, you may have to decide if that person's future may lie outside of the firm.

Setting New Business Processes to Align with Your Goal(s)

There is an expression tossed around in IT circles about "paving the cow paths." AgileConnection's website states:

> In the IT world, "paving cow paths" means automating a business process as is, without thinking too much about whether or not that process is effective or efficient. Often business process automation initiatives require figuring out entirely new ways of doing business processes—impossible prior to automation (for example, work flow automation and digital image processing)—defining more effective and efficient process highways.[21]

If you are making the transition to paperless, you need to give some thought about how you can rework your business processes to make them more efficient and effective. An example of this is asking yourself: How are you going to centralize the conversion of paper documents to PDF? If you have a small group in the firm do this for everyone, then you ensure that all documents are converted to digital form quickly and consistently. You will not be waiting for certain people to take the piles of papers that come into the firm and end up sitting on their desks and bring them into the DMS system—with all the resultant tensions and delays as people wonder when the laggards in the office are going to "get with the program."

---

21. https://www.agileconnection.com/article/paving-cow-paths

Accordingly, don't just pave your cowpaths . . . think about how you can make your systems better and faster by eliminating old outdated ways of working and take advantage of the new technologies in the office. Good consultants who have taken law firms down the paperless path can be worth their weight in gold, as they will guide you in the software, hardware, and processes best suited to implementing the paperless practice in your firm.

Learning from Your Experience and Continue to Improve Your Systems

A learning organization is one that has adopted a culture of continually evaluating and learning from their change processes. Adopting the paperless practice of law is a perfect time to implement learning concepts into the firm. As each step is achieved in a change process, ask your teams: "What went right? What went wrong? How can we do this better?" Keep a record of what you have learned and draw on that each time you need to implement a change in the firm.

When you recognize that leading, dealing with, and managing change is one of the most important skills that any person or organization can develop, then you have taken the first step toward implementing a learning (or change management) culture in your organization. Seek to build on this and instill it into the culture of your firm. You—and your law firm—will be stronger, be more adept, and have a greater capacity to absorb the changes that are thrust upon it as a result.

Celebrate the Successes

Every project has its milestones, setbacks, and successes. By positively communicating your successes, you help keep the momentum going and the change process positive. You also need to have strategies in place to deal with the setbacks in order to avoid having your project derailed by the naysayers.

Learn

Every successful change management process lays the groundwork for the next. Learn how to gather the "take-aways" that form the institutional learning for future growth. This is known as transforming your law firm into a "learning" organization that is better adapted at dealing with change.

Conclusions

OK, you have now read all the advice that we can give you on going paperless that we can fit into a chapter of a book such as this. Obviously there is a great deal more that we can go into if we were to write an entire book on taking a firm paperless. Hopefully we have given you enough information to generate the energy and the enthusiasm for taking your firm into the paperless realm.

As you stare over the abyss, recall that anticipation is almost always worse than reality. The process can be managed by properly planning, anticipating, executing, adjusting, and learning.

Don't forget involving everyone in the project at the start—and celebrating with them at the end! The firms that have gone paperless all say the same thing: It is cost effective, it enables remote work and greater work-life balance, and it allows you to carry your documents with you and access them on multiple remote devices wherever you may be. You can take your case to court and present it with ease. Moving to e-filing in government registries and tribunals is eased. It is easier—and cheaper—to store documents electronically than on paper. Moreover, it results in tangible benefits to the law firm, to the environment and to the work culture in the law firm.

So take a deep breath . . . and take that first step. . . .

CHAPTER THIRTY-ONE

Tomorrow in Legal Tech

"It's not about who has the most bullets, it's about who controls the information: What we see and hear, how we work, what we think. It's all about the information."

—Cosmo to Marty in the prescient 1992 movie *Sneakers*

"We're going to break an unbreakable Nazi code and win the war."

—Alan Turing (played by Benedict Cumberbatch) in the 2014 movie *The Imitation Game*

Introduction

It is indeed all about who controls information—and everyone today is scrambling for the black gold of big data, especially the kind that can make money and affect the relations between countries—even, as we are drafting this book, to the point that we fear that the Russians may have the ability to affect a presidential election. At the very least, there is convincing evidence that Russia is attempting to influence the American public.

So . . . are we really controlling our own info? Let us begin with the hottest issue of 2016—and likely of 2017—cybersecurity.

The Cone of Silence around Law Firm Data Breaches Shatters

We will remember 2016 as the year that the cone of silence around law firm data breaches was shattered. Breach after breach was revealed, culminating in the world's largest law firm data breach, that of Panamanian firm Mossack Fonseca. Virtually all of its data was compromised through the firm's life span to the point of breach and released on the Internet.

For years, the authors (and many others) have been saying that law firms generally keep mum about data breaches. While we have seen a few small firms abide by data breach notification laws, the larger firms generally have not, usually hanging their hat on the "we don't know what data was compromised" or the "we had an incident, but no evidence of an actual breach or misuse of data" excuses. Whether they have told their clients is unknown, but speculation has been rising that they often have not, for fear of a mass client exodus and the impact of such news going public.

On March 29, 2016, *The Wall Street Journal* reported that Cravath Swaine and Weil Gotshal, two members of the Am Law 100, were breached in the summer of 2015.[1] Other firms, not named, were reportedly breached as well.

March 29 was a tough day in the legal world. In addition to the *Wall Street Journal* article, *Crain's Chicago Business* reported that a Russian cybercriminal called "Oleras," living in the Ukraine, had been trying since January 2016 to hire hackers to break into the computer networks of nearly 50 elite law firms (almost all U.S. firms) so he could trade on insider information. The source of the story was a February 3 alert from Flashpoint, a New York threat intelligence firm. Just reading the names of the firms targeted was frightening.

Inflaming the consternation, Law360 reported on March 31 that privacy class action law firm Edelson PC was planning to file class action legal malpractice litigation against major law firms over the exposure of confidential information. Jay Edelson, the firm's founder, says the firm began investigating a class action against as-of-yet unnamed law firms over client data breaches nearly a year before the article was published.

Edelson said, "We've heard story after story from our friends on the defense side—it's a worst-kept secret that there are data breaches all the time at law firms, and there are a ton of state laws which require notification of data breaches, and the law firms seem to not care about those laws."[2]

Our own spin is slightly different—we think the firms have weighed the risks and determined that the risk of noncompliance with state data breach

---

1. http://www.wsj.com/articles/hackers-breach-cravath-swaine-other-big-law-firms-1459293504
2. http://www.law360.com/articles/778540/biglaw-in-crosshairs-as-firm-plans-data-breach-litigation

laws (and why oh why isn't there a federal law?) is small—in Virginia, as an example, your risk is $150,000 per breach—chump change for a large firm. The greater risk for law firms (we are sure) is the horrifying thought of major clients switching law firms.

Edelson also said that as his firm plans a class action, he anticipates state attorneys general and even the Federal Trade Commission may start to investigate law firm cybersecurity reporting practices.[3] Probably true—and that sidebar note no doubt added fuel to the raging fire.

Enter the jaw-dropping revelations in early April from what has become known as the Panama Papers. Let us return to the Panamanian law firm that was breached, Mossack Fonseca, which provides services including incorporating companies in offshore jurisdictions such as the British Virgin Islands. It is the fourth-largest provider of offshore services. In this breach, 2.6 terabytes of data—some 11 million files—were exposed, along with the sort of offshore hiding of monies that has become the stuff of legend in the last few decades.

An anonymous source passed the data to the German newspaper *Suddeutsche Zeitung*, which shared them with the International Consortium of Investigative Journalists (ICIJ). The ICIJ assisted in analyzing the files for over a year. The BBC says the documents show how the law firm helped clients launder money, dodge sanctions, and evade taxes.[4] Mind you, no one is alleging that all of the law firm's work involved something illegal, but the BBC's statement speaks for itself.

On April 12, 2016, many ABA members were surprised to find an e-mail from then ABA President Paulette Brown in their inbox. She was advising them that the FBI had requested the ABA to share FBI Private Industry Notification cybersecurity alerts with the legal community. It no doubt startled a lot of lawyers that the FBI was so specifically worried about the vulnerabilities in the legal industry that it would seek the cooperation of its largest association in getting the word out about threats and defenses.

In 2016, many law firm started working with the FBI's Private Sector partnership with lawyers—similar to the financial sector information sharing. The Legal Services Information Sharing and Analysis Organization (LS-ISAO) costs $8,000 per firm—a hefty price tag, though more than 100 law firms had signed up by July 2016.

---

3. *Id.*
4. http://www.bbc.com/news/world-35918844

You might try joining the FBI's Infragard (legal sector), which is free and offers helpful security notifications for lawyers, educational opportunities—and even golf outings! Check it out at www.infragard.org.

The form is a pain to fill out and it takes many months to be accepted, but a lot of solo and small firm attorneys have expressed interest in signing up. Because it is free, we expect to see a growing membership of law firms.

Will Attorneys Adopt the New Password Rules?

Another cybersecurity development in 2016 is expected to grow in 2017. You know the crazy—and impossible to remember—passwords that you were encourage/forced to concoct? The ones with special characters, lower and upper case, number, and so on? There is hope for you. New Carnegie Mellon studies released in 2016 demonstrated that the length of passwords is much more important than complexity. Who knew? The National Institute of Standards and Technology has included that recommendation in a draft report published in 2016—and we're betting that it will be adopted soon. So make your passwords 14 or more characters and use a passphrase that you can remember. But don't reuse it everywhere and do use a password manager with a very strong (long) password to manage all your passwords!

The ABA Blueprint Website

While the visionary business isn't very gratifying, by the time this book is published, the American Bar Association's planned fall launch of Blueprint, a new site for solo and small firm lawyers, should be live. The site is still limited in the solutions offered but plans to expand them. The site, much like this book, intends to help small firm lawyers find the products and services they need at affordable prices. Sounds a bit like the language from this book's preface, doesn't it? CuroLegal, the legal strategy and technology consulting firm that is helping the ABA develop Blueprint, said in late summer of 2016 that the new site will have two prongs. Quoting from a blog post by our friend Bob Ambrogi:

> The first, called Universal Solution, is for lawyers who know generally what they need but want guidance for what product or service they should purchase. If a firm, for example, wants to enhance its marketing, it would select that category and be given a list of recommended products and services.

Rather than a comprehensive list, this will be a selective list that reflects essential core products within that category. The user will click on a product to read a more detailed description and will be able to then click through to the vendor's site to purchase the product.

The second prong, called Firm Builder, is for lawyers and firms that want more customized recommendations. This will be a form of expert system that will guide the user through a series of questions and then generate recommendations. This option will also include the ability to chat or speak with a practice management consultant.

The Firm Builder feature will be restricted to ABA members. The Universal Solution feature will be open to anyone.[5]

Here's the part that worries us—reportedly the developers and the ABA are still working out the model for selecting vendors who will be listed. Our concern is that it will be based on a pay-to-play model. We hope we're wrong, because there is no neutrality in that kind of model—even with the customary disclaimer or an attempt to be transparent by noting that these are paid listings. We've seen this type of practice previously deployed and hope that revenue generation (e.g., vendor payments) doesn't trump objective recommendations.

Whatever products are included, they should be there, because like the products in this book, they have been chosen by neutral parties as the best products for the best price, with no monies (or anything else) changing hands.

Bob also reported that, at launch, the Firm Build feature will cover four areas of law practice:

1. Technology
2. Marketing
3. Insurance and retirement plans
4. Office space and virtual assistants

The site will also offer product discounts for ABA members. The developers are working with some vendors to develop pricing packages specifically designed for solos and small firms.

ABA President Linda Klein conceived the original idea for the site, believing that lawyers find the decision-making process confusing because there are

---

5. Robert Ambrogi, *ABA Says New "Blueprint" Site Will Save Money for Small Firms*, LawSites (Aug. 16, 2016), http://www.lawsitesblog.com/2016/08/aba-says-new-blueprint-site-will-save-money-small-firms.html.

so many options and not enough time to evaluate all of them. We agree with that—our concern is that vendors paying money remove the neutrality from the process. To offer ABA members a discount (which we understand will happen) is fine. Lots of state bars have the same arrangement.

The part of Bob's post that alarmed us was a quote from one of the site's developers, Nicole Bradick, the Chief Strategy Officer of CuroLegal. She said, "The principal goal here wasn't increased non-dues revenue. It was increased value to members. Period."[6] That "principal goal" language has us concerned—if the ABA takes money from vendors, it is a not a neutral source of advice. And that word will spread. If it doesn't, in any fashion, take money from vendors, the whole concept is great. So we can't predict much yet, but the authors will offer our own assessment of the site in next year's edition of this book, which shouldn't surprise anyone that has purchased previous editions.

Repeating the thoughts of ABA President Klein, we have sought over the last decade to make your legal technology choices simpler. We don't cover every product or technology—there are way too many choices, way too many vendors hawking their wares, and way too much data to ingest if you try to learn it all yourself. So we try to give "best of breed" advice with the solo/small firm lawyer in mind. We should have said "best of breed and budget conscious" advice because that is what the solo/small firm lawyer always wants. Our advice is based on what we see used in the solo and small firm environment and what our own clients use.

Access to Justice

Controversial? Always. We know we have to leverage technology and non-lawyer help to make the justice system accessible to the 80 percent of the population that can't afford it, believes in self-help, or doesn't know a legal problems exists. Pro Bono simply isn't doing what needs to be done.

Former ABA President William Hubbard created the Commission on the Future of Legal Services as he began his term, tasking it with a grassroots approach seeking workable solutions and geared to the viewpoint of those who can't afford traditional legal help. The commission's proposal for ABA policy in Resolution 105, Model Regulatory Objectives for the Provision of Legal Service, passed in the association's House of Delegates at the midyear meeting in February 2016.

---

6. Quoted in *id.*

There was a lot of pushback regarding nontraditional legal services. Opponents secured an amendment: The resolution says it does not change ABA policy against law firm ownership by nonlawyers or the prohibition on lawyers sharing fees with nonlawyers.

At the 2016 ABA Annual Meeting, the commission released its detailed Report on the Future of Legal Services in the United States, which provides state court systems and others with a catalog of innovative, nontraditional legal services in the marketplace and recommendations for new possibilities, some of which might require new rules and even legislation.

Online nontraditional legal services are clearly endorsed. Will the Report and Resolution 105 make a difference? Our crystal ball is quite murky here, because the forces of protectionism have carried the day for so long. If we had to guess, this train has left the station already and all the protectionism in the world can't stop it. We might as well hop on board, and hope simply that federal and state governments will do a good job of regulating something that has now effectively been with us for years.

For solo and small firm lawyers, there is a lesson here. If they can unbundle services and keep prices competitive, there is a way to combat the allure of nontraditional legal services and begin to fill the access to justice gap. If lawyers don't, it is clear that other nonlawyer, profit-driven services will.

E-Discovery

It is always fascinating to see what is happening in the e-discovery world. EDRM, the leading standards organization for the e-discovery industry, announced on August 24, 2016, that it had been acquired by Duke University School of Law.

For EDRM, Duke provides an institutional home with a large and respected organization, ensuring the continued vitality of EDRM. Duke Law and its Center for Judicial Studies gain resources that expand the center's involvement in electronic discovery and information governance in support of its mission to promote better understanding of the judicial process and to generate ideas for improving the administration of justice.

EDRM co-founder George Socha, who joined BDO Consulting, will remain with EDRM after the acquisition. EDRM co-founder Tom Gelbmann helped with the transition but, at the time this book is published, but has now retired. Tom Hnatowski, former chief of the Magistrate Judges Division of the Administrative Office of the United States Courts, has joined the Judicial Studies Center to manage day-to-day operations running EDRM.

Hard to believe that EDRM was founded only 11 years ago. It will be interesting to see how it evolves in its new home. We have no specific predictions here—however, in the hands of a law school now, we would expect to see some major directional changes, perhaps with a much greater emphasis on e-discovery education and a more academic approach. It will be interesting to revisit this topic next year after the dust has settled on the acquisition.

Norton Rose Fulbright's 2016 Litigation Trends Annual Survey

Global law firm Norton Rose Fulbright released its 2016 Litigation Trends Annual Survey—now in its 12th year conducted by Acritas, a global legal services market business research firm. This year's survey polled more than 600 corporate counsel representing companies across 24 countries on disputes-related issues and concerns. Survey respondents—primarily general counsel—indicate an upward trend in virtually all of the metrics relating to litigation and the broader disputes area, a tad surprising to us because litigation is generally perceived to be trending downward among smaller entities.

In this larger market, the median average proportion of litigation spending stands at one-tenth of one percent (0.1%) of total revenue. This year's survey report includes a table that gives in-house counsel the opportunity to benchmark its own litigation spend against a closer peer group, broken down by annual revenue, region and industry sector.

An expansive report detailing Norton Rose Fulbright's 2016 Litigation Trends Annual Survey can be found at www.litigationtrends.com. Highlights of the report include the following:

- The trend of respondents expecting a rise in litigation continued from recent years, as 24 percent believe the volume of disputes will increase in the year ahead versus only 13 percent anticipating a decrease.
- Companies who had no lawsuits commenced against them decreased from 25 percent to 19 percent over the last 12 months, with 81 percent of respondents being sued in the past year.
- Respondents who needed to conduct any type of cross-border discovery increased from 35 percent to 41 percent this past year. Those

needing to conduct cross-border discovery in more than half of their matters doubled from 7 percent to 14 percent.

- Companies not facing any regulatory proceedings showed little change from last year at 66 percent. However, 97 percent of respondents perceived regulators to be more interventionist during the last 12 months.
- Litigation related to contracts stood as both the most numerous at 40 percent and the top concern for respondents at 42 percent.
- Alternative fee arrangements (AFAs) were used by 60 percent of respondents, with 97 percent of them satisfied with the work from an AFA, citing better control, greater efficiency and more certainty.

Trending Now . . .

One of our favorite resources is the ABA 2016 Legal Technology Survey. Some of the stats suggest where the legal profession is heading—and with what technology.

Tablets

- 50 percent use for legal work (42 percent in 2015)
- 77 percent use Apple iPad (78 percent in 2015)
- 19 percent use Windows Surface (12 percent in 2015)
- 9 percent use Samsung Galaxy (11 percent in 2015)

Servers

- 45 percent use for law-related tasks (43 percent in 2015)

IT Staff

- 46 percent of firms have no IT support staff at all locations combined
- 18 percent of firms have one IT staff member
- 7 percent of firms have two IT staff members

Operating System

- Windows 7: 34 percent (47 percent in 2015)
- Windows 10: 30 percent

- Windows 8: 16 percent (26 percent in 2015)
- 5 percent still use Windows XP (10 percent in 2015)
- 8 percent use a Mac OS

E-mail

- Microsoft Outlook: 77 percent
- Web-based e-mail: 19 percent
- Outlook Express: 11 percent
- Apple Mail: 5 percent
- Gmail: 5 percent

Instant Messaging Software

- 38 percent use for law-related tasks (30 percent in 2015)

The top four being used were

- Microsoft Windows Messenger: 25 percent (19 percent in 2015)
- Google Chat/Hangouts: 23 percent (22 percent in 2015)
- Outlook Communicator: 17 percent
- iChat: 13 percent (24 percent in 2015)

Time and Billing Software

The top five being used were

- Timeslips: 17 percent
- QuickBooks: 15 percent
- Tabs 3: 10 percent
- PCLaw: 7 percent
- Elite: 7 percent

Case Management Software

- 46 percent reported that case/practice management software was available at firms
- 43 percent reported using case/practice management software for law-related tasks

Security Tools

Leading types of security tools used:

- Spam filters: 90 percent

- Anti-spyware: 80 percent
- Firewall (software): 79 percent
- Pop-up blocker: 76 percent
- Virus scanning (desktop/laptop): 71 percent
- Virus scanning (e-mail): 67 percent
- Encryption (files): 37 percent

Hardware Manufacturer Winners

- Dell wins for desktops (57 percent), laptops (37 percent), and servers (42 percent)
- The smartphone winner is Apple iPhone, 73.4 percent
- The winning tablet is Apple iPad, 77 percent

Cloud Computing Software

The top three:

- Dropbox: 58 percent
- Google Docs: 49 percent
- iCloud: 28 percent

A couple of points we found interesting: 45 percent of the respondents are using metadata-removal software. The figure was 37 percent in 2015. This is a remarkably low percentage, but at least it's increasing.

Although 38 percent reported using cloud computing for law-related tasks, 12 percent reported using no precautions/security measures. Alarming but not surprising.

Fastcase was finally dethroned as the most popular downloaded legal-specific app. Westlaw was at 36.8 percent with Fastcase a close 34.2 percent.

Microsoft Windows 10

As we predicted last year, we too have moved to Microsoft Windows 10—and it was a breeze. We also took most of our clients to Windows 10 over the course of 2016—and things went swimmingly. The biggest issue seems to be the extent to which Windows 10 is spying on you. If you are concerned about your privacy, you can find out how to disable some of the data collection and distribution that some folks find troubling here: http://www.expertreviews.co.uk/software/operating-systems/1404925/how-to-stop-windows-10-spying-on-you.

E-mail Encryption

Here is where we get to eat some crow pie. We predicted last year that the use of e-mail encryption would rise in 2016. The ABA's study shows that the percentage of lawyers using encrypted e-mail is actually down a tad, from 33 percent to 30 percent. The numbers don't vary much, so we can call the two numbers flat, but we are surprised.

Our anecdotal experience with our own clients is that they wanted to get e-mail encryption on board both for security reasons and to please (and reassure) their clients, many of whom are now demanding security audits of their law firms, including smaller firms. We thought 2016 would see a lot of lawyers adopting e-mail encryption but apparently that train is moving more slowly than we thought.

Cloud Computing

We appear to be "stuck" with nearly half of all law firms (more in solo/small firms) utilizing the cloud and a nearly equal number resisting it, often on security grounds.

It was helpful last year when, on March 17, 2016, the Legal Cloud Computing Association released the first set of cloud security standards crafted specifically for the legal industry at ABA TECHSHOW. It is a short document containing 21 standards—and easy to read. You can review the document at http://www.legalcloudcomputingassociation.org/standards.

Predictions here? Not so easy. We are happy to see an increasing number of solo/small firms using the cloud because they are generally better protected in the cloud than they would be left to their own devices. But the resistance to cloud computing has remained pretty firm at the larger law firms and we're not sure we see much of a change on the horizon.

Internet of Things

Bruce Schneier, one of our greatest cybersecurity experts, when asked "What should enterprises worry about when it comes to the Internet of things?" answered simply "Everything."[7]

---

7. Tim Greene, *Schneier on "Really Bad" IoT Security: "It's Going to Come Crashing Down,"* NETWORKWORLD (Apr. 13, 2015, 5:39 AM), http://www.networkworld.com/article/2909212/security0/schneier-on-really-bad-iot-security-it-s-going-to-come-crashing-down.html.

The IoT (Internet of Things) race is nowhere close to a finish line. Lawyers are connected all the time—so much so that they forget when they are connected and to what. They also lose sight of what might provide evidence in their cases—simply because there are so many devices, including cars, refrigerators, watches, and thermostats, that might provide evidence in a case.

If your law office has a smart thermostat that is connected to your network, that could be the entry point for attack. Will your firm's employees bring their IoT devices to work, thereby presenting another point of vulnerability? Sure.

The 2016 National Internet of Things Conference included a description that said, "By 2020, 25 billion 'smart' devices will be wirelessly connected to, and communicating with, each other, raising serious legal and liability issues. This so-called 'Internet of Things' (IoT) is one of the fastest emerging, transformative, and disruptive technology developments in years."

Regulating the IoE has become a concern in the United States and abroad—not only is a new legal specialty but—to remain competent—attorneys are going to have to recognize the many ways in which the IoE will affect their own areas of practice.

Competence

In 2012, the American Bar Association formally approved a change to the Model Rules of Professional Conduct to make it clear that lawyers have a duty to be competent not only in the law and its practice but also in technology.

The ABA's House of Delegates voted to amend Comment 8 to Model Rule 1.1 to read as follows:

> To maintain the requisite knowledge and skill, a lawyer should keep abreast of changes in the law and its practice, including the benefits and risks associated with relevant technology, engage in continuing study and education and comply with all continuing legal education requirements to which the lawyer is subject.

As we write, 26 states have adopted the duty of technology competence—make sure you know if your state is among them.

Some states, while they haven't formally adopted the change to their rules of professional conduct, have nonetheless acknowledged a duty of lawyers to be competent in technology. And some have changed (to varying degrees) the wording of the ABA Model Rule.

It is increasingly clear that competent lawyers must have a basic understanding of the technology they use. To emphasize that point, the Florida Supreme Court, in September of 2016, approved a rule requiring state lawyers to take technology-related continuing legal education (CLE) courses. The rule change was effective on January 1, 2017, and requires lawyers admitted to the Florida Bar to take a minimum of three hours of technology-related CLE courses during a three-year cycle. The court approved the bar association's proposal to raise the minimum number of CLE hours from 30 to 33 in a three-year cycle to accommodate the new technology requirement.

Our friend Craig Ball has joked that lawyers embrace technology as fast as glaciers melt. And with global warming, the glaciers are melting still faster. But ethical changes like these are starting to make lawyers much more mindful of the impact of technology on the practice of law—and the need to understand the technology they use in their firms.

Artificial Intelligence Hits the Hype Peak in 2016

According to Gartner, Inc., artificial intelligence (AI) hit a hype peak in 2016 with everybody and their brother/sister claiming that their products utilize AI. It also predicted (and we agree) that there will a "trough of disillusionment" as people come to understand that much of the "AI" talk is untestable puffery. Fastcase CEO Ed Walters says true AI is only about 5 percent of that which is claimed to be AI—and we concur with that as well.

What you generally see are expert systems, sometimes referred to as smart computing. Not true AI, because the machines are not learning, but being smartly programmed to reach their conclusions.

So we'll predict that we will enter a bit of a trough of disillusionment—but we, along with Ed Walters, believe that AI holds a lot of genuine promise. We simply have to understand that AI is in its infancy. We expect, within the next five to ten years, to see the use of AI expand rapidly—and to see a fairly fast adoption of AI within the legal profession. AI is very well suited to such tasks as technology-assisted review, compliance, predictive analysis, and contract management. This is not expected to bode well for paralegals and first-year law students. Much of their work can and will be handled by machines. And, in fact, the market for document reviewers has already shrunk markedly because of the use of technologyassisted review.

In 2016, BakerHostetler garnered a lot of publicity for being one of the first law firms where Watson's son ROSS, the super-intelligent attorney, began offering legal assistant support in bankruptcy cases. Where will we be a year from now? Stay tuned.

The Rise in Client Portals

Partially in response to law firm data breaches, we are seeing more and more firms embrace client portals. Anecdotally, many lawyers have told us that they were first impressed by client portals because they seemed to work so well in their doctors' offices.

They do offer a high level of secure communications, allowing you to communicate securely from anywhere with real-time notification to clients. Forget the aggravation of playing phone tag. Provide clients with documents to review, the status of their cases, and access to their invoices. The ability to do all that will make your practice seem much more modern and efficient—and reduce phone calls that are no longer necessary.

Today, many cloud-based case management programs offer client portals—a terrific benefit. The good ones all offer encrypted communication that beats the pants off of unencrypted e-mail. And as you can readily understand, simply encrypting e-mails doesn't give you all the benefits mentioned above of a client portal.

Clients adore the instant accessibility and security of client portals—and in today's legal marketplace, that makes you alluringly competitive. If you don't have a portal, potential clients (who also have experience with portals with their financial advisors and doctors) will wonder why a modern law firm doesn't have one.

Some of the built-in client portals in case management systems that we see most often are Clio, Rocket Matter, and MyCase.

Moving to a client portal is a no-brainer—which is why the use of client portals is likely to increase exponentially over the next several years.

Small Firms Largely Not Implementing New Technology: A Trend?

In a series of posts about the findings of a 2016 survey of small and solo law firm management conducted by Thomson Reuters Solo and Small Law Firm group, our friend Bob Ambrogi reported a number of interesting findings.[8]

As Bob notes, two survey questions asked firms about technology they have implemented within the prior 12 months and their plans to implement new technology in the coming 12 months. The questions asked about a variety of common categories of legal technology, such as case/matter management, time and billing, document management, and others.

Overall, 66 percent of small firms say they have not implemented any of these technologies in the prior year and 68 percent say they have no plans to implement any of them in the coming year. In other words, two-thirds of firms have not changed their technology and two-thirds have no immediate plans to change their technology.

We do not, of course, know whether it is the same two-thirds for both questions, but clearly there is significant overlap, suggesting that many small firms will implement no changes in technology for at least a two-year span.

Considering the extent to which technology can make solo/small firms more competitive, the findings were troubling. And we can't understand why they have decided not to adopt new technology.

The most common form of technology is time and billing, which 71 percent of lawyers overall say their firm uses. At firms of 11 to 29 lawyers, 95 percent have time and billing systems, and at firms of seven to ten lawyers, 91 percent do. Among solos, however, only half have time and billing. We had to chuckle at that, since we have borne a certain amount of skepticism from our language in the Time and Billing chapter in which we discuss (though not by percentages) how many folks really use Word for time and billing. Thanks to this survey, we now have statistical backing!

The second most common form of technology is conflict checking. Overall, 60 percent of lawyers say their firm has a conflict-checking system.

Just over half of firms (53 percent) have case/matter management systems. Only 38 percent of solos have these systems, while 71 percent of firms in

---

8. Search "Bob Ambrogi Thomson Reuters 2016 survey" to find the posts.

the 11–29 lawyer range have them. This is where get on our bully pulpit with clients most often, trying to sell them on the notion that Outlook is not a case management system and the advantages of a case management system are profound.

We found the survey a little discouraging since it indicates the failure to understand both the importance of achieving efficiencies and the allure that this achievement has to current and prospective clients. Hoping for better numbers next year, but this study sure doesn't support that hope.

ABA TECHSHOW 2017 and Beyond

One prediction we are confident in making is that you will reap enormous rewards by going to ABA TECHSHOW 2017—and if you missed it because you purchased this book later in 2017, mark your calendars for 2018. There are three major legal technology conferences: LegalTech New York, ILT-ACON, and ABA TECHSHOW. The case for solo and small firm lawyers going to ABA TECHSHOW was made eloquently by our friend Bob Ambrogi, who wrote in a blog post: "ABA Techshow is the small-firm lawyer's legal tech conference. The programs focus on practical topics relating to the use of technology in small firms. The vendors who exhibit there are largely ones whose products cater to smaller firms. The attendees overwhelmingly come from solo and small firms. It is, in short, where you will feel right at home."[9]

Best of all, the speakers are very approachable and happy to chat with attendees. You would expect vendors to be approachable, but we have always found them exceptionally approachable—and willing to spend a lot of time talking to attendees. Hope to see you March 15–18 at the Hilton Chicago! More information at http://www.techshow.com/.

---

9. Robert Ambrogi, *This Week in Legal Tech: The Best Legal Tech Conferences for Small-Firm Lawyers*, Above the Law (Aug. 29, 2016, 1:48 PM), http://abovethelaw.com/2016/08/this-week-in-legal-tech-the-best-legal-tech-conferences-for-small-firm-lawyers/.

Glossary

Active Directory (AD) is an implementation of Local Automatic Data Processing (LADP) directory services by Microsoft for use primarily in Windows environments. Its main purpose is to provide central authentication and authorization services for Windows-based computers. Active Directory also allows administrators to assign policies, deploy software, and apply critical updates to an organization. Active Directory stores information and settings in a central database. Active Directory networks can vary from a small installation with a few hundred objects to a large installation with millions of objects.

ActiveSync is a synchronization program developed by Microsoft. It allows a mobile device to be synchronized with either a desktop PC or a server running Microsoft Exchange Server, PostPath Email and Collaboration Server, Kerio MailServer, or Z-Push.

Advanced Technology Attachment (ATA) is a standard interface for connecting storage devices such as hard disks and CD-ROM drives inside personal computers. The standard is maintained by X3/INCITS committee T13. Many synonyms and near-synonyms for ATA exist, including abbreviations such as IDE and ATAPI.

Adware is any software package that automatically plays, displays, or downloads advertising material to a computer after the software is installed on it or while the application is being used. Some types of adware are also spyware and can be classified as privacy-invasive software.

AppleCare Protection Plan Apple's warranty with a new product is 90 days' complimentary telephone support and a one-year hardware guarantee. These can both be extended to a three-year (for computers) or two-year

---

This glossary was compiled from definitions available online at Wikipedia (www.wikipedia.org).

(for iPods and iPhones) warranty and telephone support (inclusive of the initial support) through the AppleCare Protection Plan packs, which can be purchased separately within the initial one-year warranty or simultaneously with new Apple products, mainly Macs, iPods, and iPhones.

Auto Document Feeder (ADF) is a feature in multifunction or all-in-one printers, fax machines, photocopiers, and scanners that takes several pages and feeds the paper one page at a time into the scanner, allowing the user to scan (and thereby copy, print, or fax) multiple-page documents without having to manually replace each page.

Boot Camp is a utility included with Apple's Mac OS X v10.5 Leopard operating system that assists users in installing Microsoft Windows XP or Windows Vista on Intel-based Macintosh computers. Boot Camp guides users through nondestructive repartitioning (including resizing of an existing HFS+ partition, if necessary) of their hard disk drive and using the Mac OS X Leopard disc to install Windows drivers. In addition to device drivers for the hardware, the disc includes a control panel applet for selecting the boot operating system while in Windows.

Byte (pronounced "bite," IPA: /baɪt/) is a unit of measurement of information storage, most often consisting of 8 bits. In many computer architectures it is a unit of memory addressing.

Category 5e Cable (Cat5e) is an enhanced version of Cat 5 that adds specifications for far-end crosstalk. It was formally defined in 2001 in the TIA/EIA-568-B standard, which no longer recognizes the original Cat 5 specification. Although 1000BASE-T was designed for use with Cat 5 cable, the tighter specifications associated with Cat 5e cable and connectors make it an excellent choice for use with 1000BASE-T. Despite the stricter performance specifications, Cat 5e cable does not enable longer cable distances for Ethernet networks: Cables are still limited to a maximum of 328 ft. (100 m) in length (normal practice is to limit fixed ("horizontal") cables to 90 m to allow for up to 5 m of patch cable at each end). Cat 5e cable performance characteristics and test methods are defined in TIA/EIA-568-B.2-2001.

Category 6 Cable (Cat6), commonly referred to as Cat 6, is a cable standard for gigabit Ethernet and other network protocols, and is backward compatible with the Category 5/5e and Category 3 cable standards. Cat 6 features more stringent specifications for crosstalk and system noise. The cable standard provides performance of up to 250 MHz and is suitable for 10BASE-T/100BASE-TX and 1000BASE-T (gigabit Ethernet). It is expected to suit the 10GBASE-T (10 gigabit Ethernet) standard, although with limitations on length if unshielded Cat 6 cable is used.

Cathode Ray Tube (CRT) is an evacuated glass envelope containing an electron gun (a source of electrons) and a fluorescent screen, usually with internal or external means to accelerate and deflect the electrons. When electrons strike the fluorescent screen, light is emitted.

CD-ROM is a compact disc that contains data accessible by a computer. While the CD format was originally designed for music storage and playback, the format was later adapted to hold any form of binary data. CD-ROMs are popularly used to distribute computer software, including games and multimedia applications, though any data can be stored (up to the capacity limit of a disc).

Central Processing Unit (CPU), or sometimes just processor, is a certain class of logic machines that can execute computer programs. This broad definition can easily be applied to many early computers that existed long before the term CPU ever came into widespread usage. However, the term itself and its initialism have been in use in the computer industry since at least the early 1960s (Weik, 1961). The form, design, and implementation of CPUs have changed dramatically since the earliest examples, but their fundamental operation has remained much the same.

Client Access License (CAL) is a kind of software license, distributed by Microsoft, to allow clients to connect to its server software programs.

Code Division Multiple Access (CDMA) employs spread-spectrum technology and a special coding scheme (where each transmitter is assigned a code). In communications technology, there are only three domains that can allow multiplexing to be implemented for more efficient use of the available channel bandwidth, and these domains are known as time, frequency, and space. CDMA divides the access in signal space.

Computer Monitor is a piece of electrical equipment that displays viewable images generated by a computer without producing a permanent record. The word monitor is used in other contexts, in particular in television broadcasting, where a television picture is displayed to a high standard. A computer display device is usually either a cathode ray tube or some form of flat panel, such as a thin film transistor liquid crystal display (TFT-LCD). The monitor comprises the display device, circuitry to generate a picture from electronic signals sent by the computer, and an enclosure or case. Within the computer, either as an integral part or a plugged-in interface, there is circuitry to convert internal data to a format compatible with a monitor.

Computer Virus is a computer program that can copy itself and infect a computer without permission or knowledge of the user. However, the term virus is commonly used, albeit erroneously, to refer to many different types of malware programs. The original virus may modify the copies, or the copies may modify themselves, as occurs in a metamorphic virus. A virus can only spread from one computer to another when its host is taken to the uninfected computer—for instance, by a user sending it over a network or the Internet or by carrying it on a removable medium, such as a floppy disk, CD, or USB drive. Additionally, viruses can spread to other computers by infecting files on a network file system or a file system that is accessed by another computer.

Contrast Ratio is a measure of a display system, defined as the ratio of the luminosity of the brightest color (white) to that of the darkest color (black) that the system is capable of producing. A high contrast ratio is a desired aspect of any display, but with the various methods of measurement for a system or its part, remarkably different measured values can sometimes produce similar results.

DAT72 Backup Tape stores up to 36 GB uncompressed (72GB compressed) on a 170-meter cartridge. The Digital Audio Tape (DAT) 72 standard was developed by HP and Certance. It has the same form factor and is backward compatible with DDS-3 and DDS-4.

Database Application A computer database is a structured collection of records or data that is stored in a computer system. A database usually contains software so that a person or program can use it to answer queries or extract desired information. The term database refers to the collection of related records, and the software should be referred to as the database management system (DBMS).

DDR2 SDRAM, double-data-rate two synchronous dynamic random-access memory, is a random-access memory technology used for high-speed storage of the working data of a computer or other digital electronic device.

Digital Copier In recent years, all new photocopiers have adopted digital technology, replacing the older analog technology. With digital copying, the copier effectively consists of an integrated scanner and laser printer. This design has several advantages, such as automatic image quality enhancement and the ability to "build jobs," or scan page images independently of the process of printing them. Some digital copiers can function as high-speed scanners; such models typically have the ability to send documents via e-mail or make them available on a local area network.

Digital Subscriber Line (DSL) is a family of technologies that provide digital data transmission over the wires of a local telephone network.

Digital Visual Interface (DVI) is a video interface standard designed to maximize the visual quality of digital display devices such as flat-panel LCD computer displays and digital projectors. It was developed by an industry consortium, the Digital Display Working Group (DDWG). It is designed for carrying uncompressed digital video data to a display.

Display Resolution of a digital television or computer display typically refers to the number of distinct pixels in each dimension that can be displayed. It can be an ambiguous term, especially as the displayed resolution is controlled by different factors in CRT and flat-panel or projection displays using fixed picture-element (pixel) arrays.

Domain Controller On Windows Server systems, the domain controller (DC) is the server that responds to security authentication requests (logging in, checking permissions, etc.) within the Windows Server domain.

Dots per Inch (dpi) is a measure of printing resolution, in particular the number of individual dots of ink a printer or toner can produce within a linear one-inch (2.54 cm) space.

DVD (also known as digital versatile disc or digital video disc) is a popular optical disk storage media format. Its main uses are video and data storage. Most DVDs are of the same dimensions as compact discs (CDs) but store more than six times as much data.

E-mail Spam is the practice of sending unwanted e-mail messages, frequently with commercial content, in large quantities to an indiscriminate set of recipients.

Encryption/Decryption is the process of transforming information (referred to as plaintext) using an algorithm (called cipher) to make it unreadable to anyone except those possessing special knowledge, usually referred to as a key. The result of the process is encrypted information (in cryptography, referred to as ciphertext). In many contexts, the word encryption also implicitly refers to the reverse process, decryption (e.g., "software for encryption" can typically also perform decryption), to make the encrypted information readable again (i.e., to make it unencrypted).

Enhanced-Definition Television Enhanced- or extended-definition television, or EDTV, is a Consumer Electronics Association (CEA) marketing shorthand term for certain digital television (DTV) formats and devices. EDTV generally refers to video with picture quality beyond what can be broadcast in NTSC or PAL but not sharp enough to be considered high-definition television (HDTV). A DVD player with progressive output is considered the lower end of this class, when playing a progressively encoded disc. (The maximum EDTV frame rate of 60 per second is not possible from a DVD.) The common implementations of EDTV are 480- or 576-line signals in progressive scan, as opposed to 50–60 interlaced fields per second (see NTSC or PAL and SECAM). These are commonly referred to as "480p" and "576p," respectively. In comparison, a standard-definition television (SDTV) signal is broadcast with interlaced frames and is commonly referred to as "480i" or "576i." EDTV can also refer to a display device that has a maximum resolution of 480p or 576p.

Extensible Markup Language (XML) is a general-purpose markup language. It is classified as an extensible language because it allows its users to define their own elements. Its primary purpose is to facilitate the sharing of structured data across different information systems, particularly via the Internet. It is used both to encode documents and serialize data.

FireWire is Apple's brand name for the IEEE 1394 interface (although the 1394 standard also defines a backplane interface). It is also known as i.LINK (Sony's name). It is a serial bus interface standard for high-speed communications and isochronous real-time data transfer, frequently used in a personal computer (and digital audio/digital video).

FireWire 400 can transfer data between devices at 100, 200, or 400 Mbit/s data rates.

FireWire 800 (Apple's name for the nine-pin "S800 bilingual" version of the IEEE 1394b standard) was introduced commercially by Apple in 2003. This newer 1394 specification (1394b) and corresponding products allow a transfer rate of 786.432 Mbit/s via a new encoding scheme termed beta mode. It is backward compatible to the slower rates and six-pin connectors of FireWire 400. However, while the IEEE 1394a and IEEE 1394b standards are compatible, FireWire 800's connector is different from FireWire 400's connector, making the legacy cables incompatible. A bilingual cable allows the connection of older devices to the newer port.

Gigabyte (derived from the SI prefix giga-) is a unit of information or computer storage meaning either exactly 1 billion bytes (10003, or 109) or approximately 1.07 billion bytes (10243). It is commonly abbreviated as Gbyte or GB.

Global System for Mobile Communications (GSM) is the most popular standard for mobile phones in the world. Its promoter, the GSM Association, estimates that 82 percent of the global mobile market uses the standard. GSM is used by over 2 billion people across more than 212 countries and territories. Its ubiquity makes international roaming very common between mobile phone operators, enabling subscribers to use their phones in many parts of the world. GSM differs from its predecessors in that both signaling and speech channels are digital call quality, and so it is considered a second generation (2G) mobile phone system. This has also meant that data communications were built into the system using the 3rd Generation Partnership Project (3GPP).

Hard Disk Drive, commonly referred to as a hard drive, hard disk, or fixed disk drive, is a nonvolatile storage device that stores digitally encoded data on rapidly rotating platters with magnetic surfaces. Strictly speaking, "drive" refers to a device distinct from its medium, such as a tape drive and its tape or a floppy disk drive and its floppy disk.

Hash Function is a reproducible method of turning some kind of data into a (relatively) small number that may serve as a digital "fingerprint" of the data. The algorithm "chops and mixes" (i.e., substitutes or transposes) the data to create such fingerprints. The fingerprints are called hash sums, hash values, hash codes, or simply hashes.

High-Definition Multimedia Interface (HDMI) is a licensable compact audio/video connector interface for transmitting uncompressed digital streams.

High-Definition TV (HDTV) is a digital television broadcasting system with greater resolution than traditional television systems (NTSC, SECAM, PAL). HDTV is digitally broadcast because digital television (DTV) requires less bandwidth if sufficient video compression is used.

Hubs are devices for connecting multiple twisted pairs or fiber-optic Ethernet devices together, making them act as a single network segment. Hubs work at the physical layer (layer 1) of the OSI model, and the term layer 1 switch is often used interchangeably with hub. The device is thus a form of multiport repeater. Network hubs are also responsible for forwarding a jam signal to all ports if it detects a collision.

Institute of Electrical and Electronics Engineers, or IEEE (read "i triple e"), is an international nonprofit professional organization for the advancement of technology related to electricity. It has the most members of any technical professional organization in the world, with more than 360,000 members in around 175 countries.

Intel Core 2 Duo Processor The Core 2 brand refers to a range of Intel's consumer 64-bit dual-core and MCM quad-core CPUs with the x86-64 instruction set and based on the Intel Core microarchitecture, which derived from the 32-bit dual-core Yonah laptop processor.

Intel Corporation is the world's largest semiconductor company and the inventor of the x86 series of microprocessors, which are found in most personal computers.

Internet Information Services (IIS) is a set of Internet-based services for servers using Microsoft Windows. It is the world's second most popular web server in terms of overall websites, behind Apache HTTP Server.

Internet Protocol (IP) Address is a unique address that certain electronic devices currently use to identify and communicate with each other on a computer network utilizing the Internet protocol (IP) standard—in simpler terms, a computer address. Any participating network device—including routers, switches, computers, infrastructure servers (e.g., NTP, DNS, DHCP, SNMP), printers, Internet fax machines, and some telephones—can have its own address that is unique within the scope of the specific network. Some IP addresses are intended to be unique within the scope of the global Internet, while others need to be unique only within the scope of an enterprise.

Intrusion Detection System (IDS) is a piece of hardware that detects unwanted manipulations of computer systems, mainly through the Internet. The manipulations may take the form of attacks by crackers. An IDS is used to detect several types of malicious behaviors that can compromise the security and trust of a computer system. This includes network attacks against vulnerable services; data-driven attacks on applications; host-based attacks such as privilege escalation, unauthorized logins, and access to sensitive files; and malware (viruses, Trojan horses, and worms).

IPsec (IP security) is a suite of protocols for securing Internet protocol (IP) communications by authenticating and/or encrypting each IP packet in a data stream.

iSight Camera is a webcam developed and marketed by Apple. The iSight was sold retail as an external unit that connects to a computer via FireWire cable and comes with a set of mounts to place it atop any current Apple display, laptop computer, or all-in-one desktop computer. The term is also used to refer to the camera built into Apple's iMac, MacBook, and MacBook Pro computers.

Keyboard In computing, a keyboard is a peripheral partially modeled after the typewriter keyboard. Physically, a keyboard is an arrangement of rectangular buttons, or keys. A keyboard typically has characters engraved or printed on the keys; in most cases, each press of a key corresponds to a single written symbol. However, to produce some symbols requires pressing and holding several keys simultaneously or in sequence; other keys do not produce any symbol but instead affect the operation of the computer or the keyboard itself.

Laser Printer is a common type of computer printer that rapidly produces high-quality text and graphics on plain paper. Like photocopiers, laser printers employ a xerographic printing process but differ from analog photocopiers in that the image is produced by the direct scanning of a laser beam across the printer's photoreceptor.

Light-Emitting Diode (LED) is a semiconductor diode that emits incoherent, narrow-spectrum light when electrically biased in the forward direction of the p-n junction, as in the common LED circuit. This effect is a form of electroluminescence.

Linear Tape-Open (LTO or LTO2) is a magnetic tape data storage technology developed as an open alternative to the proprietary digital linear tape (DLT). The technology was developed and initiated by Seagate, Hewlett-Packard, and IBM. The standard form factor of LTO technology goes by the name Ultrium.

Liquid Crystal Display (LCD) is a thin, flat display device made up of any number of color or monochrome pixels arrayed in front of a light source or reflector. It is often utilized in battery-powered electronic devices because it uses very small amounts of electric power.

Macintosh AirPort is a local area wireless networking brand from Apple based on the IEEE 802.11b standard (also known as Wi-Fi) and certified as compatible with other 802.11b devices. A later family of products based on the IEEE 802.11g specification is known as AirPort Extreme. The latest family of products is based on the draft-IEEE 802.11n specification and carries the same name.

Macintosh/Mac is a brand name that covers several lines of personal computers designed, developed, and marketed by Apple Inc. The original Macintosh was released on January 24, 1984; it was the first commercially successful personal computer to feature a mouse and a graphical user interface (GUI) rather than a command line interface. Apple consolidated multiple consumer-level desktop models into the 1998 iMac, which sold extremely well. Current Mac systems are mainly targeted at the home, education, and creative professional markets. They are the aforementioned (though upgraded) iMac and the entry-level Mac mini desktop models, the workstation-level Mac Pro tower, the MacBook, MacBook Air and MacBook Pro laptops, and the Xserve server.

MagSafe Power Adapter is a power connector introduced in conjunction with the MacBook Pro at the Macworld Expo in San Francisco on January 10, 2006. The MagSafe connector is held in place magnetically. As a result, if it is tugged on—for instance, by someone tripping over the cord—it comes out of the socket safely, without damaging it or the computer or pulling the computer off its table or desk.

Media Access Control (MAC) Address is a quasi-unique identifier attached to most network adapters. It is a number that acts like a name for a particular network adapter, so, for example, the network interface cards (NICs, or built-in network adapters) in two different computers will have different names, or MAC addresses, as would an Ethernet adapter and a wireless adapter in the same computer and as would multiple network cards in a router.

Megabyte is a unit of information or computer storage equal to either 106 (1,000,000) bytes or 220 (1,048,576) bytes, depending on context. In rare cases, it is used to mean 1000×1024 (1,024,000) bytes. It is commonly abbreviated as Mbyte or MB.

Message-Digest Algorithm 5 (MD5) is a widely used cryptographic hash function with a 128-bit hash value. As an Internet standard (RFC 1321),

MD5 has been employed in a wide variety of security applications and is also commonly used to check the integrity of files. An MD5 hash is typically expressed as a 32-character hexadecimal number.

Microsoft Exchange Server is a messaging and collaborative software product developed by Microsoft. It is part of the Microsoft Servers line of server products and is widely used by enterprises using Microsoft infrastructure solutions. Exchange's major features consist of electronic mail, calendaring, contacts and tasks, and support for the mobile and web-based access to information, as well as supporting data storage.

Microsoft SQL Server is a relational database management system (RDBMS) produced by Microsoft. Its primary query language is Transact-SQL, an implementation of the ANSI/ISO standard Structured Query Language (SQL) used by both Microsoft and Sybase.

Microsoft Windows is the name of several families of software operating systems by Microsoft. Microsoft first introduced an operating environment named Windows in November 1985 as an add-on to MS-DOS in response to the growing interest in graphical user interfaces (GUIs). Microsoft Windows eventually came to dominate the world's personal computer market, overtaking Mac OS, which had been introduced previously. At the 2004 IDC Directions conference, IDC vice president Avneesh Saxena stated that Windows had approximately 90 percent of the client operating system market.

Modem (from modulator-demodulator) is a device that modulates an analog carrier signal to encode digital information and also demodulates such a carrier signal to decode the transmitted information. The goal is to produce a signal that can be transmitted easily and decoded to reproduce the original digital data.

Mouse In computing, a mouse (plural mice or mouses) functions as a pointing device by detecting two-dimensional motion relative to its supporting surface. Physically, a mouse consists of a small case, held under one of the user's hands, with one or more buttons. It sometimes features other elements, such as "wheels," which allow the user to perform various system-dependent operations, or extra buttons or features that can add more control or dimensional input. The mouse's motion typically translates into the motion of a pointer on a display.

MP3 MPEG-1 audio layer 3, more commonly referred to as MP3, is a digital audio encoding format. This encoding format is used to create an MP3 file, a way to store a single segment of audio, commonly a song, so that it can be organized or easily transferred between computers and other devices, such as MP3 players.

Network Address Translation (NAT) is a technique of transceiving network traffic through a router that involves rewriting the source and/or destination IP addresses and usually also the TCP/UDP port numbers of IP packets as they pass through.

Network Card/Adapter Network adapter, LAN adapter, or NIC (network interface card) is a piece of computer hardware designed to allow computers to communicate over a computer network.

Optical Character Recognition (OCR) is the mechanical or electronic translation of images of handwritten, typewritten, or printed text (usually captured by a scanner) into machine-editable text.

Peripheral Devices In computer hardware, a peripheral device is any device attached to a computer to expand its functionality. Some of the more common peripheral devices are printers, scanners, disk drives, tape drives, microphones, speakers, and cameras.

Personal Digital Assistants (PDAs) are handheld computers but have become much more versatile over the years. PDAs are also known as small computers or palmtop computers. PDAs have many uses: for calculation; as a clock, calendar, and address book; to access the Internet and send/receive e-mails; for video recording, typewriting, and word processing; for making and writing on spreadsheets; to scan bar codes, use as a radio or stereo, play computer games, record survey responses, and as a global positioning system (GPS). Newer PDAs also have both color screens and audio capabilities, enabling them to be used as mobile phones (smartphones), web browsers, or portable media players. Many PDAs can access the Internet, intranets, or extranets via Wi-Fi or wireless wide area networks (WWANs). Many PDAs employ touchscreen technology.

Portable Document Format (PDF) is the file format created by Adobe Systems in 1993 for document exchange. PDF is fixed-layout document format used for representing two-dimensional documents in a manner independent of the application software, hardware, and operating system.

Private Branch Exchange (PBX) is a telephone exchange that serves a particular business or office, as opposed to one that a common carrier or telephone company operates for many businesses or for the general public.

PS/2 Connector is used for connecting a keyboard and a mouse to a PC-compatible computer system. Its name comes from the IBM Personal System/2 series of personal computers, with which it was introduced in 1987. The PS/2 mouse connector generally replaced the older DE-9 RS-232 "serial mouse" connector, while the keyboard connector replaced the larger 5-pin DIN used in the IBM PC/AT design. The keyboard and mouse interfaces are electrically similar, with the main difference being that open collector outputs are required on both ends of the keyboard interface to allow bidirectional communication. If a PS/2 mouse is connected to a PS/2 keyboard port (or if a PS/2 keyboard is connected to a PS/2 mouse port), the mouse (or keyboard) will not be recognized by the computer.

Radio-Frequency Identification (RFID) is an automatic identification method that relies on storing and remotely retrieving data using devices called RFID tags or transponders. An RFID tag is an object that can be applied to or incorporated into a product, animal, or person for the purpose of identification using radio waves. Some tags can be read from several meters away and beyond the line of sight of the reader.

RAID 5 A redundant array of independent disks (RAID) 5 uses block-level striping with parity data distributed across all member disks. RAID 5 has achieved popularity due to its low cost of redundancy. Generally, RAID 5 is implemented with hardware support for parity calculations. A minimum of three disks is generally required for a complete RAID 5 configuration.

Random-Access Memory (RAM) is a type of computer data storage. Today it takes the form of integrated circuits that allow the stored data to be accessed in any order—i.e., at random. The word random thus refers to the fact that any piece of data can be returned in a constant time, regardless of its physical location and whether it is related to the previous piece of data.

Ransomware is a type of malware that restricts access to a computer system that it infects in some way, and demands that the user pay a ransom to the operators of the malware to remove the restriction.

Redundant Arrays of Independent Disks (RAID) is the most common definition of RAID. Other definitions of RAID include "redundant arrays of independent drives" and "redundant arrays of inexpensive drives." RAID is an umbrella term for computer data storage schemes that divide and replicate data among multiple hard disk drives. RAID's various designs balance or accentuate two key design goals: increased data reliability and increased I/O (input/output) performance.

Remote Desktop Protocol (RDP) is a multichannel protocol that allows a user to connect to a computer running Microsoft Terminal Services. Clients exist for most versions of Windows (including handheld versions) and other operating systems such as Linux, FreeBSD, Solaris, and Mac OS X. The server listens by default on TCP port 3389. Microsoft refers to its official RDP client software as either Remote Desktop Connection (RDC) or Terminal Services Client (TSC).

Revolutions per Minute (rpm, RPM, r/min, or r•min^{-1}) is a unit of frequency: the number of full rotations completed in one minute around a fixed axis. It is most commonly used as a measure of rotational speed or angular velocity of some mechanical component.

Rootkit is a program (or a combination of several programs) designed to take fundamental control (in Unix terms, "root" access; in Windows terms, "administrator" access) of a computer system without authorization by the system's owners and legitimate managers. Access to the hardware (i.e., the reset switch) is rarely required, as a rootkit is intended to seize control of the operating system running on the hardware. Typically, rootkits act to obscure their presence on the system through subversion or evasion of standard operating system security mechanisms. Often they are Trojans as well, thus fooling users into believing they are safe to run on their systems. Techniques used to accomplish this can include concealing running processes from monitoring programs or hiding files or system data from the operating system.

Router is a piece of hardware that connects two or more different networks (e.g., LAN to WAN) to route data between them.

Scanning Resolution describes the detail of the scanned image. The term applies equally to digital images, film images, and other types of images. Higher resolution means more image detail.

Secure Sockets Layer (SSL) is a cryptographic protocol that provides secure communications on the Internet for such things as web browsing, e-mail, Internet faxing, instant messaging, and other data transfers.

Serial Advanced Technology Attachment (SATA) is a computer bus primarily designed for transfer of data between a computer and storage devices (like hard disk drives or optical drives). The main benefits are faster transfers, ability to remove or add devices while operating (hot-swapping), thinner cables that let air cooling work more efficiently, and more reliable operation, with tighter data integrity checks than the older Parallel ATA interface.

Serial Attached SCSI (SAS) is a computer bus technology primarily designed for transfer of data to and from computer data storage devices such as hard drives, CD-ROM and DVD tape drives, and similar devices. SAS is a serial communication protocol for direct attached storage (DAS) devices. It is designed for the corporate and enterprise market as a replacement for parallel SCSI, allowing for much higher-speed data transfers than previously available and is backward compatible with SATA drives.

Server is an application or device that performs services for connected clients as part of a client server architecture. A server application, as defined by RFC 2616 (HTTP/1.1), is "an application program that accepts connections in order to service requests by sending back responses." Server computers are devices designed to run such an application or applications, often for extended periods of time, with minimal human direction. Examples of d-class servers include web servers, e-mail servers, and file servers.

Service Set Identifier (SSID) is a name used to identify the particular 802.11 wireless LANs to which a user wants to attach. A client device will receive broadcast messages from all access points within range advertising their SSIDs and can choose one to connect to based on preconfiguration or by displaying a list of SSIDs in range and asking the user to select one.

SHA Hash Functions are five cryptographic hash functions designed by the National Security Agency (NSA) and published by the National Institute of Standards and Technology (NIST) as a U.S. Federal Information Processing Standard. SHA stands for secure hash algorithm. Hash algorithms compute a fixed-length digital representation (known as a message digest) of an input data sequence (the message) of any length. The five algorithms are denoted SHA-1, SHA-224, SHA-256, SHA-384, and SHA-512. The latter four variants are sometimes collectively referred to as SHA-2. SHA-1 produces a message digest that is 160 bits long; the number in the other four algorithms' names denote the bit length of the digest they produce.

Shadow Copy (also called Volume Snapshot Service, or VSS) is a feature introduced with Windows Server 2003 and available in all releases of Microsoft Windows thereafter that allows taking manual or automatic backup copies or snapshots of a file or folder on a specific volume at a specific point in time. It is used by NTBackup and the Volume Shadow Copy service to back up files. In Windows Vista, it is used by Windows Vista's backup utility, System Restore, and the Previous Versions feature.

Small Computer System Interface (SCSI) is a set of standards for physically connecting and transferring data between computers and peripheral devices. The SCSI standards define commands, protocols, and electrical and optical interfaces. SCSI is most commonly used for hard disks and tape drives, but it can connect a wide range of other devices, including scanners and CD drives. The SCSI standard defines command sets for specific peripheral device types; the presence of "unknown" as one of these types means that in theory it can be used as an interface to almost any device, but the standard is highly pragmatic and addressed toward commercial requirements.

Smartphone is a mobile phone offering advanced capabilities beyond a typical mobile phone, often with PC-like functionality.

Spyware is computer software that is installed surreptitiously on a personal computer to intercept or take partial control over the user's interaction with the computer without the user's informed consent. While the term spyware suggests software that secretly monitors the user's behavior, the functions of spyware extend well beyond simple monitoring. Spyware programs can collect various types of personal information but can also interfere with user control of the computer in other ways, such as installing additional software, redirecting web browser activity, accessing websites blindly that will cause more harmful viruses, or diverting advertising revenue to a third party. Spyware can even change computer settings, resulting in slow connection speeds, different home pages, and loss of Internet or other programs.

Stereophonic Sound (Stereo) is the reproduction of sound, using two or more independent audio channels, through a symmetrical configuration of loudspeakers, to create a pleasant and natural impression of sound heard from various directions, as in natural hearing. It is often contrasted with monophonic (or "monaural," or just mono) sound, where audio is in the form of one channel, often centered in the sound field.

SuperDrive is a term that has been used by Apple for two different storage drives: from 1988 to 1999, to refer to a high-density floppy disk drive capable of reading all major 3.5-inch disk formats, and from 2001 onward to refer to a combined CD/DVD reader/writer. Once use of floppy disks started declining, Apple reused the term to refer to the (originally Pioneer-built) DVD writers built into its Macintosh models, which can read and write both DVDs and CDs. As of December 2006, SuperDrives are combination DVD±R/±RW and CD-R/RW writer drives offering speeds of 4× to 36× and supporting the DVD-R, DVD+R, DVD+R DL, DVD±RW, DVD-9, CD-R, and CD-RW formats along with all normal read-only media.

Switch is a computer networking device that connects network segments. Low-end network switches appear nearly identical to network hubs, but a switch contains more "intelligence" (and comes with a correspondingly slightly higher price tag) than a network hub. Network switches are capable of inspecting data packets as they are received, determining the source and destination device of that packet, and forwarding it appropriately. By delivering each message only to the connected device it was intended for, a network switch conserves network bandwidth and offers generally better performance than a hub.

Tagged Image File Format (TIFF) is a container format for storing images, including photographs and line art. Originally created by the company Aldus for use with what was then called "desktop publishing," it is now under the control of Adobe. The TIFF format is widely supported by image-manipulation applications, by publishing and page layout applications, by scanning, faxing, word processing, OCR, and other applications.

Tape Drive is a data storage device that reads and writes data stored on a magnetic tape. It is typically used for archival storage of data on hard drives. Tape generally has a favorable unit cost and long archival stability.

Terminal Services is a component of Microsoft Windows (both server and client versions) that allows a user to access applications and data on a remote computer over any type of network, although normally best used when dealing with either a wide area network (WAN) or local area network (LAN). Ease and compatibility with other types of networks may differ and vary. Terminal Services is Microsoft's implementation of thin-client terminal server computing, where Windows applications, or even the entire desktop of the computer running terminal services, are made accessible from a remote client machine.

Time Machine is a backup utility developed by Apple that is included with Mac OS X v10.5.

Universal Serial Bus (USB) is a serial bus standard to interface devices. USB was designed to allow peripherals to be connected using a single standardized interface socket and to improve plug-and-play capabilities by allowing devices to be connected and disconnected without rebooting the computer (hot-swapping). Other convenient features include providing power to low-consumption devices without the need for an external power supply and allowing many devices to be used without requiring manufacturer specific, individual device drivers to be installed.

UNIX is a computer operating system originally developed in 1969 by a group of AT&T employees, including Ken Thompson, Dennis Ritchie, and Douglas McIlroy, at Bell Labs. Today's Unix systems are split into various branches developed over time by AT&T as well as various commercial vendors and nonprofit organizations.

USB Thumb (Flash) Drives are NAND-type flash memory data storage devices integrated with a USB connector. They are typically small, lightweight, removable, and rewritable.

Video Card/Graphics Adapter (also referred to as a graphics accelerator card, display adapter, graphics card, and numerous other terms) is an item of personal computer hardware whose function is to generate and output images to a display.

Video Graphics Array The term video graphics array (VGA) refers either to an analog computer display standard; the 15-pin D-subminiature VGA connector, first marketed in 1988 by IBM; or the 640 × 480 resolution itself. While this resolution has been superseded in the computer market, it is becoming a popular resolution on mobile devices.

Virtual Private Network (VPN) is a communications network tunneled through another network and dedicated for a specific network. One common application is secure communications through the public Internet, but a VPN need not have explicit security features, such as authentication or content encryption. VPNs, for example, can be used to separate the traffic of different user communities over an underlying network with strong security features.

Web 2.0 is a trend in web design and development and can refer to a perceived second generation of web-based communities and hosted services—such as social networking sites, wikis, and folksonomies—which aim to facilitate creativity, collaboration, and sharing between users. The term gained currency following the first O'Reilly Media Web 2.0 conference in 2004. Although the term suggests a new version of the World Wide Web, it does not refer to an update to any technical specifications but to changes in the ways software developers and end users use webs.

Wi-Fi is a wireless technology brand owned by the Wi-Fi Alliance intended to improve the interoperability of wireless local area network products based on the IEEE 802.11 standards. Common applications for Wi-Fi include Internet and VoIP phone access, gaming, and network connectivity for consumer electronics, such as televisions, DVD players, and digital cameras.

Wi-Fi Protected Access (WPA) is a class of systems to secure wireless (Wi-Fi) computer networks. It was created in response to several serious weaknesses researchers had found in the previous system, wired equivalent privacy (WEP). WPA implements the majority of the IEEE 802.11i standard and was intended as an intermediate measure to take the place of WEP while 802.11i was prepared.

Windows Recycle Bin is temporary storage for files that have been deleted in a file manager by the user but not yet permanently erased from the physical medium. Typically, a recycle bin is presented as a special file directory to the user (whether it is actually a single directory depends on the implementation), allowing the user to browse deleted files, undelete those that were deleted by mistake, or delete them permanently (either one by one or by the Empty Trash function).

Windows SharePoint Services, or Windows SharePoint, is the basic part of SharePoint, offering collaboration and document management functionality by means of web portals by providing a centralized repository for shared documents, as well as browser-based management and administration. It allows creation of document libraries, which are collections of files that can be shared for collaborative editing. SharePoint provides access control and revision control for documents in a library.

Wired Equivalent Privacy (WEP) is a deprecated algorithm to secure IEEE 802.11 wireless networks. Wireless networks broadcast messages using radio, so they are more susceptible to eavesdropping than wired networks. When introduced in 1999, WEP was intended to provide confidentiality comparable to that of a traditional wired network.

Index